… to *Angie*, the only one who believed…

PAPER CIGARETTE

*slices of life… when the thin line between… spirituality*
*and mental illness is blurred*

contact information:   Fernando Marques
email:                 papercig@gmail.com

snail mail:            Fernando Marques (Paper Cigarette),
                       P.O. Box 50566, Succ. Carrefour Pelletier
                       Brossard, QC,
                       Canada J4X 2V7

cover design:          François Richard
cover photography:     Fernando Marques

Legal deposit - Bibliothèque et Archives nationales du Québec, 2018.
Second edition, printed in 2019

published in 2018 by Fernando Marques

# PAPER CIGARETTE

*… el camino…*

… walked with the person I've known the longest,

but still know the least…

*… myself…*

fiction by

**Fernando Marques**

# PREFACE

... here is your chance to walk in someone else's shoes... you as the reader are stepping into the mind of a tormented man... who has had decades of life experiences... his actions of the moment may seem confusing... but through storytelling, he jumps back and forth in time... clues appear and with this you get a few more *slices of his life*... but if you want a full understanding of our main character... you will probably need to insert your personal experiences to fill in the blanks to understanding his raison d'etre... whether you believe it or not, we are all connected and experience the same things...

... the protagonist only penned one sentence in the whole novel... what you will be reading are not sentences but his thoughts... and to a certain point you will also witness the humour and play on words from the protagonist... surely the storytelling process in the novel is intentionally chaotic... life just like this novel is unstructured and perhaps at times seemingly improvised... chaos is the sworn enemy of organized thoughts, no?... erratic thinking with no rhyme or reason... there is no beginning or ending as you the reader come into a life story which is already in progress and you need to pick it up (story) and start running with it...

... this novel is written in the first person... therefore it was simpler for me to use my personas' name (Fernando or McFern) as the fictional protagonist... I don't have any academic training as a writer nor do I claim such a title (writer) but certainly a story teller who likes to stir your imagination and cut it into simple slices of life (aka shit disturber)... before going any further, brush up on your reading homework... research the internet, as to what exactly is the Santiago de Compostela (Camino) pilgrimage...

... have fun and Google it... the novel is written in a journal format... this was intentional as I felt it would be a more personal experience (voyeuristic) for the reader... throughout the novel there are references to dates, locations and even music... push the experience of reading this book a step further... discover on the internet the mentioned locations (as pictures can take you there) and especially the music the protagonist is listening to at any given moment...

... hopefully the book will affect (disturb) your mood of even your whole day... at times you may believe the fictional protagonist is not so fictional after all... this may hit a nerve when you start to recognize elements of your-self... having spent two years in the writing/making... it certainly has left a mark on me as I debated whether or not to publish it, as some stories were personally unsettling... and I must confide that at times when writing, I did blur the line between fiction and reality...

## Acknowledgements... slices of life...

*... there are not too many things that impress me... but kindness is one of those rare qualities that goes deep into me... writing is a very lonely endeavour and for the most part I would write in coffee shops just not to feel so alone... at times I felt guilty sitting at a table and consuming very little and depriving the coffee shop owner of potential revenue had the table been free...*

*... perhaps just like paintings... book writing is a craft that still leaves people in awe... via my daily encounters and exchanges with the bistro staff... once it became known that I was attempting to write a book while in their premise... the kindness and generosity displayed by these folks made me feel like an orphaned child who has been adopted and taken care of... to all those who helped me... simply said... obrigado, thank you and merci...*

Doce Infusao (Aveiro, Portugal)
Tasca Tosca (Areia, Portugal)
Pastelaria Ria Parque (Aveiro, Portugal)
Casa da Guia (Cascais, Portugal)
Sacolinha (Cascais, Portugal)
Presse Cafe (dix/30 Brossard, Canada)
P'tite Madeleine & Jessica (Fort de France, Martinique)

# NOVEMBER

PART ONE

## 2014/11/08 – Saturday (Montreal, Canada)

… well… now that I have won a battle of wits with the radio station advertising my need to buy a new car… with the cold and dreary autumn weather and other mindless drivers pitted in the orange cone festival of road repair in a pathetic Saturday morning traffic… I have found sanctuary (though brief) in the cubicle of my parked van before *exerting* my profession as a home renovator… the question arises again… *am I looking in the right place to quench the melancholy of my essence*… this is bullshit… how can I find an answer when I'm not even sure if the question is the right one… and it's not with fancy expensive bullshit, parading pompous and deceiving words that the answer will come to me… keep it simple, what happens when one follows a dream and in reality it's a nightmare…

… nope!… instead I'm here reflecting quietly while sitting on a tool box… cause the most insignificant events are the ones that build perpetual and everlasting memories… ooops!… I'm beginning to sound like an Oprah though I look more like a Dr. Phil… I'm also feeling mischievous and decided to jot this down cause it will be a reminder why I'm leaving Montreal… of course this will be a pointless journal entry like so many I plan to write during the course of a year, cause life is nothing but a series of unresolved loose ends… there is no conclusion… not even death concludes anything…

… europe endless… why do I want to leave Montreal tomorrow?… the question is more like a summary of my 54 years of existence… if I said last winter I wore a tuque for the first time in my adult life as I now find the winter unbearable then it's a Montrealer's cliché reason for leaving… though in part it does apply to me… as I sit in the cold of my truck… I have been trying to sum up my life in a few words… but the nearly frozen cerebral juices are not flowing yet, so far more like thick maple syrup… so… in the scope of the universe my life is a series of insignificant past and present events *(slices of life)* and now to convolute them into a majestic cosmic orgasmic experience is arrogant pomposity… yep!… so, here goes another breath full of hot air… immigrant parent extraction, being a lousy husband, a 3 time loving dad, die hard atheist…

… dreamy nightmare… but during a partial walk of the Santiago/Compostela (aka Camino) pilgrimage in 2013… I was plagued by intuitions/messages that changed my life… intuitions with regards to a spiritual awakening, divorce, alienated my kids, new love interest, forthcoming mental turmoil/

suffering and within the next coming year re-walk the Camino pilgrimage and also write my thoughts in a journal/diary format and maybe eventually convert my journals into a book as right now I do not consider myself a writer... and finally... a critical and puzzling intuition which I still do not know how to interpret... afterwards I have no fucken idea what I will do with my life or my life with me... today, I feel my intuitions are my guides, but more often than not I think I need psychiatric help...

... my #54 theory... I used to have breakfast every morning at the Champlain Mall shopping centre... the mall would open at 7AM but with only the food court restaurants being opened... in a purely nordic climate fashion this allowed seniors from neighbouring retirement homes to do their morning walking exercises in the warmth of the mall... just like in high school cafeterias, after their walk small groups of men, women or couples would form clics... they would sit around and drown chat in coffee... I befriended a few of these groups over the course of about 5 years... every so often, an ambulance would come to the mall and some of these people would move on to the next life and physically never show up again in the mall... ironically, so many empty chairs are quickly replaced... many conversations were had and at times listening to *regrets* was the theme... but the resounding advice was to take a chance, as the only *constant in life is change*...

... which is it, madness or clairvoyance?... being 54 and looking at the longevity of my ancestors... it is a fair assessment to say I can expect about another 20 years of life... so, taking this into account and my interaction with the seniors in the mall... it is likely that the last 10 projected years will be burdened by some illness and/or Alzheimer's amongst the most trendy, or maybe some restricting physical disability... to recap positively from a different perspective, today I have 10 good years to go... how and what do I want to do with these remaining quality years?... a bucket list of sorts?... having liquidated all my assets and debts... why not take a sabbatical year living/travelling thru Europe including re-walking the Camino pilgrimage... and because my father died 4 years after his retirement... again... I do not want my life to resemble his... I think my reasoning is both madness and clairvoyance... I'm lucky, no?...

## 2014/11/09 – Sunday (London, Airport)

... the best time to go for a walk is at sunset when house lights are on and

I can look inside people's homes… it was more to remind myself of what a typical Montreal household looks like… and how people live and also differ from Europeans… will I miss the place where I was born and raised… not sure… but, it feels like all that I know has an indirect connection to Montreal…

… Heathrow Airport… it is so cold here both in terms of the temperature and the crystal glares of people looking out the lounge windows, while waiting for their connecting flights… considering there is another outbreak of the avian flu… maybe this cold is a blessing in disguise as some viruses are of tropical temperament, I think…

… tasks… when at airports waiting for connecting flights I try to keep busy with 15 minute tasks… such as a brisk walk, window shopping, looking at people, what is served as food, reading, some tasks are double or triple such as my own lunch and coffee breaks… my game, my rules, my privileges, all this to deviate from boredom… actually, I would spend more time on my computer, but this has to be the only airport which does not have free Wi-Fi… an international class act indeed, financially speaking times are hard even for an international airport…

… on the flight over, I was awakened by the woman sitting next to me… she was playing/listening to music on her Ipod but without headphones, it was loud and Russian… with aggravated intentions to tell her to stop with the music, I saw her eyes were red from crying… small talk led me to find out she left her 2 sons (adults) behind and was moving to Russia to take care of her aging mother… jokingly, I asked if she had left her sons labelled Tupperware's with food in the freezer… to which she did… as we de-boarded I guided her to her terminal gate as she was simply overwhelmed, confused and in a panic mode with her trip…

… there is a whole area dedicated to perfume shops… do we smell that bad, when we get off the planes that it is a must we marinate ourselves with one of these perfumes… the biggest absurdity are the perfume advertisements, youthful beauty & lust, sexually intense and so perfect Photoshop enhanced bodily features… to pass time, I watch people go by and they watch me sitting here too… we share the same pass time but from different perspectives… their clothing is an indicator of where they come from to even where they are going… incredible, so many variations of the human form… this place is a small sample of the *Beatles' penny lane* world… as the people walk by, I compare them to the perfume life size posters, not one comes close to looking like anything seen on these advertisements…

... we are... each other's worst problem... Suzanne is what one refers to as an on/off rocky relationship... we went to the same high school, at the age of 14 she moved to Portugal and decades later we re-connected via Facebook... the problem with dating at my age is that we come with lots of baggage both good and bad... sometimes one cannot shake off the *bad* fast enough... especially when we are able to see ones' end of life... so unstable is this relationship, I am not even sure she will be at Lisbon's airport to pick me up... to sustain my sanity, I have to laugh at my follies... and have cab fare just in case...

## 2014/11/10 – Monday (Areia, Portugal)

... again... woke in another new and strange bed... in this small beach house with no heating and half a dozen mothball scented blankets on the bed for warmth... it has been like this for the last 18 or so months, ever since the separation... I have been renting/living in suitcase sublets while waiting for our family home to sell... last month, the house was finally sold, I took my money from the sale and budgeted a year worth of living in Europe... the idea is to re-walk the previously uncompleted 2013 Camino pilgrimage in its' entirety without any airplane ticket deadline... along with a secondary project of writing a journal (maybe book)... what will I do after this sabbatical year, is still up for grabs... mind you, my girlfriend Suzanne may now weigh heavily on my future...

... it is, so me... when I was 19, I shipped my motorcycle to Europe and drove it from Portugal to France and eventually into the UK... all in a quest, searching for some sort of serenity... after almost a year, I wiped out on the bike and ended up in a hospital bed somewhere in Spain... suffice to say, shortly after went back to Montreal with damaged body and especially soul... now at 54, undertaking another sabbatical year... again... but this time wiser, I hope... as I have started to accept spiritualism as part of my existence as it has alleviated some of my angst, loneliness and even some existentialist questions...

... the idea is to do my second attempt at the Camino walk in the spring of 2015... in the meanwhile I will live in European cities until the spring... it is to be a reflective time in my life where I will spend my time by meditating, catch up on reading, listen to TED talks and write my thoughts thru stories/journal... this will be my job for the next coming year... my *job* as I see it...

will be to write one daily story based on my reflections and personal experience... is this egotistical?... maybe... but it should be fun too, I hope...

... also some stories may be based on people's interactions, reading their body language and eavesdropping on their conversations... all this will be done while loitering in the sanctuary of a coffee shop... of course all this is refined through my imagination... no boundaries when it comes to the absurd whether for locals, foreigners or mentally crippled (plenty here too)... if you cross my path or catch my eye, you automatically may become a target for my story/journal... is this politically correct, of course not... but these journal entries are what I will call... *slices of life*...

... why choose Portugal as a starting country?... with a name such as Fernando (aka McFern) and being of Portuguese extraction, it eases my transition into living in this European continent... unlike Montreal, one only needs to buy a coffee and it entitles a prolonged stay in the bistro, which allows for inspiration and time to write... the epitome of loitering... anyway, I have the eyes of a quasi-tourist and every street has an abundance of coffee shops with their loyal clientele, which provides me with consistent character longevity where I can dissect to pieces and re-build their lives based on my creativity and merciless ego... I am their god, at least on these pages... if only for a few seconds the illusion of control is within the grasp of my fingers...

... let's face it, southern Europe is paradise most of the year with its' mild weather, European culture mindset and all... what am I doing here, really?... is it running away and hiding until I can get the thoughts in my head sorted out, my failed marriage, alienated children and ad nausea... will I ever sort them out... is this the year I will finally grow up... if anything, I wish I can stop the emptiness which has cursed me from day one, maybe I was not supposed to come to this planet in the first place... over here, I am more an alien than before... still...

... so even with great weather, a writing project and a spiritual quest... there has to be something else to bring a man such as myself to this specific part of the planet... yep!... it can only be love... perhaps Suzanne and this *love* is the cure all...


## 2014/11/11 – Tuesday (Cascais, Portugal)

... the first thing is the subtle cultural differences that fiddle with my loosening senses... been in Portugal for 3 days, jetlag is still simmering as

I got up at noon today... but coffee and toasts in the Casa de Guia café by the edge of the Atlantic ocean surely makes up for a late start in the day and the sunny 19 degrees Celsius adds to a warm welcome...

... it doesn't take long to figure out... coffee, cigarettes and orange juice (sshhh! alcohol too)... this is a culture that almost adheres to these as if it were oxygen... the first observation is that there is no such thing as a drive thru for coffee... people here get their fat asses out of the car and walk in and drink their coffee/espresso on the spot... cigarettes are rampant, though now could only be smoked in designated areas, I used to equate smoking to poorer social classes... my assumption was/is wrong, but what puzzles me now... even though they have attained a higher standard of living through schooling and monetary ease, the smoking still persists... at first glance there seems to be an abundance of idle time in their daily routines that is filled by cigarette smoking, there could be more to the smoking/lifestyle phenomenon but I will not dwell on this as I may risk taking up smoking to get the inside scoop... now, orange juice... I do not claim to be a health fanatic, but to actually see the orange juice, not out of a carton but freshly squeezed, with ice cubes being optional... just gives my day an edge...

... I will be staying here for a few weeks, I got myself a studio apartment in a small town called Areia nestled between a mountain and the ocean... from my place I could see the mountain but can only hear the ocean as it is also within walking distance... a really neat feature is my bedroom as it has a skylight over the bed... from stars to the bright sun gleaming thru, it is cause for serene and reflective moments... as I am slowly de-compressing from the a hectic lifestyle I had in Montreal prior to coming here, it dawns on me how lucky I am to be here and breathing in such experiences... and for good measure, throw in Suzanne, my love interest and life could not get better...

## 2014/11/12 – Wednesday (Cascais, Portugal)

... this is going to be the first Christmas ever I will not be spending with my kids... fuck, what is this spiritual quest and obsession that is testing me... am I to be some kind of self-inflicted martyr... a selfie martyr?... it makes no sense to me and yet I am here longing for them... it has to be a mental illness and/or madness to willingly not spend Christmas with them... and yet, I came to this continent knowing all this... where was my common sense?

... yep!... just like back in Montreal... Christmas comes early here...

whenever possible, I turn on the radio for the music but also to familiarize my ear to the Portuguese language… my preference is for a radio station called M80, which along with a healthy dosage of commercials it caters to the 80's music… which is fine by me, as it is my musical niche…

… somewhere in the 80's, when I was dedicated to buying diapers for my kids but also managed with great difficulty to save pennies to buy a CD player… Emme, (ex-wife) knew how much music played an integral part in my life, it was my hobby to say the least… at that time I had well over 300 LP's and buying a CD player would be a natural step in my hobby… we had the expenses of a new family, a newborn, a hefty mortgage… and only one of us was working, as we opted to have Emme be a *stay at home mom*… our kid(s) came first… our policy was, *we made them (kids) we raise them*… we simply did not care for the *daycare lifestyle*… it was quality of family life issue, first… anyway, I ended up buying a CD player shortly after Christmas to capitalize on the sales… the CD player was quickly installed in our home, but it was several weeks before I got around to playing a CD, as I had none… in the spring time on some Saturday afternoon, Emme tells me she will stay home with the baby and for me to go out and buy CD's and put it on the credit card… at any other time, I would probably max out my credit card with buying CD's, but now I was a father… and because of this, I only bought one as it was on sale and I was able to pay cash for it… her gesture reaped with love and kindness and to this very moment it still touches me profoundly… this pretty well sums up the person she is…

… so, gradually… when I switched from vinyl to CD, this was the first CD acquired… and because my CD collection was limited (understatement) I ended up repeatedly playing the *Joshua Tree* CD… one song in particular… *Mothers of the Disappeared*… was bombarded by the laser ray… at about the same time I had read about Pinochet (Chilean dictator) taking people who opposed his regime and dropping them from helicopters in the middle of the ocean, I can only guess they had been tortured previously…

… I think the worst living nightmare for any parent is to witness the death of ones' child, or basically outlive your child… if you ever meet a parent who has lost a child to illness, if they hold their head up long enough to make eye contact with you… you'll see the sparkle in their eyes is long gone… how they manage to go on with life, leaves me speechless…

… to have your son or daughter disappear because of political views… is… well, interpreting absurdity as reality… it is mind boggling… in a pacifist gesture, mothers of these missing children in several South American countries walked/marched around with their child's name on a placard wondering if they'll ever return home... because love for a missing child is eternal... their motherly reality slowly becomes denial before eventually being an absurdity too...

... perhaps tonight while at the dinner table, look at your children silently... they may or not, be aware that you are savouring their presence near you... you on the other hand, are not outside holding a sign with his/her name in a public protest wondering where they are... right now... for me, all is good here just in knowing mine are safe back home... even if I miss them...


## 2014/11/13 – Thursday (Cascais, Portugal)

... sitting away in this bar/cafe in the Albatroz Hotel with an un-obstructed view of the perpetually endles of Atlantic Ocean... just a few hundred years ago it was the norm/belief as everyone thought the world was flat... and once you have reached the edge you simply fall off... to think outside the box back then, could have you end up swinging from the gallows...

... my head and Ipod are one... listening to *Madredeus* and their song called *O Navio*... though this is my favourite band, I do find this song to be melancholic and it almost captures the mood I am in... it is about a man who sails off into the distance with no intention to return... a gripping good-bye to mankind back on *terra firma*... at times I forget why I am in Europe in the first place... some days everything just seems to be complicated...

... the blue sky is now a thing of the past as clouds with different tones of gray take precedence... with the forthcoming rain, there will be a free car wash and maybe even the high humidity will curl some hairs (4 only) on my scalp... the hotels plexi-glass window panes arc rattling... the agitated sea is master for now... so what... life here goes on regardless of the weather... I feel completely out of place, the homesick feeling is back this morning and to make it worst I miss my kids tremendously... negative thoughts abound, but I do my best to avoid this slump and look forward to meeting up with Suzanne for lunch...

... *Redes do Mar* (roughly translates to *ocean fishing nets*)... is a truly insignificant looking restaurant, where only locals would venture in... as I walk by the restaurant it looks more like a house turned into an eatery... in mid lunch time rush hour(s), the waiter is outside smoking his cigarette and exchanging pleasantries with other smokers... he holds the door open as Suzanne and I enter... the lamps hanging over the table are old fishing ropes with attached upside down flower baskets acting as a chandelier to hide the light bulbs... I can tell, this idea for the lighting did not come from an interior decorator but more from an electrician who has more of a practical/functional/economical then design sense...

... in a relax mode our waiter follows us in and in a make yourself at home attitude tells us we can sit anywhere... the place is practically full and it is our job to find a table... as we sit down he announces the plate of the day is cod fish with chick peas... yep!, this is the menu take it or leave it... he then asks if we are drinking wine, and we request a small pitcher (1/2 litre or less) of red house wine... he comes back with a litre pitcher and when I try to correct him it is more than what we asked for, he says... *don't worry it is the same price and whatever is leftover I will drink it*... holy shit, what a waiter and sense of humor!!!!

... while waiting for the food, I take in more of the décor, since I was in home renovation before this trip, I have a keen eye and appreciation for these things... there are 3 distinctly different areas of ceramic tiles on the floor... I can accurately determine the evolution or expansion of the restaurant, it got bigger/larger based on the floor coverings... the curtains, look as if they date back to the 70's and were once upon a time tablecloths... as I can see the generous amount of food coming our way... it is fair to say, no frills with large and tasty homemade meals... no wonder the place is packed regardless of its' simplistic appearance...

... throw in chocolate mousse for dessert, a coffee to re-energize oneself as the waiter takes away our tray with still a lot of food left over... we couldn't eat everything, simply too much... rest assured, we made every possible effort to minimize the waiter finishing off our wine... but even here, he wins... 16 euros for everything, and no tip required... we too win...

... sometimes... all I need is to look beyond the tip of my nose and get out of my self-wallowing mind set and put into perspective how lucky I am to be here... I am in for one hell of a year...

## 2014/11/14 – Friday (Cascais, Portugal)

... been here almost a week and everything still seems so foreign, especially the protocol for ordering in a café... one should never be in a hurry and even if only one coffee is ordered, it is a *carte blanche* to loiter all day... no one will ever ask you to order something else/again or ask you to leave either... such a laid back attitude... the waiter reminds me of my autistic son... slow within his displacement in this confining café... Dolce Caffé seems to cater mainly to take out food as much as this waiter is not in his element working here... he spends his time gazing and smiling at his girlfriend but his words are scarce... or is it me who is still too wired from Montreal's fast pace and impatience?... what is his *raison d'etre*... ?...

... a young guy, with more beard than body... one has the impression his waking hours are just that *waking*...all his living is done in the dark, he is an aspiring musician... from the acutely thin body and facial features, food is the least of his worries, more importantly the reason for working as a busboy/ waiter is to obtain money for his art... as his comfort level increases with the guitar, so does his creativity and experimentation with new sounds, which now devours far more sophisticated equipment... just like his passion for his art, art now requires and speaks to him in monetary terms... has he sold out to art?...

... so many fleeting friends, whose attention span can never match his... the dedication for music isolates him from people... unless musicians like him, he cannot sustain the human interaction let alone any friendships... naturally so, his circle of friends are no more than art colleagues... with one common goal which is to play music with slight variations of success obtainable from their music as an art...

... ironically... the inspiration and inevitably the main reason for his future success will be the girl who is in awe of him... the one who sits in all the time during band rehearsals... who/what does she love?... the young man, the guitar, the loud noise, the hope of success or simply the reflective moments where no one speaks and only the sounds of the edgy music can be heard... like sitting in the back seat of the car, on a long car ride, where nothing is expected from you other than looking out into the side road billboard void...

... maybe because I am a romantic and empathetic by most accounts, I will say she is there for the young man, she sees qualities of goodness in him, he is genuine in her eyes... and even though for the most part his conversation themes stem around his guitar and music... most times, she feels in his eyes she is second in terms of importance... but this is trivial right now...

... but somewhere in time, he will be plucking away some chords and will be seized by a glimpse of her darting like a humming bird in his mind... it is this, that will trigger the lyrics and melody for a song... he will eventu-

19

ally put it all together and play it for her in a private moment... his focus will be limited to his playing and singing the song correctly and there may be a very slight pride/emotion associated to his accomplishment all the while playing... but this is also trivial in his mind... at the receiving end, the young girl will be stirred by the emotions vibrating through the song... *her song*... but even in this moment she is still second in importance...

... my coffee is long gone and I have been typing unhindered for over an hour... in the meanwhile, she sits at the table in the far end monitoring his movements with only her eyes... his head is always turned towards her no matter in which direction he walks... from what I can see, these kids are in love even though they are very reserved about it...


## 2014/11/15 – Saturday (Lisbon, Portugal)

... it is so true that money does not buy happiness, but I firmly believe it buys pleasure... that is why I now find myself undertaking this one year sabbatical... a pleasurable quest for answers to my *raison d'etre*... fuck!, am I ever full of shit... using a French expression to give credence that I'm a lost soul in search of the ultimate *raison d'etre*... lol... here I go again with French...

... I live in a world of fears and they're only in my head and yet I accept them as reality... I have to constantly remind myself of the goals/reasons why I am doing this... what bothers me is that the reasons I have for doing this one year sabbatical are not even founded on any logic... blind faith... everything I plan and/or hope to undertake comes from that little voice inside, which I think we all have... unlike most people I listened and obeyed mine... is this my madness?...

... I adopted this phrase as my motto while living on this planet... *the only constant in life is change*... just a couple of years ago I was a diehard atheist and after doing a partial walk of the Camino... I returned with an epiphany... where I now believe there is life after death, because I was able to predict/intuit the death of a friends' dad... and this premonition happened during my Camino walk... and because of this event, I now found myself listening to my inner voice which also told me that I would go thru personal alienating hardships, would re-do the Camino walk and out of all this I would also write a book that is supposed to have an impact on people, my ex-wife will be better off without me... and on a final note, a critical and puzzling intuition... that something in me will die... quite an arrogant pompous order... delusional, no?

... eleven was my champagne birthday... I spent the month of March in Portugal... it was the first time I had ever seen my father cry... as he and I arrived at my grandparents' house, he broke down and cried like a baby, I had no idea he even knew how to cry... cause, just a few days before, I was hearing and channelling voices from beyond... my parents believed I was possessed by some demon(s)... and with this, my father stopped his life and brought me to Portugal for what would be a month long of exorcisms... so many weird things... all my senses were running on overtime... and I am cursed with having an incredible memory, as I write these words, I simultaneously re-live these experiences... so much so, I need to stop writing to regain my composure... suffice to say... there is another world living within our world, or is it the other way around?

... childhood trauma turns us inwards for our own perseverance... because of this, sometimes we feel others through empathy... this new ability is sometimes confounded with being intuitive... neverthelesss... when I was twenty, I had met up with a friend in Spain and he brought me to Santiago de Compostela (Camino) and told me it was a world famous place... at that time, I was nothing more than a pothead, yet when I looked around I felt and even said out loud... *I will be back*... why I said this still astonishes me... in my insomnia life , I feel this was the calm before the storm...

... Lisbon... all I know is that, unequivocally I now believe there is life after death... so, if I was to look at this logically... why do I keep on living here when I feel this planet/world overwhelms me and most of the time I feel nothing but pain... is this why I am still here, to find an answer to this, either for me or anyone who reads these stories... once again, pompous arrogance... nevertheless I still feel drawn to the stillness of cemeteries... in this city they (cemeteries) are a museum for the long gone...

## 2014/11/16 – Sunday (Guincho, Portugal)

... just another lazy Sunday morning... last night, had indulged slightly with supper, wine and conversation... for me it's a lethal combination mixing wine and conversation, perhaps it is the wine which had brought me down memory lane last night... Montreal is still fresh on my mind as I am unable to stop comparing it to being in Portugal... last night's conversations centered around being a teenager growing up in different countries... as I listened to my Portuguese friends tell me about their youth, where weekend beach parties along with drinking (mostly bubbly) were the norm as money was scarce for restaurants or anything else... it was a far contrast from what I had experienced back in Montreal, but at least the objective was the same... to simply have fun within reasonable humorous debauchery...

... a beautiful aspect of Montreal is its' mountain with nature walkways/ park, a ski lift, a manmade lake and even a cemetery... ah!... such prime real-estate for the dead to enjoy... this is where the juvenile delinquent in me would hangout on Saturday nights... we would meet up at Lac aux Castors (*Beaver Lake for those of you who are not children of Bill 101... a linguistic law imposed on immigrants as they now have the responsibility to preserve Quebec's french culture*)... just like mine, every generation has a story to tell, perhaps your grandfather told you about the time when he went to school and had to walk several kilometers to and from school and both ways were uphill too... oouff!... not the brightest kid in school, huh?... it's a great consolation that he (your grandfather) is in your family and not any of ours...

... rules... I like to think most of us can remember the 70's either as a child or as a young adult... my memory/story dates back to the late 70's... *it must be made clear*, I will not be condoning nor endorsing... but for me, the late 70's growing up in the Plateau (Montreal neighbourhood) involved refrigerator size speakers, going to arena concerts, CHOM-FM (when it played music, not commercials), long messy hair (sometimes I used the rubber band that came with the broccoli to tie my hair... yes, I had hair), smoking pot/ hashish, motorcycles were in and cool, and a really nice girlfriend named Bernadette... I did not make the rules, but I did enjoy playing by them...

... on a hot & humid very late Saturday summer night, our heads were already buzzing when one of us got the brilliant idea to play Frisbee in the cemetery, so we head up on our motorcycles to the cemetery facing Beaver lake (I will take this opportunity to boast I had a 1978 Yamaha 650 special, so cool)... there were already a few dozen bikes, we dis-mount in the parking lot across/facing the cemetery, and quickly light up another one... doubts were slowly creeping in about playing Frisbee... such as too lazy to climb over the cemetery gate/fence, catholic brainwashing & fear of evil spirits... but most importantly, the biggest deterrent was that we did not own and/or bring a Frisbee... I suspect we already had a pre-disposition to some sort of ADD (Attention Deficit Disorder)...

... so... as we stumble on over to Beaver Lake, there are dozens of bodies lying about sporadically... lying on the grass moonlight bathing... the occasional outburst of laughter could also be heard... this was a typical *déjà vu* on the mountain side, where existentialist dreamers look at the sky and mentally anguish the existence of god and when is Led Zeppelin coming back... but tonight was special, there were at least 15 people pulling down on the ski lift cable in unison, as the cable went up and down several times picking up momentum, then someone would shout to release and only one guy would hang on... and he shot into the night time air like an arrow off a bow, simply spectacular to watch... and quickly, once again we light up another one... this flying human arrow show goes on for a couple more times...

... lighting one up and passing it around, I put on my motorcycle helmet and lie down on the grass... the helmet muffles the noise around me and I quickly go into a dreamlike state... the inner voice comes back again and tells me I need to sleep/rest more and ease up on smoking pot... the conversation in my head continues with part of me contesting the *giving up pot smoking*... as it (pot) gives me a numbness feeling of happiness... this feeling, I compare it to those late night euphoric TV evangelist christians, I occasionally catch myself watching in secret... I sometimes find myself envying their happiness, as it seems so genuine...

... hey man!... I am pulled out of my zen moment by my friend Jack's voice... shouting in the now nearer distance... *you didn't see him?*... he shouts at me... lifting my head slightly to remove the motorcycle helmet... all my senses seemed to finally be switched on...*fuck what?*... when stoned I don't always articulate well... *you didn't see him?... who the fuck man?* (still not articulating)... he goes on to tell me about an emotional retard who was standing over me and staring at me non-stop... he had blue jeans and a black open t-shirt... balding with long hair and a beard, he looked like Jesus and with creepy ghostly white feet... I mustered every muscle to pan around and look for this Jesus... but every stoner on the mountain pretty much looked like Christ minus the nails in the palms... since this Jesus guy did not share his joints if he even had any, he's as useful to me as tits on a bull (now, I'm articulating!!)...

... our conversation came to a halt and our train of thought was interrupted and replaced by a loud grinding screeching noise... there really is no limit to human ingenuity... next I see humongous sparks generated by metal rubbing on metal... some guy had placed bicycle handle bars over the ski lift cable and was gliding down the cable and screaming in delight... once again, simply spectacular to watch and as we are about to light up again...

a cop car showed up at the top of the hill, and projected a powerful beam of light towards anyone lingering on the grass... we defiantly and very slowly dispersed except for a few which scurried quickly, they were betrayed by their body language because of their fast pace, I suspect they were dealers or were holding... it's not so much as getting busted by the cops, the bitch is they confiscate our pot...

... one thing is for sure, there may be a day when I too may become a grandfather, I will tell my grandchildren stories about the Plateau and that I too walked to/from school and it was uphill in both directions... oouff!...

## 2014/11/17 – Monday (Estoril, Portugal)

... as always... in a narcissistic fashion I search for a bistro where I can drop my big ass and hopefully find an electrical outlet and/or free Wi-Fi for my portable... so that I may contemplate some quirky story for my journal... yes indeed, life is demanding... I ended up walking along the ocean board-walk from Cascais to the neighbouring town called Estoril... just to rub it in, it is a sunny 20 something kind of day... a bit too hot for my liking, though I am not complaining but opted for a table inside the bistro... a little shade will do me no harm as I can still see the ocean... on the way here I walked/saw quite a few men fishing off the beach with their 10 foot long fishing rods... interestingly enough, you would think these were retired men who had time on their hands, but instead they were much younger than myself... being mid-morning, don't they have jobs to go to?...

... my dad was an outdoors man, as fishing and hunting were always an integral part of his life as best as I can remember, cause this is what we talked about to avoid those dreadful moments of silence, when in reality we had nothing in common... other than I loved him and he loved me, an unexplain-able relationship perhaps, certainly nothing a Hallmark card could coin... my dad was a vivacious mischievous child at heart and a strict disciplinary... where his belt equated in an order of importance, maintaining discipline and holding up his trousers... later as he became more portly the *discipline belt* was replaced by a 2 foot long black rubber hose, which had a steel wire mesh imbedded in the rubber, but at the extremities of the hose, the protruding metal filaments pricked his fingers and palm... to remediate, he wrapped masking tape on the ends... the fucken thing ended up looking like a twirling baton, as my brother and I paraded in front of him when he whipped common sense deep into us... of course, this was for our own good...

... other than his kids, when on *terra firma* dad (aka old man) loved raising doves and hunting dogs... the same, expected behavioural patterns/rules applied to all of god's creatures... when he retired back to his birth place (Portugal)... a small farming village called Requeixo which bordered the Pateira de Fermentelos lake... profitable eel fishing became his *hobby du jour* as in Portuguese culture it seems eels are the caviar of the connoisseurs... a hobby that paid big...

... his daily routine was taking his small boat on the lake to set and check his small eel catching nets... he was a very successful eel fisherman by all accounts and this is going to sound weird... his savvy stemmed from the fact that he thought like an eel, meaning he knew what they liked to eat and where they were most likely to be found... so, with this thinking he had placed his 10 nets in his so called strategic and profitable locations along the lake shore... and lord behold, the old man was right...

... one early morning... on his daily net reaping boat trip... as he rowed from one end of the lake to the other checking his nets... some of his nets simply disappeared... stolen to be precise... I can still see and hear him recount his story, he was still livid by all accounts... so, for the next few hours he rowed his boat into every possible nook on the lake with only one objective which was to find his stolen nets... I have to say this about his diligence, it paid off... he ended up finding just one of his stolen nets... he collected the fish/eels caught in the net and put the net back in its' stolen location... with the mid-sun overhead, he heads home for lunch, the calm before the storm...

... after eating lunch my mom coaxes him into taking a nap... my old man has brown eyes but when he is angry his eyes become icy black glass beads... I know this cause these were the eyes he had before he would whip us as kids... scary stuff, to say the least... not sure if the nap did him any good... but when he woke up, glassy cold eyes and all, he grabbed his hunting rifle and headed for the lake... he went back to where he had found the stolen net... within view of his stolen net, my fucken old man perched himself on a tree branch with his rifle in hand... and waited until someone would show up to claim the bounty of his stolen net... the sun was already setting... then some man is walking along the shore and stops in front of the net... as he leans over to pull the net my dad shoots a warning shot in front of the man's feet... the man froze, can you blame him?... this one man had stolen several of my father's nets... so, the crook, my dad and the rifle all went for a walk to collect all the remaining stolen nets... perhaps, this story is legendary in the village... no police nor lawyers, not even an inkling of revenge by anyone was ever engaged in this event... this is/was just one side of my dad... nevertheless, you gotta admire his balls, they will never float cause they're made of steel...

## 2014/11/18 – Tuesday (Cascais, Portugal)

... woke up questioning myself about living in Europe (very expensive)... and the Camino trek in the spring of next year and this whole notion of trying to write a book... I reduced my life to this one year sabbatical span... then what?... what will happen after, other than being almost penniless as I sold practically everything I had as possessions in order to come here... maybe I will go back to Montreal and re-start my construction company... maybe this is why I was not able to sell the tools before coming here... perhaps this was a blessing in disguise... even with all these doubts, I still feel strongly that divinity brought me here for a reason...

... just because I have glimpses of how others are dealing with being on this planet... having a gift of *intuition* does not make me one of god's emissary per se... nor should any of this interfere with who I am, because it is naturally implanted in me to be empathic as far back as I can remember... but all this changed two years ago after the first Camino... but still, I'm just a man and not a saviour of some kind for the masses... as I cannot turn water into wine, either...

... a book?... I'm not a writer!... I still have no idea what to write about?... maybe... will this book be about a man breaking free of his own past and re-discovering himself?... knowing very well that giving up everything he had would surely close doors and he'd end up alone like never before... how far-fetched and liberating can it be that things that were once important to him before were ultimately an illusion... it sounds like madness, does it not?... how sane is it when one claims he can turn water into wine, is it really insanity or is it faith... such a very thin line between the two... it's not always clear, if one is standing on the correct side of the line in the sand, and then again who is wise enough and dead on sure which side of the line is the right one?

... it's not always easy finding a new bistro conducive to inspiration where I can write... this bistro will remain nameless as it is the first and last time I will set foot in here, unless there is an emergency for a bathroom, at which point I'd go back on my resolution and gladly leave a dump... geographically speaking I am not sure if it's in Cascais or the neighboring Estoril town... but since there is mothball scent of opulence, the latter is most likely... does having too much money, disconnect one from reality?... does it explain, self-centred behavioural patterns?... from my experience, stupidity does not take into account wealth... other than make the act of a *stupidity* an expensive one... just a thought...

... strategic location and/or prime real estate... judging from the neighbourhood, there is an abundance of money as reflected off the condo complexes, villas and automobiles (and not buildings, houses and cars)... I always found mother nature has a knack for balancing things... and with this, quite a number of professional beggars around here... professional, because they have handmade cardboard signs advertising their misery in different languages... an international flavour to an up and coming industry... neat, no?... considering this country is in a recession and has more than its' fair share of poverty... the only viable income is from tourism and foreigners, so it seems to be the case here...

... the homeless, faceless guy pushing a bicycle loaded with garbage bags full of *whatevers* saddled to the back fender... and the intricately confusing wire/rope mess handcuffing his bicycle frame to a stolen grocery shopping cart which is also piled high with his worldly *whatevers* stored in crumpled designer brand bags too... and even in his mundane mind, he still needs more stuff, so much so that even his handle bars and front fender miraculously support more bags... and considering the summer like weather we have of late... yet, he still manages to wear several layers of coats that give the impression that his healthy looking bulky body is not anorexic...

... surely... after all he is insane with his hording about, no?... so... he smells bad, but is he insane?... he goes around in circles looking for more *whatevers* to load on to his bike... how much is enough?... people walk by him and quickly too, do you blame them?... as they too run from store to store filling in the void in their lives with *whatevers* which come in designers bags... we can never have enough *whatevers*, and they are addictive like the bi-weekly pay cheques dangling in front of us like carrots on a stick...

... what if there is a place in reality that is between the *collectors of whatevers* and *the one that can turn water into wine*... where the body and soul do not struggle but instead are at peace... and where is this place?... if only the eyes can look inwards, then we could see it immediately...

## 2014/11/19 – Wednesday (Cascais, Portugal)

… sitting here in Dolce Caffé having breakfast… from what I can tell walking here, this is pretty much a blue collar neighbourhood… and the people coming in/out are regulars as the shop keeping clerk greets them by name accompanied by a witty salutation… this morning, not having quite mastered the intricacies of the language I screwed up my order… since I was able to laugh at myself, I can also laugh at anyone because of this… and with this I was honored by the clerks' humour too… despite my linguistic blunders, it's much better being here having coffee than in one of Montreal's underground tunnel mazes, lit up by incandescent lights…

… 1965… as a 5 year old, it was the first time I had come to Portugal and it was an exposure to rural farm life in my parents' home village called Requeixo… at that time my understanding of what was a farm came from Bugs Bunny/Leghorn Foghorn cartoons or perhaps at a more evolved level, *Green Acres* TV sitcom… need there be said, more on this?… I had this perception that farms were nothing but tractors… when in fact, this is probably true for efficient Canadian prairie farmers but what I saw in my small corner of Portugal were the poor ones… a microcosm world slice of simple living, where cows were still the eco tractor and bicycles were the primary form of transportation and these folks were truly faithful to the concept of a day to day existence, with a strong belief the afterlife would be their reward…

… in 1979… I found myself, again living/freeloading in this rural village called Requeixo… cows and tractors were fighting for the right of way on the roads… bicycles are now replaced by mopeds, which by the way, was an upgrade as I've witnessed a family of 5 moving about in the village… for what it is worth, the church has a full house every Sunday morning for mass… for the young people it is a meeting/planning point for the Sunday afternoon activities/outings… with all the self-proclaimed arrogance of a 19 year old, I was just waiting for my motorcycle to arrive from Canada so that I may embark on a drive across Europe… so, here I was stuck in the village, initially, just waiting for the motorcycle… but as weeks turned into months of waiting my focus turned to these peasants… and I felt nothing but empathy, respect and for some even admiration for these people had something I could not see but felt… resiliency and tenacity…

… not being a church goer… especially on this particular Sunday as it was raining heavily… I waited by the living room window peering outside waiting for my cousin/friends to walk by on their way from church… this is how I would find out what activity/outing had been planned for the afternoon...

... in the few seconds I glanced out the window to see if any of my friends were on their way... thru the hard hitting rain, I saw this very elderly man named Jorge, plagued by deeply entrenched facial wrinkles and a *paper cigarette* on his lips protruding through the stack of freshly cut grass/hay held together not with rope but a vine... the hay stack was balanced on his arched back (burying most of his head) as he pushed his bicycle with difficulty... leaving the impression that the bike was for support and balance and nothing else...

... along with the smell of electricity in the air from the lighting discharges... a wave of emotions came through me... seeing this man, touched me in an un-physical manner... it is as if I can feel what his life is all about, I feel like I am him... god, wtf... I can feel him all the way down to my stomach, so visceral that it nauseates me... those few seconds of visual contact etched his life story in my head... to the extent, I grabbed a sheet of paper and markers, to capture onto paper what eyes do not see but perceive... the electricity flowing thru my hand/finger nerves was foreign, as it disfigured the bicycle wheels on the sheet to capture the hardship of the moment and even of his life...

... he is guided by the invisibly dim bicycle light powered by the dynamo, so much uphill struggle to feed livestock, with his living quarters on the second floor of the barn... just one ladder rung (notch) better than where the animals are kept... he talks to them as he feeds them, for they listen... sunsets will come and go, there will be no reprieve for him... they (animals) need him forever, so he thinks... he worries about dying and who will take care of his animals...

... he has... just 2 suits, one for special occasions such as mass, weddings, funerals and final departure... and the one he is wearing now, an oversized hand me down suit, in no way compassionate with the weather... he hopes his old suit lasts long enough, as the new one will eventually be part of the coffin attire with a new shirt bought specifically for the occasion by a remaining family member, if any... such an unquestioned and unchallenged existence... survival without dreams are replaced by the sense of duty... he is comfortably numb, in his struggle... is he not?

... my deep sketching thoughts were interrupted by the doorbell buzzing frantically... as I looked up and around as if I had just awoken... the sheet of paper has this drawing on it (see drawing)... the doorbell rings again... as I open the door, it's my friend Gil, from the church returning gang... and he tells me we are to meet up at the cafe in the village… unless the rain lets up, we will most likely spend the afternoon drinking… he asks me if I'm okay and I jokingly said I was on the toilet when the bell rang…

… as I put on my jacket to accompany Gil… this imprint the old man left in me, it truly fucked the rest of my day… as we walked Gil spoke incessantly and I heard his voice but not the words as I felt something was not right in my head… even as the daylight dissipated we still kept drinking… with the night crawling in to stay and with the relentless rain, all the more reason to stay here drinking… I kept buying rounds… besides, to go to an empty house with all my alcohol numbed senses is simply a scary thought for me… especially being alone as my whole being was not feeling… *right?*… what is wrong with me?…

… one of the locals came in announcing that old man Jorge had passed away… there was a moment of silence in the bistro… then the local added… a neighbour heard the animals groaning loudly as animals do when they are not fed… when the neighbour came to see what was going on he found Jorge collapsed on the ground with bicycle in hand and covered in hay… and with this announcement… shivers went through my drunk body… I felt him again, still struggling…

## 2014/11/20 – Thursday (Cascais, Portugal)

... still feel like a tourist... the novelty of being in Portugal and especially coming to Casa da Guia a mesmerizing bistro on a cliff facing the ocean... well, stifles the real reasons why I am here... which is to write a journal (book)... on what, I have no idea as I am not a writer in any way... also meet up with Suzanne... and eventually gear up in the spring 2015 for the Camino pilgrimage... my first time on the pilgrimage was in May 2013... it caused my spiritual awakening and turned my life in a living turmoil and massive confusion... maybe, I want to stay in the tourist mode as long as possible as it prevents me from facing more anguish...

... powerful emotion... so, I'm just gonna sit here and have breakfast and pick on someone at random and write something about them as I see fit... why not a story about the young woman... when I was coming in, she arrived on her Ducati motorcycle... and envy being a very powerful emotion, maybe it can trigger my imagination into writing something...

... here we have a good looking lady with my favourite motorcycle a Ducati Monster (even better looking than her)... she drives a very cool bike, but if you paid attention as she arrived on the bike and is in the process of stopping, she puts her feet down before stopping, but remember she is cute... but cute is not enough, and I agree... the color of the Ducati is a flat black... and her low cut (50% polyester, 40%cotton, 10% rayon) halter top is black too... now?... yes, we can assume she has fashion sense because her see thru uncovered bra straps are befitting her top... it can be concluded she is not color blind... on a side note, odds are very good her *undies* under her blue jeans are in sync with the rest of the outfit...

... boyfriend?... she talks to him about shifting of the gears, though she knows there are 5 gears, it seems she is unable to remember the sequence of the numbers... fortunately the boyfriend sounds as if he's from the Sesame Street era and did learn his *numbers* in the right sequence too... or perhaps it has to do with his heritage/upbringing and picking crops as a summer job... as a kid he was poorly paid on a commission basis for every head of lettuce... before, I ramble on about the exploitation, injustice and downfalls of cheap labour... let's just say he formed a union and with an equitable pay was able to save money to buy his very own motorcycle... a happy ending , no?

... we've all heard a version of the story/question... if you were to be stuck on a desert island, what would you take... considering this... here's my version of this question... if I were stuck on a desert road and the young lady riding the Ducati Monster bike showed up... and I only had the chance to have one, what would I choose?... the lady or the motorcycle (remember it's a Ducati Monster)...

... please... send me your answer by either choosing the lady or bike... and accompanied by an intelligent explanation as to your choice... the purpose for requesting an *intelligent explanation* is to give this story more credibility... basically, all I have written so far is pure shit and I'm hoping you guys are better, brighter writers than myself...

... spelling/grammar counts, and your answers will be evaluated by an international panel of newly arrived illegal immigrants awaiting deportation... who'll take some time off from sleeping on the chairs in the waiting lounge of *ministre de l'immigration du quebec* to evaluate your responses... of course!!!... there is a prize for the winner, what did you think?... this contest does have credibility... I on the other hand do not...

## 2014/11/21 – Friday (Cascais, Portugal)

... bedroom morning... did you ever look at rope, not as a whole but as a cross section... much to my amazement, it is nothing but a thinner series of strands... it's the fabric of these filaments bundled together that create the rope... the same comparison can be used for friends and maybe more with family... support from individuals around us which can make us stronger... I'm ok, with being a filament somewhere... hopefully, my kids still feel this way too...

... bedroom thoughts... I have been here a couple of weeks in this new country... arrived here with my north american mind set... and one of the first things I did was get a cell phone... why?... what I should of have done was ask myself the question *why* before buying the phone... I no longer need a phone to look at aimlessly when bored or be waiting for a friend/customer to call... this illusion that I will miss out on something will not work on me anymore and I will miss out on nothing other than bad news, so no hurry... my self-worth or importance is not based on a large number of contacts or the cell phone plan allowing me unlimited phone calls and texts...

... Suzanne goes off to work and leaves me with a kiss on the lips... with my head held high and a computer under my arm, I head off to a coffee shop, allowing my instincts to guide me as to where I should be having coffee... whether I drive, walk or take the train to the next town for a change, there is no rush... idle hands and mind are kept busy with a keyboard and reflective thoughts...

... breathing... I now have the time to breathe... my pace is slow compared to everyone, so much *hurry* in their everyday gestures... too much time, is it a curse or a blessing to have time to reflect, was it better when I was busy working and all the little trivial things which working entails... or am I better off, sitting here observing in others what I used to be like?...

... men wearing 3 day old 5 o'clock shadows, mothers dragging children with pacifiers in mouth, as if to delay/maintain the innocence of youth in a hurried adult world... the mom with the 4 year old, sitting next to me smoking her cigarette frantically while decking her espresso cup with red lipstick... all the while, verbally snapping at her kid, not to drink the chocolate milk while the pacifier is in his mouth...

... other than the weather, I now see there is no difference from where I came from to where I am now as people share the same struggles... lifestyles are the same in industrialized countries... am I becoming a spoiled *prima donna* of sorts... maybe, it is already time to march elsewhere, geographically speaking... with so much time for reflective thoughts, can they (thoughts) turn against me?... is this what it feels like to be retired?... I'm only joking...

## 2014/11/22 – Saturday (Cascais, Portugal)

... before the no smoking ban law, in public places... every bistro, restaurant or any public place was engulfed in thick cigarette smoke... at that time, the preferred hour for supper in restaurants was around 7-8 pm... I would actually go in earlier to avoid eating my supper in a smoked filled dining room... sometimes, I was so early I felt the need to help the waiters set the tables... for the most part smoking is now a health issue here and in general banned in public places... small coffee shops, mostly in villages still permit smoking in their premises... smoking is a difficult habit to get rid of, even with legislation... it must start with one's self will... otherwise all this legal jargon is just a noble attempt...

... to the best of my knowledge, this country never had a decent infrastructure when it came to telephone land lines, other than major cities... with the advent of cell phones... well, it took off... as I look around me here, it is a gorgeous Saturday afternoon in this seaside bistro... lots of couples, multi generation families... what do they have in common other than getting a sun tan on the back of their heads?... they are ALL looking/toying with their smart phones... the best way to probably get rid of the smoking habit is to replace it with another habit... hence, the cell phone phenomena...

... what is the point of watching an outdoor concert, where a man of a physically small stature like myself has difficulty seeing the stage... but to add aggravation to my size, is the hand full of clowns in front of me with their arms up in the air taking endless pictures with their phones... how many memories do you need?...

... now, how fucken annoying is your obsession with cell phones DURING concerts, don't get me wrong, as a former computer programmer-analyst, I can appreciate probably more than most the intricacies of the Apps, but let's face it the microchip in the phone will NEVER record as well as the human brain cells... for most it seems, it is a phenomenal evolutionary step that your fingers can evolve/progress from playing with your penis to picking your nose to navigating the apps on your SMART phone... but I suspect that the radiation emitted from a tactile screen has rendered you moronic (and hopefully sterile too, I and we can do without your progeny)... why watch the concert thru your miniature screen, it'll probably damage your eyes in the long run...

... so... unplug the umbilical cord from your phone to your solar plexus chakra as the information is flowing in the wrong direction... and please try this... listen & feel the music... just live *in the moment.*!!!!


## 2014/11/23 – Sunday (Areia, Portugal)

... winter... for sure I do not miss the cold winters back in Montreal... though the snow does have a pretty *effect* for a few hours... this morning I am alone in the bistro wondering what can I write about... but even more frustrating... is my being here the right thing to be doing... still so much doubt... but the idea of another winter back home precipitated my coming here... so far, I think it is all fun and games, but I need to bring into focus the true objective of my being here and dealing with it...

... my pre-retirement?... lots of retired foreigners in this part of the country... the easy climate, political stability are contributing factors for sure... but wine and food are the deal clincher... what else is left to do when retired... but to enjoy the pleasures of the flesh before the skin cells wrinkle themselves into oblivion...

... the UK chap sitting next to me is on the phone talking about Movember... where one grows a moustache during November in order to raise funds for prostate cancer related diseases... kind of pointless now, with my being here and all, though feeling nostalgic... if I were still back in Montreal I'd write something and post it on Facebook... and it would be humorous for sure...

... *Movember*... it's all about bringing back the moustache, having fun and doing it for a serious cause; men's health, specifically prostate cancer as my dad lost against it... it's a cause in which I believe and to tell you the truth the growing of the moustache is fun too, at least for most... but my implications revolving around this cause are far more noble and demanding than for most participants... one of the definitions of... ***sacrifice***... is... to *forfeit (one thing) for another thing considered to be of greater value*... so far my sacrifice will be abstinence from carnal pleasures (sex), as my wife refuses to kiss my lips, due to eventually they (lips) being sheltered by a prickly moustache... I sense/can tell you are laughing already, but this will cost you...

... being over 50... one no longer expects sex after every meal... or as an afternoon tea time snack... or between hockey periods (especially the first one)... or even as a bedtime treat before falling asleep... having said this, it still does not undermine the urges... now, it is not so much the cause that is at stake but more my ego & urges and the most critical point is the bowing down to my wife and letting her believe that she has won this battle of wills... the rule decreed by the Mrs. is simple... sex or moustache... one or the other... a choice?... yes, this is a gender battle...

... being resourceful, I turn to the global community (internet) for guidance... several resources point to the bible to succeeding in supressing manly urges... considering the bible has done wonders for priests in suppressing their urges for long periods of time, perhaps my 30 day ordeal will be a cinch... or so I thought, what I have now learned is that god has a mischievous sense of humour, cause when I opened the bible at random... which I had stolen from a motel years ago while in Niagara Falls... and up to now had been used to level my bed post... I ended up in Leviticus 18... ah! it's all about *will*, the last thing I want to read about are bible orgies... and Moses up on the mountain top collecting/waiting for the 10 commandments tablets to be chiseled out by a Joe Rockhead and looking down on his female herd of sinners exposing their bosoms... so, under false pretenses... I was conned by the bible as being the answer...

... seriously now... with 30 days of unbelievable male stamina suppression... I need motivation to persist... perhaps some financial encouragement for my cause whether you are on my side (true friends) or Emme's (spouse) side of the wit battle... either way, it is all for Movember... so, you can send your contribution by mail, or I can drop by at your convenience to pick it up... only you can save a man from having a doctor inserting a finger in ones' rectum... please, do help?...

## 2014/11/24 – Monday (Belem, Portugal)

... seriously... is this for real, it is... this is my rant segment... courts seem to be overwhelmed with families bickering amongst themselves over what they got as an inheritance from their parents... buildings are left to collapse because tenants are basically, still paying the same rent as when they first got into the apartment decades ago... high-end Mercedes run on diesel fuel, as if they can afford the car but not the gaz... shoemakers/repairs is still an art and shoes are an important element in the wardrobe... for every coffee shop there seems to be lottery outlet... chinese restaurants cater to portugueses palate, far from being authentic Chinese food...

... what is fun?... in this country it has to be football (soccer for some of us)... this week I met up with my cousin for lunch (incredibly good food), beers and eventually a sunset over Lisbon, one of the few family members with whom I have connected on a regular basis over the last few years... even though he's much younger than I (+/- 20 years) and apart from fitting into all the criteria's of being a nice guy in every sense of the word... throw in as well a great sense of humour (often a low key sly) and a profound knowledge of both Lisbon and football... to uphold my claim that he's a nice guy, he will modestly/humbly mumble he is the editor of the major newspaper which is dedicated to football and little else other than advertisements and naughty classifieds...

... how much is football integrated into the daily culture?... it almost seems there is always a football game going on somewhere, I think there are more games being played per day than babies being born, considering the recessive economic difficulties in Portugal, my cynical observation is not far-fetched... also, pretty much every restaurant has a TV showing a football game and with this, when couples enter a restaurant, men will always sit facing the TV screen as the football widows speak to their in-attentive catatonic football watching spouses...

... another annotation is the rivalry between two geographically close Lisbon football teams Benfica & Sporting... Benfica being born from the ashes of the locals and Sporting created by a rich entrepreneur... hence, the cliché both political and cultural labelling of poor versus rich syndrome... indirectly, it resonates a certain class distinction in Portuguese society...

... how to make this a better place?... I have absolutely no idea... is there anything wrong with this place other than people behaving like humans... I like to joke that the problem with Portugal is that there are too many por-tugueses... but this joke is far from the truth... this is indeed a nation full of incredible people... and at times too good to be true...

## 2014/11/25 – Tuesday (Cascais, Portugal)

... mission statement... which I seem to forget... is move to Europe for one year and live on a budget... write a journal (book)... in the spring re-do the Camino pilgrimage but this time in its' entirety... and finally but not least, make a go at it with Suzanne... one would think this is enough to keep anyone busy and yet even though I have been here a few weeks, I miss my kids... somewhat homesick, boredom has set in too, as writing my journal is a rather difficult task which requires discipline, something I lack... funny, even though things with Suzanne are going fine and I may move in with her next month... I'm still perplexed by a feeling of loneliness... anyway, today I ended up in a super store, kind of like a Walmart... glad to say, I ended up buying nothing (budget restrains)... so, I walked every isle, simply out of curiosity... with so many stacked shelves, with everything from packaging to language caught my attention... it was as if I were a kid back in Montreal... which now reminds me of a misfortunate adventure I had in a department store...

... my recollection of Kresge (the Walmart of Montreal's 60's) were the toy aisles... and actually seeing toys like Kerplunk, Gumby and Tip-it as seen on TV... though we would never dream of owning such toys, it was as close as we would ever come to them... and of course there was the Photomat machine where you'd get 4 B/W pics for a few coins... whenever we (brother and I) went with my mom... she gave us money for fries at the snack bar, we sat on the swivelling stools and drowning our fries in vinegar... yep!, we felt important...

... yeah!... I once travelled to the Kresge department store on the corner of Mount Royal and St. Laurent… as a nine year old traveling Montreal's plateau neighbourhood (world) on my own, I always had to drag along my younger brother… it's the price I had to pay if I wanted to go out on a Saturday afternoon… but today in hindsight as an adult, I realize that all my parents wanted was to have the house to themselves to be fruitful and multiply… wink! wink!…

… anyway… we wandered for hours in the store, it had one whole aisle dedicated to toys, and since we had none at home it seemed like a lot of toys to us… walking around, I was so absorbed by the items on the shelves, that when I left the store I had forgotten my kid brother, mind you I did sense fresh air flowing through my fingers where my brothers' hand was supposed to be… so I knew something was amiss, by the time I got to Sherbrooke street (6 city blocks later)…

… I never went back cause I was too embarrassed… I hope he is ok, cause it has been 45 years and I never heard from him again… anyway, the kid was far from being a marvel, but he was a surprise when my father and I heard of the pregnancy… *once again, anyway!*… on the way home, realizing my *faux pas*… certainly I could not show up empty handed and desperately needed a quick fix… I remembered there was a Senhora Maria who ran a daycare from her home… in those days every street block had a daycare of sorts…

… I stopped at a private home daycare center and the kids were all outside running amok on the street dodging cars… so I borrowed another kid (you can guess this is before $5 a day daycare kicked in)… and brought that whining critter home, the last thing I wanted was to spoil my parents lustfully good mood by announcing I had misplaced the little marvel (the kid brother )…

… in my haste, I had picked up an Asian descent kid, and no way would the old folks be fooled by this one… actually dad didn't notice, mom on the other hand… well, she caught on, but only after she tried in vain to comb his black spikey hair with lots of water to appease it, that she got suspicious…

… so I went back to the daycare again and swapped for a Caucasian this time… what?… you thought I would go back to the store to pick up my original kid brother… did you not read previously where I clearly stated he was no marvel… good riddance… this is a true story!

## 2014/11/26 – Wednesday (Cascais, Portugal)

… all the small things… it has not been a month that I am here and there are already a bunch of small things that have caught my attention… an unexpected occurrence with being in this new country is… so much free time to think… so much free time to wonder why humans are so quirky… at times I think we are all insane and I nominate myself first in this category… reading the newspapers, it is an endless reporting of medical screw ups blamed on budget cuts, never the physician himself (herself too)… doctors are seen as gods here, at least by the elderly who bow their heads in reverence when speaking with one or about one… as I eavesdrop on the herd of old ladies sitting at the next table… they compare and defend their doctors in such a way that it reminded me of my kids exchanging Pokemon cards…

… so many crippled beggars, maybe if they still had their limbs they could move to better locations… where they could increase their beggar revenue… amputations of all kinds here… one gets the feeling, hacksaws are the instrument of choice for surgeons… perhaps because it is readily available in stores and farmers markets… it must be that it is easier and far more efficient to amputate limbs than trying to mend… for one thing it is more cost effective, no?… maybe doctors simply fix god's mistakes band-aid style…

… are surgeons highly paid butchers?… who probably as kids were bestowed the honor of carving a lamb roast during morbid Easter weekends… the pride of the mother asking her son to carve out the meat on a Sunday holiday, because somewhere along the line he (son) had mentioned to her he wanted to be a surgeon… and the poor father, whose value for the family is now reduced to providing financially… as the carving honor was swiped from him… a strong mother presence along with a weak father role is a quasi-perfect setting for a recreation of the *boys from brazil*… even in this solar apex of paradise… cut throat nastiness abounds…

… driving… now the cliché is that here, they drive fast… I can attest this is exact… more interestingly is how they enter roundabouts, though we are supposed to stop before entering the circular lanes, one does not (including myself)… it is almost a dare and challenge to the drivers already in the roundabout… suffice to say, though the stop and yield road signs are physically different in shape & color… they are both interpreted as being the same, and at times even neglected (ooops!)… I think because I have driven motorcycles all my life, I have a knack for being aggressive but also defensive when driving, it helps to have nerves of steel… so, they (soon me?) drive fast to get nowhere important so as to have idle time to smoke a cigarette... and yet, when it comes to pedestrian crosswalks, they absolutely stop... puzzling contradiction...

... imagine, this will be hard for a Montrealer... shopping malls are open from 10-ish til midnight or so and 7 days a week too... electronics stores are sometimes open later... I do not... yet, have the mind set to go do groceries, say at 10 pm... and unlike back home stores are not limited to 3 employees... when buying fruits/veggies, to each item there is a code which one enters when self-weighting the items, and it generates a pricing label which will later be scanned by the cashier... when entering any store, there is always someone greeting you warmly, unlike the frustrated anorexic and/or obese (can't be both... lol) old bitch at a department store barking *bonjour* with rabies dripping saliva... yeah!, I know I am exaggerating, she does not have saliva, it's the contagious foam generated by the rabies that is dripping...

... cinema... went to see *Interstallar*... no matter what movie, it is always with reserved seating... popcorn comes with either sugar or salt... not sure about the butter... the movie is shown in its' original version with Portuguese subtitles... which I actually enjoy reading at times, as it eases my re-introduction to Portuguese... along with commercials and previews it is pretty much the same with the exception of... there is a 10 minute break half way thru the movie to allow for pipi, caca (if you are fast) or smoking...

... whether on Google, Facebook or Youtube I am now always prompted with Portuguese publicity or commercials... which I actually take the time to watch, as it is part of my learning experience... actually, no matter how serious the advertisement pretends to be, I find it funny... on a final note... the weather is always wonderful so, when driving a car, I have both windows open as I refuse to turn on the AC... thought you would like to know... go ahead, you are thinking it and why not say it too... *McFern, you adorable bastard!*...

## 2014/11/27 – Thursday (Guincho, Portugal)

... even though I am sitting in this coffee shop perched over the Atlantic Ocean, with an awesome view partly due to the windows having been washed just the other day... why do I feel homesick today?... it is not Montreal I miss but more the people I left behind... maybe it has more to do with the fact that I really have no friends here, other than Suzanne my girlfriend...

40

… with a warm latte limbering my lips… I think of not only the friends I left behind but actually people I had met throughout the years… specifically an old Italian friend from my youth, called Joe (baptismally Giuseppe)… a funny story comes to mind, which coincides with today being the day Americans celebrate thanksgiving… Joe and I had worked for the same American company, suffice to say we managed to get the day off, even though it is not a Canadian holiday… what comes to mind is the *1979 Italian Thanksgiving* day I spent with Joe and his family…

… I was to meet Joe at his house and we were to hangout and smoke some weed on this so called holiday… as I got there, he was backing out his pristine Camaro from the duplex's sunken garage, as there was a family crisis in progress… earlier that day, they had been shopping at the Jean Talon market picking up a few crates of tomatoes, and somehow they were short changed a crate… under different circumstances, his parents would take their BMW (bus, metro or walk) but this was an emergency and his parents were waiting impatiently on the sidewalk… the car is still backing up when the father gets in the front seat and motions the wife to get into the back, as you may know Camaros only have 2 doors, and in an almost comedic fashion the short stalky mother gets stuck behind the front seat and tangled by the seat belt, as this was not bad enough her husband is pulling/swinging the door shut… the swinging door had enough momentum and impacted on her girdle covered ass to poke her into the backseat… Joe, yells out over the colorful descriptive Italian insulting jargon being exchanged between his parents, for me to go to the backyard and wait…

… I walk alongside the duplex towards the backyard, empty crates from grapes are stacked along the wall with buzzing wasps… small patches of grass still remain, too bad this is not the smoking kind of grass, Joe has the smoking one on him… as I turn the corner, I see the widowed, chewed out *paper cigarette* smoking grandfather, wearing beach flip flops with black tube socks… he was collecting the broken hockey sticks from the dilapidated garden which had been used to support tomato and/or bean stalks… he muttered a few words in Italian, I just nodded & smiled, as I do not speak the language… he handed me the sticks and picked up a broken zucchini off the ground and placed it in front of his open fly/zipper and gestured a sexual innuendo and laughed profusely… funny indeed, even though his wife passed away, the man still has the desire to procreate, I guess it is evident that from his clothing to seducing a zucchini, he is now lost without his wife…

… Joe just spent over 2 hours dealing with his neurotic parents at the market, and I what seemed to be an eternity with his grandfather... when he (Joe) returned we lit one up in an emergency manner... as we sat on the wooden picnic table in the backyard, soaking in the last rays of an autumn sun... the buzz had... well... set in... when we were interrupted by his father, he came out to the yard wearing house slippers, gray dress pants and a sleeveless undershirt, with his wet slick hair combed back... the undershirt straps cut into his hairy shoulders, he looked like a monkey on an organ grinder, which made me laugh... the old monkey man came awfully close to us... I think he suspected we were high/stoned and I was still trying to control my laughter... so!... the 3 of us ended up, unloading more tomato crates from the car into the basement where he also made wine... to ease the tension I initiated small talk with the monkey man and asked him if he added whisky to the wine during the fermentation process... he looked at me with a gleam in his eyes... I sensed he was impressed by my question/knowledge of wine making... while Joe unloaded the crates by himself... the monkey man/dad and I spent the next few minutes discussing his wine making process and had me taste his various vintages and concluded his monologue with inviting me to stay for supper... considering I am buzzed, drunk and have the munchies simultaneously, I accepted...

... I was glad we were having supper in the basement kitchen, as I would find it challenging to go up the stairs to the showroom kitchen... the monkey dad dragged an old metal/plastic chair covered in duct tape and which has seen better days and is now probably used as a step ladder to replace light bulbs... nevertheless, I still felt I was handed the king's throne... immediately *we* the 4 men sat down... and the mother removed the *paper cigarette* from the grandfathers' mouth and taking a second glance at the table making sure nothing was missing, she sat on the edge of her chair in a state of alarm just in case she had to get up quickly if food would ever be lacking... here I was having a theoretical Italian thanksgiving dinner, and these folks without pretentious fanfare invited me to share their food, completely unaware that today was a holiday of *thanks*... as the mother walked behind me, I said the food was very good and thanked her... she whacked me on the head and said *you cutta you hairrr...* between courses, I looked at this quasi-dysfunctional family and wondered what bonds them, certainly nothing Hallmark can put in a card, cause there are no words... but there are several variations of something called *love*... go figure!

## 2014/11/28 – Friday (Lisbon, Portugal)

... does time fly when being idle... ???... indulgent gluttony... every time I come to Europe I go through a phase which usually lasts a couple of weeks where I return to and even discover new restaurants... I find here, food is almost an art, other than the young kids which eat at McD's and Burger kings... everyone seems to take the time to eat elegantly, and by this I mean real cutlery, wine and finely cooked cuisine...

... suppers are always my best time, which usually starts at 8:30 til 11-ish... and I think I have mentioned this to some of you already... starting with the breads and even the butter served as appetizers... and throw onto the table too an assortment of olives, pates/spreads and an endless array of finger foods... by the time, the main course arrives, at times we are no longer hungry and yet I still indulge myself...

... *entrecosto* aka spare ribs... there is this one restaurant in the Cascais town center called Dom Pedro which has what we feel are the best spare ribs... and unlike the restaurant back home where the ribs arrive at your table within seconds of taking a first sip of beer... here, I actually waited at least 45 minutes, makes me think that perhaps the cook had gone to some farm and slaughter the swine himself... it is during these long silence free minutes that one starts nibbling on all the appetizers...

... never been disappointed, the wine lists are about as big as the yellow pages in Montreal (slight exaggeration here)... unlike remembering jokes, I can never remember wine brand names... even so, I always ask for a pitcher and/or bottle of the house wine and astonishingly so, it is divine too, but never the same from week to week... the owner prides himself in choosing the wine vintage of the week...

... the most extraordinary resto discovery was in Lisbon itself... it is called Mercado da Ribeira... it is composed of two identical twin buildings... in one half there is an indoor farmers market type of setting, the closest thing I can compare it to would be the Atwater market in the peak summer months, but it is like this all year round... the other half of the market is a food court... the size of it is an overwhelming, wow!... but here is where it gets interesting and memorable... take any food court found in a shopping mall back home... the difference being, 5+ of the restos are owned and operated by renown local TV chefs... as you walk by the different food outlets, it is not students serving/working but what seems to be professional cooks with pots gushing out all kinds of hypnotizing scented steam vapours... throw in a wine shop in the court as well... what you will NOT find are paper plates, waxed glass cups or plastic cutlery... ALL food is served on real plates with cutlery... when you get your wine bottle, you also get wine glasses... you can eat or you can just get yourself a bottle and sit there and simply drink... when you are finished eating/drinking, you get up and leave... someone (busboy/girl) will clear away your plates etc... I saw friends, couples, even families with small kids and they all end up in the food court after shopping... to meet up and indulge their afternoons in large & long family style tables, over food and conversation...

... this architectural space has a double function both as a provider of food and more importantly it fosters a community spirit as it is located in a residential area away from the tourists... for me, this was a truly privileged discovery and for some reason, I wished my kids were here to see/enjoy this too as there's even a sushi shop... a choosing dilemma indeed...

... and as I lay here in bed, balancing my laptop on my bulging stomach as I write this... it is now time to back off my gluttonous mode so that I may return to a flatter stomach... as I reflect on the month gone by with its' lingering summer weather, my gastronomic indulgences and the never ending worry if I'm doing the right thing in being here... waiting for spring weather (season) to embark on my Camino pilgrimage... it just hit me, after my sabbatical year... will I be able to integrate back to my old lifestyle, now that I have tasted this side of living...

## 2014/11/29 – Saturday (Cascais, Portugal)

... I spent my afternoon in the Albatroz Hotel bar... there is an unobstructed breath taking view of the ocean as I type these words... interestingly... the chairs are upholstered with a picture of the Beatles from the Sargent Peppers Lonely Heart Club Band album cover era, I speculate they had stayed here at one time or another... for centuries Cascais is/was a beach town resort for monarchies from different countries... today the hotel seems to accommodate tourists from high society who seem to linger perpetually... I couldn't help but observe on my way down to the hotel that there is a sharp contrast in housing built by the historically rich compared to the very modest local fisherman's housing... Cascais is not your typical Portuguese town as there are way too many foreigners at any given time... they stifle Portuguese traditions with monetary related lifestyles... the irony is, I am a foreigner too...

... a disadvantage of being in a foreign country, despite my personal situation and its' beauty... is having no friends... though Suzanne has lots of friends, for the most part they are single women... mind you... this would be good if I were single and not with Suzanne... and I do miss going out with other couples... today would be our first outing with another couple... finally, someone with whom I can discuss football, power tools or hell anything else other than tampons, feminine *staying fresh* hygiene or shampoo hair care...

... we were invited for coffee/drinks at Carla & Pedro's... being of a curious nature, I always had the idea that the best way to learn a language is to watch the local TV, but to learn about people is to go into their homes... it is where people are most likely to open up the door to themselves too... inside scoop... interesting couple in the sense that between themselves there has been half a dozen marriages or so... yep!... hobbies come in all shapes and sizes including divorce related real-estate such as their house...

... I get out of the car... and push (open/close) the iron gates leading into a driveway laced with a series of tree canopies... just a few meters past the gates there is a mausoleum to my right with the year 1840 engraved into a stone placed over the ornamented doorway... I get back in the car and think, "oouuff!... creepy"... and to lighten my mood, the Flintstones comes to mind with the episode where Fred & Barney must spend a night in a haunted house... at the gates, there was still daylight but now as the car tires crack the gravel road as we park, dusk has now set the mood as we approach their elaborate 200 year old house (so I guess)...

... everything about the house is big, and I am just going to briefly mention what I see as I walked towards the front door, you can use your imagination to fill in the blanks... chimney, gables, gargoyles, and *gothic everything* and already an uneasiness is setting in my stomach... one thing is for sure, the first owners/builders wanted the world to know how rich and powerful they were and probably considering the superstitions of that time, it probably warded off potential robbers...

... as our owner Carla opens the door to us, I try to grasp the size of the immense entrance hall (dimly lit)... as my eyes panned the room, of what seemed like endless walls, I finally rested my eyes on the spiral staircase... wide enough that if this where a sorority house, some drunken student would drive a Volkswagon Beetle up the stairs... everything about the house was original other than some electrical wires running along the baseboards... as she welcomed us in from the drizzling rain hitting our backs, she apologized for the mess as her latest cleaning lady also quit on her... to ease the moment, I said she had an extra-ordinary house and that I would work for free cleaning her house just to be able to explore it... we all laughed... yeah, I know... I'm adorable...

... our hosts guided us into a foyer type of room with Louis XIV type sofas... they were old and smelled their age too and had seen better days... nevertheless, the whole place so far had all my senses reeling, and I was not limited to my 5 physical senses either... this building was alive with the past, I could feel it... a few drinks later and lots of giggles... and I still had an uneasiness in my stomach... I gained control of the conversation and turned to the hostess with precise questions as our host Pedro was more reserved (women in general love to talk)... did she know anything about the original owners... ???... she said the original owners were Italian and had come to Portugal... and built this house as a summer resort/holidays... as the backyard also had winding stairs along the cliff leading down to a secluded sandy beach... but a subsequent family generation had at first abandoned then sold the house... as it was rumoured to be haunted... and it remained empty for many decades, even after being sold...

... I jokingly said... *well, you are living here, but apparently your maid could not*... without knowing, I had put my foot in my mouth... my comment must of hit a nerve as both our hosts bodies' simultaneously jerked on the sofa... and asked me if I felt any presence in the house?... not quite... I am not a medium by any means, but I do have a knack to hone in on invisible energies... I am quite good at dowsing as I had done this successfully several times in my youth... Pedro, interrupted and said all he knows is that he does not like living in the house...

... I think... sometimes are instincts are acutely aware of what we do not see or understand as humans... Carla on the other hand wanted a confirmation that she was not alone in feeling there was something in the house, she was adamant it was a ghost... I said to her that when I first walked in the house I felt an energy coming from the second floor... and with this her eyes opened wide and she pulled me out of the sofa, leading us up the stairs... at the top of the stairs was a sort of reading room which connected to the hallway leading into bedrooms... just standing there and looking down the hallway, I told her there was an strong energy coming from the room in the far left... I felt Suzanne coming into my bubble, as slight fear was setting in her too... Carla wanted me to go into the bedroom, but I declined instinctively... as I walked around the reading room... I felt myself walking through what seemed like an invisible light ray of energy shooting up from the floor into the ceiling... as if it were a light beacon, and stepping in and out through it the hairs on the back of my neck would rise with shivers down my spine as I heard faint voices murmuring...

... I grabbed Suzanne's' hand and turned to our hosts thanking them for their hospitality and heading back down the stairs... in the vestibule... protocol dictates that we kiss on the cheek on departure... as Suzanne was about to lean forward and kiss Carla good-bye on the cheek, I jerked and pulled her hand towards me, making it impossible for them to kiss... still holding her hand as if she were a five year old child, we both stepped outside and I just waived good-bye to our hosts... Suzanne, gave me a puzzled, if not an angry look... I just said, they are contaminated and we got in the car...

... it's my safety net... a form of auto-protection... my body is here, but my mind wanders, under the cover of conversational nods... I will be the first to admit it is mentally unhealthy to perpetually drift... but I do and even re-create their reality in my head... so farfetched a story and even entertaining... my world fills in the blanks of theirs... they live in a world of materialistic opulence, I used to be one of them... do I hide in my head as a denial of my past?... perhaps... or am I afraid their world will suck me back in after the Camino... after all, I too am contaminated...

## 2014/11/30 – Sunday (Areia, Portugal)

... bought a lottery scratch ticket and newspaper... my lottery *losing streaking* is still intact, at least this is consistent in my life... even in the Sunday newspaper there is no truce on domestic violence, road accidents and corruption... though more than usual, pictures of nude women in the arts section of the newspaper... is distorted sexuality, art?... interesting... neither me nor any of the people in the bistro look like the nudes I saw in the newspaper's art section... should my bleeding heart be dismayed with the human race...

... breakfast couple... how far can we let our bodies go to waste?... mr. personality here has a tummy big enough to shelter a dozen or so anorexic babies from the rain... hell, he can even hide them inside if we were in nazi Germany... if the suit he is wearing is his Sunday best, he needs to take it to the cleaners… what anxiety triggered him to let himself go, cause surely he was not born this way… also, this fascinates me the most… when was the last time he saw his penis?… does he go about feeling it as if he were reading in brail?… what about sexual desires, or is it an *out of sight, out of mind*?… what is wrong with me, so mean and judgemental…

… beautiful… very beautiful indeed… though with low self-esteem and quite evident too, a personal *insecurity* mind set… her clothing is tasteful and conservative but very modest… prudish would best describe the way she dresses… with high heels and a tighter skirt emphasizing her sensual curves she could have any man at her feet… and yet, she is with him… did they meet up before his physical change, if not… why settle so low for such a bobbling man… or scary as this may be, is this the best she has ever had, or was he simply the first…

… as he interacts with the waitress behind the counter, the small talk is extremely and I must emphasize this… extremely loaded with undertones of kindness… I am beginning to feel like an asshole who had misjudged him… mr. personality is in fact a very nice and kind man… fuck, was I wrong… what is biting me on the ass?… envy?

… the beautiful woman… which had accompanied him into the bistro, found a table and quickly pounced on the napkin dispenser and set out to wipe down the table, and grabbed the tabloid newspaper off the next table… this speaks volumes about her… she flirted through the pages… it was evident she had very little interest in the news, it was simply a filler until he joined her… a challenging counter, barely did his arms reach out beyond his stomach to grab the coffee cup saucers… the cups must have been nearly overflowing… cause his jerky moves shook the saucers/cups which caused the coffee to run over on the sides, and this for both cups… he smiled sheepishly at the waitress and his coffee *faux pas* was evident to her as well… as he approaches the table, his smile widens even more and it is reciprocal… his coffee *faux pas* was amusing… it's as if… this is an insignificant comedic mishap…

… it dawns on me now… the courteous/kind exchange with the waitress… and especially the beautiful woman's response to his smile upon seeing her… it is nothing else other than they are in love… the man is happy, simply happy cause in his eyes her presence is all of the world he wants to know about… being accepted as is, denotes true blinding love… napkins in hand, she waits as he places the coffee cups on the table… he places the first cup in front of her (gallantry is still alive here) and she remains still… and once the second cup finds a resting spot on the table, she reaches out to clean his overflowed coffee cup and then proceeds to clean hers... holy shit!... such a simple gesture, but the sequence of the gesture has my eyes watering...

... sitting here in this café surrounded by dozens of people at any given time and despite all these good folks here, I feel very alone... how I wished for someone to wipe the overflowing coffee from my cup... what is biting me on the ass?... woke up in a strange world and alone too... this here is not my world... and the novelty of being here seems to be running out... it's getting harder for me to justify the reason for my being here... but it all has to do with the spiritual epiphany from when I did the Camino pilgrimage in 2013... though lonely insanity is prevailing at the moment...

* * *

# DECEMBER

PART TWO

## 2014/12/01 – Monday (Lisbon, Portugal)

... decided to come into Lisbon for a change of pace... though I write short notes/stories in the form of a journal everyday... I feel what I write has no substance... it is all fluff and hopefully entertaining... one thing is for sure, I'm not writer material, maybe more of a story teller... maybe I could do stand-up comedy if I were funnier and not shy... opted to take a city bus tour along with a slew of UK tourists... it was nice to hear english being spoken... even our tour guide made me feel I was not in Portugal with her impeccable command of the english language... quite a beautiful city both in terms of architecture and history... did not even know there was a synagogue in the city, let alone a jewish community... but what got me thinking was the Santa Apolonia train station... it was here at the age of ten, I rode my first train... and with this floods of memories cascaded from my archived sub-consciousness...

... we grew up in Montreal's plateau, which at that time was a blue collar workers neighbourhood... it was a mix of mostly French & Portuguese as the previous generations were mainly Jewish but had moved to newer areas of Montreal... though at that time most landlords were still Jewish folks renting to the newly arrived immigrants such as they were themselves once upon a time too... I feel, it was understood, almost like an unwritten rule amongst immigrants coming to Montreal... we all need a break and some kindness... eventually as economic times improved for the Portuguese immigrants, they started buying the houses from the Jewish landlords as they were getting on in age and their children did not care for these old buildings...

... I can still remember our landlord, a tall Jewish man always dressed in black or dark suits and always wore a hat, must have been a fashion statement or some sort of piety, I feel it was the latter... 2 things impressed me... that this very old man had once lived in our flat as a kid... and that he was a kid once upon a time... he came once a month to get the rent and my dad would always invite him in for a glass of wine never moonshine... I'd watch/listen to the old man's heavy steps follow my dad into the kitchen... and as the men sat at the table drinking, he would complement my dad on how the flat was well kept and clean and how he wished he had more tenants like my dad and at the same time complained about the other tenants who according to him, left a lot to be desired... in time, the old man did not complain for much longer... nor did he collect the rent ever again... as his son-in-law took over this inherited task...

... one night in february... my mother worked the afternoon shift and got home around midnight, which was past my bedtime during school days... but on Fridays, I tried to stay up and wait for her cause as a 10 year old it was quite the feat and at times we would even watch the midnight movie on TV too... my brother was an epileptic, and was spending this particular week in the hospital as his carrousel of daily pills to control his epilepsy had turned on him and caused additional seizures... so, I found myself in the evenings alone with my dad that week...

... the flat we lived in was basically, one long corridor from the front door to the kitchen which was at the end of the corridor/hallway and all the rooms were off to the left... architecturally speaking it totally lacked imagination and it was more function than esthetics design... another down side to it which I found depressing was it had almost no natural sunlight, so we had the lights on, no matter what time of day it was...

... that evening my dad had stepped out to the annexed shed at the back of the house, as he had made himself a wine cellar of sorts and he was in the process of transferring the wine from barrel to bottle... it was his hobby and I do remember the pride he had in his wine making skills... so, I was sitting at the kitchen table by myself finishing off my bowl of soup... as I sat at the table, I faced the long dark corridor with the barely visible front door at the end of the hallway... sitting there and looking into the dark emptiness, as I had done so many times before, I could not help but to think that this is what it must be like for the blind, to see nothing but darkness...

... the lack of activity with my spoon allowed enough time for a film to form on top of the cold soup... my next option was to flush the remaining soup down the toilet before the father guy would return and give me a lecture about starving kids in Africa... as a kid I thought... *hey!... instead of sending money to feed starving kids... get unemployed nuns over there to feed them... or better yet,... why not send an airplane ticket and get them out of the shit hole they live in*... with the soup now flushed away and I made sure no drips betrayed me back to the table... I went back to my chair and sat there with the empty bowl in front of me... not sure why I was still at the table, maybe to show my father I had eaten everything while he was gone... *I know it would be lying*... or maybe, what was usually next for me after supper was home-work and I was simply procrastinating...

... while in the kitchen, it was the only room in the house which was lit... as I sat there quietly and looked into the hallway... I distinctly heard footsteps in the hallway walking in my direction... I stood up and froze, with shivers running down my body as I tried to focus on my legs in getting me out of there… the footsteps were getting closer… to say I was scared shitless is a major understatement… I don't know how, but I managed to run outside to the backyard and to the shed where my dad was fiddling with his wine… he saw the undeniable look of fear in my face… even as I write this, I can still sense the fear which was in me… I told him I heard footsteps in the hallway… he darted out of the shed and ran head on to the kitchen, his courage facing the unknown totally impressed me, he was scared of nothing… I tagged along behind him, I simply did not want to be alone… but he was so fast, I lagged behind…

… when I got into the kitchen, he was nowhere to be found and all the lights were still off with the exception of the kitchen… as much as I could force my eyes to see in the dark, I saw him going into every room… he came back to the kitchen and told me there was no one and the doors/windows were closed… of course, he claimed I must of imagined it and as he cleared the bowl off the table asked me if I had any homework… I told him that I did not imagine it and that the footsteps were real, I was still shaking with fear…

… he accompanied me to my room and I turned on the light immediately, I was not into walking about in the dark as fear was still raging in me… imagination or not… I grabbed my school bag and stuck to my dad as he walked out and switched off the light… we sat down at the table and I unpacked my bag and spread out a few books and started the motion of doing homework, he sat in front of me blocking my view of the hallway… he just stared at me, he saw I was still afraid, but said nothing… I can only speculate he did not understand my fear, after all he was a tough guy, scared of nothing… he said, he needed to go back to the shed and tidy up things and that he would come back right away… he looked at me for some sort of sign, approving his departure… I just kept my eyes down on the books & homework… he got up, but I did not want to raise my head for I knew I would be facing the dark hallway again…

… with my unfocused head plunged in homework… no sooner did I actually read a line in the book that I heard the footsteps again… this time they were coming very fast in my direction… it sounded like they (footsteps) were angry with me… my chair was now an obstacle and it went flying out of my way… as I darted out of the kitchen and back to the shed… I ran into my dad and told him it happened again… he just stood there and looked at me… he did not run out like the first time… I knew he did not believe me… and yet, so much fear looming in me…

… we walked back to the house together… I would not leave his side… at times he stumbled because I was so close to him… he asked me to put away my books but I kept one eye on him at all times… we ended up in the living room watching TV… as we always did on Fridays since I did not have school the next day… I ended up lying on the sofa with my head on his lap… then it started… I felt as if someone was putting sand in my eyes… it hurt and wouldn't stop… I cried uncontrollably… he walked me to the bathroom to rinse my eyes… but it happened repeatedly all night… I kept telling him someone was putting sand in my eyes… I suspect by this time, he was anxious my mom would arrive from work… later… both my parents were up in arms… I slept on the sofa that night with both of them next to me…

… I can only imagine as worried parents they were probably up all night… the following day, I was terrorized again… but this time I would stop in my footsteps and come to a complete halt… as if I froze solid… I could not move my legs… this went on several times… my father grabbed me by the shoulders and looked at me straight in the eyes… I saw him as if I was far away, in the distance kind of imagery… I was way back in my head, so far away from him… my dad looked angry… I felt myself saying I'm sorry for making him mad, but my words did not come out…

… my dad shook the body I was in… I felt the shoulders swaying back and forth… why couldn't he hear me?… then I heard him shout at me and ask… *who are you*… then the voice of a grumpy old man answered in lieu of me… *you know who I am*… I felt the old man who had spoken was inside of my body… I was filled with more terror than my small body and mind could handle… my dad seemed to know what was going on… he understood, I was possessed by a demon… my dad turned to my mother and said… *he was leaving for Portugal with me*…

… we got in the car and went down to Dupuis Freres, a department store of that time… we ended up buying luggage and some clothes and that evening we went over to a friends' house where we all slept… on Sunday night my dad and I got on the plane… I could not explain it but I felt to be sharing my physical body… eventually, ended up sleeping on the plane to Lisbon… I was still sleepy in the taxi ride from Lisbon airport to the Santa Apolonia train station… he and I ended up spending the month of my champagne birthday year going from one exorcism to another… from cigarette smoking witches, herbal teas, healers, and priests who demanded more proof… and of course family/neighbours who knew of someone who could cure me… was I finally able to cough out/expel the old man with a coarse voice?… to this day, I'm still not sure… but it permanently left a bad taste in my throat… in hindsight it was just an exorcism festival… for me…

## 2014/12/02 – Tuesday (Cascais, Portugal)

… for the patrons… only one newspaper is available in the bistro… and just like in kindergarten one must learn to be patient, courteous and share as well… but several times I have witnessed 2 seniors jump out of their chairs and just as adversaries in a credible wrestling ring, they make a grab/rush for the newspaper whenever it becomes available… but today, I was actually pushed out of the way as the old lady made a dash to get the paper before me and/or the other senior citizen… the staff behind the counter witnessed this… we all looked at each other sheepishly… it was later, when I was paying the cashier that I was given the inside scoop about these 2 old farts and their newspaper fiasco…

… so here goes their story… of course, I will stay true to the general facts as much as I will embellish them with my version of their story… why?… simply, to make my life more interesting, as Christmas *without my kids* will be here in a few weeks and I need to distract myself before I too become a miserable old fuck like them… me… with headphones looping *Octobre - La Maudite Machine*… I'll spin the tale and lose myself in the music, as it touches a nerve in me…

… *she's*… in her late 60's (retired school teacher) but still very mobile, a short woman who wears high heels based on their height potential as opposed to beauty, functionality, cost or even safety, considering this country is one big mess of uneven cobblestone sidewalks… motorcycle helmet, best describes her hairstyle… it is so plasticised by hair lacquer, it is far more water repellant than a duck's feathers… not one plastic hair is out of place too, in the hair world, one strand or dis-entanglement is viewed as an outcast from society… when she talks and moves her head about, chunky flakes of dandruff fly off in all directions… reminding me of typical snow storms in my native Montreal… pretty from far, far from pretty, if you get my flakey drift… by all accounts she is a waste of oxygen… and her being a spinster, reassures me she will not be taking anyone other than herself into her ludicrous world… her last (maybe only) romantic encounter was with the clerk at the pharmacy…

… *he's* a pre-retirement engineer, who found himself laid off after 38 loyal years with the same company… his termination notice came via an attachment in an email, during work... he struggled to open the attachment, as he was ill at ease with computers in general... later that evening at home with the help of his son, he finally opened and read the email attachment... his new found poverty, encouraged him to take the first job he is now qualified for at this stage in his life... as a clerk, stocking shelves in a pharmacy from Monday to Friday, as the weekends are reserved for students who better qualify for this task but are unavailable...

... the pharmacy he worked in was located on the ground floor of the retirement home where she lived... along with laxatives, tissues and hairspray, the shelves required constant replenishing of these items... it was during his daily hairspray shelf replenishment task that their paths first entangled... maybe her heels were not high enough and/or in the elevator she was at eye level with a flatulent asshole in front of her... a bitch by all accounts, she was in pungent mood as she came down to the pharmacy to purchase hairspray... so, brace yourselves as this is the saga's pivotal or high point... as he handed her a hairspray can... as to avoid having her jump up to reach the high shelf... somehow when their hands connected... she then barked... setting claim to politically safeguarding the importance of her high rank in society, dignity and virginity... suffice to say the human touch was not welcomed...

... our clerk, did not care for virginity as his was long gone and forgotten nor was he keen on society because as a professional he was now reduced to a blue collar worker... no, what made his persona unbalanced was his dignity being attacked by her... being mal treated by this foolish woman... he suggested to her... why don't you offer yourself a battery operated toothbrush, there is a pre-Christmas sale today and you can surely use it as a vibrator...

... how will I ease you into the idea that things are back to normal for our engineer, as he was fired verbally and not virtually... and their courtship in a newspaper format now continues in the bistro... gotta love the human touch... Christmas is all about humanity and people connecting with one another...

## 2014/12/03 – Wednesday (Lisbon, Portugal)

... cabin fever... today I went back to Lisbon... being here before yesterday and with the city's Christmas light decorations... it reminded me of Montreal and Christmas moments with my kids... I can shake off or ignore a lot of things in my life, but not my kids... this is the first Christmas I'll spend without them… it's a weird feeling, such an empty feeling deep in my gut… don't know how I will manage on Christmas day…

… though feeling melancholic… my newly acquired taste for Lisbon, drew me to Vasco da Gama shopping mall… for Christians churches are the house of worship… for the rest of us our houses of worship are banks with the best interest rate except at Christmas we switch to malls and overpay on everything we purchase… bank's compassion versus priorities… on average 45 cars are seized per day by creditors… folks prefer losing a car so that they may continue to pay cellphone and cable bills… which would explain why electronics stores, even today are busy with shoppers… ended up in a book store just browsing Portuguese language books but my command of the language is still limited… they did have an English section, it reminded me of French book stores in Montreal with a small English section hidden away not to offend language purists… how re-assuring to know, globalization does not neglect or ignore stupidity…

… co-incidences… came across a book about alien races and such… not that it was particularly interesting, meaning I would not pay the 24 euros… so, I just flipped through it… my fingers flipped the pages and stopped on this one page… was it accidental I happen to stop here?… *the number 11 is a master number and represents inspiration, illumination, and spiritual enlightenment*… okay, interesting… flipping more pages, I stop on the characteristics of what is a starseed child… shit, this hit a nerve in me as I recognized myself in almost all the criteria… these are the points I jotted down from memory… they will be etched forever in my mind…

… they have an intense sense of loneliness…

… they feel like they don't belong in their earth family…

… they have a fascination with the stars and feel as though their home is out there, but they can't remember where…

… they begin to question the ways of earth at an early age, usually around age 10… many are the black sheep of their family…

… they are drawn to metaphysics seeking answers to why they feel so alone and why they don't seem to fit in on earth…

… many have an adversarial relationship with the parent of the opposite sex…

… the majority of starseeds have the facial shape of their mother but the remainder of their physical body is like that of their fathers… this is done for a reason…

… lower than normal body temperature and inability to handle heat…

… the majority of starseeds carry the Crystal Gene… once activated, the crystal gene allows for clearer guidance with beings on other dimensions… it acts as a guidance system of sorts, keeping the individual on course in their respective mission…

… many feel drawn to do grid and vortex work… through which energy may pass…

… sinking into the bookstore's plush couch… things began to correlate in my head… my exorcism(s) experience as a 10 year old, finally found an explanation… and today of all places and time… as 2 days ago I forced myself to re-live my experience in the journal… could it be, no it has to be… synchronicity or a *meaningful coincidence* between/amongst unrelated events…

… when did it start for me?… born with an intense sense of loneliness… what am I doing being raised by this earth family… I belong and come from the stars… these humans behave strangely and this I knew early on in age and along with this endless reading of books about metaphysics and my quest for answers… perhaps I was looking in the wrong place and/or time… and this was compounded by what seems like an eternal contradiction to my parents… all this struggle (from an early age too) to finally discover I am a starseed child…

… so what is a starseed child doing?… or better yet, what was I doing in the Santiago de Compostela pilgrimage (aka Camino)… looking for a *raison d'etre* to ones' life, what else?… for years I wondered why I was not like everyone else, I certainly felt painfully alone and even isolated when interacting with people, they just made no sense in their words, actions, illusions and suffering… what a confused vulgar lot…

… *a starseed child comes to earth to help and improve mankind's existence*… I always helped people, this came natural to me… Suzanne would often remark I went way out of my way to help others… but now to read that I have *gifts to share* with others such as in the areas of healing, channeling and spiritual education… shit!… I'm just a quasi-humble man, and do not appreciate myself or my own abilities… how can I help others in this way… this is simply too much for me to accept… too much responsibility…

… eleven… and how the number eleven has both astral and spiritual meaning… and it also happens to be my birthday and I spent my 11th. year (birthday) in Europe after experiencing what now seems to be a spiritual awakening and my parents in their infinite wisdom of christian beliefs thought I was possessed and had me running thru Portugal from one exorcism to another...

... in my mind... this was troubling information, I was not prepared to believe it... my logical mind kept coming up with other explanations... though I did ponder buying the book... my logic denied its' purchase... stepping out of the mall, I grabbed a taxi parked by... why did I have to look at its' license plate?... it had 11 FM 69 as its' identification... naw!... I just added 69 for comic relief...

## 2014/12/04 – Thursday (Sintra, Portugal)

... night time angst... as I stand on the window ledge with my weak left arm hanging on to the window frame... my right arm pointing/raised to the stars in the sky... as I peel out backwards from my physical body and float into the supporting night air... I see my watery brown eyes and my right arm/hand trying to grab me... but it goes right through the new me... I am free...

... another dream... it's the same old shit... why am I escaping my earthly body again... what is out there that draws me, almost every night... is someone calling me, or trying to tell me something... why can't I hear... this endless fight between body and soul... was I put here against my will... a starseed?...

... no destination... took Suzanne's car and drove... country roads winding through small towns had me seeing a road sign for Sintra... co-incidence, knowing Sintra is famous for its' ghost stories... dating from the times of Romans and Moors... and since it is nestled on a mountain side... it was a strategic military location... goes without say, surely a few battles were had here... even on a sunny day, the place is eerie... found myself a teahouse and sat in a corner... people walking in, mostly alone and sitting down to sip tea... is tea the drink of solitude... one day I'd like to open my own tea house back in Cascais...

... the roads... had me passing next to a cemetery... so much beauty, mausoleums old and new... ornamented grave stones and the freshly placed flowers... such care for the dead, was it so when they were alive?... is it an obsession we have with death... do we fear it so much that we repress it... we live in denial but I can't... am I the only one who thinks like this or do I have a death wish... the dreams of leaving my body... could it be my soul has seen something better elsewhere and simply wants to leave… maybe, the earth life realm is seen as a running gag by the rest of the universe…

… her funeral… with her in Portugal and me in Montreal… the nursing home did not take into account there was a 5 hour time difference… the announcement of my mother's death came at the proverbial 3 AM… being yanked out of bed, I for one cannot react or articulate very well… on the phone, I was numbed by the news… in hindsight, it was a form of denial, but I immediately started planning the overseas trip for the funeral…

… making ends meet… prior to her death… she had already made a pre-arrangement with the local undertaker of her native village where she wanted to be buried, in the same grave as my dad… I guess, with her living in the retirement home where death is the breakfast topic of the day… she had enough foresight and time to plan hers, this says a lot about her, does it not?… but in reality, she did not trust me or my brother with her funeral arrangements… somewhere in her loving heart, she thought we are nothing but fuck-ups… the undertaker first and foremost is a farmer… he was stacking hay, when the retirement home called him to come and collect her… efficiency being his *modus operandi*… he hopped on the hearse mobile to pick her up… hurrying back to his farm with her corpse in the back… he parked the hearse in his driveway and got back to his hay stacking job… this was her last suntan, in a parked hearse… can you say BBQ… such fucken irony, no?

… real thing… before closing the casket… I touched her to make sure she is dead… quite annoying… waking up in a buried coffin with a sun tan and no one to show it off to… as the lid closed, I could not believe this shrivelled woman was my mother… she always prided herself in having her nails done… and now her fingers tips were nothing but a nauseating blue…

… one size fits all… my father's grave was made of granite slabs… it was about 6 feet long and maybe protruded a foot above ground level… a headstone too, with trivial data such as birth and death dates… this info, leaves a lot to the imagination of who this man was… the top granite slab had been removed so that my mom's coffin may be placed on top of his… together at last, she moved in without his permission too… the opening was not more than 4 feet and her coffin was nearly 7 feet long… no way her coffin could be dropped in horizontally…

… slip and slide… improvised yellow nylon ropes are looped through the coffin handles… myself along with volunteers lift the coffin up off the gurney… not that it was heavy, but it was very awkward to manoeuvre using only ropes… we had to lift it up on one side so that it may go through the

61

opening at an almost 45 degrees/vertical angle... once the coffin inside the grave/hole... we had to level it off horizontally and let it go down slowly... I was dressed in a suit and tie... hot sun, intense un-coordinated manual labour... and the incredible difficulty in getting her coffin in the fucken hole... along with the absurdity of the cemetery festivities... without looking back I shuffled my feet on the gravel path lifting dust... the cemetery iron gates, had no intention of letting me out... push or pull was to hard a decision... instead I had to fight them so that they may open...

... surreal... lost in both thoughts and direction... somehow found my way to the car... with car door ajar and the endless chiming demanding the door be closed... sitting in the front seat and listening to the chime... it annoys me but I do not know what to do about it... with a vast selection of useless thoughts flashing in my head... I stopped on one... for sure she moved around when we lifted and lowered the coffin... and she's all curled up to one end of her box... pretty sure there was no seat belt of any kind... imagine the look on the face of those who may one day open the coffin... they will think she was still alive when buried...

... chime of silence... loosening my neck tie... more blood and oxygen rushed to my head... and with it came a solution to drown out the door chime... by turning on the radio... the song... *Israel Kamakawiwoʻole - Somewhere Over the Rainbow...* came on at that very moment... it hit me that she was gone... there was no longer any need to suppress my emotions and I broke down... and now opted to believe she was in a better place...


## 2014/12/07 – Sunday (Areia, Portugal)

... still don't know how I will manage Christmas without my kids... Sunday melancholy, actually I coined this feeling as the... *Sunday blues...* first became aware of this mood when I was still in grade school... it was a typical Sunday evening and I had still, not done my homework for Monday... I'd promise myself to wake up early Monday morning and work on my homework assignments... but because I truly enjoyed sleeping until the very last minute... so during my slumber I made an executive style CEO decision to stay in bed and live with the consequences of not having done my homework... in hind sight, I made the right decision... an irresponsible quality of life...

... my daughters' question was simple enough... *what day is it today...*

but I had to have a convoluted answer for her... and watch her face mimic my response, all the while keeping on a serious face... it was hard for me not to laugh, but I always did end up doing so... other times, all their (childrens') questions were always answered with... *NO*... if they whined the *NO* answer would stick, but if they justified/argued their demand/position without crying I was open to changing my answer to a... *YES*... this was great for me while they were still young... but by teenage years... my... *NO*... was not an answer and I now had to justify my response with an explanation... oh my god, I had created mini-lawyers... because they were exposed to my warped sense of humour, and now claim there will never be enough money or time for a psychiatrist to help them...

... when my kids were young, the beauty of the wife working the evening shift allowed for my kids and I to bond undistractedly... and we bonded tremendously... we would sit around the turntable, and I would play... *Vangelis - 1492 Conquest of paradise*... I'd improvise a story using the music as a background... the sailors/ship would be reaching the mysterious shores... with the background music of choir vocals & drums... the sailors jumped off the ship and into the head high water, and struggled walking to shore... as they imagined my words accompanied by the music... their eyes were completely focused on me... and of course, I would get into my skit/routine pretending to fall asleep and snore real loud during my story telling... need I say, laughter became contagious... afterwards, wrestling with no parental supervision ensued... and wouldn't you know it... it's all fun games until somebody loses an eye... after being all wired up by wrestling... for the next song, we'd play... *Sex Pistols – EMI*... and shout the *EMI* refrain at the top of our lungs... could never quite understand why they were so wired up, when it came to bedtime... you'd think they'd be tired from so much playing... I certainly was...

... school humour... at first I did not quite understand the concept... I'd walk the kids to the bus stop... wait for the yellowish bus and push my kids up the steps and watch their crying faces squeezed up against the folding glass doors... I thought, that this was it, good riddance... but no, that bastard of a bus driver brought them back every afternoon... it got to the point where I gave up... and told the kids to go to the bus stop by themselves... as I could no longer endure the daily dis-appointment of them coming back home...

## 2014/12/09 – Tuesday (Cascais Portugal)

… why not?… it was just another lazy Tuesday morning, I was lying in bed alone and Suzanne was somewhere in the house doing the domesticated tasks which only women judge to be important and men take for granted… but she was like a mouse, extremely quiet so as not to disturb my sleep… her goodwill thoughts and actions are mute, as I lay awake…

… the room was quite cold and somewhat dark, and the European shutters allowed some sunlight to dart through the little hole openings and with the wind taunting the trees, the sunlight beams were dancing in a kaleidoscope fashion as the tree branches/leaves occasionally interrupted the sun beams… the room felt almost like it had a disco strobe light without the noise, cigarette smoke, vain egos and endless array of body odours camouflaged by man-made scents…

… my lower back was acting up, as it gets sore when I spend too much time in bed and/or had wild sex the previous night… as I lay flat on my back and with this I slide up my feet so that they rest flat on the bed and my knees are high up to put some soothing pressure on my lower back… I was somewhat in a relaxed contemplative mood and also felt happy with myself at this very moment in time, it was one of those unspoken pleasures… I placed my hands together on my chest, as if I were praying or in a more morbid, humorous sense, as if I were lying in a coffin… actually, I thought to myself as I laid there, what it was like to be lying in a coffin with an erection and the morticians were unable to close the lid… would they cut it off or drain it, but then the logical side of my brain kicked in with a motherly tone and reminded me that all bodily fluids are removed from the corpse, hence depriving me of any joy and using matriarchal guilt to ruin my fun moment… no matter…

… the mild and bearable lower back pain was still persistent… not enough though to hamper my good mood or mischievously absurd thoughts… I slid my hands to the side and laid my palms flat on the bed… after a few minutes I felt my back was numb of any pain, but now I was also feeling my legs, from the knees down were getting heavy, and my soles seemed to be springing roots downwards into the mattress, so much so that I no longer was able to clearly distinguish where my feet were making contact with the mattress… ok, I was curious to see where this would lead… I took a few deep breaths, and let myself go willing and allowing my torso to merge with the mattress too… it was soon after if not simultaneously I felt my head getting heavy and sinking into the pillow... only my eyes seemed to be awake yet with closed eyelids... as for the rest of my body, it had its' own agenda...

... the eye of insight... or the third eye, lit up inside my head with a bright silver like light... I found myself going down, in a vortex kind of way... as my body remained intact but only the inside of my head felt as if it were spinning... such a blinding light hitting my third eye and it was getting stronger... I can hear the sunrays coming through and pushing their way in through the shutter's holes... so much energy, which my third eye can now see and even feel... it wants me... this energy wants me, I belong to it... shit, I am not comfortable with what is going on, it feels to surreal and I'm even fucken scared... then these words came into my mind... *get out*... it were as if I had started a silent dialogue in my head, but I could only listen... *leave it*... then the overwhelming sensation of me as a kid... all excited to go out and play in the snow, as school was cancelled due to a major snowstorm... hundreds of images darting in my head of our parents hovering over us, as my brother and I are lying on the bed and they are helping us put on our bulky snowsuits with a full body zipper... scarves, tuques and gloves are floating around us... so much excitement, all four of us are in a good mood, simultaneously too... such a rarity...

... overwhelm stop!... I shouted silently and with this the images were gone... it was as if I now understood... I'm stuck in it, got to get out and let go, don't I?... and with this I sense my very own body has a full length zipper on the skin... I need to unzip... I see myself pulling the zipper open from head to toe... I heard myself laughing, as I thought I had never seen this zipper in a mirror reflection nor had any woman I ever slept with... you think one of them would've noticed, no?

... with the zipper opened and now it even disappeared... my mind went blank... I felt myself weightless and even quite luminous... actually I felt transparent... I feel myself rising out of my body in the shape of a ball... as a ball of light... I know I am floating, I just know... should I open my eyes before un-rolling my body... I cannot see anything other than my own light... opened my eyes as I started un-rolling my body, I see the ceiling... and as I spin myself to look down to my body on the bed... from the corner of my third eye I catch an image/glimpse of my parents, laughing as they are excited the kids are going out to play in the snow and they'll spend the afternoon having sex... bastards!... and I smile...

... I see myself lying in bed... my god, so fragile a being, is this really my form?... grabbing the body's hand and placing it against the headboard it wraps its' fingers around the post... I feel safe now that my physical body is anchored... so, I can find my way back upon my return... and with a thought... I hear a sound similar to the one a jet makes when it breaks the sound barrier, the body on the bed jolts and I move at a blurring speed through the shutters...

... spectrum... difficult to determine if it is me who is moving or the pixels points of first dark and then light colors... the pixel points surround me no matter where I look, they follow along with the scope of my eyesight... I'm not scared though I think I should be but at the same time I feel very mellow and buoyant... oh! so cool... and the uncanny thought of not having a soul entered my mind and caused me to feel even more weightless... the pixels began to merge into clusters and metamorphosed into a gorgeous blue sky and an ocean... I was floating between sky and ocean... I somehow propelled myself down to touch the water... hot, the water was hot and in the distance I saw what appeared to be white steam floating over the ocean and coming my way... thoughts, ideas or intuitions are coming into my mind, faster than I can manage and this urgency is due to the white steam coming my way... this white steam is not a good thing at all... not so much as fear but panic set in and I screamed silently *I want out... I want out NOW!...*

... traffic control... with a jolt I felt myself back in bed... slightly out of breath, I was scanning with my mind the extent of my body... like turning on the ignition of a car as one listens to see if the motor is running well without any strange sounds... information was still coming into my mind... it was not new information as some messages were repeated to what seemed like dozen times... *I'm to be the voice of the soul rebellion... my intuition gift is to communicate with my soul and even (also) help people and ease their suffering...* how can this gift be to help mankind when here I am and can't even help myself... so now I'm supposed to be some sort of Mother Teresa who by the way left before finishing her job on this planet... I'll just put this in the journal/book and hope it is useful for someone who may read this... I'm not comfortable with any of this...

## 2014/12/10 – Wednesday (Cascais Portugal)

... okay... as I sit here alone... in this pouring rain but warm afternoon in a coffee shop located in Cascais's tourist area, it is called Sacolinha and is well known for its' fine assortment of pastries... along with a very modern and refined chic décor where waiters are dressed in black slacks and pristine white shirts...

... as I look out the window, I see another restaurant across the alley... the other resto is called Tasca da Villa (with good food too), its' awning is struggling to maintain its' shape with the hard hitting rain... though the outside tables are snuggled under the awning awaiting customers, they are all empty as patrons prefer being inside... at this time of the year, tourists are few and mostly locals and residing foreigners linger in coffee shops...

... the bistro I am in has automatic sliding glass doors... as the hard rain comes down, the large water droplets trigger the magic eye to open the doors repeatedly... almost as if ghosts are coming into the bistro, but prefer using the open door rather than going through them, laziness has no realm limitations...

... with umbrellas opened wide... as people walk in front of the windows... their stride is unhurried, and why would it be, it is only rain and it will be here for the next couple of days too... why not make the best of the situation... the only time their pace is accelerated is when they skip over the water puddles...

... redemption... why do I feel this notion?... due to a warm rainy day?... is the rain a cleansing element... can it be that today of all days, rain is to my soul what the morning shower was to my body?... but, I am indoors... am I privileged?... my life has been pretty much trivial, meaning other the importance of being/ trying to be a good father... I went through the same things like most of us such as working, saving for a rainy day, investing in RRSP's, insurance policies, annual vacations etc... and coasting along in a life which was monetarily easy and by this I mean putting food on the table and providing shelter... and not buying new cars or a large TV screen... my priorities were never about materialism, other than a motorcycles of course...

... where I differ from mainstream... is that I said, *stop!... this is not what I want anymore...* actually, this was and is still all good... but right now, at least not for me... it felt as if I was able to predict the future, my routines were well established and comfortable... all I needed to do was coast with the flow... there is something in me and it goes as far back as I can remember which is not so much as not being satisfied... but more an un-quenching desire to know, to wonder, to understand within reason, and an endless feeling that as soon as I know something there is already something else capturing my attention... for a while, this even applied to my relationships with disastrous results... boredom is my curse...

## 2014/12/11 – Thursday (Cascais Portugal)

… luxury… it's safe to assume the funeral industry is thriving… with an over populated planet, customers are an abundance… the joy of one is the misery of another… and the flower shop next to the cemetery is also a flourishing business… as fresh flowers/plants are placed weekly on graves by family members… here, the dead are treated like royalty, either due to respect or regret/guilt… for most of us, the only time we get to be in a Mercedes is either in a taxi (industry car of choice) or a hearse… the Mercedes hearse van has a big bow window on either side… making enough room for the coffin but also flower arrangements… despite the morbid context, one has to appreciate the fact that it's quite pretty and ever so colorful against an all-black vehicle… almost trendy in design… I disapprove buying flowers for the dead or even for a birth… the targeted recipients do not care for the gift, but their entourage will be apt to evaluate the *love* based on the flowered monetary value…

… fellow feeling… up until the death of own my parents… whenever I attended funeral homes I would stare at the corpses and I'd get the sensation they were still alive and only I could see this… their bodies would not move, but their lips and eyes did… I'd listen to them and the range of topics varied from fear, anger, irritability, loneliness, and comically enough even sexual frustration… in the pecking order of the universe, I was still on top of the food chain… and being egotistical and not at all envious of their situation, in the end I'd say… *better you than me, see you later*… maybe it was delusional thinking and I alienated myself from the world beyond… if they (deceased) want kindness and compassion then look for it on the other side because the *love boat* on this ocean is sailing off without them…

… earth prelude… out of respect for my friend Carmen whose mom passed away, I went to the funeral home to pay my last respects… other then the polite chit chat at social functions, I did not know the deceased lady very well… so I anticipated that mourning for her death would not be more difficult than wearing a black piece of clothing for the occasion… today, when I think about my attitude the only possible conclusion I could reach was that I was a *fucken asshole*… no sooner did I find myself in the middle of the room in the funeral home… on one side of the room there was a loud commotion… a grandson crying his head off for the deceased lady… the young man was surrounded by family members trying to console him with no success… on the opposite side was the open casket…

… can heaven wait… I could not see the deceased lady as I was too far away... but yet, the deceased woman was in my head... she was frantically going around in circles telling me to go and talk to the grandson on her behalf... if he looked into my eyes, he would see her and calm down... my head swung repeatedly from one side to another... first looking at the open casket and then the grandson... my ex-wife was standing next to me... she clutched my face between her hands and asked me... *what is happening*... I was scared... so fucken scared and my ex saw this... I asked her to drive me home... in hindsight, I admire my ex-wife even though she did not quite understand me at times... she did recognize I had some sort of cursed gift, even before I admitted it out loud to myself... I did not attend the funeral, which was seen by some as being politically incorrect even discourteous... other than my parents, this was the last time I set foot in a funeral home... and from this point on I only attended funerals where the casket is already closed...

... star dust... when my dad died I did not engage with him at the funeral home because my mind was cluttered with grief... and yet, there were so many things I wanted to say (ask) to him... later, I made a mental note that when my mom would go... I'd drill her for info but in the last years of her life I spent a lot time talking to her and after a lifetime, we finally bonded... the day my mom ended up at a funeral home I did not want to know anything, for the memory of Carmen's mom was still fearfully etched in me... days later, while alone in the car listening to music on the radio... I asked out loud for her (mom) to give me a sign that she was okay... the radio switched to a religious program/station without my touching the dials... I took this as a sign, as she was a devout catholic...

... insight... we go through life thinking and doing things and for the most part we do not pay much attention to them because they are not unique... we figure everyone else must be doing the same in one way or another... and it was with this mindset that I thought we all had some sort of empathy, maybe some with a bit more to the point where it is defined as intuitions... I just thought I was a sensitive person and could sympathize with others quite easily... it was not until I did the Camino in 2013, did I realize I was not like everyone else and for the first time I started taking my intuitions seriously... something in me awoke or better yet a barrier came down and I was able to feel others with too much ease... and to the point I was overloading myself by allowing all these empathy feelings or intuitions come into my mind and at times feel someone else's bad moods as being mine... it was a living hell for a while...

... secret card... it's one of those life mysteries... we all come onto this planet through the same channels but once here some are successful and others flounder... in hindsight, I had always recognized my intuitions as no more than empathy or imagination... but since the first Camino, my intuitive abilities have excelled... years after Carmen's mom passed away, she came through me again while I was walking the Camino... she was bearing an announcement for me to pass on to Carmen that her dad was on his death bed... this story is still too emotional for me to write it down today, but I will get back to it... nevertheless, to be able to know/see when someone is going to die, was more intuitive ability than I was able to handle... eventually, word got out about this specific intuition... people/friends shunned me, because of disbelief or simply thought I was crazy and must be avoided... either way, it was nothing more than a two-sided coin of fear...

... tell somebody... naively I thought my intuition gift could help people but their negative/fearful reaction caused me to isolate myself... and added more emptiness... I was overwhelmingly alone as I had no one to confide in... then... as a parent there was a growing *new fear* in me... what if one day I intuit the death of my children... there is no doubt in my mind I would not be able to handle it... now, my capabilities scared me... by this time, I was avoiding touching/hugging my kids for fear of picking up some vibe off them... it took me over a year to control and/or shut down and be able to block myself from people's vibes... this was a new skill I had to learn through a spiritual center's counselling and meditation techniques...


## 2014/12/13 – Saturday (Cascais Portugal)

... little thing called love... it distorts reality and perception too... though Suzanne and I have been having rough patches... maybe because we were dating via skype for about 2 years, with occasional meet-ups... sometimes, the one on one contact can set things right... undeniable, the chemistry, and the feeling of *deja vu* that we have been together before and the intoxicating overwhelming feeling of being in love defies all common sense and behaviour... moving in together, should set things right...

... meaningful purpose... on my way to your home I was thinking about how I want to hold you near me, just feel your loving warmth, nothing complicated or dramatic... just two souls, finding asylum from the worldly madness... I think I have mentioned this to you before... our bedroom is our haven where the world has no access to... where we and just we alone can dream and live in a pure love and compassion for one another... to hold you snuggly... where you can sleep peacefully knowing that as long as you are in my arms, no harm will come to you... loving, protecting... all the while caressing your face and twirl your hair with my fingers... for I am in love...

... you are the most beautiful person I have ever met in my life... I fell in love with a woman that had me mesmerized by her intelligence and which I truly respected and only to find out what a beautiful lover you are... your body has me humbling to the beauty of the human female form... your gentleness and daintiness subdues all my insecurities and I give myself to you... body and even soul, cause within you I am finally home... I am nothing but a mortal in love with an earthly goddess... hold on to me Suzanne... no one will interfere, I will not allow it... for I love you with every breath that flows thru me...

## 2014/12/15 – Monday (Areia, Portugal)

... this time of year is taking its' toll on me... it will soon be the first Christmas, I spend without my kids... though my youngest daughter was supposed to join me in Portugal, at the last minute she decided to cancel... I feel her anger towards my divorcing her mom and my coming to Europe has simply not subsided... this saddens me to no end...

... sometimes I find myself thinking that perhaps ending a marriage after 33 years was not the wisest thing I have done... but at the same time, I simply was not into being married, the novelty was no longer there for me... though we brought 3 kids into this world, they're now adults and I felt I was just coasting in this marriage... waiting and wasting time... I was restless in every sense of the word... my only consolation, is that we still managed to remain friends after the separation... we agreed it was pointless spending the last few years of our lives bickering... I may of fallen out of love with my ex, but in terms of respect and admiration, this will never dwindle... I had met my ex-wife Emme when I was 21, I had just arrived from Europe, after spending almost a year riding my motorcycle throughout the continent... back then as today, I am still looking for myself, with only existentialist questions as baggage...

... as the expression goes... *adventure is deadly but routine is dangerous...* yep!... with the mindset of a 20 something travelling throughout Europe on my Yamaha 650cc motorbike for a year in 1980 was a bigger than life anar-

71

chist undertaking... common sense, maturity and logic combined did not sway me from my grandiose scheme... a reckless undertaking in homage to being young and living life without worrying about fitting into society, as I was the *society*... with basic ethical values that being nice to people was all that is required of me and you know what, it made for good karma too... yeah!, all good and well but let's face it... debauchery, weed and to a lesser extent booze was also an integral part of my scheme... this was all within the context of *my society* rules... hey! I didn't make the rules or did I, but I do follow and even re-adjust them when convenient...

... so, in 1980 at age 20... riding my motorcycle from Portugal to southern France (and eventually hitchhiking to UK, loved punk music)... though, always seeking warmer climates and it was also quite a long, long journey which required several days... this was the time before Ipods and entertainment was self-made, not bought or served by a young nerdy clerk *(with too much acne to work in the cosmetics section)* from an electronics department store shelf...

... with the roaming thunderous sound of 650cc's jolting quiet country roads into chaos... your adorable yours truly would sing to pass the time... now, I will be the first to admit my singing voice leaves a lot to be desired... and when I sang at our house my brother would implore me to shut the fuck up... justifiably so too... but here I was, somewhere in Europe with a motorcycle wrapped by my testicles and my head locked into a motorcycle helmet with a fogged up and saliva drenched visor... belching this one line... *I'm a juvenile product of a broken working class*... as this was all I bothered to compose/memorize... perhaps it was selective memory as I felt only this line was a propos...

... this resonated so true... at that time, this was the extent of my understanding politics... a pro socialist where the wealth is shared, it was not until I started working and saw all the paycheck deductions to support our social system... that I began to get slightly greedy and changed my political view, as I felt my monies were being miss-used...

... today, 54½ years old (an adorable 54½, I must add)... still an anarchist (less hair) but with slightly more money in pocket... the ethical values unchanged except with the addition of spirituality and even more kindness... setting off again on a one year journey seeking answers to my existence on the Camino route... but this time with the notion, there is more good to people than the bad I read in the daily tabloid newspapers...

... existentialism?... will I find the answers, of course not... as having all the answers defies the purpose of living... what I will find, is that life is simply too beautiful and perplexing and that it (life) works better if there is love especially self-love... so, I will indulge myself in the absurdity of looking at questions with no answers available in this life form... but unlike my youth, I will do this without debauchery or weed but will only plunge into *vinho* this Christmas to drown my sorrows... will I ever grow up or even believe what I wrote?... never, as I still have childlike dreams...

## 2014/12/19 – Friday (Areia, Portugal)

... Portugal with un-insulated and un-heated century old houses... it is colder inside the house than outside... now this is great for this beach country summer mentally... but with global climate change denial, house building protocols are far from being true to *times, they are a changin'* reality... hospitals actually have a crisis with hyperthermia cases... still I rather sleep naked with several layers of blankets than invest money in a pyjama... after all I am a Canadian, hey?...

... nights... this is an old country, with its' share of violent hardship history... sure, you can read about it in books and even get a glimpse in a museum of what life may have been like for these long gone folks... but I prefer looking at buildings, close my eyes and use my senses to talk to me... it is these feelings I pick up from these old houses that linger in me... and when I am in a calm or zen moment they come back to talk to me... repeatedly... the dangers of too much meditation... is being lost... like when I used to smoke pot and get stoned... sometimes, when too high one could end up out of touch with earthly reality...

... in the nightly insomnia, the silence can be heard... so intense a feeling that those of us who have ever experienced this, can also leave their vibration impregnated in long forgotten bedroom walls... I am never alone in my silence, they follow me... who are they, that haunt my night time... an extension of me before I was me, a past karma catching up with me... even with a new body, as if this would hide who I was or did... they find and recognize me, just like old friends drinking in a bar, who never know when it is time to leave... they beckon me into their misery, these cannot be old friends... restless, agitated... can they not forgive and forget, not even turn the other cheek when slapped, of course not... as there is no other cheek that can be turned... cheeks require a matter, physicality for which they are not...

… now what?… as my silent insomnia becomes a permanent state of mind… I feel them about me, as shivers escalate up my spine, I know this is *them* screaming for my attention… and as my silence irritates them, their numbers increase to voice their acknowledgement, their *raison d'etre* that no longer is… fools in the midst of a halo mist surrounding me, so many… all is invisible, from their long lost past existence to my current feelings… why does blame, have no boundaries, limitless?… I could never be sorry for what I did in a past life… even if it was *I*, it was never the *I* of today…

… perpetual insomnia… now dissipates and my eyelids drop, I now find myself joining them… facing an old and revengeful justice… night, followed with only a short reprieve of daylight… and soon with another night of anguish forthcoming… I am tired of my *spirituality* awakening…

## 2014/12/20 – Saturday (Cascais Portugal)

… gloriously sunny market day… Suzanne and I were in the car heading for the market, it's our Saturday ritual going to the market for fresh produce and sweets too… cliché scene… car windows open and radio playing loud enough… what comes on the M80 radio station… *Zucchero – Per Colpa di Chi*… immediately recognizing the song opening with its' animal sounds… pumping the volume to the max… love this song especially the piano… language of passion… though my Italian is limited to several key swear words and I have no idea what he is singing about, nevertheless I do appreciate the melodic language… funky rooster… the first 30 seconds of farm animal sounds in the song's beginning or as I like to call it, *what St. Léonard would sound like on any given Sunday morning had not an imperialist mayor of the 60's banned raising farm animals in the inner city*… such fond memories of oppression…

… dad bonding… come to think about it… when the Jean Talon market was still run by/with Italian shops and real farmers from Le Nord du Quebec… as a kid, I remember Saturday mornings with my dad and him parking his car on Henri Julien street and stepping out of the car and hearing a rooster crowing from some defiant backyard owner nearby the market… was the rooster crowing/complaining about the lack of hens or was it because his fate had already been pronounced as the guest of honor for the Sunday lunch… either way, his happiness was beyond his control… if any consolation, it would be a short lived honorable death, I am sure the owners palate would salivate upon returning from church and bursting into the house and be engulfed by the smell of roasted chicken with a side dish of potatoes... now, I am not a church goer by any means but I am a free loader, so... if any of you are planning a Sunday chicken roast... hey!... invite me, I do have adequate table manners and would even fake saying grace before lunch if there were a certainty that a drumstick would end up in my plate...

... adolescence... or carefree days... I'd avidly travel the metro system/ stations in order to attend Sunday lunches at anyone of my friend's homes throughout Montreal (invitations were optional)... I must admit, though I tasted several ethnic variations of the roasted chicken dish, and I must insist that by no means am I an expert... BUT... for my palate, the Portuguese had the best chicken and I think it had to do with the fact that they added... *chorizo piquante (spicy sausage)*... into the roasting pan... mind you the elongated phallic like chorizo snuggled amongst the potatoes looked like a penis with multiple testicles... not too pretty, but oh!... ever so tasty and almost an erogenous satisfaction for the mouth... not sure what else I can add to my delusional story except to say that I will be free on Sundays for lunch... actually, I am free all year long as I have no social life... I wonder why?

## 2014/12/24 – Wednesday (Cascais Portugal)

... believe?... believe in Santa Claus... believe in god or the devil... believe in the Virgin Mary making a cameo appearance on an olive tree... believe your parents love you un-conditionally... believe in any of the 3 dogmatic religions from the middle east, as they all emerged from the same corner of the world when making up a religion was in vogue... believe in the end of the world... believe in salvation... believe in the Montreal Canadians... believe whatever you want... cause I believe humans simply like to believe... it is in our nature to believe... and believe what we believe... because we are a cluster of neurons determined to believe at all costs... *I believe this will be the last Christmas I spend without my kids...*

... subdued... my first Christmas with Suzanne was loving, quiet and serene... it is so hard to shake off 33 years of married Christmas memories... not about being married but about the kids... isn't this what Christmas is all about, a time to reflect on the mishaps that had occurred during the past year and laugh about them too, over the dinner table conversations... the art of storytelling... my girls were very good at pointing out my follies... especially, like most men buying the wife's Christmas gift on the eve… expensive useless crap bought under the pressure of a doubled parked car with a sensuous voice over the shopping mall loudspeaker announcing closing time is with minutes… the voice fell short of saying… *com' on you dummies, you blew it again this year*…

… facetious… being an ex-veteran of the *married life*… I've learned the hard way… of course, how else will a man learn, there is no book on this… that there are certain gifts which are not appropriate for nesting under a Christmas tree… I had the chance to learn this after about 33 attempts… and I am still optimistic that one day I could/will get this concept right… but not just yet, as I find that there still is humour to be found in giving an inappropriate gift…

… receipt… now, seriously… *yeah right!*… for you newbie husbands out there… avoid offering the following gifts… *unless of course you want them for yourself*… in general make sure it is something that does not break, and that the packaging is reinforced… this will make the *refunding* easier… though I suspect Walmart & Dollarama have become lenient on this issue… personally, I like offering power tools (DeWalt or Bosch) they can take a substantial amount of abuse and come with the option to buy a prolonged guarantee… this could be handy… as once you move to the doghouse… you may start upgrading/renovating your new home… but just like your real home, the renovations will drag and most likely never get completed… the wife may throw you a bone when she is in desperate need of having something fixed or she may call a competing handyman… and give you the bill… having worked for myself as a handyman… I know this for a fact, as many of my female customers are in this type of predicament…

… solidarity… motorcycles are always good… a his and hers motorcycle is a very nice way to spend time together… but if you have to compromise on the expensive motorcycle you want, then just buy the one for yourself… and she can occasionally tag along on the backseat… this will only happen once she cools off… so you may wait a few summers before she hops on… a blessing in disguise, no?… I cannot emphasize this enough times… never and I mean never… never, offer a baseball bat… this can, what am I saying, this will be your downfall and most likely your last gift too…

… Christmas is for kids… no matter how old mine may be… Christmas without them is not the same…

## 2014/12/25 – Thursday (Cascais Portugal)

... nonetheless... love my wrist watch, it has such... *ex*-... sentimental value... it was kinda of a Christmas gift from the ex-wife... I was heading home late one night after drinking with a few buddies and I was feeling pretty good... in my moment of bliss a dark thought entered my giggly mind... I just remembered it was gonna be Christmas soon... and I had forgotten to buy my ex a gift... so I pull into a Petro Canada gas station to pick up some flowers or a... *Mae West, a palm size cake...* or anything that would be perceived as a Christmas gift... the only thing I found was the watch and a gift certificate for a car wash... I kept the watch and the rest is now history, so I hope... knowing women in general, they always bring up the past when in an argument... what I should of have bought was a calendar and then I would see Christmas was still a few weeks away...

... Montreal winter... one year, just around Christmas time... we had a major snow storm and people posted an endless amount of pictures of the mediocre event on Facebook... as if we have never seen snow in our backyards... unless you lived on another planet... or in Europe, *land of the whiners & imposed austerity measures for the poor...* 43cm may sound like a lot but it really boils down to 16 or so inches... to put this into context, the size of a Portuguese non-piquante chorizo sausage stretched out on the BBQ...

... marital snow removal... sure my ex-wife tried endlessly to get back in the house during the snow storm... I repeatedly shouted through the living room window... you are not coming in until the driveway has been cleared of this godly discarded snow... sometimes, I think she annoys me on purpose... especially during my self-imposed TV marathon of mediocre Canadian sitcom re-runs imposed by the CRTC and subsidized by my tax dollars with story lines/plots of an elementary grade 6 student caliber... ramming crap down one's throat is not conducive to promoting Canadiana...

... Solomon's wisdom... now, you may think I am a mean old ogre... but after she shovelled the driveway and with only 2 steps left to clear... I reasoned that... with hers tears of fatigue crystalizing on her eye lids... it was best to let her in as it was already close to 11PM & her productivity was slowing down... but under the condition that she would get up early the next day to finish the job... as I wanted to be at the coffee shop around 7AM... as I had several calls to make to my customers to cancel my jobs for the day... one cannot travel to work with this kind of snow... at first I was concerned that I would not be making any money that day... then figured with the ex-wife going in to work, my income would still flow in... who needs UIC... when one has marriage with low or no contribution premiums...

... farcicality... so, after spending nearly 4 days of pretty much locked in front of the TV... a change of pace was in order... what better way to ward of the winter blues... your eyes are not deceiving you... yours truly decided to BBQ with -14 degrees Celsius... I don't want to brag, but I personally cleared the snow off the deck, prior to firing up the propane gas grill... if you guessed... it was a chorizo on the upper grill and bifanas (pork steak) on the lower grill you are akin to being Portuguese... now enhance the experience one notch up by imagining the smell of the smoke... suffice to say, the bifanas had been marinating in *vinhos d'alhos* (garlic & wine) overnight... mmm-mmm, smells and tastes so good...

... no nonsense humour... to quote my dear ex-wife... the beatings will continue until moral improves as she does not do the *snow* or *BBQ* thing-ees... this story is pure wishful fantasy... having said this, I hope she does read my story... otherwise her *colher de pau* (wooden spoon) will find another mission in life other than being used to stir soup... oh! shit... I'll send her a copy of this story... after all, I live dangerously... *que deus me ajude,... foda-se, a colher de pau vai mágoar!...* (use a software translator)

## 2014/12/26 – Friday (Cascais Portugal)

... for a typical *4 generations Portuguese family*, what a gloriously beautiful day... so, today being friday December 26, 2014... the bridge day between Christmas day and the weekend... it is not a holiday, but judging from all the folks strolling on the seaboard walk, one can only speculate, either they took the day off as a vacation or the wiser ones called in sick, hence having the day off at the expense of their employer... of course, being a predominantly christian country they love thy neighbour as long as their boss is not their neighbour...

... snuggly greyish dressed seniors are shuffling about as well, hanging on for balance and support on the baby strollers of their great grandchildren... after all, even the staff at the retirement home need time off so as to get their chance to cater to their very own parents... and is it asking too much from family to pick up their aging mothball scented parents on this supposedly contrived family holiday... it's almost symbolic if not ironic that both babies and the elderly require the use of the stroller... what goes around comes around, no?

... and what is a stroll on the seaside boardwalk without the constant connection to a smart phone... other than the babies and/or elders, the whole lot has a phone in hand pending a text message or even the rarity of a human voice coming thru on the receiver, the voice's sound waves will blast out encrusted dust particles from the receiver holes... of course some will stop to sit, on one of the numerous benches or even retaining walls to figure out the operational mechanics of their phones, these of course are folks who treated themselves to a smart phone for Christmas and where more excited to show it off than learn how to operate them... along with the disgruntled loving words of *stupid phone* and the constant bombardment of the tactile screen with the index finger... one has to wonder, why put up with this frustration and our need to be connected, on this supposedly day off... is it not quite insulting to be surrounded and ignored by family members, as the phone has priority during this family walk... with phones in hand, wouldn't it be practical that they be solar powered too?... just in passing, I had seen a baby with a toy cell phone...

... at least here the walk is in the great outdoors with the sun reigning over the ocean and a salty warm breeze clearing out their congested cigarette nicotine drenched lungs, between cigarette inhales... ah! mother natures' feeble attempt to restore health to an uncaring chain smoking, fiscally drained population... well, at least for today they are out of the shopping malls with its' fake cotton snow tarnished by colorfully glittering confetti... why such ugliness to convey the consumption spirit of a Nordic continent in a Mediterranean country?

... today, young parents can be less stressed and even more cherishingly caring with their kids, such a drastic change from the shopping mall a couple of days back... witnessed in the mega grocery store, a series of ridiculously funny and quite embarrassing *enfant roi* scenes... the art of whining/crying was exposed intensively in every other isle...

... in isle 2 the child was with his knees dragging on the floor all the while trying to free his wrist from the clenches of an infuriated mother... or the little girl in isle 4, inside the shopping cart experimenting with contortionism and defying gravity by extending every limb over the edges of her mobile jail and by dropping her fat ass on the bag of flour bursting it open creating a white cloud which would make a cocaine addict think he were in heaven...

... isle 6, the lovingly disciplinary, resonating palm whack on the head from the freshly manicured finger nails, which does nothing but to increase the whining volume... how I wished I had seen what childish act had warranted such an assault from the highly refined stylishly dressed mother with hair emanating a scent of both higher education diplomas and money... what brought her to this child rearing Neanderthal level, was it her Bluetooth capturing subliminal reptilian signals from outer dimensions...

... isle 12, watching a 3 year old boy... he frowns when his dad places a bag of chips in the shopping cart, which does not meet his seal of approval... but the audacity of the little boy shined when his dad was not looking and he escalated the shopping cart and withdrew the bag of chips and threw it on the bottom shelf... a silent victory, indeed... anyway, on Christmas day a truce will be called and every mischief/grievance will be forgotten and ironically even rewarded with a gift...

... blind... as the sun continues to shine, absorbed by its' sole task of expulsing its' un-judging rays upon these folks... now, it seems that these kids, highly skilled in the art of *tantrum*, all got brand new shiny bicycles for Christmas... as they make their way, clumsily riding and ineffectively dodging any passerby with the echoed shrieking warnings from the parents to be *careful*... as their parental units simultaneously, were sheepishly shrugging their shoulders apologetically to the injured yet smiling pedestrian... not one bell or horn was heard from these bicycles, which indicates these bikes were bought in these recession times from large surface retail stores where personalized customer service is null, otherwise one would hear and see a bicycle bell... along with remote control dune buggies and tethered airplanes flying low... the futile earful cacophony is drowned by the pounding waves against the rocks...

... parents are segregated by gender with the stroller as a dividing barrier... both genders were looking into the opposite distance, with a few words exchanged every so often, this was the opportune moment during the mundane chit-chat to glance over at the phone in hope of something and/or anything!... before their eyes shifted back to the crowded horizon and looked forward to *nothing*...

... I am one of the *nothing* in their horizon as I sit here unhindered by all this... looking at the beautifully bluish sky... in the hope of seeing my kids in the invisibly blinding sun...

## 2014/12/30 – Tuesday (Areia, Portugal)

… anyway… woke up feeling like shit… undertook a lengthy meditation yesterday afternoon where time and space ended up having a whole new meaning… suffice to say, in my night time sleep, I was far from feeling alone… via the meditation, perhaps I left behind me… an open passage to the other side… ?

… galloped my way to the coziest bistro in this neck of the world… what a blasting rainy day… so, the day started off in another coffee shop next to my old house called Tasca Tosca… impossible to be sitting outdoors today… as the rain was washing away any remnants of bread crumbs off the bistro tables outside, depriving the local birds of their daily nourishment source which sustains their lively hood… how will they now manage, as they got used to the ease of getting their food off human crumbs… as opposed to eating insects, which would explain why there are so many flies finding refuge in the coffee shop and pestering me… oh!… read between these previous lines, as it draws a parallel to a humans' unbalanced modernization of our environment…

… Tasca Tosca… interesting coffee shop, its' layout and décor has an edge similar to an old Montreal loft, playing mellow english lounge/jazz music… it is run by very friendly young people, which gives me the impression it is almost cool to be working here (almost a Gap brainwash mindset)… though the décor is nowhere as eclectic as say Olive & Gourmando in old Montreal… it still does have a blend of modern industrial architecture with vintage Portuguese artifacts… sorry, as I wished I had my camera to give you a glimpse of this place as my words do not render it justice…

… last summer I spent my vacation at a Club Med beach resort in Turks & Caicos, it had lazy relaxed waves crawling onto the shore… the nearby beach here is called Guincho… and nowhere that gentle, it is more like a menopausal woman cursed with an unexpected menstrual cycle, with a good dosage of cramps kicking in too… whoa!, that was a mouthful… suffice to say, the beach is in a bitchy mood too… please?… no complaining about sexism, this is humour & nothing more…

… no matter what I write to distract myself… it keeps coming back, I am not able to shake it off… this feeling which rendered my night sleepless and now seems to affect my waking hours too… wtf… leave me alone… all night I felt nothing but *aloneness and it was not mine… sure, it is easy to say I have been here too long with too much time on my hands and am probably going through something similar to cabin fever... I know what I felt, it was an unreal reality...*

... I am not qualified to explain what I felt as I do not have any of the technical mambo jumbo jargon... and as I try to calm my mind by reflecting and writing the events of the last few hours... all I know for sure, is that there must be some sort of after life where we may linger for whatever reason... I am going to give this a positive twist so that I may get on with my day in a normal fashion and especially remove the fear this *unknown* has caused me... I don't know and cannot remember where or what I did, or was during the meditation... I cannot explain how I know this, but I was not asleep either... as eccentric as this may sound, perhaps I met and had interactions with other beings, and maybe I eased their *aloneness* for a while but they did not know it was a temporary thing I was doing with and for them... maybe they want more of me, if so... it will be on my terms and not theirs... no one or anything is going to rule me, my essence abides by free will... regardless of any divinity... this is not bad for someone who was a hard core atheist just a few months ago and is now more confused than ever before...

* * *

# JANUARY

PART THREE

## 2015-01-01 – Thursday (Areia, Portugal)

... dancing myself... even though I have a massive headache from a hangover and every time I strike the keyboard its' resonating strokes creates an intense pounding in my empty echoing skull... right now this is the emotion *du jour*... as for any other emotions I may feel during the new year... depending on the availability, I'll either consult a psychiatrist, the liquor store for the weekly specials to solve my problems or divinity... I know, I am all heart with myself... last night's party was oddly strange... when speaking Portuguese, people picked up on my accent and questioning ensued, I was a novelty because I can speak three languages... add to this that there were other foreigners and some were feeling homesick... needless to say, we ended up forming an alliance with the consumption of booze as our common platform to drown sorrows...

... oceanic coffee shop... taking in deep breaths of ocean air... I was hoping this cool air would clear my head and maybe drive down a notch the nauseous feeling in my stomach... but like pretty much anything in life... *you reap what you sow*... usually this time of year I plan for my physical checkup within the next few months... interesting how I take care of my body but do nothing for my mind other than indulge in alcohol... this is also the day when most reflect on the year gone by and maybe make resolutions... I'm no exception to this concept... but go a step further and examine the path the previous year left me on... along with this day of reflection, I also need to confront my fears... notably, the second experience I had with Carmen's mom while I was walking the Camino in 2013...

... hat trick... even as I sit here in front of my laptop... words fail me as to how I will start recounting this experience... within a few afternoon hours while walking the Camino, everything in my life changed... the way I see it, the Camino is divided into 3 phases... :

the first is the *physical*... aching muscles and foot (shoe) blister festival... unknown/new town every day... where is the albergue (Spanish for refuge or hostel)... what kind of people will you meet in the dormitory... where to eat, if there is a restaurant nearby or do you snack on whatever the local convenience store may have, usually bread, cheese and cold cuts... wash clothes and hope they'll be dry for the following day...

... the second phase is the mental... all your preconceived notions of how things should be in your world are scrapped as now improvising is the new agenda... things like work, school, airplane return deadline all seem so futile because for the first time one's daily life is simple... get up, put back on yesterday's smelly clothes cause everyone else stinks and so do you, walk, eat and sleep... and most important, enjoy the view cause this is truly a case where it is not the destination but the journey...

... 3rd... once you have uncluttered your mind with phases one and two then kicks in the third phase which is what I call the *spiritual*... by this time you are walking in a Zen state of mind... so intense is this phase that you are in a perpetual introspective and meditative mood... at that time I did not know this, but be careful as this state of mind opens the door to the other world...

... drive away... not only was everything up to this point in my life made clear, both in terms of accomplishments and failures... but it was the lucidity perspective which had me smiling... love may be a drug but hope is the driving force... I knew by this time I was well into the *phase three* of the Camino... it was also the first time in weeks the sun was brilliant and warm... I was in sync with my environment... after a quick sandwich lunch by a roman built bridge, I started walking and the path followed alongside a river... and I was thinking how lucky I am to be here, such beauty... only the river water, insects and my footsteps graciously and harmoniously disturb the silence... then... the relaxed happy thoughts swirling in my mind were snappishly interrupted... starting from behind me, I feel the spirit of Carmen's deceased mom go through me... fear bullied into every cell of my body... I stopped in my footsteps and started crying uncontrollably... though I did not see her or anything for that matter... I did feel she *(her spirit)* was going around me to enter me again from the back... it was as if she had swung through me and missed the target... instinctively I braced myself for her reentry... and with a thought I asked *what the fuck do you want?* ... again tears bolted out of my eyes... but this time she left a message in my mind about Carmen's dad... *his candle light is dimming... his candle light is dimming... his candle light is dimming... he needs Carmen... he is scared...* I did not do this but the thought/message ... *his candle light is dimming...* was associated and/ or equated with his death...

... coming home... I don't know how long I just stood there... but when I started walking I was still having outbursts of tears... I felt different, it was as if a part of me had left with her... the feeling I had is something in me sneaked out while I wasn't looking... but now the idea that I had to relay this message to Carmen was burdening me to say the very least... how do you tell a friend... *hey! your dead mom just told me your dad is on his death bed and he needs you...* by now the path opened up into a country road and I walked slowly and zigzagged as if I was inebriated... I did not know what to do and was buying time, hoping for a fucken miracle to solve the previous miracle... my analytical/mathematical mind kicked in with logic... what just happened was my over active imagination which took control for a few minutes... my survival instincts took over and the emotional and logical voices in my head raged until I said to *shut the fuck up*... shuffling my feet on the road... hoping time and distance would be never ending...

... heaven and earth... fuck me, what am I going to do... without a computer nor any prepaid phone time left... now I feel I must contact Carmen and explain what happened and for her to take it with a grain of salt... would she understand? ... would I, if someone called me with this kind of information? ... how could I be so happy one minute and in a living hell the next... I can now see the little village where I had planned to stay for the night... with the sunset crossing the threshold as I reach the village gateway... I look up to the sky and in a desperate tone ask... *give me a fucken sign*... and shit, no more than a few paces into this insignificant village I see a paper sign on the coffee shop window... *INTERNET*... I laughed out of relief... then... it started again, I paced back and forth in front of the café debating whether to go in or not as voices in my head were arguing the pros and cons...

... the wave... I'm insane, an idiot, and a fool as I push the door open to the café... behind the foosball machine, I see a computer all the way in the back... as I sit in front of the paying computer... I'm not sure if it is located back here for privacy or that the foosball is more popular... I drop a coin into the slot machine/box to start the computer... as I wait a few long seconds for the unit to warm/start up... my mind goes blank and I realize I have no idea what I'm gonna write Carmen... all I can think of is that I'm crazy... the screen comes on and I open an internet session and start a new email addressed to Carmen... without any cuing, I see the blank email screen... my fingers are on their own, as if they were being borrowed for a few seconds... I look at the screen to see what my fingers are typing, because I still had no idea what to type... the first typed line appears... *these are not my words*... next, I see the message I had received showing up on the screen... my typist fingers are faster than my reading eyes... with a few screen flickers, the email closes up and the word *sent* is displayed... this was the end, when I was not even sure when it started... at this point, the email is virtually on route to Carmen in Montreal... somewhat stunned I say to myself... *what the fuck have I done...*

… people have the power… for me, most of this was all hearsay… Carmen received the email and went into a panic mode, and justifiably so… she called my wife at the time asking her if she knew anything about the email, its' content and what I was up to… it had been days since my wife heard from me therefore she was of no help… Carmen's dad had re-married and moved overseas… she calls him and it's the stepmother who answers his cellphone… she confirms that her dad is very ill, but did not want to worry/alarm his children and kept his illness a secret… shortly after… Carmen calls a family meeting with her siblings… the evening in which they are all together, discussing what to do next… they receive a phone call from the stepmother announcing her dad's light had gone out…

… earth prelude… days later when I finally was able to reload my cellphone… my wife told me about the passing… she had many questions for me, but I avoided saying anything as I was in a *state of disbelief* … add to this, that for the last few days the growing and worrisome feeling that something was missing in me kept amplifying… this is hard to explain… I felt different in the sense that I was somewhat incomplete, as if part of me disappeared… but now more than ever, anyone I met… it was if I was able to take part of their essence and put it in me as if I had space for it… and actually I was able to feel what they were feeling… and at other times, I felt as if I was sending myself messages disguised as intuitions… notably to re-do the Camino and write a book were the recurring messages… at the time I thought how absurd, I am not a writer… and today I still think I'm not a writer but at least I can jot down my thoughts in a journal…

## 2015/01/04 – Sunday (Cascais, Portugal)

… wallowing in confusing self-pity… in 2013, the summer after the Camino… I spent the summer in my house… still living in the family home… though my ex-wife and I were not together in any matrimonial way… other than announcing and acting upon our separation, everything else in my life was plagued by indecisiveness… I was still trying to come to grips with what I had experienced in my so called spiritual epiphany, but at times I would think of it as the *big fuck up*… word soon got around that I had been able to see death… and I felt very self-conscious about this… to the point where I felt alienated and feared because I can talk to the dead kind of thing… though, so far from the truth…

... why am I here... funny even to this day, and almost 2 years after I am still affected and afflicted with my coming here and trying to put all of this history down on paper... and at times feel that in a masochistic way I will do it all over again with a second Camino pilgrimage... will it affect my relationship with Suzanne?... though I always felt that Suzanne and I have been together several times in previous lives... is it possible that in this life I'm on my own?...

... during the summer of 2013... I did not work much in my home renovation business... my mind was not into it anymore... just enough to pay off the bills and support the household... but it was not long before I was dipping into the credit card to round off the month... Sundays were always reserved for my company paperwork, but this too had changed as I would just sit in the backyard... why is it, when I look back upon those Sunday afternoons in the backyard I think of myself in the third person... is it my higher-self kind of thing?... sometimes, when I write in this journal I feel I am in a dream... again, as if these are not my own words...

... this is when you are sitting in the backyard on a Sunday afternoon, lingering in a plastic yet comfortable chair... the good thing about the chair is that it has a rather large arm rest... where you can place/rest your glass between sips... suburbia, just the word conjures images of single family homes surrounded with the madness of fences... as the need for a fence approves a sense of safety and security, how foolish can it be... look around and all you see are flowers and bushes, none of which are good for smoking... just for pleasing the color palette of the eyes... nice house, but your heart is no longer here and nor do you belong here...

... time has come to move on... another sip, to drown the thoughts... move on to something else... the bohemian mind asks, how did I ever end up in this situation... no idea, just walked into it kind of thing... *right time and place* scenario... without much thinking or planning... ended up in a lifestyle, mind you much good did come out of this, but like everything else, nothing is forever...

... now... all alone with an empty glass and the bottle is in the house... this is the new lifestyle... no one to help me... need to get up for the refill... or are you losing yourself in a wallowing of thirsty self-pity... a thought?... if you can get up for a refill... take it one step further and walk out of the of the backyard... there is something beyond the fence...

... choice?... my choice is actually easy... as my arrogance knows enough... there is something on the other side of the fence and maybe it's not so good... but, staying within the confines of the fence... would be my mental coffin...

## 2015/01/05 – Monday (Cascais, Portugal)

... being in Portugal this time of year has its' perks... for me, amongst other things it has to be the warm sun in lieu of a blistering snow laden cold, as it is back in Montreal (plateau neighborhood) today... with empathy juggling my childhood memories of my old neighbourhood and a snowstorm back in 1969 ... a time before parking vignettes *(the time sharing condo concept applied to abstract parking spaces, where you pay and end up owning... nothing! )* where Portuguese was the official language on the plateau until it got replaced by bourgeois... this is the story of Senhor Joao and Maria (is there any other Portuguese name for a woman?)...

... it is believed Senhor Joao drove an Oldsmobile Delta 88, being of a small stature he had to place a cushion on the seat so that his nose would not rub on the steering wheel... on a tormenting stormy winter snow day, one had to dig out parking spaces... he had parked his car illegally up the street and set forth to dig himself a parking space in front of his duplex ... it gave him a feeling of re-assurance to be able to keep his used & prized Delta 88 within eye sight... after all it had a doily on the back seat panel, handmade to measure by Senhora Maria... since they were unable to have children, she had a lot of free time...

... after an hour or so of digging out snow, he had himself a geometrically accurate rectangular space for his car... he placed the shovel in the middle of the parking space so as to mark his territory and set out to get his car and drive it to his newly chiseled parking space... when he arrived, some filho da puta (son of a bitch) had put his car in HIS space, and to add insult to injury the shovel was gone too... with rage now flowing in his veins ... he drove the car several times around the block and the other car was still in his spot... on the next street block, he drove his car with such a velocity into a snow bank that the impact created itself a parking space although his car was precariously balancing at an angle... no matter, his prime directive was to confront the vile parking space free loader thief person... he got to his house and dodging clothes lines/ropes (to hang and dry clothes) in the hallway ... he made his way to the bedroom window to see and hopefully catch the parking space ladrão (thief)... long minutes passed by and his impatience was now fuelled by anger...

... anda ver, anda ver ... Joao!! (come and see) his wife called out to him... once again he dodged the clothes lines in the hallway and upon reaching the living room... he sees his wife sitting on a plastic covered sofa and eating a homemade rissois (Portuguese version of a pizza pocket) and dripping azeite (olive oil) on her enormous cleavage, he thinks to himself what a fucken slob... once, in their monthly saturday night sex sessions (if you want to call it that... oufff!) ... in bed he couldn't help smelling lemons and was not until he fondled her breasts that he found a lemon scented fabric softener sheet... though they had a dryer, she preferred hanging clothes on the hallway lines/ropes and use the bounce sheet to prevent her tits from sticking together... on the TV newscast they were showing the snow storm... she had called him to come and see the snowstorm on TV... this is what one would call a Kodak/Mastercard moment, you should of seen the look on his face, priceless...

... our friend heads back to the bedroom window... once again hitting the clothes lines in the hallway and breaking one... as he looks out the window, there is now another car in his spot... foda-se, caralho (procreation and penis explicative)... he now turns his back to the window and leans on the very small window ledge... despair has set in, as his eyes pan their bedroom, he sees his golden lacquered imitation wood frame wedding picture (almost poster size) over the bed board ... he remembered the argument this picture had caused at the Galicia Portrait Photo shop... the Spanish owner had 2 versions of the picture, one au naturel where her facial hair was the focal point on the picture and a second with time consuming touch-ups to hide the black grizzly spots... of course the latter cost more, though they ended up getting and paying a substantial amount for the one with touch ups... they thought the Spaniard would end up placing the au naturel picture in his window display without paying them some sort of royalties... of course the savvy Spaniard did no such thing as he wanted passerby customers to come into his photo shop studio and not be repulsed by a such a woman...

... you are wondering why he would marry such a woman?... Canadian immigration gave preference to married couples... yep! a shot gun wedding Portuguese style... on a side note, the picture was taken soon after arriving in Canada and her wedding dress was already too small... though they were only married for a few weeks, she was already exploding into obesity... of course, the bigger she got physically the more there was to love, if you want to give her size a positive twist... cap in hand ... our snow hero Senhor Joao...

walks out the door and this time was completely unhindered by the clothes lines, as his posture of despair made him physically smaller... he now heads out to the next street and try to fix himself a new parking space where he had left off his car in anger... once there he realized he did not have a shovel, and his rear tires made no contact with the ground... his car was floating in the air... he heads back home, pours himself a shot glass of agua ardente (moonshine) and catches the last few minutes recap of the weather report calling for more snow...

## 2015/01/06 – Tuesday (Cascais Shopping Mall – Portugal)

... woke up in anger, don't know what I did or saw during my sleep, but it was not good as it is still lingering in me... it's the same old shit, I cannot tolerate myself... actually I feel inferior and hate the way I look and feel inside... the body given to me is ugly, the personality it came with is also really dumb, vain and insecure... a true loser by humans standards, a waste of oxygen by all accounts... the feeling of me in this dysfunctional body is taking its' toll... what the fuck was I thinking when I accepted to take this body, had I given it more thought perhaps I would of made a better selection, no?... for sure!

... it feels like a baby's hand inside an adults' glove, what a bad fit... my soul slushes from side to side inside this physical water based body... it is like I am always holding on for dear life inside this shaky body... so much effort put into stabilizing myself, that if there was any pleasure to be had within being in this body, I would surely miss it as "me" is busy holding on to this shell for dear life...

... someone, something help me... it is and never was about loneliness... it is the aloneness I feel all the time... this un-controllable fear of being alone on this planet and yet here I am alone with fear and all... I still manage to exist and lack the courage and determination to end this life... which pretty much explains why I am still here... oh! I'm a really funny guy and in more ways than one too...

... all the beautiful people... so busy maintaining the beautiful that they turn out to be the side effect result of endless shopping... maybe shopping malls should be regarded as functional, hands-on museums with every store being a canvas both visually and musically as there is always music being played so that a customer may be distracted and manipulated into impulsive purchases... along with the shops will be the food courts with a variety of colorful trays from the noisy fast food restaurants… each tray color representing its' respective restaurant… of course, there are also kiosks dispensing coffee, where small tables only have 2 chairs … it is here you will find me, sitting alone in one of the chairs and looking at the beautiful people…

## 2015/01/08 – Thursday (Areia Portugal)

… sitting in my favourite coffee shop called Tasca Tosca… just read about the Charlie shootings in the paper and from the corner of my eye, caught a glimpse on the TV… in this little town of our world, this atrocity is seen as a human waste, in the occident the bells of religious & political implications are clamoring, for sure … now the TV goes eco with the green of a soccer field, as worldly misery and sadness has a life span of about the time it takes to down an espresso while standing up… the morning customers have their own misery, with a recession at hand weighing heavily they carry their own strife, with money being so scare and being able to treat themselves daily to a 55 cent espresso coffee, makes them feel they can still afford a luxury in their mundane life… and with haste they shuffle out the door and merge into a bus stop flock…

… religions like any other industry have their own protocol or procedures that dictate (I insist on the word dictate), but unlike commercial industry which periodically revise and upgrade their internal procedures to adapt to the current times as this is how they are able to survive… but if no change is adopted, nothing but chaos and/or collapse ensues… and this goes for mankind as well as the only constant in life is change…

… no loving god or prophet/preacher would ever demand killing as a means to resolve a disagreement… with this the 3 terrorists/men who committed the shooting of 12 humans for who have now left loved ones behind temporarily… how noble, to honor and defend a defenceless God Almighty… but at the same time for the victims, God is not our friend… what has their murderous action gained other than fuel more misguided hatred… I'm not wise enough to write something that will resolve our problems… I wish what I wrote made sense, but it is cluttered with emotion and I cannot think clearly… would this justify me wishing harm on the terrorists?… but on this planet it seems that cluttered thinking is clear…

… blind lab mice … 3 frustrated men who's momentary lack of human emotions and probably human contact too, rendered them so revolted, isolated and hostile that they allowed themselves to be brainwashed into a distorted ideology, because they left the thinking to be executed by others... had they spent their energy in helping others or even try to make the world a better place instead of wasting their time auto-fucking their assholes with the barrel of their rifles... these men are human and I cannot forget this but unfortunately they are clogged with their own shit... ego, makes you live in fear... indeed what a shameful mess for ALL of humanity...

... when caught and they will be caught... whatever their outcome, it will not appease my anger because I cannot be angry with someone who is sick... as the end result of their capture will not bring back the dead nor restore any positive fate in mankind, as the so called justice is a disguised vengence... my dismay will linger forever... I am not alone here as these men are someone's children and I am sorry to say what a waste of oxygen they turned out to be...

## 2015/01/10 – Saturday (Cascais, Portugal)

... all my life... there are no two ways to say it... my spirit was being stifled and probably even dying before its' time ... what the fuck was I doing trying to be like everyone else... ignoring what I always knew deep in me that we are not alone in the universe and even on this planet... I can feel them looking at me... especially at night when relaxed, where I was always ever so fearful... it was not until I was introduced to spiritualism and more precisely meditation, after my first Camino pilgrimage ... that I began to understand and eventually, the slow learning curve of re-wiring my thought process that I began to master my fears...

... not the first time... window shutters closed... the room in complete darkness... as I laid in bed straining my eyes to see in the dark... I began to see these dark shadows flying about like a hawk visually seizing its' prey before a descent... these shadowy things were in front of me and over me flying in erratic patterns... every so often there were minute sparks, like those generated by sparklers on birthday cakes... but the sparks were always to my right, could not see the source of where the sparks were being generated, though I tried... can't say I was comfortable with this... but I also accept there's more to life than just the physical realms... and here's a positive attitude, why not all live in harmony... this is the best I can do for now when dealing with extra-sensory perceptions...

... last night I had a couple of beers while on an outing with Suzanne...

nothing that was out of the norm, in terms of alcohol content... it was just that I was very relaxed, calm and/or probably just mellow... but I have found being this relaxed is almost like being in a state of meditation... it seems to open portals too... in general, I'm more receptive than usual...

... yesterday though... was particularly more disturbing than usual... as I felt one of these dark shadows slipping into bed between us and making himself (felt it to be male gender) cozy... it seemed to be cold and gelatinous in nature and was spreading out like liquid glue using itself to connect Suzanne and me... as if all three of us were to be one... scared for sure... but I also felt angry, pissed off and thought you fucken bastard... in an authoritarian inner voice, bawled... Enough!... and the intention of the word and thought was understood and encompassed that they were not welcome and to get the fuck out... feeling a shiver of detachment... at this point I asked Suzanne to open the blind/shutter slightly to allow some moonlight in... as I panned the room with my eyes open, I saw nor felt anything... some deep breathing... I closed my eyes and clutched Suzanne in my arms as if I had to protect her and quickly fell into a deep sleep... but, I knew she felt something was amiss...

... intrusions... this was not the first time it has happened, and if I put enough thought into it, I can probably remember other intense feelings of intrusion... though this time, it got brash... this is how I perceive these entities when they disturb me... it's an intrusion and nothing else... I especially did not like the entity getting in bed with us... just like a school yard fight, after being thrown the first punch, one gets up to finish the fight... I know I went after them when I fell asleep... didn't like these fucken bastards invading me, they have no business here...

... I know my dad was with me, because I always perceived him as being my guardian/protector ever since I came back from the Camino... I always turn to him for help and/or guidance in moments of confusion... in the morning, Suzanne said she was also telling them (entities) in an inner voice to get out... as she too, felt I was struggling with them...

## 2015/01/13 – Tuesday (Fatima, Portugal)

... Fatima... a Sunday drive done on a weekday... and why not stop here, as for one it breaks the almost 3 hour car ride and also I needed to pee... the timing could not be better...

94

... left the car parked in one of the multiple large, pounded earth parking lots... completely void of any shade... this place must be a scorcher in the summer time... as I walked to the shrine I could not help observing this arid land is now home to large hotels, elaborate avenues lined with coffee shops, restaurants but mostly religious virgin Mary related souvenirs... from t-shirts to statuettes of her and anything in between which can be sold to a believer...

... as I crossed into the open asphalted space of the shrine, besides the overwhelming immenseness of the place was the smell, could not quite make what it was... anyway, there is a large church in the northern edge of the open space and to the sides an assortment of buildings both modern and of traditional architecture, either way they seem out of place...

... burning candles... the smell which at first I did not recognize was that of burning candles but it also reminded me of when I was a very young kid and we would buy live chickens at the market and they were killed and plucked of their feathers before our eyes... so, this had been my introduction to death, I certainly did not grow up thinking fowl grew in plastic and styrofoam packaging... candles are given out for free, in a designated building you can light one up in honor of a departed love one or for some hope/wish ... and it will burn for a few hours and I can only guess the wax is recycled, due to the yellow/tarnished color of the free candles...

... the tree where the Virgin Mary was supposed to have appeared to the 3 shepherd (children) is now gone, back in 1917 or so, after the apparitions (UFO for some), some of the 70k people who had witnessed the sun dancing in the sky, ended up depleting the tree into oblivion for souvenir purposes (maybe like the rhino horn as an aphrodisiac)... so, where the tree once stood... an open air chapel was erected, a combination of modern structures and amber color stained wood ... the color reminds me of the church benches piety... the altar of this chapel is a little stone house, kind of like a toolshed with a statue of the Virgin Mary encased in glass... why the glass boxing is a mystery to me...

... another mystery ... 3 secrets/messages were handed to these kids by the Virgin Mary... two of which were revealed... and here is the clincher for me, in 1960 or so the Vatican decided the third message would not be revealed... somehow the guys back in the Italian walled resort, knew better than divinity what is good for mankind... maybe, had the third message been revealed... today I would not witness people burning candles or praying while walking on their knees or crawling/dragging themselves on their bellies out of desperation for a miracle... a few years ago the message was released but speculation claims it was hacked ... who or what can we trust?... probably, the third message was withheld simply because the male dominance in the church were unable to adhere to what the last survivor (woman) may have to say... even if the message comes from divine infinity...

... as I walk back to the car, I glance at the souvenir window shops and see black and white pictures of the 3 shepherd kids ... the pics do make a good case for child labour, after all these kids were herding instead of being at school, no?... sorry to say, but the children were far from being photogenic like realtors... so, not commercially viable in terms of selling T-shirts with their pics as an imprint... at least their parents loved them I'm sure, though the younger ones died shortly after the apparitions... the eldest one became a nun until her death... whatever has transpired I hope they have found serenity... in the meanwhile I will keep looking for it as I have not found any serenity here nor in me, yet...

## 2015/01/14 – Wednesday (Aveiro, Portugal)

... as I sit in this tea house called Doce Infusao (sweet infusion) sipping my recently acquired taste for tea... which is not so much the beverage, but the ritual and calmness associated to savouring tea... this corner shop has very little wall due to the large windows and an atrium architecture infusing sun rays from all angles... serenity in its' décor and the sweet jazzy music being played softly and my waitresses Tania and Sandra, glide about smoothly rendering them almost invisible...

... as a small kid the first time I came to Portugal... I fell in love with the city (Aveiro) and did not even understand why... today as I look out the windows and see unique buildings that have been here for eternal decades... if the buildings were a book, the only word one could read off the pages would be neglect... endless rent signs in vacant shops, the multitude of banks on its' main artery are now replaced by Chinese discount knick knack stores and there are lottery vending kiosks everywhere selling a mathematically impossible dream of monetary joy... this country has been in a recession mode for a long time... not only is it seen, but one can feel an eeriness in the air... but all this makes for an economic tourist attraction...

... memories now flood my head ... trivial things like meeting my grandparents for the first time and feeling their unfounded affectionate hugs crushing me and their clothing smelt of mothballs... my grandparents lived on a freshly scented manure farm and sounds of farm animals day and night did cause me some sleepless nights as I thought I'd be attacked by one of them... yeah!, I was a wimpy sensitive city kid...

... also!!... way back in 1965, at the ripe old age of a very dreamy mature 5 year old kid... we got on the plane in March for a month of dysfunctional family vacation in Portugal... at that time, my vision of the world was limited to the black and white babysitting provided by our television set... couldn't understand why my dad wanted to see my grandfather when all the stories he would tell my brother and I were about how much he was hit with the belt...

... when we left the farm to visit Aveiro, a city with a population of +/-100k ... this was a major outing as it was a whole 12 km trip from the farm... the whole family squeezed into the car, my car seat was someone's lap... other than the fact that it is occasionally considered the Venice of Portugal because of its' canals (on a side note, on low tide the canals enchant the air with a sewer smell)... it's simply, a typical city like so many others...

... but... for me, as that 5 year old... I found myself in parks and public spaces with my arms stretched out as if I were a plane running/flying about... as if my winged arms were picked up by the wind and lifted me up into a déjà vu feeling of freedom... this city resonated in me, it was new to the eyes of the 5 year old, but not to my soul... the colors, the sounds and even the smells came to me with an air of familiarity... of course... such serenity and momentous joy came to an abrupt halt...

... my loving dad did not hesitate showing his true colors to impress my mothball smelling grandfather... by applying unlovingly the palm of his hand to my head... the impact destabilized me and I nearly crashed into my mom... she grabbed my arm and with an aggressive jolt had me standing upright instantly and she reprimanded my younger brother too, though he did nothing except stand in fear...

... so... spiritually speaking... it is said... we choose our parents as part of the learning experience on the earth plain... what purpose does it serve my apprenticeship to behave as an adult at the age of 5 other than stunt my emotional maturity later on in life? ... why these people as my parents? ... how in hell did I get mixed up with these foreign earth beings... deep down I know my parents loved us beyond reason and in hindsight there was no need for being violent... but when I associate empathy with my dad, who did my father have as a role model other than my grandfather... my grandfather, the man who at 12 years old ran away from home permanently because of the beatings my great-grandfather gave him... all I wanted that day was to fly... maybe they did too, once upon a time...

## 2015/01/15 – Wednesday (Aveiro, Portugal)

... new town... feeling out of sorts today... feeling lost, settling in is never easy for me... my guide is a little paper note pad, with endlessly adjusted to do lists... for a change of pace, I stepped into a church for a bit of serenity... actually it was more to see if maybe I could meditate... existentialist questions abound again... regarding me but also my relationship with Suzanne... there was an ongoing construction site next to the church, competing for my attention with its' festival of jackhammers... sometimes, I have days where one is best just giving in to the new and re-adjusted plans... with this in mind I went to the movies instead... in the darkness of the theatre one forgets the real world... but as I sit here ignoring commercials and the turn-off your cell phone jingle... my thoughts go back home to my youth, to happier carefree times... or so it seems, as I romanticize them as such...

... down to an art... teenagers sneaking into a cinema... we all contributed money for one ticket... and one of us would go in and open the Exit fire doors for the others... here is how we eventually got caught... the fire exit corridors leading to the cinema were made up of unpainted concrete... in our way in ... our shoes would pick up the dust, once we got in the theatre... our dusty shoes would leave footsteps printed on the dark carpet... all the ushers had to do, was follow the footsteps pointing to where we were sitting... busted!!!!...

... professional delinquency... like most of us growing up in a Portuguese blue collar neighbourhood in Montreal during the summer (circa 1970's)... if your parents did not send you to Portugal to experience the torment of living in a dung infested dairy farming village... surrounded by fashion conscious grannies dressed in black widow garb... along with Sunday morning sunrise masses... WHO GETS UP AT 11 ANYWAY?... and local village girls uncomfortably wearing their Sunday best hand me downs which can deter a young male from any sexual desires ... get the picture?...

... lucky me... yep!... I got to experience a summer of creative mischief in Montreal... it was great, at least for me... on a warm lazy weekday afternoon... we would park our asses on the door steps of some house facing the back doors of the porn cinema ... and wait... and watch the brown fire exit door from the theatre, a cinematic porn emporium... when a customer would come out through the door... I guess their shame was too much, one always showed up... as soon as the door opened and the customer exited... we ran (darted) to catch the door before it closed... yes, once we had the door under our control, we sneaked in...

... nobility... once inside we had no intentions to watch the movie... nope... we had far more intellectual aspirations / notions... we actually placed ourselves on stage behind the screen... once again our patience was a virtue... we waited for an erotic seen to be projected... keeping in mind they only ran pornos... we did not wait long... so, one cannot say we were actually virtuous in any way...

... team work... whenever an intercourse sex scene came on... we would push the screen in unison to create a 3-D effect... the screen would swing back and forth... creating the ultimate viewing experience for the audience... yes!... we had invented the next cinematic attraction... the 3-D effects were anti-climactic as they could not last long enough... as we were chased out of the theatre shortly after... but to this day, I always wonder if the viewers appreciated our avant-garde high tech efforts?... what I retained the most from this... was that I did not know that the screen was see through until then... did you?

## 2015/01/17 – Sunday (Agueda, Portugal)

... sermon... on this Sunday morning... for all you pot smoking space cadets out there and even for those still stuck here... and those who are now using beer bottle bottoms as sunglasses, due to the hangover... for those who feel there is more to life than simply sustaining Revenue Quebec's monopoly... and the Catholics who are presently sitting in church yawning, and trying to convince themselves it is a necessary evil... for those who can see beyond the tip of their noses... for the lucky astronauts (still very few) who have stuck their heads outside this epic planet... for those who think there is more to the sun other than mostly hydrogen & helium... for those on this planet cursed with empathy and loneliness too... for those who cannot see and/or imagine beyond the blue of the sky... we are but a fraction of a sand grain in the universe, and yet how can we be so pompous... into thinking wine has no side effects the next morning... this morning my head is throbbing, last night it was my lower head...

... jackass... it would be impossible for me to pass up on this journal entry... within a certain variation pretty much everything is a déjà vu... as kids we were already heavy coffee drinkers... whether we ate Corn Flakes or Alphabits we would add coffee to the cereal/milk combo... tea cookies were dipped in coffee... and a day old bread, was cut up into spoon size pieces and in a bowl, we would mix in the bread, sugar, milk and coffee... mmm?... I wonder if this would explain why we were hyper?... my mom worked the afternoon/evening shift, which left my dad in charge and of course his wild unconventional culinary skills... he was a firm believer that ice cream was no good for us as the cold caused cavities... but being a loving dad, he liked treating his boys to sweet treats... in his infinite wisdom, he would warm up homemade red wine, add a heaping of sugar to it and then we would all dip bread pieces into the warm mixture... today, we would probably label this as a fondue... the following day, my mom would desperately try to wake me up for school (grade one was a nightmare for me), she actually would sit me on the kitchen table and dress me, I was zonked out and pretty much unresponsive... can you say hangover?... occasionally she wore the manly skirt in the house... ice cream came back on the menu, coffee was still a staple, but wine was out...

... glass eye warmth... politicians say it best... the family is the most important resource we have... our children are our future... education is our number one priority... of all the species on this planet, we are the most intelligent, so it seems... yet at the first chance, we hand over our kids to a daycare institution to raise them... of course we will haggle the daycare fee too... we want more money for other important things which amazingly I cannot remember any examples... but I'm sure it is worthwhile... parents seem to confuse love, nurturing and responsibility with guilt... kids are dumped at daycare/schools earlier than birds feed themselves... even before dawn cracks, parents are already left with a long day to earn money and guilt...

... quality time... last night had supper alone, at a family restaurant... family because it was past 9:38 PM and it had quite a few children... and quite an assortment of kids that became my new entertainment for the night... because up to now my choices were the big TV with soccer or my silently friendless phone... some patrons were still walking in as I raised my hand in one combined gesture to order another bottle of wine and wipe Suzanne from my teary eyes... a 5 year old enfant roi... dictating the policy of pacifier versus a spoon feeding mommy with high gloss crimson whore nail polish... on another table, grandparents sitting quietly as a father scolds his kid for being stupid/dumb and waiting until supper to do his homework on the res-taurant table... for a candlelit dim kid he mouthed off his daddy was always too busy to help him... most tables had smart phones next to the fork for the kids to play with or take selfies stained with finger prints... along with the nice clothes they're all wearing tonight which will not be worn tomorrow as it's incorrect to wear the same clothes 2 days in a row... the next person to see these clothes will be a bored & frustrated clerk at the dry cleaning shop ..., no wonder this country is third in the world for the consumption of anti-depressants... at least these kids were not at home dipping bread into sugared wine...

## 2015/01/19 – Monday (Aveiro, Portugal)

... I came up to Aveiro,... for I was out of touch with who I am after a disagreement brought on with my girlfriend Suzanne... this town, is where my parents came from and where they had lived their final years... and since I am so far away from my native Montreal, I had hoped I can resource myself here, but it's not much of a conversation going on while I stand in front of their common shared burial plot/grave... for the first time, I had the final word on whatever we discussed...

... one week has gone by and the longest conversation I had was with a taxi driver and the only exchange worthwhile retaining was that of a classical music radio station... my vocal cords will surely seize any moment from lack of use... my ears, ache from being plugged with earphones ... come to think of it, I hide in my IPod...

... what is happening to me?... I've noticed ... I am becoming very re-clusive... I find myself walking around looking for a coffee shop and making sure there aren't too many people inside, I cannot handle the noise or being surrounded by humans... today I went to the mall to do some groceries and maybe eat in the food court and before I know it there are so many folks everywhere that I walk into to a movie theatre to escape... and yet, I feel the need to talk or exchange verbally, so I think... cause my actions contradict my way of thinking...

... furthermore... actually, today I went into a church intentionally and try to clear up my head... I think, the last time I went into a church with a purpose was when my daughter was baptized some 20 years ago... to put it mildly, I am not a faithful customer of the church retail shop... I just sat there for almost an hour... alone, not sure god knew I was there or maybe he did not recognize me since it has been so long since I've come to see him...

... again... even I'm worried about how reclusive I have become... I have found new ways of comfort with church and tea drinking, but mostly inner peace through meditation... I avoid people at all costs... I find myself living only in my head... I need to build up the energy/determination to get myself out of my un-healthy comfort zone...

... is it possible to be in love with a woman such as Suzanne and she in love with me... and yet we somehow cannot get along... is it because we are both in our mid-fifties and have encrusted stubborn inflexibility... maybe, we can/should just shrug off our egos for a while, cause time and even life is running out on us... love does not need to be silent and I must speak up...


## 2015/01/20 – Sunday (Aveiro, Portugal)

... another Sunday morning bored and cursed by loneliness, while in the crowded coffee shop terrace... though the coffee (latte) sets the mood for a well-tempered start to the day... it does not fill the immediate/current void in my heart, and especially today the city noise was hard to ignore on my way here too... the city is taking its' toll on me, I need to find my center, a zen place with quiet sound... so, meanwhile... I feel empathy creeping in, what is there around me now, which I can pick on and unmask... ?

... there!... a young chap sitting a few tables over ... wearing a military green dress button shirt, blue jeans, and black loafers... though I feel the colors are off a bit, the kaki green and blue jeans clash but at least it looks like comfort wear above all... the wearing of the sunglasses all the while eating probably stems from the fact that he wants to look around without being noticed by the victim... in his own benign way he is a predator, aren't all men predators?...

... a woman just joined him and is sitting to his side (why not across from him?) and is quite petite and submissive looking, the word frail comes to mind... compared to his physical aggressive demeanor, it indicates she is insignificant during sexual intercourse... I can guess she was in the bathroom when he ordered the food and started eating without her... this lack of courtesy points to there being an overtly comfortable setting between them, but also a dwindling if not decayed love relationship...

... she must of have spent a bit of time preparing herself, based on the over worked hair and make-up... all this effort in vain too... cause other than remotely pleasing herself, no one will notice her, she is a run of the mill woman... it is not her looks but mostly her posture that makes her dim amongst the crowds...

... perplexing... she is thin without any misplaced fat, I sense she feels she is beautiful... too bad, her validating image of herself is based on fashion magazines with anorexic touched up models... and here is the coup de grace... the defining moment where she feels she is a modern empowered woman... the opening of the purse, and the retrieval of her cigarettes... drawing one out, with ease from having done it very often, she lights it up by herself as the gallantry of her man has long burned out... the phallic symbol between her fingers burning away... is just that... a fleeting moment of self-importance... the eventual cremation, will be the final burn, her very own carnival of light...

... wtf ... is wrong with me... I feel such bitterness on the tip of my tongue waiting to be vocalized... my head is heavy, so much unresolved anger... finish off my coffee and will head back to any church and seek external quiet and maybe even find internal silence...

## 2015/01/21 – Wednesday (Aveiro, Portugal)

... walking around taking pictures of the city, but this time I only photograph buildings and street views one would never see in tourist advertising... the beauty of the city is undeniable, but my sense of mischievousness has me looking at things differently...

... oh!... what a flashback... in a remote side street I spot a barbershop I had been to with my dad when I was a kid... since, I needed a haircut/trim my beard and it has been over a week since I have had any type of real conversation with anyone... what better place to simply talk ... though I thought I would be telling my story, it was in fact the barber who did all the talking...

... alarmingly so... the clock on wall was ticking loud... the barber and an old man sitting there seemed oblivious to it... the old man was over 80 years old and had been the previous owner who had now sold the barbershop to its' current owner a Brazilian man... from what I perceived the old man still hung around the shop out of habit and probably a combination of boredom and loneliness... since he is not holding scissors or a comb, I guess he has too much time on his hands, nevertheless he is still part of the décor... and for the time being, it is physically...

... I do remember the shop from my childhood, but at that time I did not register the place... all I do remember was the cape being too tight around my neck and yet little hairs still fell on my back causing endless itching... the place is slightly depressing in appearance, maybe due to the décor or lack of... in the waiting area is a red velour sofa with its' cladded wood panelling base... once upon a time ... this sofa was definitely in a living room somewhere and was fixed up for a second life in the shop... the mirrors are chipped away on the edges with brown rust color decay... the double neon light fixtures hanging off the ceiling and walls have a plastic cover that has yellowed over time, adding more melancholy to the shop... the walls are baby blue in color with an assortment of gray wall tiles added on at different times, depending on the re-modelling du jour...

... escape Brazils' violence... in talking with the barber a very proud family man... it is obvious he came to Portugal to make a better life for his family... and as he mentions the academic, professional and now family life of his own children... one can still denote the unselfish parental sacrifice but at the same time feel the man misses his homeland... history repeating ... surviving hardship in a new country for the family... this is pretty much the life of an immigrant... my dad did the same, but he was lucky as he got to come back to Portugal unhindered...

## 2015/01/22 – Thursday (Aveiro, Portugal)

... Aveiro... by my standards is a small city... with industries located in the outskirts ... even the outskirts used to be farmland but demand for factory space changed the landscape ... this is progress, cleaner jobs allowing for more consumption... when it comes to farming local produce is replaced by importing from EU mega producers... during the daytime, it is a student galore festival... a city with a mega university campus and a handful of high schools... looking at some of the high school kids they all look high with their app covered eyeballs... for those who will eventually attend university, will also get to wear a black suit with a cape (uniform)... a power trip of sorts for the young student, a status symbol... I'm sure wearing such an outfit dates back to some historical tradition... but so did being barefoot and pregnant... some of us have moved on, without the need of a university education/ritual... what better occasion to parade their pompous black uniform suits then during the hazing rituals...

... 1967... back home in Montreal... my only time in grade 2, nearly failed the year... as I grew up speaking Portuguese at home and had a hard time learning English... we used to go to the library from our boys school... it was quite the field trip every second Wednesday... of course, it was exasperating for the teacher trying to control 2 dozen rowdy boys who couldn't care less about books... we were more fascinated with crossing intersections where there were traffic lights... of course, there was a Pakistani lady who worked at the library and she had a Bindi, a dot of red color applied in the center of the forehead ... such a far cry from what we were used to see at home...

... jump to 1972... with me songs have this knack to bring me back to a time and place... 7th grade, the gym in the girls side of the building (we did not have mixed gender classes)... where we have some themed school dance and the gym is decorated... the windows are partially covered up... initially for décor (dark and naughty) but in reality it made the place sweltering hot... girls on one side of the hall, the boys on the opposite wall... then the Beatles – Hey Jude... comes on, a 7 minute plus song, ideal for slow dancing if you're leaning against a girl with an unpadded bra... over the music you hear wet shirts peeling off the walls, as the wimpy now self-confident boys make a move to ask a girl to dance... if successful, 2 sweaty bodies become one... and create new heat, as if the place was not hot enough... which could lead to a romantic spark... the following day the matchmakers (friends) are at work on your behalf asking/confirming ... does he/she like me??...

... know it all... then of course there was music like... Michel Pagliaro - J'entends Frapper... an edgy raunchy rock song... very few were found on the dance floor... for most were back to their regular positions along the wall... playing air guitar singing/shouting the refrain ... what became of these students... are they engineers, computer programmers, construction workers or school teachers... perhaps still playing air guitar somewhere... cause they still have the innocence of a child... ah!... perpetual youth of mind alone, not body... rituals of passage will be here forever...

... new media... has anything changed other than faster technology... what does this technology do for us... does it work on a human level... may be... it was at these dances where I first became aware of Suzanne... shortly after she moved to Portugal, eventually becoming a school teacher and a mom... little did anyone of us know we would meet again some 40 years later via Facebook… with the Atlantic Pond separating us, we managed to connect… is destiny being persistent and keeping up-to-date with technology…

## 2015/01/24 Saturday (Aveiro, Portugal)

… Suzanne… after exchanging a few emails, we had planned our get together this afternoon in Aveiro… our discreet rendez-vous was to meet at the Hotel Moliceiro, it was to be an afternoon of discovering each other after a few weeks of being apart, would we in a few hours be able to uplift our spirits so neglected by our daily predicaments, lovers' quarrels and obligations?…

… as I sat on the edge of the bed full of self-doubt, and wondering if you had changed your mind… I looked out the window, the sky was gray, it had a melancholic, almost palatable velour like texture… those were once upon a time white fluffy clouds, now beaten by heartless cold weather… I see your car pull up into the parking lot… you can't believe how glad I was to see your car, for even I worried about you driving all this distance from Cascais…

… you knocked lightly on the door, as if you didn't want to wake me up from a deep sleep… and I'm already at the door waiting for you… there really was no need to, but I let you knock anyway… I didn't want to seem over anxious… you smile at me naughtily as you walk in, I suspect you are wearing something sexy underneath your coat… you carefully look around the room, as you grasp the layout, you also visualize the architectural characteristics and décor of the room… I think at this very moment it dawns on you why we are here… I see you rubbing your hands as they are cold, I put your hands together, and wrap my warm hands around yours…

… we are standing facing each other, the closeness, the intimacy we were both lacking, hit us like a tidal wave… holding our hands close to my chest, my right hand leaves the finger melee, and gently caresses your cheeks, you kind of sway your face and follow my fingers and the back of my hand gliding along your neck, face, and ear… I gently press by lips against your forehead… I now feel the gentleness of your arms going over my shoulders, as not a word was spoken as we simply stood there, just embracing, as only lost lovers know…

… I was just lying in bed, staring at the ceiling and the smoke detector alarm, wondering what goes into making this apparatus… I'm still amazed how we as humans manage to put all our resources, skills and differences together and create such things… why am I thinking about alarms? … after all

I am here lying down in bed... ... as my mind wonders off racing again about another abstract thought, it finally hits me... am I happy?... when I feel this way, everything around me feels excessively wondrous!...

... there is a light scent of your perfume in the air, it plays with my sense of smell, I can feel my lungs bring in air and at the same time making an effort to capture more of the delicate scent... I close my eyes for a second, so as I can focus on all my other senses... I hear hearts beating and can feel a pleasant pressure on my chest... without moving my head so as not to disturb my comfort position... I see you, with your head lying on my chest, your arm over me and my god you are sensuously beautiful... Leonard Cohen's song *there is a war* is playing on the Ipod... how fitting when he sings... *I guess you call this love, I call it service...* am I really happy here or anywhere for that fucken matter?

## 2015/01/27 – Tuesday (Belem, Portugal)

... it's a vintage 60's style coffee shop... which has seen better glory days probably around the time it was built... but today its' worn out décor caters to the bus loads of duped tourists, who through the travel brochure were informed they would be stopping at a café... surely the brochure did not mention the combo of javel water & urine scented bathrooms... nevertheless, it has large windows with a view of the Jerónimos Monastery (worth the visit) and the CCB (Belem Cultural Center)...

... this is not the first time I have been in Belem, I had come a few weeks ago (maybe months) as Suzanne insisted we visit a nearby pastry shop renowned for its' flakey custard tartlets... my palate caters to dark chocolate therefore I was not engulfed by the pastry... Suzanne, on the other hand ate hers and mine ... as if it were not enough she was still debating whether to have more... due to her swollen stomach, it was our cue to return home... but, I did make a mental note to return to Belem for a second visit...

... as I sit here jotting down some notes for my journal and all the while plugged to my IPOD... is it a coincidence that with almost 3 000 songs playing at random, Mozart comes on as I see his poster across the street on the exterior billboard of the CCB, today would be his birthday... life is full of these quirky mysteries, surprises and synchronicities... back in the days when I was married... I had rigged a radio in the bathroom which would play music when the bathroom lights where switched on... the radio station was also synchronized to CJPX a classical music station par excellence in Montreal... so, there I was sitting on the throne of my kingdom... with the gates locked so as not be interrupted by the wife and/or kids... completely undisturbed while my mind wandered in the calm of classical music...

... now... not all of you have the technical savvy to set up a radio in the bathroom and/or kingdom... perhaps you are sitting by an electrical or gas fireplace conveniently started with a press of a button from a remote ... snuggled under a comfy blanket reading a good book (could be a bible too)... or you just got home in the wee hours of the morning and are still buzzing high and feel the onset of the munchies... all of a sudden you get the bright idea to get an early start on breakfast by eating cornflakes before going to bed ... or of course, the classical and socially approved debauchery of a nauseating hangover ... and you eat only the inner white part of a Weston (POM is also acceptable) bread slice hoping it will soak up the alcohol in your stomach... all the while listening to an incredible piece of music by Mozart... you start wondering about the picture of our man Moz you had seen at some classical music event... his pointy facial features, frilly clothes and that awful puke white wig...

... since, you will not say it, I will... did this guy ever get laid?... seriously, I know I am no prince charming but come on Moz, did you turn on chicks with your magical piano fingers? ... cause I think not even Miss Clairol can help you with your hair/wig... we have all heard the expression ... history repeats itself ... isn't it interesting to see his outfit is quite similar to what Austin Powers wears... unlike his music which will last way beyond infinity... I along with this gibberish text, just like Moz ... will all be short lived... and maybe, just maybe ... depending what funeral home your remaining relatives can afford or think you deserve for your last sun bound day on this planet... perhaps his music will be on the menu as the undertaker plays it during the funeral wake, but at such a low politically correct volume that not even the dead can hear it... what a waste... I know all this is convoluted, but it is an integral part of my imagination, warped sense of humour, and desire... will anyone listen to me now and not later... I hope history will not repeat itself, and my last wishes will be respected...


## 2015/01/28 – Wednesday (Lisbon, Portugal)

... a sunrise... my days are long... there is only so much reading I can do… my walks are always soothing… have not been able to find a quiet place or church for my meditation… despite all this I do think I'm lucky as all I need to do is reflect on my life, and try to write something which would hopefully have some meaning until I embark on the Camino pilgrimage… plugged into my headphones, I listen to music and the songs trigger memories… most are absurdities of days gone by…

… sadness in my heart… when I think I had to give up my musical career as an accordion player because the instrument was too heavy for my puny body to carry… mind you later in life… I thought about picking up the bass… but I was too lazy to make the effort to learn how to play… come to think about it… I'm a pretty good drummer… as long I use one limb at a time… when I'm required to co-ordinate my 4 limbs then I suck as a drummer… but not to worry… if I cannot play, I can listen… we all have our quirks after work… some will get home and turn on the TV… others beat up their kids… some hop behind the stove like robotic servants… I'm addicted to music and I try to find a CD and/or a song in particular which will reflect the day gone by and hopefully define the evening…

… teenager collectivism… in a Montreal sports bar watching TV athletes… with only fat drunks or anorexic baseball cap males on a weekday afternoon… endless car publicity selling happiness with a ludicrous association to freedom… biggest let down ever in history… this is where I would meet a guy who sold me hash for over two years and I was never sure of his name… one could say he was part of the décor… after all he brought in customers to this stale cigarette smelling low end bar… for appearances I always bought one beer but drank from the bottle… in my circle of friends… just like in Friday lottery pools in the office… there is always a designated money collector and buyer for the group… being willingly un-employed I was the official pot buyer and I would get to smoke for free… perks of the trade…

… Beatles – A day in life… this is one of those songs from my delinquent juvenile days… hard to believe… I can assure you, I did not live a sheltered life… every Friday, a group of us would always meet up in Jack's flat, on the 3rd floor on St. Laurent/Villeneuve streets… on the street level was a store - knitting crap, I think … I never found out if anyone lived on the second floor, I guess no one did, cause we played music really loud and never heard a complaint to this effect…

… the flat was sparsely decorated, whatever little decorations it had, they were either hand me down to found in the family garbage artifacts… quite eclectic to say the least… though I must say we did have an extensive assortment/collection of ash trays... big smokers, if you get my drift... during the course of the evening... as the haze intensified and was circulated by the LP record spinning turntable doubling as a fan... this song was part of our weekly ritual... just before the munchies set in... where we would most likely end up at Pines Restaurant... for pizza and chocolate cake... of course... with chocolate ice cream too...

... long note... the interesting point to this song is the last perpetual (at least it seemed back then) piano note at about the 4:22 minute mark... it was almost a contest to see which one of us can hear the note the longest before it faded out... sure, I agree what a pointless endeavour when sober /straight... but this was not our case,... so our high absurdity can be reasonably justified... the winner of the contest was determined by the honor system... the last one to say... I can still hear it... was the self-declared winner... one thing I did learn was... as per the quote... never argue with idiots, cause they bring you down to their level and beat you with experience...

... always told my kids... if I ever catch you smoking drugs you are in big trouble... not because you are smoking but because you did not share with daddy... it would not be smoking pot that would have me concerned but more their hanging out in bars... especially a dive...

## 2015/01/31 – Saturday (Aveiro, Portugal)

... so much to do... but no thoughts could organize my to-do list... the paper table cloth is my canvas... gibberish thoughts about loneliness abound on the paper... again even snuffing out would require some sort of thought flow... where is my higher self?... do I need help, not for long... will drown everything, soon enough...

... pressed against the corner in the café... my only two friends who protect me are the 2 walls on each side of me... the harder I squeeze into the corner the more I feel loved and protected... these walls are talking to me... a drunken hallucination?... the walls will soon be embracing someone else... perhaps the new customer will feel my impregnated essence... all that can remain here... a fading energy of what I was...

... bistro semantics and body language... look at all these faces... do they not see their ugliness?... how do they go on day after day... I would envy them if it were not for the fact I know more than they do, such fools... should

I help them, such a hassle… they're too lazy to get out their misery, let them be… simply because I am too lazy to care… is not laziness a sin…

… with heavy eye lids… as I glimpse over the final notes and scribbles on the paper table cloth… will anyone understand my reasons… so much alone drinking… would they complain about the fuss of dragging me out feet first… it'll be their problem not mine… so many ugly smiling faces… wish I could smile too…

… her day… today would've been my mothers' birthday… and she left a damaged package behind… no fabled love is coming from above, not even from below… mother gave birth to me… as a free being… but locked me into her manic depressive world… that is why I'm always anxious/concerned or trying to please others…

… the majority of everything we did was crap… a Sunday afternoon drive to her work… dad in the front and my brother and I in the back… sound of her heels sinking into gravel as she steps out of the car… too busy with her reflection on my back window… a tender kiss sent into the car is transparently obstructed… good-bye loves expressed with the cool warmth of a tree branch wave… such warmth compared to the sunrise of the morning… with wooden spoon in hand… lashing in mind … a dash under the bed to tremble from the pain… or bathroom door locking behind me for protection… this was our war… for now a truce… but damage done…

* * *

# February

PART FOUR

## 2015/02/09 – Monday (Aveiro, Portugal)

... what is a trip to Aveiro without visiting my local bank... can you sense my forthcoming sarcasm... banks in this country were second to the Vatican in terms of prestige and wealth... recently... unlike the financial wizards hidden in the *Vatican City* State walled enclave within the city of Rome... these Portuguese banks close shop due to corruption and ineptitude... but I must give credit where it is due, the ATM machines are light years ahead of anything back home...

... my bank branch is still on the same street corner, though it has undergone massive renovations and an equal amount of name changes due to takeovers, it is nevertheless where I store my pennies as I cannot trust them with more than this... I enter the bank and head to the courtesy counter, I see it is the same young woman who served me the last time I was here, 4 years ago... there is more of her now, as she has put on quite a bit of weight, I guess for her husband it only means there is more to love... my request is quite simple, just a change of address... I hand her a printout with my new Montreal address on it so as not to spell out street names which are completely foreign to her... she fiddles for the longest time with her computer, she is unable to modify my address on her system... apologizes profusely and asks to make a copy of my printout so that she may submit it to the appropriate channels... refined bureaucratic jargon but I love it... coincidentally, I first dealt with this bank when I was 10... when it opened its' first branch in Montreal...

... puzzlin' evidence... in 1970 the first Portuguese bank (caisse populaire now) opened between the magazine kiosk and Alfa Pizza on Pine Avenue... to promote the bank opening, they (bank representatives) came to our elementary school OLMR (Our Lady of Mount Royal) and had a raffle per class just for the Portuguese kids... the winner would get a new bank account with a $5.00 deposit already in it... AND I WON... my intuition guessed the right number... humm?... was I a gifted intuitive child... not sure... adorable for sure and I had a full head of hair back then too...

... mind you, at 10 years old I was introverted but already wise to the ways these earthlings maneuvered... I just wanted the money, I did not have any plans for the money, but I already knew that leaving it in the bank, was and is and will never be my style... went to the bank with my dad cause he had to sign papers as I was still a minor... got my bank book, it came with a transparent plastic sleeve, which I thought would be better for storing my hockey cards... my dad did not allow me to withdraw any of the money,...

I truly perceived the money as being mine and did not appreciate his imperialistic authority over me... guess what?... of course, I defied him... did you really think I would succumb to this earthly fascism concept?... so, the next day I went to the bank with crumpled bankbook in hand (left the sleeve at home with hockey cards)... the middle aged bank teller wore a suit and tie, the suit was probably one or two sizes too big... I guess when he went with his wife to buy it, she probably said it was a bit big, but that he would eventually grow into it... judging from the grease stains on his neck tie and protruding stomach... she was a wise woman...

... I wanted to withdraw the $5 and close the account... this was unheard of and the teller along with the bank manager leaned over the counter to see who was this little guy (adorable me) making such a demand... they actually had no procedure for closing accounts as they had just opened the bank... the teller informs me... I can only take out $4, cause there was a $1 administration fee for closing the account and he retained the bankbook which I wanted to keep as a souvenir... I exclaimed *caralho!!!!! (Portuguese explicative for penis) in anger... I felt short changed... and to add insult to injury (robbery too) they also called my house to inform my parents of my colorful metaphoric language and the missing bankbook sleeve...*

... are you wondering if my dad gave me a well-deserved beating for withdrawing the money?... no, not he... but my mom who answered the phone call from the bank, was quick with the *colher de pau* (wooden spoon)... she did not tell him (dad) just yet, as to what I had done... the mother unit, demanded the money but I refused to give it to her... the beatings continued until she got tired and exasperated... she then ran into her bedroom crying and asking god why he gave her such a demon child... on my behalf, I will admit I can be stubborn... and it's not one of my best endearing qualities...

... years later... when my dad was on his death bed, I told him what I had done, thinking I had to clear my consciousness ... I kept a safe distance between him and I, when making the announcement... cause even if he was in a very frail state, he still had a nasty backhander (after all he had years of practice dispensing *bolachas* on me)... he signaled me to approach the side of the bed... I leaned over cautiously, anticipating any jerky move from his hand... cause, when I told him, I had kept my distance, I learned this from experience... he muttered softly, that he had gone to the bank after me to argue the one dollar fee, he got it and kept it... lol... I leaned over cautiously, anticipating any jerky move from his hand... ... his eyes shifted/pointed to the night table drawer... as if to say the dollar was in the drawer... I felt this wave of happiness come over me, I was touched by what he had done... as I pulled the drawer open, I see the bankbook sleeve with hockey cards and he mutters *I spent the dollar... caralho!!!!...* upon his face, came the biggest smile/smirk I had ever seen him make... and with this he closed his eyes permanently...

## 2015/02/10 – Tuesday (Aveiro, Portugal)

... my daily ritual, as I now see this as being my job... is to walk down from my apartment to the Doce Infusao bistro for breakfast and where I will spend most of my day writing until basically closing time... my route takes me through Infante Dom Pedro park... it is a throwback to the aristocracy of 1862 with its *Art Noveau* style... today, though somewhat neglected probably due to the recession... its' massive old trees, winding paths along ponds, ducks and its' doves singing just adds an edge of mystic serenity to the place... for me doves are a reminder of my dad as he had raised these birds as pets... and as I stand for a few minutes watching ducks with clipped wings prancing in the pond... I feel my dad's spirit is with me, I hope he is cause I am not doing well today... as a feeling of loneliness abounds and is no longer a feeling but a reality...

... nearby the park, there is this house or actually the ruins of a house with only a partial front wall standing with an ironically locked door... graffiti on the door reads... *you cannot put your (h)arms around a memory...* images of my kids when they were very young sustain me when I have down moments... but it is getting harder to maintain the images in my head, and now the agonizing realization I no longer have a family which was my resourcing... as I watch a pair of ducks engage in a courtship ritual, a feeling of numbness takes over my body with only my eye lids still functioning to clear away dwindling tears... shit, I'm not even able to cry... how fucked up am I?...

... an ultimatum to commitment, I cannot give her what she wants... yesterday... I had decided again, to put an end to my relationship with Suzanne... for now I live in my writings or in my head... there is very little space in between for anyone or anything else... though, I need someone to believe in me and she was the only one who thought I could pull of this book writing endeavour... somehow, people seem to run through my life like sand through fingers... never really ever having any long lasting friends and now with Suzanne gone too... she was my last human interaction... I have no friends here or anywhere... what does this mean, should I seek medical/psychiatric help?...

... last night put some music by Einaudi... and just sat on the sofa trying to meditate but instead slumped into a wallowing of self-pity... the wave of loneliness and aloneness combined was strong enough to push me off my eighth floor apartment balcony... then logical madness was gaining ground... if, I now have proof and believe there is life after death, what am I doing here on this earth plain (realm) as it no longer nourishes my soul but instead intoxicates it... at this moment, I felt a poke on the back of my neck, I turned around and saw no one, after all I was alone... but as I thought about this curious poking sensation, my dad came to mind... and the poking came with the feeling as if someone cared...

... before anything stupid becomes a reality in my feeble head... I went to the noisiest bistro I could find... I needed to be surrounded by people and though I did not interact with anyone... just sitting amongst this rowdy football crowd without the isolation of my Ipod headphones... simply needed the external voices to remind me I was not alone... cause now I was scared to find myself alone either here or the next world...

... when the waiter started placing chairs upside down on the tables, it was time to take my glare off the table top... funny, the annoying noise of chairs being jolted was soothing... I felt ok... nothing was changed or resolved in my life... I just felt ok, now... right now, this was good enough for me... got home and took a very hot shower... and imagined the hot water pouring on my head like white light protecting me... it felt ok...

## 2015/02/13 – Friday (Aveiro, Portugal)

... waking up I looked out the patio door in my bedroom... fog was blocking my 8th floor view of the skyline... rain is forthcoming... made a mental note to take an umbrella when I go out to protect my bald head from the rain (lol)... I got out of bed and did not yawn or grunt as I did not want to acknowledge my aching bones... I woke up in silence... I miss my little girls running into the bedroom and jumping on me with giggles to spare... faint memories, is this all I have left?...

... as I sit on the edge of the bed, I see myself in the mirror... don't recognize myself, who is this man?... old too?... who is inside the empty shell... I seem to be disappearing, it looks like I lost weight again... I have been in

Portugal for the last 3 months, all I do is write, eat and when not constipated either mentally or physically, I shit too... I don't sleep enough, I know this... but it is hard to sleep when all the writing ideas come during the night... I am just a vessel, not a writer, I'm just the physical fingers connecting *them* to a computer... the only time I feel I am doing something for myself is when I brush my teeth... this is not my life but *them* reliving or accomplishing theirs through me...

... friday the 13th... is this date supposed to mean something... it did back home... what the fuck am I saying, I have no *home*... all I know is a place called Montreal, which is where I had a home... home used to be a 5 bedroom bungalow, with as many or more bathrooms, family rooms, dining, kitchen, living rooms combined, but mostly animated by people... soon I will need to give up my current one bedroom apartment to move into a hostel bedroom with a private bathroom as this is the only luxury I can still afford/find right now... it seems as time passes, my living quarters are getting smaller, eventually from 2 suitcases down to a final coffin, a one size fits all... residence... every time I move house something dies in me... nevertheless, I will tidy up the apartment...

... I put on my wrist watch and realize it is close to 3pm... I find I am losing track of time more often than usual... I need breakfast or something... gearing up to leave, I set my Ipod to play on repeat... *Einaudi's - l'origine nascosta*... stepping outside it is raining and I did not bring an umbrella, no matter... walking and lost to the sounds of the music rummaging in my head, I find myself in front of the church where I meditate daily... hunger aside, I go in instead...

... no sooner am I sitting down on my usual bench... a slew of old ladies with mops and rags start cleaning the church... 2 of the women actually moved around with forearm crutches while dusting... ended up moving twice to another bench to avoid them... finally gave up on the meditation and walked out... one of the women apologized for interrupting me, I just smiled politely...

... raining... I stood in the church door portal... watching traffic manoeuvre rain and pedestrians... I had no destination other than maybe get some food or write, but even this was not a priority... so, I leaned against the wall and watched cars, people, gray sky and rain blend... two men ran under the portal to shelter themselves from the rain... one pulls out a cigarette pack and offers his friend a cigarette and then points the pack in my direction...

it is a blue wrapping with bold letters... *SG sem filtro*... I declined the smoke but the packaging reminded me of one I had seen for the first time as a kid...

... back in grade two... wait?... I remember the desks now... the table (desk) and chair were attached together by a metal bar and one was not able to adjust/move either one, allowing for more sitting comfort... it was fine for me, cause at 7 years old I had a small build stature... one morning, the desk next to mine had a new student... the new kid was almost twice my size and he simply could not squeeze into the seat because it was so tight against the desk... he looked lost, uncomfortable and the English language was foreign... and with just cause as he was a newly arrived immigrant from Portugal... as I found myself staring at him, he had sideburns and a peach fuzz on his face and most likely in the terminal phases of puberty... obviously he was much older but was put here as language integration classes had not yet been invented... when the recess bell rang, I motioned him to get up and follow me... we did not talk much, but once outside in the school yard... he pulls out a cigarette pack, takes a cigarette for himself and then points the *SG sem filtro* cigarette pack in my direction... I declined the smoke...

... your guess is as good as mine as to what ever happened to this young man... my guess is, if he's still alive, odds are he's coughing up a lung somewhere... hardships, come in all sizes and flavours... in hind sight, all we had in common is being... so out of place...

## 2015/02/14 – Saturday (Aveiro, Portugal)

... slept from 2 to 6 AM... my diet of espresso coffees, chewed paper cigarettes and keyboard fingers has to change... how long can I sustain this mode?... remained in bed, with eyes wide open while my mind plowed through every thought in its way... more revisions are required to a story written back in November 29 as I understood the murmuring voices... I need to stop my mind, it is out of control... I cannot be mad, as I can see my madness, maybe I am just losing it... what day is this?... why can't I remember days anymore... when I worked as a computer programmer, numbers, dates and chunks of programming code were always on the forefront of my mind... now, not even the day, let alone a date... got to get up, but don't know why, habit I guess...

... morning stillness... as I get dressed... gently brush the aching cavity, wash the face of the stranger in the mirror and spray some light scented cologne, given to me by Suzanne... I can't even remember her face,... it strains me to think of her... heading out to the bistro for my breakfast, it is still too early as it will only open in an hour... opted to get the popping corn left in the cupboard by the previous tenant... I'll feed the doves in the park, a sort of breakfast with dad... since these were his favourite birds...

... corn feeding in the park... entering the park, I hone in from where the dove singing originates... throwing some corn on the ground the doves land in front of me... they do not fear me, I guess this is not the first time they deal with humans... as I drop more corn on the ground... and at the speed of which a negative thought enters my head, the park bully pigeons swoop down on the doves and corn in a territorial claim... first the doves then I, we leave the corn to these rat size vultures...

... pecking order... there is something fundamentally wrong with the concept of creation... why does it have to be big fish eats little fish bullshit... it makes no fucken sense, this epitome of cruelty... furthermore the accepted practise of god worshipping... why does man have to be subservient to a god... does any kind of divinity require us to obey with heads down, are we all not equal... I am sure this worship concept is not godly but man made... no god could be so vainly petty... are we not equals, but with different objectives... our objectives vary from planet to planet or a reincarnation, no?...

... strangers on my route to the bistro are my acquired friends... I have never spoken to these strangers but just seeing them almost daily, I feel a connection to them and besides they accepted the invitation into my head... the ghostly street sweeper in her bright yellow florescent rain gear overcoat... a middle aged lady with long jet black dyed hair, protruding red lips on a paper white complexion, I nicknamed her my morning vampire... my street sweeping vampirette is scooping up dog shit in the public square nookie... as arts & crafts merchants set up their tables for an outdoor sale... if my kids were here, I'd buy them anything and/or everything they wanted... I miss them so... looking around, the square is decorated in a festive mood with red ribbons and red heart cut outs...

... coincidence?... my earphones exude the music of *Daniel Belanger – l'autruche*... it dawns on me, the ribbons, hearts and the abundance of red, it's the 14th... Valentine's Day... yes or no?... for the last few days I've been ignoring my ringing phone and the text message alerts... I know they are from Suzanne, and I don't mind the ringing, it lets me know she is ok... I know/ feel she wants to make the 3 hour drive to be with me, she does not want to give up on us... I wanted to give her an answer but I was unable to operate the phone, as I found all the phone buttons confusing... besides answering her in any way would be a step back into her reality... and I prefer living between the sanctuary of my head onto these pages... it's easier this way... I think...

## 2015/02/15 – Sunday (Aveiro, Portugal)

... at the time I had left Cascais unexpectedly to come to Aveiro... was for no other reason than Suzanne and I were at odds... I came to Aveiro simply because there was already an element of familiarity, having been here when my parents were still alive... her insecurity demanded some sort of relationship commitment... I on the other hand had just left a 33 year marriage in order to pursue a spiritual epiphany... but because of my marital break-up I became alienated by all who were once my so called family/friends... and with just cause... those who ended up being hurt by my actions, did not see the storm coming... actually neither did I... suffice to say... with my love for Suzanne dissipating through a sieve as well... I now find myself completely alone, in the truest sense of the word... all I have going for me is this writing project and in a few weeks the Camino... then what?... I do not know... fuck it... I came this far, let's see where this will all end up...

... she's so beautiful, smart, funny as hell and poetically creative... so many qualities one could love and be in awe of her forever... and I did... but with so many qualities, all it takes is the one of being insecure... and worse yet letting her insecurity run, control and ruin her very life and even mine... I found myself walking on eggshells, when with her... I was no longer being natural, no longer being me... it takes more than love to sustain a relationship, it takes trust too...

... so, over the last month... I plunged whole heartedly into my writing... I worked on it pretty much day and night... I tried going to the movies, but even then the movies did not sustain my interest as I was always thinking about what to write and how... it is such an obsession... I became a recluse by all accounts and did not even realize until this weekend when Suzanne insisted on coming up to see me, it being Valentines week-end... but it was too late for me as I had... too much free time on my own and without human contact... too much free time for thought...

... reality... was when she showed up, she seemed a stranger to me... comically, I was actually shy of her... as if I were a small kid, I was unable to make eye contact with her... it border on fear... I felt like a critter from a hole who just saw daylight in a very long time... I had by my own reckoning deteriorated... her coming here shook me up... I am still obsessed with writing and even more scared to face the reality I am alone... truly alone...

## 2015/02/16 - Monday (Aveiro, Portugal)

... the tension was more than I was willing to put up with... 6 AM and my eyes are wide open, not seeing but hearing the rain bouncing off the balcony tiles... Suzanne was sound asleep and I restless both in body and mind... I get up and walk around the apartment, like a fish in a tank I look out the windows from my 8th floor apartment... I need to get out... as I get dressed her voice echoes the same phrase... stay in bed... and I mumble repeatedly, I need air... not one of the most intellectual conversations ever known to the human race... mind you the echo versus mumbling combo says a lot about my state if not ours...

... once outside... my first breath is filled with cold damp air, reminds me of autumn in Montreal... looking at my watch, dismay sets in as the bistro I go to only opens in a couple of hours... with drizzling rain as my only friend... I walk downtown where I suspect a pastry/bakery coffee shop may open this early... approaching downtown and looking up at the drenched gray clouds... I see a glow, a neon light glow to be precise... this neon glow was coming from the coffee shop... how intense was the glowing light?... so intense a blind man could see his shadow... cataracts are burned off... the type of glow airplane pilots look for as identifying landmarks... and if the conditions are right, may seem like the Virgin Mary appearing over an olive tree to 3 homely kids whose parents sent them off to some remote field for herding entertainment... as I sit there alone reflecting endlessly that I am here because she is back home, why did I leave?... after tanning alone under the neon lights for hours... customers are now coming in... unbeknownst... soon to be victims of my creative malicious observations...

... since history repeats itself... it's the same old scenario here in this coffee shop... three very old ladies with overdone pumped up hair styles... aging aristocrats who are as ugly outside as inside... my judgement is not solely based on the physical appearance, but on the conversation I hear emanating from the aerosolized stool odor floating over their pasty burgundy lipstick encrusted coffee cups... at night their pillows act as hairdressers, therefore they must sleep like stiffs in a coffin not to misplace a hair until the morning when complimented by another overdose of hair spray... so much so that any flying insect who had the misfortune of flying into the hairspray mist trajectory would be crystalized instantaneously... in the insect world, this is a worse death than impacting on a car windshield...

... with such blindingly vulgar golden engagement rings and wedding bands... though they may be married, who would fuck these sleeping stiffs with brittle cunts... the only husbands who could crack and fuck women like these are men who can afford hookers who'd willingly lick their urine scented vulture head shaped cocks... at night two contemptuous beings who were joined together by the sanctity of the church's worst, still unpunished pedophile priests... this spousal sin sleeping in the same bed with the accumulated warmth of 3 day old semen stuck to anal linings...

... this is where plastic grocery bags though environmentally and politically incorrect may serve a purpose... in the advent of a surprise rainfall, leaving the coffee shop to get into their son-in-laws car without getting rained upon on the plasticised pumped hairdo, the bag serves a second purpose as a hair protector... so, that favourite green slogan of ecologists... re-use... may actually, be contained in reality...

... our hero... you know I'm referring to the son-in-law, right?... is there no soccer game today or is he that amorous of the mother-in-law, that he would actually step out on a rainy day just to pick her up at the coffee shop... such a noble and caring endeavour, for one to care about the old lady but equally or more, be concerned about her hair getting wet... seriously, was he ever exposed to a high dosage of hairspray that seized his brain synapses from impulsing... our hero is here because the wife (a clone of the old lady) did not ask but told him to pick up her mother... the technological illiterate mother and daughter team have mastered enough smart phone skills to make our hero's life a misery...

... maybe he has reached a point of no return, those few minutes of driving the car until reaching the coffee shop are a meditative lapse of time... the repetitive orchestrated sound of the wipers, squealing against the wet glass, transport him if only for a brief moment to a numbing serenity... for this seductive and inducing rhythm comes to a braking halt when he stops the car and the impact of the old lady's non-musical hands are fighting with the locked door handle which distorted the soothing musical melody...

almost there... he has not yet reached the point of no return... cause now he is driving back home with a barking hairdo sitting next to him... soon he will be sitting at the table, being fed and taken care of... his future is in front of him... as he looks meekly at the enormous hairdo supported by a dry raisin body thingy... he sees his future in the mother-in-law and his present in the wife... is this his point of no return, where he must make sure to have money for hookers...

## 2015/02/17 – Tuesday (Aveiro, Portugal)

... voices carry my words back and forth... I am the only one who hears these voices as they are locked in my head... with each voice there is a unique opinion on what I should do... I am the custodian of these argumentative dialogues and I am incapable of managing this unruly screaming crowd... Suzanne left this morning...

... officially... to be alone again... soon I'll move from this nice apartment... to a one hole bedroom with connecting bathroom, with no room to fart... such is my new coffin size residence... at times I think this is a sign of the times to come very shortly... I feel unfit to spend more than 15 minutes in my cell... I fear my night time phobia contemplating an eternal sleep... all my possessions fit in 2 suitcases... but I now feel it is too much... I always wear the same 2 t-shirts and jeans... if the clothes are not on me they are washing... will I find my lost spiritual center as my material world assets are reduced...

... absolutely... there is no doubt Suzanne and I are ethereal lovers... we already came down with baggage, but our separate time here has added more than either one can carry for the return trip, a curse from the onset... anger, her vexing pettiness brought on by insecurity, my detached unsympathetic reaction... love and trust go hand in hand, but not when we want to wear white gloves... she is unpredictable as I am probably a bi-polar door mat... this could be the only explanation to justify why I lost all of my self-respect...

... what now... with her gone... I find myself wishing for some kind of woman who, at my late age... will she understand and give me my space to evolve... could she be a muse, perhaps... is this all I have to offer or be for a woman?... a selfish man with a yearning obsession to find a spiritual balance in my life and all the while try writing something meaningful as an egotistical legacy?...

... all of you... leave me alone... my life has no meaning, all I have is this spiritual quest via my writings... inadvertently, all the people I loved... I... busted their comfort zone sky high, for this I'm perpetually sorry... a reversed Midas touch, which is now my guilt and curse... now, with fear in my head... what if the Camino does not materialize anything...

## 2015/02/18 – Wednesday (Aveiro, Portugal)

... yesterday afternoon I got a text message from Suzanne, vowing to make things better between us... the message eased me, it was the placebo I needed to hear as I used it to reduce my over charged synapses... the afternoon looked, well optimistic...

... it was past 2 pm when I stopped writing, causing me to almost skip lunch... I left Doce Infusao bistro feeling defiant and contradicted myself by walking in the opposite direction of the restaurant, even though I was quite hungry... found myself walking the quiet residential back streets... the occasional car with its' tires on the cobblestones contributing to the city noise and my notion that I am not alone... found a Jehovah Witness hall snuggled in a basement of an apartment building... I stopped to read some preachy sign about the end of the world, when I looked up to the sky and realized we were having very nice weather after a week of rain... with such a sunny day, could the end of the world be delayed, at least for another day?... the streets felt eerie with lack of people and once again, quiet too...

... changed direction and headed towards the resto... the negative emotional slump I was in this morning was now being replaced by a physical grumbling hunger sound in my stomach... walking through the tourist area in Aveiro called the Rossio Quarter... busloads of Spanish tourists were crowding the streets along the canals... improvised sweet bread vendors on every corner using boxes as a make shift table to display their goodies... even saw a hefty blond woman roasting chestnuts on mobile charcoal grill/oven... the charcoal smoke convinced me that chestnuts could be lunch... approaching the vendor, I noticed that the smoke which seduced me was marinating her blond hair into a state of being smoke smelly, limp and without shine... her hair would be a challenge for an haute coiffure contest...

... chestnuts in hand I headed for the canal, and sat on the wall overlooking the water... just saying I removed my coat and sat on the wall basking in the sun, says it all... so many kids dressed up in costumes as if it were Halloween... their parents wearing wigs and/or masks... looking at the time, quickly realized the children had the school day off... shit, the last few weeks

I had been so out of touch... today is carnival day, a sort of semi-holiday for most...

... walking around... not one unoccupied chair or table could be found on outside terraces... as folks settle under the afternoon sun... cigarettes packs are passed around the table as people drink, smoke and share both cigarettes and conversation... so much harmony... how I wish my kids were with me sitting at one of these tables, we would probably discuss their Halloween experiences and how I always managed to trick them into giving me a few candies...

... as I watched all these people... a feeling of well-being came over me... though I am alone and for the most part slightly melancholic... the energy in the air is contagious and I took it in too... it dawned on me what a privilege it is for me to witness all this... especially the silliness and laughter coming from the children... my goals of writing and soon walk the Camino trek is synonymous with my newly improvised mantra... positive feeling... an upbeat feeling... embracing the forthcoming unknown... for sure one of hope... and maybe love... but love in the most un-imaginable context...

## 2015/02/19 - Thursday (Requeixo, Portugal)

... sweet unrest... the invisible alarm clock I never programmed went off... the alarming wake up call, summoning me from slumber... I feel as if I'm back home with the ex-wife, this life I have been having was not mine or real... I hit the snooze button disguised as a night table, granting me a 10 minute reprieve until it goes off again... those projected 600 seconds of improvised fantasy life, will belong to me... creating a clean slate in my mind which can now project everything and anything dreamt uncensored, it will make me happy, it must... I'm not alone in bed or in life... I feel her next to me and we define our space in bed... and yet I sprawl myself, with my 4 limbs looking to touch her body... her warmth... her love...

... thoughts of the work day ahead light up in my dreamy world... is it more writing, and about what?... I am tired of writing... fuck, I'm not a writer!!!... but are quickly extinguished and replaced by lottery sums of money and the ease of life, but what ease is this... I already had the comforts/ease of life that, the diligent working responsibility provided and I was ungrateful... again, nothing now... seems clear... selfish thoughts of maybe hitting the snooze button a second time if I forego shaving and go for the bad boy look... but I now sport a beard... inner clock interrupts... letting me know the alarm will... ring again and soon... please, just a few more milli-seconds of irresponsibility... let me be... I sink deeper into the pillow and latch on to what is left of this sweet unrest...

... stepping out of the shower... sliding open the shower curtain caused enough of a breeze to dry my hair... looking into the mirror... being bald, no hair, no me... what is this thing I see in the mirror... it is not human... it is dead...

... with money so tight this month, the taxi cost me 20 euros to go back to my parents' village... Requeixo feels and even looks like a ghost town, if it were not for my taxi driving through on his way elsewhere... walking around the small streets seeing my grandparents houses which meant something to me in my childhood as we had spent vacations/summers here as kids... now they are empty or completely abandoned, either way peeled of any soul... went to the cemetery, it is the home to all my family now... the last one to move here was my mom in the spring of 2011... the only year I had delayed my visit because I was attending night time school and only ended up seeing her at the funeral... the hefty woman had shrunk in both girth and height, which made her coffin lighter... a useless blessing in disguise, no?...

... spring for me was always melancholic... the last dozen years or so prior to her death, I would visit my mom in Portugal annually (and sometimes twice) and would stay in an Aveiro hotel along the canal... I would spend a few daily hours with my mom at the retirement home or as I called it... death's waiting room... in the evening I would have supper alone and sometimes with relatives... but it still left me a lot of time to ponder the cliché term Life... jetlag, insomnia, homesick and shear sadness/helplessness to see my mom decomposing in front of me had me up at all hours of the night and walking along the canal streets in Aveiro... I found myself night walking endlessly and absolutely aimlessly... with so much emptiness in heart and mind, the need to fill the void/solitude had me looking at the most mundane things and remembering them all... when she passed away, a little of me died too, and now for whatever reasons I associate Aveiro with her memory... hence, homesick for a home that is not even mine... maybe this too, is why I came back here now... nothing lasts forever, just like pain and life... but both of them leave an imprint somewhere in the universe...

... in a country with coffee shops at every corner... this is the only village in Portugal with just one coffee shop... unloading my backpack of my shoulder and pulling out my laptop and setting it on the table... looking around, seeing 2 dirt covered scruffy faces sitting over bottled beers... what can I write about?... there is no life left in this village or is it me...

... walking 12 kilometers back to Aveiro, feeling like a little boy, a sensitive one too... watching the tips of my boots emitting a soothing rhythm to match the melodic words chirping in my head... why did you give birth to me... my home is reduced to this backpack, and it is getting heavy... with no place to call my home and I'm still one of the living... where are you?...

## 2015/02/20 – Friday (Aveiro, Portugal)

... everything now is about staying mentally fit... I find it is so easy to fall into despair... with Suzanne now out of the picture, she was the last connection I had... it is a strange sensation not to be lonely but to simply feel alone... how long will I last?... sure, I smile at the girls serving my tea, but little do they know I will soon be walking beyond Santiago to Finisterre (a coastal town)... according to the Romans, they believed it was the end of the world... maybe it is my end too... will I be normal and blend in or never be the same after this... everything I ever loved were my kids and I lost them too... will they understand me or/and ever forgive me?...

... the coffee shop seems noisy this morning... even the crunch of my toasts cannot shut out these folks... I plug my headphones and read the paper... same old shit... it almost seems there is a pattern/recipe to this tabloid newspaper, it seems to expect a daily dosage of the same events so that it can easily plug the news into their pre-established format... news are not sanitized... they do not hold back on showing blood... which would explain the survey, if people would fight (join the army) for their country and the percentage of those who said yes was very, very low... I guess having violence shown to you explicitly... you think twice about getting involved in a fight, especially someone's else...

... with hunger and a movie on my agenda for this afternoon as part of my plan not to go insane... I head for the nearby shopping mall called the Aveiro Forum... a Romanesque style building including condo complexes at both extremities... one even has a direct view of the cemetery... the rest of the complex is an outdoor shopping mall, with shops, cinema, food court and even gardens on the roof... and in true roman colonization style, it is built along a canal...

... with rain... logistically it was easier to eat in the food court and then go to the cinema... order soup which is in itself a meal... the tables were packed with future generations of noisy students... there was a rectangular table for four, with only a pregnant woman... I asked for permission to sit diagonally from her, she nodded yes... we ate in silence, looking everywhere except at one another...

... I see an old man standing near the soup kiosk with a tray in hand... he is looking around for a place to sit, but it seems more like he is scouting the tables... if I were to listen to my empathy... I would say he's looking for a table where he would not be refused a seat... without asking... he ends up sitting next to me and facing the pregnant woman... for a second I thought she would get up and leave... there's still a strong sentiment of respectful politeness in this country... probably remnants of fascist submissiveness or even as far back as aristocracy...

... hand me downs... a suit jacket with large shoulder pads and dirty trousers... all this with mis-matched colors... top off the wino GQ ensemble with a black baseball cap... he bathed recently, there is a pleasant manly scent... though there's a week old stubble on his flaccid skin... and high blood pressure skin tone does not compliment him in any fashionable way...

... quite a short old man... he leans into the table, almost as if he was a child and his mom was behind him and pushed his chair against the table... he alternates, eating a spoon full of soup and then one of fruit salad from a plastic cup... whatever is eaten, he makes a slurping sound... I feel sorry for saying this but it looked like he was eating out of a trough... picks up the bowl and then drinks the soup... and with a flash he gets up and leaves, with half the soup remaining in the bowl... maybe he did not want to fill his stomach with food to leave room for booze...

... I share/exchange a pity smile with the pregnant woman... looking at her I can't help and think that he was someone's baby at one time... was he loved?... nothing happens for a reason... I feel and believe divinity likes to give us clues, a kind of prankster at times... maybe there was a message here for me or even us three sitting at this table... could it be interpreted... the unborn baby being my past and the old man my future... what I was and what I will be... thank you divinity and by the way go fuck yourself...

## 2015/02/21 – Saturday (Aveiro, Portugal)

... nights are the hardest time for me... it's when the feelings of loneliness intensify... last night... it was only 9 PM and had already settled in my room for the night... at first I thought of going out to a bar, but I fear I will lose myself in alcohol again... knowing myself, I will end up there soon enough... woke up at 1 AM and admired the poorly plastered ceiling... the admiration is for the one who did this shit plastering job and got paid too... after some reading and 3 channel surfing on TV, my attempts to fall asleep failed... instead meditation calmed my mind enough to fall asleep...

... got up very early... just started walking in the quiet streets as the brisk cold wakes up my senses... decided to look at the buildings not as an architectural interest but as homes... real people live here... thought of the 3 houses I had shared with my ex... had no feeling of nostalgia whatsoever, even the last house which we designed... why can't I feel any emotional attachment...

... ended up at the farmers market... well, it used to be a farmers market... until EU sanitation standards pushed the farmers out and brought in merchants instead... long gone are the butcher shops with exposed animal carcasses hanging from hooks... saturday market shopping used to be the domain of wives only... things have changed as men and/or women are now shopping alone and only for themselves, judging from the portions they buy... men look sad and women angry... sign of the times???... family sunday meals must also be a thing of the past for those shopping here...

... observations induce memories... as kids, wearing our sunday best clothes for mass... we would come home to the sunday meal... as we entered our house we'd be engulfed by the odour of a roast mom had been preparing while we were at church... for the most part my parents were together out of spite... so mommy criticized my daddy constantly... our parents never did anything together, including mass... today was no exception, as she kept nagging him to spend quality time with us, in my opinion her advice should also apply to her...

... stifling emotions with food... on sunday afternoons mom worked at the Airport... at that time, the surrounding area of the airport was somewhat still forested... so, we drove her to work and my dad took us to some field near the airport where the trees had been recently cleared/cut down... a lumberjack paradise... neatly stacked tree trunks and branches piled into high mounds... surrounded by 3 to 4 feet of pristine white snow on the now de-forested field...

... to our dismay... our dad took us hunting... he sat on top of a branch mound poised with his rifle... he told my brother and I to walk over to a shrub and shake it, he claimed hares were hiding there... yeah right!... we were small kids and to complicate matters we were still wearing our Sunday best clothes which were not practical nor comfortable to walk in 4 foot deep snow... we were drowning in the snow... we were 11 and 12 year old whiners stuck between being boys and manhood... we knew enough to know this was not fun for us... we finally managed through the snow to reach the shrub... we shook it with the tips of our fingers as snow kept falling off on us... within milli-seconds a hare pops up and runs across the snow... the old man shouts for us to stay put and not to move an inch... the tone of his imperative voice made sure we would not disobey...

... at first watching the hare quickly hop over the snow... then focusing my eyes on him (dad)... sitting calmly with his rifle against his shoulder... aiming and also slightly swaying the rifle barrel... the one thought in my mind... I hope he misses... was interrupted by the shot's loud bang... I looked to where I thought the hare should be... I no longer saw it...

... crowbar... separating the boys from men... this was not a game or sport for him... with a serious face and voice tone to match... he told us to get the hare... again... my brother and I struggle through the snow in search of the elusive hare... at first all I saw was a big red spot contrasting the white snow... as we stood there we looked at one another without saying a word... those seconds seemed eternal... the old man then shouted something to the effect of... what are we doing... we looked at this bugs bunny framed by really red blood... its' body still pulsating even though there was no head to be seen anywhere... unable to take my eyes of the hare... I hear my brothers' voice... you take, you're older, you're the man, you have pubic hairs... in hindsight I can laugh at what he said... but, did I want to be a man at this moment?...

... it had no head, nor did I feel my own head... I approached it cautiously as I still felt it may get up and go... I did not want to stop it from running away... the old man shouted something... fuck, his voice annoys me... at this moment, I think my brother echoed the old man's words as it removed his involvement from picking up the animal...

... heavenly warmth... feeling alone, I was alone with my fears too... I picked it up by the hind paws... they were so warm and cuddly soft... don't know why but I raised my arm as high as I could... as I held it up, not to show it to the old man... but felt it's (hare) warmth coming down thru my arm and reaching my chest... with heat waves being emitted through me, I felt its' last pulses of life... with the last pulse and in an unprecedented defiant tone... I shouted to the old man... I'm going home!... we sat in the car with not one word being said... detachment, felt nothing but detachment...

131

PAPER CIGARETTE

... hare festival... on a lighter note... since my dad was an avid macho hunter... it was up to my mother to gut and remove the fur from the hares he had killed and brought home... this was something she hated doing... so for over a week, she would serve hare for supper every night... to the point where he could no longer see, let alone eat it... from that point on, he gave away most of his kills... and when need be, he would gut his own hares whenever he felt like having it for supper... but the bastard, built himself a v-shape hook to hang and gut out the hares, and because the animal was hanging, he would pull off the fur as if one would be removing a t-shirt... why didn't he build this for her?...

## 2015/02/22 – Sunday (Aveiro, Portugal)

... mixed bag of emotions... what is happening to me?... if I am not writing, all I feel is an overwhelming sadness, so intense my stomach hurts... since I have ended my relationship with Suzanne, I haven't spoken in 5 or so days (I think) other than ordering food in bistros... walking to keep busy and also clear my head and maybe extract inspiration from the cloudy skies... when writing, I forget about the me and live in the typed pages... it is better than any reality I can deal with...

... walked through crowded and busy streets... it left me indifferent... the downtown core was set up with tables where anything could be sold... like a garage and/or rummage sale... from quasi-antiques to just plain crap... neglected or discarded artifacts are now re-branded as antiques... a new life given to what someone ended up thinking at one time was shit... this whored capitalism leaves me unhindered too... wake up man, feel something!!

... sitting on the edge of the canal... the water is a dark murky green with an intense foul smell... mullets swim near the surface and along the canal walls... maybe they want to get out... the fish are coming to the surface and gasping for air... I can almost relate to them... the other day in the bistro, the table next to mine... the mothball scented Spanish tourist seniors, cut a series of farts... the kind that makes you grow gills so as not to intake oxygen directly from the ambient air...

... took to one of the small streets... watched the young man walking ahead of me asking passersby not for cigarettes but money... one would think he was Ebola ridden from their reaction... he was a colored chap with a heavy Portuguese accent which probably has him coming from one of the former

African colonies... he turned back several times and saw me but never approached me for any money... and here I am desperate for conversation, no matter what circumstances... I just want to know if my voice exists... actually thought of buying him a sit down lunch and talk to him... but his clothing attire would not allow him in any restaurant even a McDonalds... simply that unacceptable by any standards...

... no walk is complete without a stop at the church (not mass)... I always try to go to a church on a daily basis as it is a quiet place where I can meditate... once seated in a comfortable position, I glance at my watch to see the time and then close my eyes... before plunging into any meditation, I ask to maybe get a glimpse of my future... if not... at least help me through these difficult times in my head, and even in my life... I can feel my feet anchoring the ground and my head lifting up like a hot air balloon... within moments I'm deep into the meditation... then black out!!... this is where time disappears and I can't remember a thing... when I come out of this black out, I find myself hovering inside my head and looking out through my third eye... mentally asking to see or have some glimpse of my future or anything for that matter... but all imagery is blurred... once a thought or image did peer through the blur... a woman's' name starting with the letter... E... she is supposed to have an impact on me... before leaving the church... looked at my watch and had spent over 20 minutes meditating... where did I and time go?... perhaps... an alternative to relying on faith... maybe consulting a psychiatrist... ?...

... are the best thoughts contradictions?... at one time the plan was to visit Barcelona and Madrid and do some writing there... but right now I feel incapable of such an undertaking as I couldn't manage nor bare the language barrier where I would not even be able to talk to bistro staff... then stay in Aveiro or start the Camino walk immediately... if I am to be alone, might as well be on the Camino... at least in the evenings I can always talk to other pilgrims in the hostels... but at this time of year to sleep in cold dormitories and occasionally only have cold water for showers is more than I can handle at this stage in my life... I feel so old... is going on 55 old?

... mom & pop type of restaurant... walked around checking out all the daily menus of a handful restaurants I usually eat in... never before had money been a concern... but now I try to get my money's worth from the one restaurant meal I eat per diem... lamb on the menu... this was my favourite Sunday meal when living with my parents... thoughts for tonight... I need to define again why I am here doing all this... I'm losing my focus... am I on a spiritual journey or just a martyr by my own doing...

## 2015/02/23 – Monday (Aveiro, Portugal)

... dwindling optimism... again this morning... the question, why am I here... during my first Camino pilgrimage in 2013, I had a series of intuitions... a sort of a forthcoming blue print for my life... at first I shrugged it off as being delusional... but then I intuited the death of Carmen's father... this was for me an epiphany moment... for better or for worse, I heeded to the intuitions... resulting in, my divorce, alienation from my kids and friends and a never experienced sheer loneliness... and aloneness, the feeling of not belonging to this planet...

... insult to misery... it has been almost 2 years of emotional hardship since the first Camino/pilgrimage... and now as part of my so called blueprint... I have to re-do the Camino, write a book which is supposed stir/help people... for a while I had Suzanne's support to my writing endeavour... she believed I could do it... with her gone out of my life, I feel more insecure than ever before... I don't know if I have what it takes to write... I do write, but I have no idea if it is even worth the paper it is on... the aloneness of all this is what is bringing me down... why do I need or want someone to believe in me?

... Aveiro... turned out to be a can of worms... a Pandora's box... it made me open up all kinds of repressed memories... some to sordid to even write down... is it because in my adult life I coasted along for the most part... is it payback time?... if it is, then it's very cruel... at times I reason that, since I believe there is an afterlife of sorts, then why stay in this realm... or simply said... I'd rather not be, than be alone... this is making more and more sense to me... maybe I am procrastinating or my ego won't give in until the second Camino/pilgrimage is completed... whatever it may be, I fear the logic of my thought...

... hey doc!... I look at my behaviour like a doctor places his fingers on your wrist to measure/count your heart rate... spending evenings in the mall... eating only soup, should I not be hungrier than this... sometimes watch the soccer games on TV, on the overhead screens... watch people walk by to fill my emptiness/voids... and now paranoia too, I meticulously discard any printed paper with my stories on it... almost like the stories falling in the wrong hands… at times a sentiment lingers in the back of my mind… maybe you are not used to being the center of attention, but take a step back as you'll soon rock the world… with convictions and behaviours questioned… be who you want to be not what others want…

… right about what?… as I look around at the bistro customers… from their body language, facial expressions and especially the tone of voice… what is the obsession with always being right in a conversation… is it self promoting?… is it mediocrity being validated… I miss familiarity… it's only an illusion things are better in Montreal or anywhere else… but I also know as soon as I'm back, I'll want to be elsewhere… I'll never be happy because I am not at peace with myself… I feel tortured inside… what have I learned so far… love oneself first?… success to a happy life is to have friends and feel loved in a quiet fashion… I have none of this in my life right now… I'm a walking dead… and besides, I will never be right anywhere…

## 2015/02/24 – Tuesday (Aveiro, Portugal)

… not bitterness… my breaking-off with Suzanne… not angry with her in any way, in fact I still love her very much, god do I still love her… her insecurity caused mistrust… she would need to resolve her insecurity first, before anything else… it will be difficult for her to correct years of damage, maybe impossible… mistrust of men… probably started with daddy issues, something which is not easily resolved… perhaps, we will re-connect in the next life… in the meanwhile, I'm nursing a damaged and not a broken heart…

… today… it seems all the women in the bistro have very masculine traits… femininity is hard to find, they seem to think they need to compete with men… maybe they are right as I have never seen so much machismo… even the young couple sitting at the next table who remind me of white trash Portuguese style… new parents indeed… the father looks like a joe cool bozo where the only woman who would ever sleep with him is a fat cow… nothing at all can be said about her choice in men either… shit, they have a baby together… what hope does the little girl have with these parents… as a parent I was not one of them, and yet I managed to alienate my daughters… and yet, sensing so much frustration, revolt and just plain anger coming from him… no love… a feeling of being trapped… but honing in on her… just maybe she is able to calm him down in his worst moments of anguish… maybe she believes in him, she actually seems to be mothering him... too bad... he will betray her with the first women who sees him breathing...

... why such a phenomena... the 50 shades movie is in the media non-stop... is this a publicity coup... if so, kudos on the marketing... newspapers have related articles on the front page almost every day... sex does sell, well too... maybe my perception of Christian prudishness is erred... and with this I will try to write erotica too,... and why not even throw in a subliminal message too... see if you catch on?...

... you just sat there exasperated as I installed small lamps under your kitchen cabinets... having rushed all morning running errands and even rushing home so as to let me in to do your electrical installation... sitting there and having coffee while watching me work... letting off a loud sigh of relief... loud enough to get my attention anyway... I asked if everything is alright?... saying, you kind of envied me, being my own boss and all... well, it has its' advantages... maybe your problem is trying to have control of situations when there really is no need to... you sometimes have to let go, which you said... was easier said than done... it all depends on your state of mind... are you willing to try something new... are you opened minded enough?... and how much is enough... you inquired... blind faith... I replied with a smirk... there was a pause while you interpreted the gleam in my eyes...

... motioning for you to clear the kitchen table of its ornaments... you're wearing a t-shirt and cut-off jeans just like in porno movies... asking you to lie belly down on the kitchen table... you hesitate... remember, your will to control is the source of your anguish... you hesitantly lied on the table... getting behind you and pulling on your ankles to align your knees with the corner of the table... from the corner of your eye... you saw me removing my jeans and underwear's... you began to feel quite aroused and slutty... walking around the table to face you... I began snipping wires while standing in front of you and every so often letting my semi-erect cock rub on your face randomly... I looped the wires around your wrist, and as I tied the other end to the table legs I shoved my cock on your lips, hard enough to force it in to your willing wet mouth... by now your wrists and ankles were tied to the table legs... stepping to your left... my hand glides up your leg, from your ankle all the way up to your jeans and under your shorts... two of my fingers slid deeply into your moist pussy... so, pleasurable that you raised your ass... but with my free hand I slapped it down... ouch!... pleasure and pain and now your senses were reeling...

... I started opening every drawer in your kitchen... you asked what

I was looking for and I ignored your question and walked up to you and put my cock in your mouth... with no resistance... I went back to look into the drawers and found scissors... the look in your face turned to concern... once again I forced you to suck my swollen cock... but I sensed you were not focused on the task at hand... I said I was going to cut away your jeans and maybe your undies if they weren't sexy... then I proceeded to cut off your jeans in half down the middle of your ass... while you sucked hard on my cock... throwing the scissors on the counter and stepping back from you...

... you saw me looking around, wondering what next... stepping behind you and pulling your thongs to the side and started to french kiss your asshole deeply... my warm tongue made you raise your ass... I pulled back and you tried in vain to raise your ass... but your tied limbs held you down... when you laid back down... I plunged my hot tongue forcefully into your tight asshole and rolling my tongue around in your hole... I stopped... and you heard the freezer door open and the breaking out of ice cubes into your sink... I returned to your ass and inserted my tongue, just as your hole began to expand I inserted a cold ice cube... my cold finger now slides into your hot wet cunt... the doorbell rang, and we froze and stared at each other!...

... not sure if I will have the guts to leave this in the journal... to be seen or not... no costly toys were used in this story other than electrical wiring... which proves, great sex starts in the imagination... think about it?... think about what?... isn't love or lust all about some form or another of control... and this also goes for religion and any fucken thing we tend to abide by... everything we believe in is a manmade religion which is synonymous with control...

## 2015/02/25 – Wednesday (Aveiro, Portugal)

... all that I had gained in terms of spirituality, intuitive abilities and serenity... after Camino, was pretty much gone by the end of 2014... almost 6 months of emotional turmoil with family and friends, an outcast in all respects... I was no longer able to maintain my spiritual serenity... I lost all sense of purpose in life too... worst yet, later on I stopped meditating and ended up debilitated myself spiritually... becoming my worst enemy... my ego got in the way when I mis-used my intuitive abilities when going on dates... did not know I could even use it for this... yet with all this, there still

137

persisted endless, intensifying questioning leading to disbelief and denial...
spirituality fucked my boring and mundane life...

... a wave of change... unexpected message... last evening on my way to
the shopping mall... unable to be alone any longer, I headed towards the mall
to be surrounded by voices and welcoming noise... a young girl no older than
15... a student carrying a 3 ring binder in front of her with arms wrapped
around it... on the top of the binder one could see and read... are you satisfied with an easy life... what we choose to believe, is this our reality?... who
else can see it?... would they be seekers/wanderers like me... maybe she was a
soul mate from a previous life delivering a much needed message to us/me...

... an intuitive message may feel like a surprise... for me, I now know and
understand my intuitive messages come via my subconscious and must cross
the obstacles of my busy conscious thought traffic... this is where the my difficulty or blockage lies... but when walking and the peacefulness on Camino
path... it triggered the quietness and serenity of my conscious mind necessary for intuitions to come through in hordes through the subconscious...
unhindered by thought/consciousness obstacles... I like to joke that I can
read thoughts if they exist... not until recently, did it start to feel like I am
tuning something good... but never sure if it is empathy or intuitive abilities...

... high... school smart ass... if I sin all my life and just before I die... I re-
pent, would god forgive me and let me in heaven... I got kicked out of class
for this statement which was not even of my creation... hell, I didn't want to
be in any religion class, just like I wanted to attend French school instead...
the politics of the time had me cornered doing what I did not want... the arrogance of my youth has been replaced with humility... and today... slowly
but surely I am tuning back into my spirituality... the discipline of meditating
is slowly setting things right... it has been a long time... but sometimes I can
feel again... by this my intuitive senses are coming back and I can feel energies coming from people and things... energy in a form of warmth...

... meditative serenity... sat there just watching the mall being closed
down... shop keepers rushing to leave and lingering souls like myself having
difficulty parting... with an un-necessary dramatic breath... I plugged myself under the headphones with Dead Can Dance – Summoning of the Muse
on repeat mode... the tempo has been set for my walk back to the inn room
solitude...

... ingenuity... foggy, night time quiet... blurred lighting from lamp
posts... cobble stone sidewalks artistically laid out with white limestone and

black basalt stone designs... by an unknown labourer who probably does not recognize the artistic worth of his skill... probably with only one concern, meeting the rent deadline... so close... less than 5 minutes from the inn... I did not feel like going in just yet... admiring everything in my sight and thinking mankind can do wonderful things... Aveiro is alive with history... I can feel it's vibrations as I am in tune with my environment...

... sitting on a bench... on the pedestrian street called Rua da Coimbra... this street used to be a busy merchants' artery in its' heyday... small shops have closed up as customers moved into malls... preferring prices over attentive customer service... recessions affects lifestyles not just people... looking down at the sidewalk... cobble stones pounded over time and in waves but still snuggly joined... looping patterns of black stones on white as far as the eyes can see in this fog... to my right on the second floor of a community center... women in black chorale gowns rehearsing silently in my ears... as close as mortal angels can get to the heavens...

... not alone... so many street benches and yet was lured to this one... it faces an abandoned building... a 3 storey building with a vacant shop on the street level with a sun curled rental sign... three guillotine windows per floor... the left side window on the second floor no longer has its shutters... the lamp post next to the bench, lights up the room inside... the layered wood plank ceiling... only odourless from where I am sitting... the room is alive with an abundance of emptiness... I can feel her trapped inside and unable to leave... lost just like you, I am not the light...

## 2015/02/27 – Friday (Aveiro, Portugal)

... change... the only constant is change... the wave of loneliness is in a upwards direction... in order to change its orientation to downwards... decided to move to Lisbon to experience living in a dynamic city which up to now I had only seen as a tourist on several occasions... Aveiro is very nice and did open up a lot of stories/memories... re-living not necessarily traumatizing child hood experiences but then again not pleasant either... sometimes I think life is just an Olympic hurdle race... a fast paced series of obstacles we surmount... an argument with Suzanne catapulted me to Aveiro, a blessing in disguise for it energized the draining, writing inspiration...

... moving day... around the 10th of March... a day before my birthday... as if this is still an important event in my life... in the past, I always took my birthday as a day off from school and/or work... and have been doing this since the age of 16... a nothing day, a day where I would do absolutely nothing or almost... a day dedicate to moi... as I was on the computer confirming the apartment and train reservations... all I have to take to Lisbon are my 2 suitcases and even that I found was too much... I need to cut down on my belongings... I have a suit, dress shirts, and shoes etc... why do I carry these around with me?... some charity can use these clothes and the beneficiary would also look debonair... a wave came through me, I used to be a monk in a previous life...

... mayan calendar... it kind of started around December 2012... not sure if it had anything to do with the Mayan calendar... though I guess like most people I do have a keen interest in the archaeology of the area and even era... especially with all the hoopla in the media about the calendar and what I regarded as convoluted theories about the end of the world... having worked as a computer programmer during the Y2K fiasco, which some claimed would be the end of the world too... change is the only end of something, with anything that is remotely mystic... I can honestly say, I did not know what came over me, it was almost like an obsession, a steady drive to a goal which I did not even know what goal this was... I just knew, I had to join the gym... why the gym?... first I did not feel I was overweight or out of shape... but I could stand a little more exercise as it could do no harm either... finally in January of 2013, I caved in to this relentless obsession... I joined the gym...

... meeting with a gym staff member... the young man went through his well-rehearsed routine about showing me around the place... and asking me about my previous experiences (if any) with gyms... should I tell him I am here because an intuition of sorts brought me here... to answer his question... the only gym I could think of was some 40 years ago in high school with a gym teacher which I perceived as being a former Nazi... with a pointer stick, who enjoyed whipping students' legs to motivate us... the gym instructor smiled politely... not sure what went over his head, the Nazi reference or pointer stick pain... so... the young attendant starts talking to me about setting up a workout routine tailored for me, including cardio and weights... out of the blue... I interrupt him and say all I want is the treadmill and nothing else... he looks at me with a stunned look... he goes back into his description of the gym's many features... no, no stop... all I want is the treadmill, I just want and need to walk... that is it... all I got from the instructor was the contemptuous look that the customer is always right...

... wtf... in late April 2013... a chance meeting with my old friend

Manon... out of the blue... she told me about her Camino pilgrimage she had done decades ago... that evening the random thoughts were coming together that I must embark on this pilgrimage too... did some research on the internet about the pilgrimage... all I had going for me at that time was that I was physically fit... finances were the major issue as a home renovator, spring being my busiest season... I fiddled with the Camino idea, of maybe doing it the following year or if things would line up properly maybe in the late summer or even fall...

... woke up... on the morning of Wednesday May 8th, 2013... do not know how or where the thought or should I say... order... came from but I knew I could not wait and had to get on the pilgrimage ASAP... that morning I got out of bed... headed directly for the travel agent and booked a flight for Sunday night... re-worked my workload schedule to postpone or cancel job/work commitments... that evening, announced my plans to the family... they went into shock, too put it mildly... shopped the next few days for adequate clothing, back pack and hiking boots... I had to break in the hiking boots, nearly slept with them for the next few days...

... mental illness?... I had to endure my families' concerns... in hindsight they were right, even I could see their point of view... had I gone mad?... no one or anything would stop me... my wife was alarmed beyond belief, at one time I turned to her and said... you are asking me to choose between you and god... you already lost... I don't know where this came from, considering I was a diehard atheist at that time...


## 2015/02/28 - Saturday (Barra, Portugal)

... weekend... gambled on the partially blue-ish morning sky and headed for the beach towns... biting my lip, as the taxi meter spun at the speed of a hamster on steroids racing the Ferris-wheel... hoping to unhinge it and catapult it's escape out of the cage... screeching windshield wipers pushing rain aside... the only winner was the taxi driver with fare and a free carwash... so much rain... even the driver parked/stopped the taxi on the sidewalk as close as possible to the bistro doors... so much inconsiderate free rain... surfers on the beach completely unconcerned with getting their hair wet... like in a weekday movie theatre matinee, I am alone in the bistro... the waiter walks around with a face of regret for coming in to work...

... loneliness... this will eventually kill me, even when surrounded by people… with a population of over 10 million… I'm still emotionally and/or socially disconnected from those around me… language barrier is perhaps a contributor… unlike automated breathing, I need to remind myself the havoc loneliness is playing in my head… a lurking danger…

… fear… a mentor of an emotion… all my dreams, my repeated dreams were always about fear… facing an enemy either human or not… at the crucial moment in the dream, it was evident I'd die… even knowing this… nevertheless, in an almost kamikaze way I'd attack my enemy… never fleeing… and at the moment of death in the dream, I'd wake up… whenever fear presents itself in my life… it was an easy decision, all I needed to do was face it… regardless of the consequences… maybe had I ran away, there would not be so many fuck ups in my life… still, I regard the emotion as a positive one… except when dealing with women… the fear of rejection by them can reduce my self-esteem to such a low… it paralyses me from operating normally… my Achilles heel… is it a mommy issue?… surely she walked all over me at one time…

… failure… not responding to my existence but instead creating it… am I setting myself up for failure?… is this not the higher self-free will concept… the ability to deny failure… simply said, a gambler… for me to consider and even attempt to write a book… need to trick my mind that I could… boost the ego to believe in myself… regardless of what I believe in… there's more to this life thing than what I can see… so, go beyond what I can see and into the unknown…

… love… as a young man existential questions abound… the endless why am I here… for the most part I was selfish where mainly, my well being counted… got married, became less selfish… it was all for my spouse, her well-being before mine, but the questions pursued… all my existentialist questions came to a screeching halt… my rasion d'etre became my kids, and I enjoyed their company like I had never experienced with any other humans… why can't I hold on to this… especially with the women I choose to love, they seem to slip through my fingers the fastest… with such cold and decisive separation, am I human?… except my kids, they are my only love constant… go back in time… if I could go back in time it would be to their youth… I need not be younger as I will always be a kid no matter what age… all I want is to be a father again… perhaps to ease my pain… life without love, or caring for others… especially for myself is just pointless…

\* \* \*

# MARCH

PART FIVE

## 2015/03/01 – Sunday (Costa Nova, Portugal)

... stayed in hotel... cheaper than cab fare back into town, but this is not the reason why I stayed... yesterdays' soaking rainy day on the beach was soothing... I had not planned to stay overnight... no change of clothes or toothbrush either... I think I was the only guest in the hotel... beach towns are dead during winter... I got up very early... showered again and headed down for the hotel lobby where breakfast was being served... gulped down a hard-core coffee with a self-made thick marmalade sandwich... in a hasty walk and eat mode, I headed for the beach... in a hurry for what?

... blinding fog... fog over the ocean, perfect weather for landing UFOs... and a light mist, wet enough as it made me feel as if I had been sweating... from Barra, I walked to the next town called Costa Nova... the beach connects these two towns... neighbouring towns and not one soul on the beach... I owned it all, and at the same time I had nothing that was mine... waves were so loud, a rock concert without lights... despite the crashing waves, I still felt the serenity I had experienced when walking *El Camino in 2013*... at that time I also had a critical, puzzling and unsettling intuition that something will die... *have yet to figure out if it is me or in me*... maybe this is why I rushed out of the hotel, to take in whatever time I may have remaining... anyway... in my head, I'm always at odds with everyone... with those who used to love me or may still do... since I cannot look at life simply... to be able to see humans' qualities & faults... without being a bleeding heart or too paternal... who wants to save the world... so, better off here alone...

... Costa Nova... got off the beach and headed into town... felt the need to meditate and sit down too as it had been several hours on the beach... saw a church tower, and made my way to it... from the outside I heard there was a Sunday mass going on... did not even remember it was Sunday... so my meditation was out... but I headed in, out of curiosity and in search of a sitting place... the place was quite empty... found myself a bench near the door, as I felt I was intruding... mostly elderly folks... grasping at the last years and checking in with god... mumbling prayers perhaps to guarantee a place in heaven... come to think of it, we do not live very long... this month celebrates 50 years ago, I came to Portugal for the first time at the age of 5... to a certain extent... a life time came and went... but where did it go... 50 years later and I still feel empty... where did it or I go wrong?

... a 12 year old... we spent our summer vacation, mostly on this beach, and its' endless sand dunes... my brother and I along with a cousin... the

3 musketeers kind of thing... my parents were busy with purchasing real-estate and we were left alone most of the day either here or back on the farm with the grandparents... to ease their guilt, they'd let us spend the day on the beach and with pocket money too... we'd buy homemade chips off a travelling vendor who'd walk up and down the beach with a basket (full of chips) on her head all day long... a steady diet of coke, chips and ice cream... or if you prefer a cavity festival...

... if not on the beach... we'd be left with our grandparents to look after us back in the farming village... since my brother and I were the Canadian grandkids... we were allowed to do anything... even get away with murder... we'd walk in the barns and boots creamed with manure would not stop us from walking into the house... they simply did not dare to exert any control over us... all we did was play and eat... if we did not like what was being served for lunch by the grandparents... we'd head over to our aunt's house for French fries and eggs... though I feel I'm running out of time... so much did happened in my lifetime... am I just ungrateful and/or greedy for more...

## 2015/03/02 – Monday (Costa Nova, Portugal)

... atonement... one more hotel darkness... even with another slowly gouged breakfast, it was worth another night... why is it we only think of the beach in terms of sunny warm weather... so much more an intense experience in rough seas... with grey sky isolation... the waves pounded by heavy rain... clothes soaked... waves hammering my shins and challenging my equilibrium... to stand on the shore oblivious to the water dripping sunglasses... no need to see clearly, as all the clarity I needed was being diffused in my head...

... the beauty of getting older... besides grey hair (even under Miss Clairol or Grecian formula miracle makers) and wrinkles for all of us... is the wisdom to become calmer in almost everything we do... why be in a hurry when going to a restaurant, unless you want to help the waiters set the tables... with almost being 55, is that we have about 35 years of history as adults... and man, even as an adult did I ever fuck up too...

... but somewhere in this span we popped a few kids who are now seeking their turn to be adults... should we tell them, not to worry and life is pretty much a joke... but most of all laugh at misery... if anything it is your own, and yours alone... did we listen to our old folks?... probably not... if anything we looked at them with a puzzled look and had the audacity to say I am not like you and it will be different for me... youthful arrogance and even pompous attitude... once you have a few of your parents lying horizontally 6 feet under... the youthful arrogance now seems so misplaced...

... you know what... forget about being in a hurry... your-self absorbing personal misery... and anything else you deem important that does not and will absolutely not fit in your coffin... what you need to acquire are great memories... these do not take up space in your head but they do make up the essence, which is you... and which you take where ever you may end up...

... put *love and passion* into everything you truly believe is important... and by default you will have *beauty*... and for most of us... the first sign of this was your newborn child looking at you for the first time... as they stare at you and look at your soul through your eyes... asking themselves, *why this guy as my father*... nevertheless...


## 2015/03/03 – Tuesday (Aveiro, Portugal)

... spiritual emptiness... a disease, maybe I was sick... when married I would be lying on my pillow... thinking, there has to be more to my life than this... get up in the morning and leave my eyes closed... physically push myself to work... stuck in night time home bound traffic, felt it did not last long enough... slouch into my indented couch... watch TV and finally go to a crowded bed... and of course socialize on weekends... is this living or existing... why go through with this, simply said... my 3 children and the responsibility of one being autistic...

... woke up in a fetal position... not sure why but instinctively this is not good... beach weekend... bathing in yesterday's rain left a souvenir... woke up with a sore throat... if it were more than a sore throat... who would help/ take care of me now... not even a sympathetic caress... if my doctor ever announced I had a terminal disease... on my way out of his office I would not take the elevator down to the lobby but up to the roof and jump off... on a lighter note but just as important... always told the ex-wife, if I ever wear the combination of shorts, tube socks and sandals... do the world a favour and shoot me...

... old breath... I'm tired of this *Bed & Breakfast*... it's so small... how small is it... it's so small that when lying in bed I can piss in the toilet and not miss... farts ricochet of the walls and ceiling perpetually... ended up smelling the same fart over and over as it flew by my nose... it had an amplified echo too...

... new breath... moved to a another Bed & Breakfast this afternoon as my loneliness requires a new address for entertainment... funny thing the young woman running the B&B... her name is Elsa with a capital 'E'... could she be a prophecy to my intuition... wait and see... with the move out of the way... headed to the local park with its' pond and birds... with a handful of throat lozenges... figured I would spend a little time in a quasi-nature setting... somehow the loneliness is not as intense there... on the way picked up a few soft sweet breads as a snack and as a consolation for the sore throat... yeah!, I'm a big baby... aren't all men?

... playing god... stood on the park bridge which crosses over the pond... saw a catfish swimming below... dropped a few crumbs of the sweet bread... with every piece of bread dropped, the number of fish doubled... at least three dozen or so of catfish fighting over bread crumbs... never imagined such aggressive behaviour from fish... ducks announcing their arrival with imposing quacks... daring pigeons and doves landing on the bridge railing next to me... even ants took time off their busy earth moving schedule to see what the fuss was all about... fear and hunger for survival...

... pecking order... when I think about it, every possible species that exists on this planet can feel fear but only humans know of love as well... so, do I succumb to my fears and be limited to this planet... or choose love and go beyond the blue sky... there is nothing holding me back here, let me fly away... but first let Elsa take care of me for the night...


## 2015/03/04 – Wednesday (Aveiro, Portugal)

... as industrialized humans... we have had nothing but contempt for the planet and even ourselves... and this since the beginning of time... now, will we change?... I don't think so... but I'm curious to see how far we will go/reach... one thing is pretty sure the planet will be here forever, as for us... well, I'm not so sure... maybe we will leave behind the only thing that sustains us, whenever we have it... the essence of love... as it lasts forever in time and space...

... yesterday moved into a B&B... after one night of living hell... low price rental... no heat whatsoever... not even the concept of what a heater may be... instead 6 layers of blankets on the bed to technically keep one warm… nor the weight or the number of blankets kept me warm, instead they crushed my body and prevented blood circulation… bathroom with no walls… after a shower, pubic hairs could not be dried as they froze to a crisp… the intuited big E was not just for Elsa the loving attendant, but also Escape an Extra-marital situation… hence the risk of interpreting intuitions combined with emotions… spent this morning moving to a third B&B… spent more money too…

… felt my day was wasted in dealing with the move to a new B&B… with… a plenty… disorganized thoughts spent some time fiddling on the internet… Suzanne had sent me emails several days ago… looking at the sent dates, it dawned on me how disconnected I allowed myself to be with the outer world… with such hunger for her, I savoured her emails breaking the ice… both of us now realizing it is hard to be apart… we felt each other's suffering even though we're 300 kilometers apart… two limitless souls with no concept of distance…

… souls… floating in the air, without the sense of fearing heights and never grounded… just floating freely where ever the wind guides them… whether high up or down below there is beauty in everything… so much childlike silliness when bumping into one another, as if everything is a pretext for effervescence…

… it is with this unchartered happiness… as you scoop down, grab my hand and lift me up into your floating soul universe… at first we are two entities… but as the heat of our passion for one another intensifies… we slowly melt into one loving soul… no need for individuality, we are two minds in sync and loving as one… as if this was the way it was meant to be… finally the connecting moment had come to fruition… like floating on my back in the middle of the ocean… alone but far from lonely… surrendering to the waves, as I have now surrender myself to you…

## 2015/03/05 – Thursday (Agueda, Portugal)

… mass production… if we start off with the notion that some humans are not the cream of the crop… erratic in their thinking, selfish and truly aspire to love their creature comforts especially money… having money… gives us the sense of being in control & powerful… for a human ego this is an addictive feeling… then why are we surprised when poor or rich folks try to screw the financial, political and even religious systems… politics no longer, are the result of the populous wishes... but those of a few elitist who have money... so get your hands on enough money to be an elitist... and you will coast thru life with ease though not necessarily happily, but with ease nevertheless... if you are unable to make money, then turn to god for the illusion that your life is worth living too...

... having said this... there is always a few who do not follow dogmas or the norm of the masses, these are the ones who inspire me... the rest of them... well?... hopefully, they just make me laugh... and in this family run bistro, a microcosm of the world... with all three family members working behind the counter and the action is non-stop... as I look at them I wonder, is this what humans look like... am I one of them in any way?... gonna write a journal entry, finish my coffee and get out of here before I lose fate in humanity, including myself...

... a father... a short and stalky man, with a protruding stomach to match his height... with squinting eyes magnified by his glasses... most of the time, he looks over the glasses, maybe this is so as not to wear out the lenses... thinning hair combed to the side, just like his mother had imposed on him at the age of 4... a necktie whose knot was only made once, by the clerk in the men's wear... wearing a sweater vest with vertical stripes to distract the peering eyes from his extended gut... did he learn this visual fashion trick himself?... not likely, as it was his wife who picked out the sweater... she bought it without his presence being required... deep inside, he thinks it'll appeal to other women too...

... the mother... she would make more sales if it were not for her high pitched voice... her piercing vocals crack and melt customers' encrusted earwax... with short curly hair, a throwback to the late 1950's, grayish brown with white roots... all her curls are counted and accounted for... so much control over the positioning of her hair, that she forgets to be a woman, a human... much taller than her husband... with bulging eyeballs beaming like a lighthouse over the tables and customers... making a mental count and keeping track of what has been served... at the end of day, her mental calculations have to match the sales registered in the cash drawer... she definitely is the mastermind behind her empire... but being in a male dominated culture, her inept husband is the figure head of her empire...

... only son... in his thirties... a tall, slightly hunched back chap... very dark circles under his eyes, kind of gives him a sinister creepy look... he writes with his right hand, yet his left arm bicep has more muscle mass... conclusion, his favourite pastime could be internet porn and left hand masturbation… coming in this morning and carrying a grocery paper bag with neatly packed small Kleenex boxes… speculation would lead me to believe one is for his night table and another for the desk in the living room where they have the shared family computer… taking this one step further, the Kleenex box on the desk gets replaced more often… he blows up with his breath the empty grocery paper bag… and crushes it near the waitress who gets startled/ shrieks with the loud popping sound… the mother overstepping the husband coaxes him into remembering he is the manager… he comes over to the waitress and reprimands her forcefully for making a loud shrieking sound… no mention of the paper bag popping either…

… a nobody… the waitress downplays the verbal attack with a chuckle… she looks over at the patrons seeking a glimpse of approval and/or alliance… she could head home tonight with mounted resentment… her impatience and frustration may be felt by her little ones… or the husband will get an earful and wish for a lottery winning to save his wife… will she be able to leave work behind, once out of the bistro… or take it home with her…

… ethics, little big word… an honest reaction and yet she got chewed out by the manager… woman, you did nothing wrong except not stand your ground… could the manger be the problem when all he did was bark without knowing why… does he dream of a life where he is not henpecked… would he recognize it if he saw it?… let me guess, he wears a tie as a phallic symbol cause his peanut brain matches his penis size… competing for time on the family computer with his son… his computer sessions are loaded with porn too, most likely big breasts or asses, cause his petty life is so pathetic… that he relishes his fantasies in human anatomy which is bigger than life… when you need to put someone down in order to validate your insignificance, you are not a manger… nor much of a human… what you are, is a waste of oxygen, because you know what you did was not correct…

… understanding… whether day or night when I float around humans… looking at them in disbelief and ask myself… are they unable to see the beauty that surrounds us… all they are concerned with is their pettiness, maliciousness, absurdity, materialism & jealousy just to name a few… it seems to sustain their raison d'etre… perhaps I'm a snob and/or not a team player… cause I do not quite fit in… the fact of the matter is that I've been re-incarnated so often that I'm beyond these simple mortals… is this a curse or a blessing…

… human vulgarity… on a final note, I do not judge… who am I to judge anyway… but I will always challenge myself, when watching them… perhaps re-think my perspectives and convictions… but for sure, it opens my eyes to other ways of thinking too... and for this I am grateful... the day I stop learning, might as well die... maybe when it will be time to go again, what would I take as a lesson learned from this...

## 2015/03/06 – Friday (Aveiro, Portugal)

... believing... sitting here in the coffee shop on a Friday afternoon... with a text message from Suzanne announcing her coming to Aveiro... another chance at being US again... with nearly two months of failed reconciliations... what endures in us so much that we are unable to part... no need for a wrist watch or a cell phones' additional function of time display... so many clocks and deadlines monitored by the sunrise and/or sunset... do we really need to be reminded subconsciously of fleeting time?

... she... my time is unlike all others... it is quantified by my being with you... and yes, time does torment me, when away from you... for every spasmodic shift of the dials, a little bit of me gets taken away into a hollowness... those seconds of ME where I am deprived of you... never knowing the beauty of being measured by you...

... she... time is unrelenting... it has no human emotions... for if it did, it would not tick by me as you are so far away... it would stop, and allow me to catch up with you... maybe, even cheat and go back in time, extending our time together... sitting here and concentrating hard to forget or even stop time... my heart betrays me and pounds the beats of time... reminding me you are not yet here...

... she... never too late... why now as a mature man?... did I start to hold hands with you and feel it is an imperative that it must be so and not up for negotiation or even reasoning?... am I hanging on to you... as an assurance for me in knowing that I will not lose you again... is my love for you something new to this current lifetime... or has it been going on for eons... lunacy would be to believe this love is new... I'm going out on a limb with my heart, again...

... she is Suzanne...

## 2015/03/07- Saturday (Aveiro, Portugal)

... night delight... when the night is no longer mine but ours... with Suzanne on my side, I feel the world is no longer a concern... I let myself feel, she is there for me, she cares... I'm very aware of her fears with regards to me... I do not have a good track record when it comes to stability with us... I'll be the first to admit it... for what it is worth, I feel the time for change is now... thinking I'm ready... can't really say what triggered this attitude change in me... perhaps the separation was a phase I needed... I came out of this lost lapse of our time more frustrated and even sadder then I was before... regrets I have plenty... therefore a change is mandatory...

... missing you... my life was crumbling before my very own eyes... I knew it, saw it and did nothing about it... wished for someone like you to come into my life... but saw no one in my immediate entourage who remotely came close to the woman I dreamed of... I thought I had as much of a chance to win the lottery as finding someone new... my objectivity caused me to see I was in a dead end situation... and I found myself simply wishing to blow away with the dust... I became a smiling lifeless body...

... not ready... this feeling of void... precipitated the thought of leaving for the Camino... in a spiritual quest, to this day I'm still not sure why I embarked on this pilgrimage in the first place... and now doing it again, felt it was a salvation from my loneliness... but your coming to Aveiro to meet me... if I were to take a guess I would say it was divine intervention... and on time too, I was simply distraught... almost to a point of no return...

... courage... in the midst of all this, you show up... I will never be able to explain the impact you have on me... you went from someone nice to know on Facebook to someone I want forever and beyond... my mind and heart were shut... you poked in and stirred things up... when it comes to emotions, humans can be cruel, very cruel... but not all of us want to be like this or are like this... I have seen and lived this cruelty already... I now deserve something better... I finally found love, and I am hooked on life...

... you can hold on to your fear of me leaving you... or you can drop it and go for the loving feeling instead... ask yourself... how do you want to spend the rest of your life... now that you have given me a second chance at being happy... my choice is clear, I want the loving feeling as long as it is with you...

... for you are in me... incredible... you bring out the worst in me but by the same token, you can bring out the hidden loving gentle side of me... for so long this side lingered in the shadows... occasionally prying it's head out of obscurity... just like a scurrying mouse it retracts within itself very fast...

for at times, for the world is cruel and would enjoy nothing more than to see me endure pain...

... in silence... I love the idea or/and feeling of giving all that I am or can be just for you... the moments where you sit against my chest and my arms around your waist, with your back to me, you are faceless... just like in my life long dreams of finding a woman... I hoped and maybe even knew she existed... in my odourless and colorless dreams she was faceless too... as I searched so many a woman for this elusive face and found none... and now here you are sitting against me and faceless... it is not the face that I should of have been looking for but the unconditional loving essence... as I lean forward and rest my face into your hair... I feel your vibrations sending shivers down my body... your comforting reassuring love comes from within you... this is your beauty...

## 2015/03/08 – Sunday (Luso, Portugal)

... fountain of random thoughts... the town of Luso synonymous with good quality mineral water... the water flows freely from self-serve fountains... as I watch you filling a plastic bottle from a fountain spout... what would be the first thought... the most elemental one in my life at this very moment... I love you... can you blame me for loving you... compounded with a mischievous smirk, as you proclaim yourself to be irresistible... I like the pic I just snapped of you... it captures your sweetness, innocence and an angelic Suzanne all at once...

... your radiance... with the sun brighter than it has been in days... lunch in the Bucaco Palace Hotel terrace... wine flowing into our glasses... the opulence of manicured gardens beneath us... am I too romantic for wishing you near me... to feel your nakedness and probably listen to you talking about unimportant important trivialities... your voice soothes me... sometimes I think you speak so much, just to stop yourself from repeatedly blurting your true feelings of how much you are in love too...

... assimilation... it would be for us just to hug... where your breasts press against my chest and we are so close... not even a sliver of paper can slip between our bodies... our prime 1 + 1 does not equal 2... as in we now share one heart, one endless closeness, and such an intense loving moment, can only exalt itself into a loving interlude... where the tenderness of the moment is consumed... caressing a natural loving gesture... not one of lust... but two bodies connecting physically... as our bodies act as the bridge allowing our souls to meet again...

... it has been a long and arduous separating wait... perhaps our waiting can be measured in days, weeks and then months... but for our souls the wait had no notion of time other than an infinite timeless wait... such tormented souls, reconnecting thru our intense physical love making... filled with loving passionate desire for one another... and the humility, as the intenseness of the moment brings us to such an emotional state of unearthly pure love... unparalleled for any mortal... for a few seconds, we are allowed into a godly world... we are privileged, as this is beyond primitive mankind...

## 2015/03/09 – Monday (Areia, Portugal)

... never the same... yesterday, came down with Suzanne, and stayed at her place over night... this morning headed to Areia for breakfast... computer in tow, went back to my favourite breakfast bistro... it has not changed and how I used to like being here... but not today, it feels different because I am different too... the familiar faces are just that, familiar... no sooner that I finish breakfast, I'm out of there... drove around, until I came to another bistro... quieter... typed for a bit, but the thoughts and words were not flowing... I think I miss the madness and depressive state I had while in Aveiro by myself... why is it thoughts and ideas come out fluently when I feel down... does writing need to be emotionally destructive...

... trough festival... it wasn't long before the lunch crowd started clamoring into their cell phones... when this happened in the bistros back in Aveiro, I found refuge in the church and meditated during the lunch hours... besides, it was easier to meditate on a quasi-empty stomach... in fact, what I liked most was having a mid-afternoon lunch when people were on their way back to work... a Pisces in the truest sense of the word... against the current... of the two churches I know here... both have their doors closed... as if praying is an organized activity for Sunday mornings like soccer is for the afternoons... maybe meditation was a placebo, but it worked on me...

... motivation... I must admit I was caught off guard... had I not done the Camino Pilgrimage in 2013... and invoked the divorce, selling off the business, house and cars etc... I would be the first to admit I would not be here waiting for spring weather for a second attempt at the pilgrimage... turning 55 years old in two days... ideas about the duration of life start coming to the forefront... quickly the thought of having another 20 or so years of life left to live put things in perspective... do I coast or do I dare to dream the remaining years... is what I'm living now a dream... or a nightmare in a dream?...

... at what price... the danger or blessing of the Camino trail... is that it forces you to simply walk all day and think, and think surrounded by serenity... and it imposes upon you both a mental and physical breakdown... once you have experienced this then (and this is the best part) lucidity takes over... my lucidity spoke volumes... once I had peeled off the layers of fear accumulated over the decades and focused into making my intuitive dreams, the reality... and this was how I left the trail behind me... and here lies the problem, the rest of the planet is far from being like the trail...

... blurred vision... the lucidity lacked clarity when no longer on the pilgrimage... my actions caught everyone of guard, including myself... but I do see the humour in all of this... and with this thought... perhaps we should all do the Camino trail... but can we risk the whole experience turning this into a dogma... and who knows maybe you too will have an epiphany of sorts... and lose what you once perceived important...

## 2015/03/10 – Tuesday (Lisbon, Portugal)

... Lisbon... just the name of the city conjures my reeling senses... in previous years, whenever I came through this city it was always as a tourist... and as such, I would also look at the buildings and wonder, who lives here... what is there daily lives like... such a mix of decrepit and very old buildings snuggled by modern aversions of what a dwelling ought to be... like probably everything else, money dictates and limits the promoter in selling an appealing condo with the bottom line in mind...

... organized chaos... my apartment is in an area called Saldanha... tree lined streets struggling with cars for space... sitting in the apartment looking out the window as I write... before me an undefined open space with tall trees... surrounded by old buildings with boarded doors and windows... I'm sure at one time these dwellings were someone's pride... conclusion being... pride lasts as long as its' owner, buildings perhaps slightly longer... about 500 meters out in the horizon is a new sky scraper with an overlapping helicopter platform on its' roof... the new looking down on the old... is this not what we also do...

... their world... stepped out for a few grocery necessities... walking

155

around discovering stores and bistros as I looked for a grocery store... finally found a grocery store with a small and very discreet entrance... no large bright neon sign of any kind announcing/promoting it... but once inside it is as big as anything we have back home... an underground grocery store with flooring ramps taking us deep into this subterranean city belly... picked up some bottled water, as the tap water in the apartment is not appealing to a couple of my senses...

... our world... what would be the barometer for a city... the number of homeless or the lack of homeless... on the way into the grocery store I had seen a homeless man lying down in front of the grocery store vent... he was warmly dressed even though this is a 25 degrees Celsius kind of day... paradise for most, but he is clueless... on the way out I dropped by and gave him bread and fish patties... he looked at me stunned and muttered thanks... for sure, I cannot be the first to do this... afterwards, went by the market and picked some fresh produce... on my way home I handed the same homeless chap an orange... asking him if he enjoyed the bread and fish patties... he could not remember the food I had given him nor me... he forgot me as much as this city forgets him...

... noise... later on the day I went out for a snack in one of the bistro terraces I had spotted earlier... besides with such a hot summer like day, a draft beer on a terrace is a quality of life perk... the bistro terrace is quite crowded for a Tuesday afternoon... the waiter sets the pace for the service... my thirst and patience are at his mercy... with one cold gulp down, I calm back into my chair and simply watch... the fast and noisy driving... the smell of diesel fuel in the air... cars and people with somewhere important to go, judging from the displacement speed... yet a truce at the crosswalks, as both drivers and pedestrians judge one another with mis-trust... with a month long stay planned... I wonder, if my romantic perception of this city will last...

## 2015/03/11 – Wednesday (Malveira, Portugal)

... morning smile... spent the night at Suzanne's place... can being... in love... be considered as a birthday gift... why not... today is my birthday, the insignificant number 55... if I were still in Montreal, I would've scheduled my medical annual check-up in the morning... then spend the rest of the day off by doing something I enjoy... such as going to the movies or shopping for some personal trinket... but being in Cascais with Suzanne... while she was at work I took her car and drove north until I'd spot a coffee shop... ended up in a little town called Malveira... with the hot summer weather... sitting in this tavern watching some downhill ski competition on TV... the tavern owner looks at me intensely... he is not used to having customers who look like foreigners nor do not have a construction worker sweat scent... only I know of the humour going on here... the laughter is only in my head...

... 55... so here I am on my birthday, waiting for my kids to drop me a birthday wish... and debating what I'm doing in Europe writing a journal/book and contemplating the Camino pilgrimage... all my logical reasoning tells me I am nuts... but my instincts still persist to carry on with my plans no matter how ludicrous I think they are... why do I feel Jesus died for somebody's sins but not mine kind of thing... though everything is going well in my relationship with Suzanne... and I know how lucky I am with having her in my life... yet, I feel I have accomplished nothing with my life... but as I juggle my memory for the last 35 or so years of my life... for the most part I was restless and always searching for something... will the second Camino trek finally ease my quest?... or maybe the solution is not to be found on some trail but somewhere inside of me... everything points to the latter... even my confusion is unstable...

... smiles... small talk with the tavern owner along with a second beer and to sweeten the relationship the tavern keeper throws in complimentary salty lupini beans... a few friendly words with the 3 elderly men on the table next to me scratching their lottery tickets... I'm not alone amongst these strangers... I like this feeling... it temporarily downplays the pain of missing my children... they made me feel I was worth something... as a human... I really have no idea what the future holds... but, I hope my kids and love be in my life... otherwise, it is all pointless...

... not the first time... when I was twenty... I shipped my motorcycle to Europe for a one year sabbatical... started in Portugal and went through Spain, France, England and back... working at odd jobs to keep myself afloat... after a nasty motorcycle accident I ended up back in Montreal... met my ex-wife, got married and had 2 children... 10 years later I find myself leaving my young family behind and flying off to Iran to work on a one year engineering mining project... upon my return, I enroll in school in computer science... our 3rd. child is born... in my mid-forties I had enough with working as a computer programmer analyst... the computer screen stifles me... radical change for creativity... I start my home renovation company... and both money and ease of life are an integral part of me... but now, more than

157

ever I feel empty... especially when my children are asserting their independence as young adults... the void increases exponentially... by this time it is 2013 and my first Camino pilgrimage throws my life into a chaos... or was my life already in chaos but I was too dull when it came to seeing it...

... now... I find myself spending my birthday with only Suzanne... with my only future plans being to write and a second Camino trek... then what, with no job prospects of any kind, what future as a man can I offer Suzanne... am I being fair to her?... happy birthday McFern... only you can complicate your life... and you know what... you're good at it... must be from all the experience you acquired over the years... for god's sake... lighten up man... indeed, I'm my worst critic...

## 2015/03/12 – Thursday (Lisbon, Portugal)

... career... with my apartment in Lisbon and Suzanne living 30 kilometers away in suburbia... I decided to experiment and do the train commute from Cascais where she lives to Lisbon where I write as a job... it feels like I go to work and at night come home to her... it kind of reminds me of when I worked as a computer programmer and would travel into Montreal via a suburban bus... with suit and tie, a portable on my lap or a book I lived the part along with my fellow neighbours and travellers commuting... where they unhappy like me, or did this lifestyle seem acceptable to them... the only reason why I did it was for my family... at times I did not feel like much of a man... but before anything else, I had to be a father and provider... this ingrained notion I could never shun... with the love I have for my young kids, I could never run away... but deep inside, I felt sooner or later I would collapse...

... with train tracks paralleling the coast line into Lisbon... as I sit there alone and in a contemplative mood... the ocean to my right and to my left a mixed bag of buildings either new or old... such extremes in architecture and/or urban planning... it's as if there was money to build these edifices but never any money to maintain or renovate them... considering the economic state of this country, there seems to be just enough money for food, cell phones and/or cigarettes and nothing else... which explains the exodus of young university graduates looking overseas for employment, even with symbolic government incentives to stay... symbolic incentives such as patriotism do not put much more on the table than food... considering the age of planetary materialism we live in, flag waving is antiquated...

... mood swing... arriving at Cais do Sodre train station, I must now take the metro into the core of Lisbon... on the metro platform, I walk by a few British tourists... with an already formed opinion of how dirty Lisbon is... I wouldn't quite agree with them on this... though I'd take it one step further and say it reminds me of east block cities after the communist downfall... crass aluminum architecture slapped on concrete structures with an endless array of clothes lines displaying the social class of the apartment occupant... for the dozen of homeless and cripples I have met on my route begging for money, such an apartment would be a lap of luxury... nevertheless, this visual misery drains my empathy rendering me numb and indifferent... only when I reach, not necessarily opulent neighbourhoods that this city shines brighter than the sun...

... metro... the Lisbon metro being something completely new to me... I follow the herd into the underground... is there an international etiquette for metro behaviour... the train car doors open and people shuffle in... the morning silence is interrupted by the whistle warning the doors will soon be closing... on an ironic note... the whistle sounds like the one a soccer referee would use... co-incidence in this soccer worshipping culture?...

... jaundice... the lighting in the train is somewhat yellowish... facial complexions look ill... with heads plunged in some sort of personal pad or telephone connecting one with the real world up above... others hiding behind the newspaper headlines of corrupt bureaucrats...

... independence... with an abundance of empty seats it eases the avoidance of human contact... mis-trust followed by a tight clench on hand bags... direct eye contact is avoided, instead one's eye sight is projected above a head and the glance down scans the passenger... is the darkness of the tunnel also in their hearts...

... underground community... speaking to the passenger nearest to me... asking him about the next stop... my mispronunciation of the metro station name has him and everyone in the vicinity pitching in with assistance... their hard faces are smack of sympathetic smiles and the validating feeling of doing something good... maybe, also demonstrating their knowledge of the metro system... as if all the years of travelling the underground resulted with this one instance of helping me... as I step out of the metro car onto the platform... inside folks are pointing for me to go left... gotta love these people...

... despite all the difficulties these people may or may not have... every time I interact with them, their kindness is legendary... in contrast... does not say much about my friends' silence on my birthday... yesterday...


## 2015/03/13 – Friday (Lisbon, Portugal)

... stability... woke up this morning... grateful for what works in my life and optimistic with what needs to be improved will one day come to fruition... came into Lisbon this morning, feeling confident with my public transit traveling in this foreign city... I feel like one of them... a lisboeta... being Friday the 13th, has absolutely no superstitious meaning like back home in North America... good or bad luck, my life goes on...

... how true... I do deserve good things... but the problem seems to be when to recognize the good things... is there a wonderful life ahead of me... considering I am 55 and looking back at my genetic lineage... if I can milk another 20 or so years I'll be lucky... when I read self-help slogans like... *something you've worked hard for*... considering I'm lazy by design... can I really expect something?... I always dreamt not to be a pain in the ass... but considering I am now writing this... is it a given my dream will not materialize... so, will I... really get what I wanted... when I have yet to define what I want...

... my god this is so true... and it happened again this morning... when I got up and went to the bathroom and looked into the mirror... even though my eyes were still covered with that yellow stuff (rheum)... even through this blurry eyelash filter... I saw myself and thought modestly... Mcfern, you are adorable... I know, hard to believe huh?... not that I care what you think of me... what counts is what I think of myself... so... how would an adorable man like myself look for an unfound soul mate... of course... why not?... use these pages shamelessly to find... the one... so here goes... at least it is cheaper than using the UN-Matched dating site... cause once they got a hold of my credit card, they would not let go and charged me despite my cancellation requests... for a company that sells human interaction... no human answers their phone lines...

... I'm a 55 year old moderately romantic chap and a Pisces too... very creative and extremely unpredictable... I like long walks on the beach, but since it (beach) is far... I go to Home Depot and walk on sand bags to get that sandy beach feeling on my soles... I love cuddly romantic evenings by an electric or gas fireplace, as long as I get to hold the fireplace's remote control...

... my speciality is romantic candlelight suppers... carefully selecting (on sale that week) the right flavour of low sodium Campbell's soup served exquisitely from the can... but I do wrap a decorative ribbon around the can to embellish the mood as we dip our previously used plastic spoons into the lukewarm soup... please note, one of the spoons is cracked, I will use it this time, then you (chivallary)... and Airwick has the most enchanting scented candles which are not just for the bathroom... in cold winter days, I open the car door for you... so that you may get out to push the car... the door latch is broken from the inside...

... seriously, I am a gentleman who still believes in chivalry when convenient... that is why at the movies we can share the popcorn I sneaked in from Dollarama... which was placed/hidden in your purse without your knowledge... yep!... if anyone out there has a free heart... you know I'm an adorable catch...

... alas!... sorry to say, but you are too late, for on this delusory Friday the 13th... it is not the lack of women who have come into my life and loved me, as I loved them... no, the dilemma is me loving myself that is always short lived and I drag the ones I love down into my conundrum...

## 2015/03/14 – Saturday (Cascais, Portugal)

... tension... on our way to the Saturday morning market for some fresh produce... our couple thing is not going well... switching on the radio... to break the uncomfortable but welcomed silence between us... one of my favourite albums... Pink Floyd – Wish You Were Here... is being played in a tribute format... not sure it was as a commercial success, especially since it came after Dark Side of the Moon... I actually remember saving money to buy this album (late 70's)... since my coins were few, I was extremely selective with my purchases... often, I would ask my mom for additional money... as an impetuous 16 year old teenager... when I listened to the lyrics I'd think/ agree... I'd rather die than live a mediocre life... and today, mediocrity is almost acceptable, as long as you have a loving mate who tags along for the ride even in silence... then again, perhaps my reasoning at 16 could hold true today...

... deal breaker... being a rock music fan as if it were a religion... buying

Pink Floyd albums in a trendy Phantasmagoria record store was cool... but buying an Abba album for my mom because it had a song called Fernando... well, it did not fit my wannabe cool image... principles, integrity and whoring... I needed and wanted money to buy records... so I would end up buying her the record and in return she would throw a few extra coins my way... for my mom, the name Fernando meant a lot to her... not because it was my name, but the name of her first boyfriend/love... while dating my mom, this chap had moved from Portugal to Brazil and due to the inefficient postal system of that era, the letter exchange dwindled to the point where he ended up finding new and improved love in Brazil... can the postal system really be blamed for the failed relationship... ?...

... delectable... if you never heard the Abba song Fernando... then you are in for a treat... it was released in 1976... later on, international covers were also recorded as my mother had a French and Portuguese versions of the song... it was such a huge hit that even on my cell, it's the ring tone... I know... it makes me all the more adorable...

... delinquent... it was the spring of 1976 and I had just finished high school for the year... having spent most of the school year wasted... my parents in their infinite wisdom felt it was best to send me to Portugal for the summer... and to spend quality time on the grandparent's farm... they concluded my friends were influencing me into drugs... I did not have the nerve to tell them that it was the other way around... as their son was the bad seed in the lot... suffice to say, a free trip is a free trip... and besides I was exempted of the drudgery of a summer job... yet, was provided with pocket money for my overseas stay... can life get any sweeter?

... sweet injustice... after the Montreal to Amsterdam flight... there was an 8 hour layover before taking off to Portugal... do you suspect I was the one who made the travel arrangements... ouufff!... so much time in Amsterdam... surely not to be wasted in an airport waiting for a connecting flight... this was the time before the Euro currency fiasco kicked in and I did not have any Dutch money (guilders) on me.... so, I left the airport and just walked around in the city... I ducked into an alley, and nearly bumped my head on a café sign... POT CAFÉ... I know, what a pleasant surprise, duh!!... I looked through the glass window... the place was packed... I could hardly distinguish the human shapes as there was a thick smog and it was permeating through the door frame cracks... my keen sense of smell quickly analyzed/ identified the scent as marijuana smoke...

... for non blondes... with no Dutch money in pocket... I figured if

I walked in and pretended to look for a table that maybe I can rush a few lungs full of smoke... with every inhale, my smile widen... I guess, it caught the attention of the brunette sitting at a table, she motioned me to the empty chair in front of her... we shared a water pipe... it was far from romantic... though this tall brunette reminded me of the Abba singer... which I found was the cuter one of the two singers in the band... but I also guess, when stoned the mind can play tricks as they were both gorgeous ladies... anyway she was much older than me... we talked... mmmm no, actually she talked as by this time I was so high and not able to articulate a syllable let alone compose words into a coherent thought/sentence...

... lost... time and space was no longer in my control... and I had a flight to catch... I asked her for the time... she pointed to the clock tower outside and it had a drummer boy figurine beating the hour on the drums... she asked... Can you hear the drums Fernando?... yeah! I can hear them, but I'm not able to maintain a count... she laughed and I added it would make a good line for a song, no?...

... happenstance... Can you hear the drums Fernando?... is the first line to the song... is it possible that inadvertently I put into the collective cosmos the opening line?... I never got any acknowledgement or even royalties for coming up with the opening line to the song... this is not an issue as the best things in life are free... wonder if the brunette I met that day, thinks of me when she hears the song... I am sure she is thinking of me as I'm simply... that adorable...

## 2015/03/15 – Sunday (Sintra, Portugal)

... changer le malaise de place... Café de Natalia in Sintra... decided to come here for breakfast without Suzanne... as the sweetness of her voice irritates my rancorous ears... sometimes I think we are ghosts in human form... trying to re-live a past love... so much anger towards her... but anger from the past... a betrayal anger... she is demanding too much of my time... her teaching job allows for empty time between classes... she wants me to fill in the clock points between the numbers... she reminds me of those lonely people in the park walking their dogs at night... both dog and owner with drooping faces... realizing all they have is each other in the dark...

... freedom... like plant roots growing circularly in a transparent glass vase... we're prisoners of ourselves... stability versus instability, I've always been the latter... dragged my ex through hell and now bringing in Suzanne too... I have no plans for the future other than write and the Camino... then what?... spend my days writing my thoughts when my thoughts do not believe what I write... once beyond, writing and the Camino, if there is a beyond... is it fair to make her wait too... and wait for what... with her insecurities of loneliness or my leaving her for another woman... despite telling her, writing a book is not the place to meet women... I feel I am a prisoner in this one or any relationship for that matter...

... convoluted fuck... the Camino first broke the physical, then the emotional and finally the spiritual... the emotional is people attachment... or as I see it, being shunned by mortals... what happens when one leaves the pilgrimage with a broken spirit and goes back to reality... a spirit which has experienced an epiphany is a broken spirit in the physical world... is my spiritual awakening a detachment from oneself... the latter opens the flood gates to another world... welcoming earthly death... granting an insiders' opening to the collective above...

... still earthly bound... at 55 years old... having acquired the taste for being self-employed... I cannot see myself working for anyone else... plus the cultural and language barrier if I stayed in Portugal... not sure about the book thing either... too farfetched as an idea to earn a living of any kind with it... so, what can I offer... too old to find a job here other than open a business such as a tea shop but this will require capital... therefore must return to Montreal to my home renovation business... and for how long?... would Suzanne wait... would I wait?...

... space... a table with a napkin dispenser, an ash tray, phones, cigarette packs, 2 plates with sweet crumbs feeding flies and tempting daring ants, 2 coffee cups & saucers, noisy cutlery and 4 tangled arms... such is the crowded table next to mine with only two occupants... at first glance this may seem insignificant and usually attributed to young people in love... which in itself is considered the norm... and why not, as we like to attribute things into neat little categories... how we love to associate customs and gestures with category groupings... it gives us a sense of understanding and controlling our environment... and do we love to control, it is in our nature... just like the need of oxygen... or as the couple locking each other's hands...

... my point... what about a 55 year old man... why would I now at this ripe age hold a woman's hand... is this not reserved for young lovers... is this amorous display apropos for my age group or even gender... can it possibly be considered as simply being juvenile?... and how can one determine what is the norm when judging the love between a man and woman... am I, perhaps trying to re-live some fragmented youth... how does the world perceive a mature man holding a woman's hand... is he henpecked by her... my crowded table is empty without Suzanne's arms...

## 2015/03/16 – Monday (Lisbon, Portugal)

... deja vu... it feels like I have a job as a writer... hopping on the commuter train and going into Lisbon to write... reminds me of my commuter days, when I used to leave Brossard suburbia to work in Montreal... tailor made suit, shirt and phallic tie, freshly shaven face and an assortment of cosmetic odours from soaps to colognes... the power trip of a computer programmer... so much importance given to the appearance, to command believable respect when I'd contradict my boss during a meeting... how often, my arrogance shined when I'd say... I don't want to say you are wrong, but then again you are not right... he (boss) should of fired me... back then, I really needed to get out of my comfort zone to see myself and what is really important...

... privilege... traffic light restraint... I waited for the light to turn green before crossing... others did not as they were in a hurry to get to work so as they may dream about their future summer vacation... at my relaxed pace, I declined to make a run for the train... I have no wrist watch as time is of little importance at this stage in my life... and besides the trains run often enough... headed for a coffee shop instead... found myself a table, where I would have a view of customers coming in and out... I do this for writing inspiration but also, it makes me feel less alone... this morning I find my empathy is running high and out of control... I feel everyone I look at, so I often bow my head... there are other times when I sense people are staring at me... do I remind them of a celebrity or do they see the light glowing in me... I don't recognize this glowing light in me, is it kindness... ?... nope...

... a 30 something child... he sat near the front door and the overhead TV... but awkward like a 12 year old boy, during the clumsy puberty growth phases... he watched TV and the door whenever it opened... the volume was set to off on both... not sure any sound would stop him from fidgeting... he got up and walked in my direction... a small man but with a full set of curly hair that gave him some contradicted height... he walked with a curved back, leaning to the right... he stuttered, if I could give him a cigarette... gently nodding my head as if to say... sorry, no... but always making eye contact with him... I wanted to get into the world inside his head... the husband and wife café owners were quick to reprimand him on how impolite it is to inconvenience customers and that the next time he would not be allowed in the shop... and with this he was quickly back at his table of four... all his friends are sitting in the 3 empty chairs... society's roaming outcast... hookers are the only ones who'd sleep with god's rejects... who can love him?... his frustrated parents?... who riddled him with corporal punishment disguised as love... as they cannot contain their own helplessness in thinking they will die... and leave this adult child to fend for himself... they will not die in peace or ever have peace... with the complicated process of unlocking the cigarette vending machine... and leave a pack on his table on my way out... his world was getting into me from a distance... as is my detached kindness in offering cigarettes...

... random... with no train in sight at the station... I sat on a street bench which allowed me to have a diagonal view of the station... since I knew the next train would be at 9-ish and I did not have a watch... with time on my hands... I watched the station for any indication when I would need to get going...

... commendable... across the street from me was quite a sight... over 40 people waiting in line for the unemployment office to open... most were holding attaches cases, maybe some were recent Christmas gifts as they looked to be in a pristine state... the school bag for adults... though we may be adults, it is sometimes hard to give up our childish notions... unemployed 50-ish... fairly well dressed family men and women... I wonder if any saw their unemployment forthcoming... or were they just struggling with making monthly ends meet that they did not see beyond the tip of their noses... ignorance being bliss, some were probably planning vacations... quite a rude awakening indeed...

... courage... with a woman's bicycle in hand... the man with his pants bottom tucked into his socks to avoid getting caught in the bicycle chain... in one hand a manila colored envelope... probably with a neatly slipped in CV... his homework for the potential employer... with the other hand he chains the bicycle to a post... the old and rusty chain, links his/her bicycle to a solid reality... no young people in line... either it is too early for them or they have taken McJobs somewhere... is coming here a distraction to ease the heaviness of being unemployed... a placebo to cure a depressive mind...

... boxcar... doors are opened by a bland faceless public servant... with

grim faces, a sluggish walk almost like an un-orchestrated funeral procession... struggling for both a synchronized march and dignity... all the while
suspicious of someone else inline getting a job or their job... there is no
brotherly love to be seen in this herd... but just down the street... a Brazilian
woman is giving out flyers and asking passersby if god is in their life... she
certainly is early to rise to do god's work... maybe one from the unemployment flock will be drawn to her calling... a mineable straggler in a weakened
state... isn't this how a dogmatic governmental god likes them...


## 2015/03/17 – Tuesday (Lisbon, Portugal)

... grippe d'homme... nothing like being sick to appreciate health,
though just the flu... but it dampens days, nights and even some aspects of
life... is it because I have a headache and a runny nose that I did not see nor
smelled it... but sure felt it... dog shit... all you can step on, it's free... the two
annoying traits... is no one scoops up their dog's shit... and the street name
signs are for the most part, hard to find... even harder to read during the day
and invisible to the human eye at night...

... un-conditional love... the homeless man who sleeps outside the grocery store has a name... Francisco... I've been giving him food almost every
day and he still looks surprised when he sees me... if I could have just one
wish is that he remembers me... it's an ego thing on my part... but it would
mean a lot to me... if he could distinguish that not everyone is uncaring...
for Francisco, I do not want to be just a face in the crowd... is the respectful passing dog looking out for him?... a connecting sniff, and the animal
moves on to shit elsewhere... just before I hand Francisco some food... an
old woman is lecturing him, that she can only give him 50 cents... he is oblivious to the bitch's condescending words and extends out his palm in quasi
permanence... judging people is like comparing the number of sins we each
carry... I'm always at a disadvantage as I feel I'm the world's biggest sinner...
such low self-esteem cripples me but at the same time assures me that I can
remain humble...

... failed paternal power trip... just a couple of years ago... I did not believe in god... therefore thought I had to do his work here on his earth... by
helping the less fortunate since god was neglecting his responsibilities... or
is it I just liked people especially society's underdogs... homeless people just
like children do not wear masks... they do not worry about being found out

they are fakes… as adults we hide in the self-images we project of ourselves to the world… all fake… what happens when we are exposed?… my marital rupture was a result of my being a fake… faking my marriage as being genuine when it was deceitful… to the proud eyes of my children, their father was a fake… they did not contact me for my birthday… I feel I lost… the people I cherished the most… my walls crumbled but worst yet, my foundations disintegrated…

… esoteric observations… my morning walk is directed by silent intuitions… a city of surprises… hidden treasures… art nouveau in building architecture and landscape… pedestrian's walkways with bistro tables creating an obstacle course… snuggled restos… city parks created before automobiles, which now interrupt traffic circulation… even residential ghettos similar to post-communist eastern block countries… found myself back in this restaurant where years ago I once had lunch… is it to write about the customers eating here… not in the mood to observe lunch time people… so, let them be… my cousin had introduced me to this restaurant… food was terrific, even though he did not eat much as he was in an avid gym training program… which he eventually dropped as he wasn't allowed to smoke while on the treadmill…

… the 50 cent sweetness… the woman next to me in the restaurant is the same one who had lectured Francisco… claiming the fished she had ordered was over grilled/cooked… demanding the waitress have it replaced… a regular customer as the waitress knows her by name… her plate is taken away silently with only her voice clamouring echoes throughout the restaurant… is this the result of old age, frustration or loneliness?… a 60 something… balding woman with a short boyish cut combed back hair… a widow as she is wearing 2 wedding bands… dark tinted glasses which makes her look unfriendly… she wears brown pants… a men's dress shirt hidden by a loose tan colored wool sweater… her frown dissipates as her new fish arrives… friendly words are exchanged with the waitress… since her fish plate came back so quickly… I can only speculate the cook flipped the fish over to the other side and had it returned to her… an optical illusion of happiness…

## 2015/03/18 – Wednesday (Lisbon, Portugal)

… commuter perception… it's somewhere around 8 AM when I pass the coffee shop inside the train station… a city worker wearing his reflective green safety vest is polishing a beer... is this his night cap before going to bed as he has just finished his night shift... or is it his breakfast of champions before heading off to work... neither one of us shows signs of yawning...

... the regulars... there is a certain type of commuter, who stands on the platform at a very specific location... usually middle aged male office workers... when the train arrives they are lined up with the commuter train doors... as if they had made reservations for a specific car/seat... should I be impressed or sadden with the result of such a practice... this is a game where there is no spontaneity... does it, to distract from the pathetic routine... for sure it is... efficiency... in getting to work... but if this is the highlight of his day... then there's no efficiency in life...

... right or wrong... should I sit on the right side of the commuter train and have the ocean view on my way to Lisbon... or do I sit on the left side and look at the manmade manicured landscape... such architecture of opulence only to be interrupted by decrepit buildings... that this opulence came about at the expense of another... commuters shuffling in, looking at empty seats to see if any newspapers were left behind... the only newspapers are the free tabloids which can be picked up at every station... but it seems to be beneath the commuter to do so... but once in the train, even this still free & obsolete tabloid is worth gold... free tabloids left behind on the seats with just enough to read between stations... no one picks them up from the stands in the stations... nor do they want to be responsible in keeping them to drop off in the recycling bins... what if I left my journal entry on the seat... is this part of a book or my final testament... would this scribbled paper be read like a newspaper and/or would someone take it home to further study it... I don't belong here, so many people and so noisy... I'm an alien in your world...

... dimness... metro station darkness... I am different from them in the underground, as I have the time to be here and observe... they are on the move... and I watching the gray metro car with blue doors... like a kid seeing airplanes for the first time in an airport... a metro blind man... walking through metro cars... begging for money... in a clear and explicative voice... with a melodic rhythm... I followed him when he came out of the metro wagon... and he went to the platform on the other side... waiting for another train in order to go back in the direction he came from... are these his stations, his turf... as I have also seen a blind woman in some other stations...

... late 30's... 3 women on a metro car stripper pole discussing their boss... their obese breasts make it difficult to graciously hang on to the post/pole... anyone else around them is free standing as they also make it impossible to squeeze another arm pass them to hang on to the pole... the conversation is a series of verbal attacks on their mutual boss... every lashing brings gleam to their personas as they validate themselves by putting the boss down... if only they could see that their boss... is a confused authoritarian... the boss is even scared to lose her job... insecurity... power struggle with herself and management... but it easier to dehumanize her, it makes the 3 little pigs feel better about themselves...

## 2015/03/19 – Thursday (Lisbon, Portugal)

... answerability... of course to fill our laundry washer up with water we had to connect the hose to a bathroom faucet... on the inner side of the drum was a black line (water mark) to indicate the maximum water allowed in the drum... the filling of the machine was a manual process and someone had to watch it fill up and turn off the water when the mark was reached... as kids, my brother and I were cursed with this boring task... and it goes without say, we were always fooling around and sometimes we were inattentive and the water overflowed... I guess you can already anticipate that from this point on the colher de pau (wooden spoon) came into action as a bonus while we'd mop up the floor with towels...

... fish bowl... why would we put up with the verbal and physical abuse... we were just kids... and we were stuck with this neurotic woman as a mom... no matter how much we mopped up... there was water all over the place and my brother and I were stuck in this cracked fish bowl with her... drowning under her pressure... I may stop, commuting to Lisbon and decide to sleep here in town... it did not go well with Suzanne... and I can see her point of view... her and her home are impeccable... does not matter what I do or where I will live... need I always be restless unless medicated?... the trigger for all this was that I installed some shelves for her... I felt it was like still being married... I did not mind installing the shelves at all, actually I enjoyed it... but the overwhelming feeling was that I let down Emme (ex-wife) and may one day hurt Suzanne too... well, it had me running again... maybe, she is unaware that we are imposing expectations and roles on one another...

... non-chalant... on this particular morning I was heading down to the train station as per usual savouring Suzanne's cold kiss on my lips... but at the last minute decided to have breakfast first before getting on the train to Lisbon... bought myself a newspaper, sipped coffee and let the toasts melt in my mouth... after breakfast, instead of catching the train to Lisbon... walked back to Suzanne's place to install the rest of the shelves... on my walk to her place saw a taxi driver parked and asked for his business card... I installed the shelves, packed my bags and called the taxi... no mess, no fuss, bags in trunk and on my way to Lisbon... joked with the taxi driver... that I was running away from home as the domestic violence was intense and my hand was hurting from so much hitting... the driver was not sure of my humour or caper... to me the logic was undeniable... even to a madman, there is always logic in his actions... how else can we justify, corrupt bankers, politicians, religions and wars...

... unleashed... there is a calmness about me today... almost as if I did not care or worry about anything... a go with the flow kind of day... no watch, train or calendar dictating my pace... and to boot, I feel very mischievous too... yet, I see beauty in ugliness... and there are so many ugly lost souls in downtown Lisbon... but everyone I see, I can find beauty in them, no matter what... European cities have their fair share of public spaces or squares and Lisbon is no exception... where else would the homeless hang around... got to a public square with a gigantic statue of a pompous horsed king... much more imposing than the like of Mussolini or Hitler sepia portraits in train stations and/or presidents portraits in post offices... but not as imposing as my mother stuck in the bathroom with her two sons mopping up... and her swinging a wooden spoon at us... so what did I learn from this experience, surely something memorable which escapes me now...

... the dude... this city square is a meeting place... for the homeless to exchange strategies in extorting money from tourists and share their earnings with the less fortunate... the vents from the underground parking offer warmth and refuge... some vents are big enough to accommodate a family of five... a seller & buyer paradise location for trafficking pot... the latter applies to me... negotiated a chunk of hash with a wannabe Rastafarian Portuguese dude... the kid had class as he left me holding the hash and my cash as we went looking for someone to break a 50 euro note... hash in pocket, I joked with the dude not to deposit the money in a bank... as some people lost their savings because fraudulent banking CEO's got incompetently greedy... why are so many folks at the bottom of the ladder suffering with lost savings... start at the top with the CEO and confiscate his belongings to pay off the lower echelons... even for a CEO, poverty could be a new beginning...

... Neptune & Trident... asked a cop for directions to the nearest tobacco shop, after all he was just standing there probably bored... with mischievous irony in my head, I actually felt like asking if he had rolling paper... he pointed to the round about that had a water fountain with Neptune... that there I would find a tobacco shop... and of course, divinity in all its infinity had the Trident pointing my way to the tobacco shop...

... gift wrap... as kids, our Christmas gifts were never wrapped... and not at every Christmas did we get gifts... I think, it had to do with someone being nice as per the jingle... anyway, just before a happy Christmas, we'd go with my dad and pick out a gift/toy and bring it home and start playing with it immediately... hand in pocket warming and softening the hash... I came upstairs and immediately rolled a joint... mixed a lethal dosage of hash and cold meditation... and thought if I could detach from the physical body... I could look from the outside and maybe see wtf is wrong with me... I felt my spirit trying really hard to separate from the body... struggling to leave but it was chained to the body... it kept yanking the chains in hope they would break... but knew they would not break and this very thought would make it yank the chains again and again... in utter desperation...

... journey... still sitting upright on the sofa... having slept with clothes... woke up feeling cold and startled... in a slow motion setting, went into the kitchen and fried 2 eggs for supper... the house was quiet but I was not alone as I ate... and thought this was a glimpse of what my Camino trek would be like... I must be the mis-understood middle child of my higher self... I no longer want to leave my body and not return... is it too late, as I feel I've never really been in me... I need to live in love and not fear... my parents did the best they could, did I do the best I could with my children... I created bad, but I certainly can create good too...

## 2015/03/20 – Friday (Lisbon, Portugal)

... alone... I suffer in silence with this persistent cold... do not remember ever being this sick due to a cold... could it be this flu and my being in a foreign country... that my immune system has not yet developed resistance... which cure process should I go with... go down to the pharmacy for more medication... or submerge myself in brandy... the latter would only be cost effective (what a culture and country)... but truth be told, I am concerned... and delirious at times with waves of hot flashes and intense sweat... during the day, falling asleep on the couch... and waking up irritated because of sleeping with clothes and still feeling cold... no one, to throw a blanket over me...

... in silence... when I returned from Camino in June 2013... I was not able to sleep, insomnia was my only companion... as all those who knew me, no longer knew me... even I did not know myself anymore... it had gotten out of control... like a wild fire with only smoke... my prediction of Carmen's father being on his death bed... pretty much scared away my entourage... whenever I'd still meet these folks, it was pretty much as awkward as extending condolences at a funeral home... how could I expect them to understand me as I no longer recognized what I had become... I was of no help to anyone or myself... simply fucked... and thought about checking into a mental institution... just drive up to the door and beg them to take me in... instead... in desperation I Googled spiritual help...

... downtown... on a very hot summer night, I found myself downtown looking for the spiritual center... so many people walking around and also sitting on terraces drinking... downtown Montreal has a festive tone especially during summer... I was oblivious to so much happiness around me... not only did I feel like a foreigner in the very city I was born and raised... but completely out of touch with this planet and what I regarded as its' inhabitants... what am I here, where is the old me... on the internet site it was announced they had a workshop at 7H30... I had no idea of the cost and understood very little the workshop content... as I stood in front of the building and thought... if they ask me for an extravagant membership fee plus all the dressings... then this place is not a spiritual center but a place of business... once inside... the $10 fee was to cover expenses for the local and also fund charity work in Africa... the nobility of the place eased my apprehensions...

... the circle... with 2 instructors and a dozen students from truly all walks of life... we sat closely in this large room... the chairs were placed in such a way to form a circle... first we were asked to place our hands on our knees and close our eyes for the meditation... the neurotic thought of my wallet being stolen entered my mind... but was dismissed as I had left it in the car... even in a spiritual place, I still retain vile human qualities... dream like soft music was played... the instructor combining music and with her suggestions... created images of physical relaxation and serenity one can follow in their mind for the purpose of the meditation...

... my agenda... at first I listened to the music and instructor... the floor and my feet became one... but out of nowhere, I found myself zooming away, at top speed from the body sitting in the chair... it took me a while to realize it was my body too... holy fuck... as I moved effortlessly at an incredible speed in a dark space like environment... I saw faces coming at me, at first human than alien... I knew I was not sleeping... and then, everything went pitch black... the next thing I know is that the instructor was raising her voice slightly for me and maybe some other student to comeback... I heard the voice and words, but was slow to make sense of them... eventually, I reopened my eyes with a lot of difficulty, almost resisting the request to do so... we all had a chance to share our meditation experience within the group... most, if not all created images in their minds by what was being said by the instructor... after sharing my experience, I was asked if this happened often... I stated this was the first time I ever meditated... I got the feeling the instructors seemed stumped...

... exercise one... I sat on one of the six chairs, which were turned around to face the wall... those of us sitting were given blindfolds... the lights were turned off... the instructor then placed at random one of the six remaining students behind each chair... those who were sitting, had to non-physically feel the person standing, placed behind us... so, I had to try and hone in on the energy of the person standing behind me... and possibly come up with some sort of message or intuition for this person... and if at all possible, also determine who was the mystery person standing behind my chair...

... the projection... the process, basically involved meditating again and see what I was able to capture in my mind about the person standing behind my chair... with my eyes closed and blindfolded but this time, somehow did not allow myself to get into a deep meditation... I was very self-conscious that my previous meditation was completely different from those in the group... I wanted to blend in with the group and not stick out as a freak... at first I saw a bright light in my mind, almost blinding... it was almost like a cinema show being projected on the inside of my forehead... then the light went off and the place seemed the color of midnight blue...

... then my mind's screen lit up again with snapshot images... a young woman floating in a fetal position... though I could not see her eyes, I knew she was crying intensely... so much sadness in this woman... I physically felt her pain in my stomach... I was becoming her and I needed to back away mentally from her... suicide, suicide, suicide, echoed... she was wishing for death, she wanted to end her pain, she wanted to end her life... this is not me, and I demanded to see the face of the woman floating on my minds' screen... it felt too real and painful... all I wanted was to see her face and get out of the meditation... I was scared shitless... this meditation thing is not for me... I want out... the last image I saw was her face... her eyes sent a jolt of anguish down into my guts...

... real dark... still sitting in the chair, I opened my eyes in the blindfold... I just sat there waiting with my eyelids getting stuck/rubbing into the blindfold... what the fuck is all this... I knew what I saw in my mind was real, this I knew for sure... am I believing my imagination, have I really gone nuts... the instructor spoke, it was as if her voice came on over a loud speaker... only half way into what she was saying did I understand the exercise was over and that those standing were to sit back down and that the lights were gonna be turned on... after which we removed the blindfolds and turned our chairs around...

... a carbon copy without a filter... those who were sitting/blindfolded, now had to share what they saw, if anything... I said it as I saw it... and pointed out to the young lady across on my far left as being the one in my images... with this the young lady got up crying, slurred out a few words to the effect that what I said was true and it was also very personal and that no one was supposed to know... she ran out of the workshop in an emotional state... one of the instructors went after her... the other instructor came to me and in a harsh tone said that whatever intuition I get that I must filter it before speaking it out loud... I could not apologize enough... and repeatedly said this was my first time in a workshop and did not even know what I saw was an intuition... I so much wanted to blend in with the group, but instead found myself having all eyes on me...

... comrade... another student (woman) joined our conversation... the woman said that she too had felt the young woman's pain earlier in the evening, before the start of the workshop... as I looked at this woman now speaking... I blurted out there is an older man in your life who is very mean to you... the student/woman froze and eventually said that her ex-husband was much older than her and they were going through a bitter divorce... the instructor told her to get away as I was capturing all kinds of intuitions and was not able to control them... I felt I was in a mess... I apologized to the woman, and again to the instructor and went looking for the young woman who had run out as I also wanted to maybe explain myself but for sure apologize too... after the workshop, I got a crash course on what was happening to me...

... it has a name... mediumship... what the Camino trek had re-opened up in me was the ability to feel/see things in other people... without using and even going beyond my 5 senses... and the focus is on my third eye as the entry point for perceived info... the third eye being located on the middle of the forehead just above the eye brows... okay... nothing was solved in my life, other than now I did not feel so alone... and someone took the time to listen and explain... but now a new thought was growing in my mind as I went home... if I had an intuition about Carmen's dad coming to the end of his life, plus the fiasco this evening... what if one day, I can foresee the death of my own children... this mediumship gift... is too much power for me...

## 2015/03/21 – Saturday (Lisbon, Portugal)

... lord of the flies... went down to the church this afternoon, was in need of meditation... but the church is closed on Saturday afternoons... I guess god needs a rest too... perhaps after all he may be Jewish like his son... it is not so much that I can't meditate at home... but in the church I feel less lonely... also, the Sao Joao de Arroios church has a very modern architecture... simplistic lines and a concrete if not industrial feel to it... quite a drastic contrast from most of the churches I have visited in my lifetime... though it does have the same feel as the St. Joseph Oratory in Montreal, but with a lot less opulence... so, might as well go back home and meditate...

... god's creatures... as I come out from meditating... I see this swarm of flies, just half a dozen or so... hovering in the middle of my living room... I sink back in the couch and watch them... they are here every day hovering in the middle of the living room... never do they fly around or near me... there is plenty of foods at one time or another on the coffee table... yet, they maintain their aerial trajectory... but the biggest quirk, is at night time they disappear... I never see them and do not have any idea as to where they go... but the next day, they are back... even when I walk through the swarm, they move out of my way... a Moses kind of syndrome when parting the sea...

... exercise two... I continued attending spiritual workshops during the autumn 2013... in one of the workshops we were blindfolded in the hallway... in the main classroom before our arrival, the chairs had been set up haphazardly to act as an obstacle course... also, in the classroom the blinds had been drawn and the lights were off... the instructor led us by the hand one at a time to the classroom door... he opens the door, and tells me to use my third eye as a guide... the objective is walk across the classroom and reach the wall on the opposite side without bumping into a chair... I did not know how to go about this… I took a few steps and felt my hip scratch one of the chairs… it then felt as if I recognized the chair's energy… and from that point on, I navigated across the room and reached the wall unhindered…

… exercise three… we started off with meditation and instead of playing music one of the students is a yoga teacher and she chanted in order for us to meditate… she was able to see our chakras… especially mine as I did not want to come out of the meditation, again… she hovered around me, to breathe hard and to come out of the trance… during the meditation we were asked to focus on the third eye… I came out of this with a headache, but it was an intense feeling and better than any pot I had ever smoked… also learned that evening, the key to communicate with the other side is via meditation… is this my key to communicating with the spirit world… ?…

… practice… next we did the chair exercise again… where I sit down, close my eyes and another student stands behind me… this time I had to get the first letter of the person's name who was standing behind me… what I saw was a white horse and a white unicorn along with the letter H as in Hernani… an exchange student… indeed, he was the one who had stood behind me… Hernani is some sort of monk in San Sebastian (Spain) and in the monastery he only wears white… the instructor believes the unicorn symbol was a symbol for me… a symbol of magic, miracles, purity, innocence and enchantment… at this point, I'd add humility too…

… guide… later after the workshop… the monk Hernani and I sat face to face… he leaned forward, and whispered in my ear in a foreign language… he sounded like an old priest, a very wise sounding voice too… did not understand the words at all, but felt he was taking pressure off me and felt shivers down my back… it was emotional and spiritual all in one… later on he told me he has a vision of me, tearing down barriers… at that moment I equated this with my divorce… but in hindsight, it was beyond the physical world the barriers which he referred to…

… why me… that evening on the way home I wondered… why at this age do these mediumship qualities come to the surface… or did I always have them?… what am I to do with them…

## 2015/03/22 – Sunday (Lisbon, Portugal)

… numb… Suzanne's text message was wreaking anger… chemtrails were being sprayed in Cascais… especially on this sunny afternoon with the beaches being crowded... she was asking if I had seen any planes over Lisbon spraying mind bending toxins... and to stay indoors... lovely thought, is it not... fear is a slavery... and as far as I am concerned, only the physical body is affected by these chemicals... whether I stay in or outdoors, I do not like my body as it's only a temporary shell... luckily, either way I was and am doomed...

... caretakers... if we are served shit but are told it is chocolate... do we know we're getting fucked?... what about the chemtrails this afternoon over Cascais... it's a beach day, most if not all... do not want to look into this conspiracy theory... but is not a theory an educated guess?... the career homeless man in the train station this morning too... looking at the turnstiles with their green and/or red flashing lights... green light you are allowed in, but not with red... with no money nor time... yet his red, shot eyes craving to jump over the turnstiles... with no physical destination whatsoever... but maybe, the turnstile is a portal if he gets through without triggering either colored light... a password of sorts to get to the other side... wait, still waiting and more waiting... his indecisiveness to react is typically human... eventually he must let go of his earthly train ticket...

... expanse... though this body has been brainwashed... I do function well enough in it... but it certainly does not need to be polished and pine scented like a car... it's value is in the mileage, the more the better... I feel and why not even know my soul will betray me... it will leave without me... unless I out smart it... could I do that?... can I get out and hand the baggish outfit of cells suit to my soul on my way out... I could live forever in my thoughts... memories are eternal, no?...

... ambidextrous... at about the age of 12 years old... my brother and I are playing with a tennis ball against a neighbour's bricked house... left being his weak arm, my brother throws the ball and hits the glass window... the sound of glass popping and breaking was also a neighbourhood shriek... a community neighborhood watch affair... with the whisper of broken glass falling... my father comes out to see what has happened... naively honest, as we were never taught to think for oneself... once the blaming fault established... the existentialist question of good versus evil in the same entity became evident... my father's endearing tone of apologetic words promising the neighbour to pay for the damaged window... and with the same breath now void of any oxygen... with such harsh words, that it got my brother running back into our house seeking the illusion of safety...

... architecture... since I did not break the glass... why would I go home... so, I stayed alone in the shelter of the big city street... as my fucken old man gets in the house... he turns around as if he had forgotten an annoying something... his eyes gripped and told me to stop lingering and get in the house too... reluctantly, I followed him into the house... I did not feel whole... I was already breaking up... swooshing away parts of this physical body trapping me inside... we lived on the second floor... once at the top of the stairs, if you turn left is the kitchen and then the bedroom my brother and I shared... and to the right of the stairs are the living room and his bedroom...

... children... reaching the top of the staircase I faced a wall... my eyes focused on the white wall color... I could see all the miniature bumps and ridges which had been imprinted by multiple paint rollers, a silent history of sorts... all the while... my left ear picked out the sounds of my brother crying in bed in entangled whimpering sounds of fear... my right ear... picks out his heavy steps coming towards my direction... I take one step back to my left and lean against the fridge door... the warmth of the cold metal surface presses against my body and soothes me... through the heavy steps... I hear the quiet sound of him folding his belt in half... once folded he pulls both ends and snaps it... a greeting of sorts, an ego power trip of the absurd, a father/man encased in raging isolation... at this point, I did not know if I would get whipped too... but I did not take a chance... I pressed myself harder into the white fridge door... my chameleon proficiency made me disappear... I became one with the fridge... I allowed the compressor vibrations to fuel my heart... to sustain the body, while I stepped out momentarily... my very fear prevents me from saving my younger brother... I hate myself...

... youth?... when I came back... I found myself on my bed looking at my brother lying down on his bed... he was in a near fetal position... the black & blue bumps and ridges on his skin branded the belt mark signature on his back... it caused his skin to ache when stretched and even the bed sheet I put over him was excruciating... my body was intact... my gift of disappearance saved me this time... the little man in front of me was full of fear... the old man was nowhere to be found and probably was also full of fear, alone in his bedroom... even the silent smell in the house imposed fear in any daring airborne molecule... the silence persisted until mother arrived from work... a few adult words could be heard between them... soon after, the mother person is now rubbing oils on his small back to ease his pain and trying to console him... but I feel, he is just a shell now and that my brother is also gone... he managed to escape too...

179

… instant adult… a few days later I was called to the principal's office… he and my brother's teacher wanted to know why my kid brother was walking like a crippled… and I thought… I'm just a kid too… so, fuck off… I miss hugging my own kids… their touch goes through this shell and touches whatever humanity is still left inside of me… otherwise, I would've been long gone…

## 2015/03/23 – Monday (Lisbon, Portugal)

… timepiece… take the time to listen… love you… you love me… you forgive me… forgive you… and this takes me to spend the night with Suzanne… it brings me to a morning dreamy state, allow me to indulge myself in this, during an insomnia interlude… I am losing control, I am unable to worry about my future with regards to mundane issues like employment, income, retirement and so forth… even my plans for the sabbatical year of writing and Camino… seem vague like drizzle in a summer rain… nothing consoles me right now, other than the thought of us…

… sitting with Suzanne in her bed, snuggling in the corner by the window… she leans into me with her back and my arms wrap around her delicate frame… no need to fill my head with thoughts of responsibility… in this exalting zen like moment, our bodies are nothing but an amalgamation of one… *invisible to the eye*… just a loving energy…

… as we look out the window, from your celestial apartment all we see is the tree canopy and the eternal blue sky… what lies beneath the canopy is the chaotic human world… which for the moment we cannot see and therefore all that remains is the reassuring blue of the sky… as we snuggle tightly… we know we do not belong below but above in the vast outer rims of the planet… it is frustrating, even limiting for us to be restricted with a physical body… as if our bodies were a piece of clothing… they (clothing) fall of our essence and we find ourselves lifting and floating away through the window… with no fear of heights, and especially no fear of the unknown… we find ourselves gliding into vastness…

… meia de leite… the day announced itself well, I slept in until 10, and an outstandingly beautiful day too… left for Lisbon with a lingering kiss from Suzanne… went for coffee with newspaper in hand… and read that a newborn baby, if it is deprived of human contact it would first give up eating and eventually die off… it's as if nature, had a humane approach to life and a survival criteria… my afternoon was plagued not by loneliness but aloneness... everywhere I went I saw people and they all had human interaction with one another... I don't want to be alone, but then again I don't want to be here without writing either... as I feel I am wasting precious time... but I do miss her so much...

... flush... I took a nap after speaking on the phone with Suzanne... and slept from 6 to about 7:30pm... I woke up suddenly with her calling out my name in my extremely deep sleeping state... it sounded and felt so real, the tone of her voice was one of alarm... as if to warn me of something... my evening was horrible, such an intense sadness... I felt that while I was sleeping that I had left this planet and there was no coming back... but the sound of her voice pulled me back here... restlessness, sadness and more... ended up at a coffee shop around 9-ish in an attempt to alleviate my morose state... just felt things got worse...

... just got back home... did my night time coffee ritual and then went to work for about 20 minutes of writing... on the walk back home... found myself wishing for a clear blue sky... the night time stars seemed sparse in the sky... this was a warm evening... though slightly breezy... all this to say, as I took in deep breaths of air... I found my olfactory senses searching for her perfume with every puff of air entering my lungs... this is when it dawns on me... how my life is empty without her... I love her, beyond all physical senses...


## 2015/03/24 – Saturday (Lisbon, Portugal)

... set the tone... as a very young man... I had worked for my father-in-law in landscaping... not a wise move when dating the boss's daughter... it was a small company where most of the labourers were Portuguese... and due to the harshness of the work, to say the least they were not the most refined lot of people... on my first day of work... I got picked on because I did not know how to handle a pick/shovel or mix mortar and dated the boss's daughter too...

... a tall silence... he was a Frenchman... born and raised in Quebec... he saw me struggling, and said to me with a sly smile... puis Fernando... with these two simple words he set the tone about the absurdity of work in general and probably life as well... I felt like I had gained an ally who merited my outmost respect... though he came across as a mild mannered man... he was a force to be reckoned with... what he did as work did not matter, as all that counted was what was inside his mind... the body is a tool and it can handle work... with our lunch time chats that followed... his charisma has touched me in such a way... it is/was a life lesson... for it (life) is an absurd concept and all we can do is simply laugh...

... my turn... when I looked and listened to my Portuguese co-workers... always having fun at my expense... but then it goes too far, as they are downright malicious... in my infinite wisdom, it is never their fault... but the fault of their mothers who gave birth to them... I imagine these workers growing up on some third world rural farm back in Portugal... and their mothers getting up early to milk the cows... the husband (father) would do it... but it would be traumatizing to see similarities between the cow's and his wife's nipples... besides, the husband is nurturing a hangover with his thumb in his mouth or in his itchy asshole... either way, the IQ is the same...

... rise and shine mommies... in the early hours of dawn... they train with a milk canister on their heads... and later on in the day the water jug is a chapeau for an afternoon outing... all this is part of a rigorous non-olympic physical training... mind you it is not just training... the afternoon trek also involves socializing by the public water fountain... where a herd of head wrapped in a handkerchief mommy babes gather to exchange pleasantries during the bitch club reunions... such as malicious gossip... lament about their hardships especially about the husband thing they married and of course their unruly children who happen to be a spitting image of the moronic father...

... progeny... all bitching aside the mommy heads back home/hut with the water jug skillfully balanced on her head... once she has killed the chicken... plucked and now boils the water she just carried... to wash the chicken and get it cooked for the ungrateful family supper... of all those who will be at the table for dinner... the chicken is the only one who washed... the last of the remaining water is used to wash dishes... if there's enough water leftover, maybe she'll wash her feet before getting into bed... but it is not a big deal, just a perk... as she (mommy) lays in bed... looking at the lump of a husband lying next to her... who did not listen to a word she said all night... she wonders, about her life and prays to god to help her get out of it... considering god is supposedly a man too, odds are he hears her as much as her husband does... maybe her landscaping laborer son will save her one day...

... career choice at 50+ age... I was waiting for the traffic light at the intersection to turn in my favour... being perched high up in my van/truck I looked into the lane and saw a man popping open the dozen or so recycling bins… scavenging for what I would perceive to be plastic gold… in the very last one, he finally found a coke bottle… in a very relaxed pace he headed back to the bicycle leaning against the wall… placed his new found bottle in one of his saddles… to be more accurate, worn out plastic grocery bags… disturbing as this scene may be, he is someone's son… for me it was more unsettling cause the man seemed to be my own age… was he here by choice?… what went wrong in his life… or was this the lifestyle he aspired to?… or was it simply the born at the wrong place and time scenario… is there a fate for the poverty stricken and a fate for the well off?

… balance… what does the bank and church have in common?… they are both houses of worship… don't remember where I picked up this line… but suffice to say it had an impact on me… why does my bank CEO earn over 11 million per year… does anyone really deserve such a salary for milking my money… and not making any of it trickle back down to the trodden?… and that pope chap in the Vatican indulging in absolute opulence… in my youth during the catechism indoctrination… the brief cameo appearance of the Christ character preached socialism and not capitalism… does the pope really need robes stitched with gold… I am sure if he shopped on Chabanel schmata street on a given Saturday morning, he could find a robe at a bargain price…

… still my turn… until the CEO or pope fall off their pompous thrones… I'll take it upon my bleeding heart to improve things within my scope… my intervention will be a grain of sand in an hour glass… but it is a start and even if time flies…

## 2015/03/25 – Wednesday (Lisbon, Portugal)

… exhaustion… if I were to make it as far as the edge, have I gone far enough… actually why limit oneself by stopping on the edge… why not push the envelope… would falling be bad… simply because it is perceived as being bad?… why not make the best of it and enjoy the fall… can't this be another type of getting high as you go down?…

… new direction… all newborns, no matter where… all have one intrinsic ability in common… to suck, preferably a female nipple too, it would assure survival… if the infant already has everything he/she needs to survive… why then the thirst to learn and acquire more… is this also part of the programming, to seek learning and experiencing… I love and adhere to this unquenchable drive... when did the drive reach the edge... what happened to us, that we have now stopped... is it because we are adults or cowardly fools?... I dare you to have the courage to walk into a retirement home during meal time... watch seniors resort to sucking their food through a straw... as humans is this the full circle of physical life?... fuck, I refuse to believe and/or accept this outcome... if and when I reach the edge, I will jump, not because I am insane... but the contraire as I will not finish my days here as I started them...

... straw-less... there will always be edges to what we do... you jump off one and another edge shows up... this is simply incredible, and what a ride to... what differentiates us from any other species is that we can have the ability to jump... and even enjoy the ride... this is what it means to be human... as always, true living is taking chances, risks... even if means failing too... laugh at failure... better yet, my very own failures... cause these are the funniest... this journal is a failure, what the fuck do I care... and for my food, I don't want a straw just yet but would not mind a nipple or two to gnaw on...

... boyhood... on my 2013 Camino trek... walked a few kilometers with a Greek chap by the name of Kostas... the mid 40-ies man was in turmoil... his girlfriend wanted matrimonial commitment... and he was still a boy at heart... we walked most of the morning together... he was probing my mind, as I had been married for 30+ years... the novelty and longevity of my marriage appealed to him... I did not open up with him, as I did not tell him I was on the verge of a separation... I figured, let him enjoy it and find out like the rest of us, that nothing lasts forever...

... GPS... as we walked, conversation ensued intensely... and because he was adamant that we use his GPS to direct us on the Camino path... we ended up missing a crucial turn... as I looked at the mud ahead of me on the dissipating path... I did not see any foot prints from other pilgrims who had supposedly walked this path earlier that day... instead I saw small claw imprints in the mud... a dog or deer I thought, hopefully not a wolf... the road-ish path came to an abrupt end... a cliff, with sliding mud... he wanted to continue... I pointed out the lack of human foot prints... he paused, and put his GPS back in his pocket... what is the point of rubbing it in that we screwed up... we walked back about 4.5 kilometres... at which point we found a yellow arrow pointing westerly... our error totaled 9 kilometres and over half a day's walk in pouring rain... let it be... laugh it off...

... pause... we ended up in a restaurant mid-afternoon for lunch... as we sat and ate, my mind was being made up... as not to get involved with anyone on my pilgrimage... I let him know that after lunch, I was going to go solo on the walk... Kostas left and I found myself alone, looking out the restaurant window... I actually found beauty in seeing the rain run down on the glass window... a tall Germanic man enters the restaurant huffing and puffing... he throws his backpack into a chair and sits down next to it... exasperating his hot breath in frustration... besides being tall, lean and apparently in very good shape... he looked to be well into his 70's with a full set of gray hair... a bygone poster boy for the Aryan race... part of me was saying to mind my own business... but I got up anyway and went over to talk to him...

... barriers... I asked him if he spoke French or English... he said he was more inclined to English... at which point I asked him if everything was alright... he said... it has now been three days that he started his pilgrimage and the rain has not let up... tired and wet, he is not sure if coming on this trip was a good idea... I said, that the Camino will first break him physically, emotionally and eventually the spirit cracks too... then between small chit chat to make him laugh... I let him know that I had just made a 9 kilometer blunder and laughed it off... I said the most important thing in this pilgrimage is that our hair looks nice even when wet by the rain... he looked at my bald head... and with a slow reaction, laughed out loud...

... sign language... as his lunch arrived... I got up to leave and get on with my walking... I looked at him... and pretending to spit into my palm... I ran my hand with the make believe saliva over my bald head as if I were styling hair... he laughed and I then waved good-bye... days later I saw him outside another village... he just looked at me... pretended to spit into his palm and ran his hand through his hair... we both laughed but never exchanged a word... I knew he was doing well...

## 2015/03/26 – Thursday (Lisbon, Portugal)

... easter break... so many kids with their grandparents... on the streets and in any bistro that can appease the kids for a sweet re-fueling and also resource tired old feet... from the look of some grandparents... an afternoon of TV for the kids and a siesta for them... it will be a long day for them, but at the end these old folks will say that it was fun having the kids... and so, this is family life... Suzanne is a high school teacher... and I do get quite an earful from her about rowdy kids... but at the same time, there is always two sides to a coin... some kids probably need a break from frustrated teachers whose wages have been frozen for nearly a decade... is it not a contradiction and even an insult government corruption abounds as public servant wages are frozen .

... snowball effect... watching all these kids gulping industrial dosages of sugar laden cakes... these kids are so full of life... at their age I was introverted and so quiet... even in a classroom I would find myself resting my head on the desk with closed eyes... and plunge into a serene state of mind blocking any outside noise whether human or not... with my head down and my closed eyelids pressing against the desk top... I drifted from this body...

... indoor blackboard... I began to see a light show projections on the inside of my eyelids, geometric shapes in a kaleidoscope background... it is almost like a 3-D visual effect... please note, no hallucinogenic drugs were tested on animals prior to my usage (lol)... yes, it is all me floating inside my head... I get a flashback to my second grade teacher Miss Moore (aka fucken mean bitch) holding her pointer stick to the blackboard and talking about point A and B in space... and if you join these 2 points you get a segment and then she goes on about rays, plains and geometric eternity...

... emergent... all this geometry means nothing to me... and I absolutely have no sense about abstract points in space, certainly not at this tender age... as my 7 year old mind wanders off to glimpse the reality of the tangible sunshine rays coming thru the window... it's beauty and almost palatable calling... I find this zen moment came to a complete halt by the tears gushing out of my eyeballs... as I see her pointer stick thru my blurry vision winding up again with a whiz sound... and coming back at my hands resting on the desk... as I look down at my hands I see the stick impact on my fingers and leaving its' redness imprint signature...

... recess... my solitude continued in the school yard during recess... but at least I was *adult free*... the teacher tells us to go out and play... and after recess we would go to the bathroom... which even in my young mind made sense... since we'd be thirsty from being outside and upon returning to class I'd stop to have a drink from the water fountain which was located in the bathroom area... all good... not... when the bell rang drastically announcing the end of recess... we had to line up in front of the school in two parallel lines and enter the building in an orderly fashion... yep, seven year old military core... of course the line was crooked and rowdy too... fuck we were kids, and all boys too... we were punished by having our bathroom privileges rescinded... can you imagine, the lethal combination of full bladder and thirst... I ended up peeing in my pants while in class... and to add insult to injury, I was still thirsty... who put this adult in charge?...

... time... at my young age, the only... *point*... my parents insisted upon was that everything could be explained by simply saying... *god's will*... this was a conversation stopper in our household... if I could go back to 1967, I would say to her (teacher)... not to envy or shatter my naïve wonderment about the world... nor vent her frustrations on me simply because the lithium free batteries in her vibrator went dry before her climaxing... take your phallic pointer stick and shove it where need be...

... influence... as my mind re-hashes *(interesting choice of words here, no?)* her geometry lecture... tonight it finally became... *oh! so clear...* an epiphany of geometric proportions began projecting within my eyelids... I finally understood what she talked about in grade two... as I shut down the computer... for a second or so I saw my reflection on the screen... I wonder... if I connect her letters, point A and B... will my head be somewhere in space permanently?...


## 2015/03/27 – Friday (Lisbon, Portugal)

... sweltering... what a hot day... while here in this Lisbon terrace as I sit facing the Atlantic ocean within the reach of my breath... god, it is breath taking... foreigners pacing about unsure where to sit, or look... completely out of their comfort zone... with phones in hand... taking pictures awkwardly... to bring back home... to show others what a great time they had... as they show and bore their office colleagues with the miniature picture of the grandiose Atlantic ocean on their intelligent hi-tech primitive phone... ironically, they think to themselves how anxious they were to get home when they're away... but somehow need to prove to the viewer how great a time they had and even to themselves...

... vacation... why do people travel... every moment seems stressful... the constant feeling of getting lost... the language barrier when they did... and worse of all... the food, so foreign and at times unsatisfying... this is when they would indulge in a bag of cookies brought from back home... the comfort food of the gods... as if the real god lived only in their now foreign home country... like any true god... the entity always finds an excuse to abandon you in a moment of need... gotta love the deities... they never go on vacation with you... can't afford the expense... let alone the hassle...

... jealousy... tourists with money and little else to show... the echoing repetition of the mis-pronounced words read off the menu... the waiter looks at them with an air of contempt... even though his attitude is what they (tourists) will take home to describe the people of the country... the waiter is an ambassador... who bites the hand that feeds him... what an arrogant envious motherfucker... but I gotta love his attitude... the poor but proud ego... all show now, but when at home he looks out the window as the cold night air rushes in... and wonders when he will see the money in his hands to replace the faulty window and shelter his child from the cold... it is at this moment he feels humble, and perhaps reflects why he is one of the have not of this unjust world... little does he realize he is a struggling parent... like any other...

... fatherly love... our arrogant waiter swallows his pride and humbly immigrates to an industrialized country... as the love for his motherland is unquestionable but at the same time the motherland is a bitch when it comes to provide a quality life... an outcast in a new land, he makes Quebec his new home... his bank savings are the barometer of his success... months later, he has more money than he ever had during his whole life and hence his new religion emerges too... the sweetness of money now brings his family to join him too... in the new country his children grow up as he grows down...

... make belief... our waiter is now a senior citizen... his children are somewhat ashamed of their roots... the father is a reminder of the old country... they see the old country as a place to visit one day, but not more than that... out of sight, out of mind... the children drop off the father in the Portuguese community center in Montreal... an old elementary school refurbished into both a new church and retirement home... the rest of the building becomes the community center for the undesired parents...

... for whom the bell tolls... converted classrooms are now home to all sorts of activities/courses... the old and aging are ushered into the new life of the classrooms... since the whole community center was the mastermind of caring Catholics... the whole place is bombarded with all kinds of religious symbols... one would of course expect crucifixes... but they were bought in such large bulk quantities... that in some of the old classrooms every wall has its' own crucifix... in the evening, some of the classrooms are dedicated to arts & crafts... quite a noble undertaking... keeping seniors citizens out of mischief by catering to their creative side...

... idle hands and the devil... can you imagine these seniors roaming our city streets spreading gossip of all sorts... and probably end up in some Azorean grocery store in the basement consuming beer, smoking cigarettes...

and obnoxious conversations where nothing is discussed other than contradicting one another... not good... better off keeping these old bastards busy and what better way than... to have them cut out crucifixes from cardboard and have them paint it afterwards... but now the dilemma... to find a wall on which to hang this newly made crucifix... as every classroom already has an abundance of crucifixes...

... nearly Easter... of course... they can take their (crucifix) to their children's house when the rare Easter Sunday lunch invitation comes in... this is when these old folks scrape off the mothballs from their suit, (the good suit, coffin ready version) and go out to lunch with family... on the way, they try to remember the grand children names... and perhaps they will give their newly made colored paper crucifix with a Portuguese inscription to one of these little kids... but thanks to Bill 101 the little kids of oppressed immigrants are now attending brainwashing French elementary schools... anyway... these cute little bastard type grand kids will denounce our hero (waiter, father, immigrant and now useless grandparent) to the St. Jean Baptiste Society whose new mandate will now probably include religious crucifying policing along with Italian pasta menu surveillance...

... nowhere... what an incredible shit load of verbose waste I just typed... maybe our waiter is better off accepting the unjust world and remain in Lisbon... for me this is another boring Friday afternoon... let's see what is playing at the movies later on before nostalgia fever sets in, and I start, missing my kids...

## 2015/03/28 – Saturday (Lisbon, Portugal)

... fortunate... woke up this morning thinking about where I am... besides being in Lisbon, and living a bohemian type of life style... I wonder about my family and friends whom I left behind... none understood that I wanted to live a dream now... and not like them, when they'd retire... while they are back home saving money, I am here in good health... and modestly spending the savings I have accumulated over the years... at the end of the sabbatical year, I may not have any money to sustain this lifestyle... but I will have the memory of it... as time goes by... I do not care if I die, it is after all just a body... I now know enough to believe I will live on eternally... and that this physical life is just that, a physical life... the real beauty is in the essence form... and I hope to feel and even see more next month while on Camino trek...

... times past... my Lisbon apartment is a living history... the creaky floor planks... the echo of the high ceiling rooms... plaster mouldings and cornices... cracked walls and flaking paint chips... poorly lit doorways with grinding hinges from the heavy wooden doors... a unique scent of humidity emanating from the plastered walls... but best of all the music is playing loud... Madredeus – Guitarra... the guitar calling from afar... which carries ones' spirit throughout the house until the music is found... and yes, this is an exquisite song... it makes me want to lift my arms and fly away like an angel... up and above is where I belong...

... flashback to 1978/79... I would like to take this moment to apologize to my downstairs neighbours for imposing... my Punk music (mainly Sex Pistols and Ramones)... as their daily breakfast music for many months... in retrospect, eating cereal to these fast and aggressive beats... got them out of their house quickly... I am sure my dear neighbours were either anxious to get to work... or come upstairs to punch me out and kick the speakers in... if the latter was the case... then I once again, apologize for not hearing the doorbell... music was so fucken loud... sorry...

.... music catalog... and now, re-direct this story to the present and then another past... random music... my Ipod is programmed to play randomly one of almost 3 000 songs... I like the fact that there are no pre-programmed music playlists... one never knows what will be the next song nor the type of music... classical, rock, alternative, pop, soul, new age, etc... suite... I have a tendency to always associate songs with a time/event in my life... AC/DC - Hells Bells... brings me back to 1980/81, when I was travelling thru Europe on my motorcycle and ended up in the south of France for a few months...

... self-centered 20 something... like in any good story, there should be some element of romance... sorry, this is not a good story, so one has to settle for lust... nothing could be more palpitating/exciting for a travelling delinquent then to meet a French girl for a short lived infatuation smothered in both physical & mental sexual innuendos... it seemed like an eternity of endless sleepless nights... that's how powerful lust can be... come to think of it now... I would drink REDBULL, if it contained lust instead of caffeine... anyway... she started her grocer job at 6:30 in the morning... so by 6AM we were already in the bistro ordering café-au-lait with hot croissants...

... stamina... after a night of obsessive debauchery/passion and not more than an accumulated total of 19 minutes of interrupted sleep... I was to say the least and understandably so, simply tired & sore... I needed to wake up and/or be more alert... cause I would be driving her on my motorcycle to her work place... of all things, the bistro had a juke box... I would borrow a franc (French currency) from her, cause I was always conveniently broke... I always selected Hells Bells by AC/DC... because it was the only English song in the jukebox...

... priority... with music playing and as I was about to sit down at our table... I placed both my hands on the table to assist myself to sit/lower myself down (remember, I am tired & sore)... she would clasp my hands with hers and gaze into my eyes in a dreamy awe... now I can understand her point of view... cause I know, that even back then I was adorable... but in front of me is my café-au-lait & hot croissant... which I cannot eat/drink because she is still holding both my hands... the coffee aroma is intoxicating me and triggering my inner voice to scream inside my head...

... linguistic conflict... though all my schooling was either in English/French... my inner voice always speaks to me in an Portuguese... perhaps I should consult a linguist spiritual psychiatrist on this... but I am afraid this may open a whole new can of worms... interestingly enough... my inner voice kept reminding me... only my visual and olfactory senses were enjoying breakfast... to further enhance my distraction from hunger... I paid attention to the song lyrics... how coincidental and/or improbable... is it that this was the only English song in the juke box... to a certain extent the lyrics are fittingly a propos about my lustful hunger ordeal... yep!... life is still good cause it has an ironic or even sarcastic sense of humour...

## 2015/03/29 – Sunday (Lisbon, Portugal)

... camaraderie... as a teenager I got a lot of slack from my friends back when... because I listened to French Quebecois, punk and classical music instead of the corporate rock like Styx, Toto, Bad Company, Queen etc... music which they remained loyal to and so did I... but how can one only listen to one type of music, why limit oneself...

... withdrawn... as a kid in the 60's... in our house we had CFQR radio station playing constantly off some big brown cabinet radio unit... mostly smooth easy listening type of music... being quite an introverted kid, absolutely not a team player by any means, while my brother stepped out to play street hockey... I enjoyed the solitude of a Sunday afternoon and the music...

I'd dissect the song/music... almost feeling I'd be able to oversee the recording and even improve it... on other occasions, I would turn the dial, seeking the faintest sound and listening for anything out of the ordinary... maybe aliens like me are doing the same elsewhere...

... not my world... I was arrogant perhaps even elitist but things of this sort, just come to me naturally... and don't you know it, my happiness had an expiry date... that is until a parental unit stepped into the room and order me to go outside for fresh air... in hindsight, these being typical Sunday afternoons... odds are they (parental units) wanted to be fruitful and multiply... no new siblings ever came from their encounters...

... the peasants... I ended up joining my brother who was playing street hockey... my elitist curse as a kid... was that I would look at street hockey as no more than running after an orange ball... I completely failed to see/enjoy the intricacy of the sport... in retrospect, I really missed out... but even today, I still feel the sport to be redundant... guess, I am truly wired differently... and am still, in no way a team player...

... solution... as an adult, when once upon time I was married... in our bathroom at home... I had set up a radio that when you enter the bathroom and switch on the light... the radio comes on and the dial is set on CJPX 99.5 classical music... so whenever I am sitting on the porcelain throne... classical music accompanies me in all my endeavours... I am to a certain extent like one of Pavlov's dogs trained to associate bowel movements to classical music... perhaps drugs are in order... as long as they are of an organic nature... my body is a temple, blah, blah blah... no evil goes in me, but sure does come out...

... benchmark... music is the only thing that makes and takes me everywhere... it triggers memories of both time and place... I guess we all have songs which mean something to us... from joyous moments to regrets... but in the end it is nothing but a memory... but life being what it is... aren't memories all we end up with...


## 2015/03/30 – Monday (Lisbon, Portugal)

... furious... as an elementary school kid... my walking to school was generally a bullying festival... on my way to an English school, I would meet French kids on their way to a French school... derogatory words were heard, with weather permitting snowballs flew as anger projectiles and occasionally

fists were shared... this was my introduction that territorial linguistic posses-
sion was not limited to cats spraying piss to mark their territory...

... apology... I really don't see an issue here... I was born in Montreal
(1960, Notre-Dame hospital, in the gay ghetto) and am of Portuguese extraction... therefore, in an ascending geographical pattern, first I am Montrealer,
Quebecer, Canadian, but this means nothing to me... I am Pur Laine, cause
I was born in Quebec... this is MY definition of a Pur Laine... but if the definition of Pur Laine is that your ancestors came from France during the colonization of Quebec and pushed out of the way any Amerindians who spoke
up... well, then sorry... as none of my ancestors were prostitutes, mentally
handicapped, or jailed criminals shipped off to the Nouveau Monde... all my
ancestors have in common with these first colonists is poverty...

... what matters... is that I'm a citizen of this beautiful planet and stuck
here as in everywhere else with petty small minded ridiculously absurd humans who make politics a religion... simply put, I was born a human with the
only instinct to suck on a nipple or any facsimile... whether language, some
form of nationalism or religion these are all manmade institutional concepts
that one either acquires thru education or stumbles upon thru birth... nothing belongs to me and the best part is that I belong to nothing...

... anthems... while in elementary school... in the very late 60's with the
advent of Expo 67 and perhaps the Révolution tranquille indirect influence...
there was a wave of patriotism in school... maybe the directive came from
higher up, I simply do not know... what is for sure... is that every Friday after
the lunch bell... we would line up in the school yard and prior to going back
to class we would first sing the national anthem...

... advertisement... now, this is where the pleasant memory kicks in for
me... keeping in mind, that mini-skirts were in fashion... my classmates and
I would line up in front of the gallery that lead into the main office... the
stairs and deck were made from steel, and the platform was constructed with
evenly spaced bars... the teachers would stand on the metal platform and
initiate the singing of the anthem...

... out of tune... though I am musically inclined, this song (anthem) did
not do it for me... what did it for me were the 4 legs of 2 teachers wearing
mini-skirts... which one could see thru the bars... along with a handful of intellectual 7 year olds... after the singing, we would rush and push each other
to get under the metal gallery and look up thru the bars and see the teachers
underwear... as if we saw anything... what came out of this nonsense was the

uncontrollable laughter when one would brag that he saw a brown stain on the undies...

... anthems & advertising... it is not money, business or governments that are the issue as these are just invented tools for our era... no, it is the most basic element which is the human being and its' series of emotions/desires... control, thoughtlessness, greed, primary self-interest and selfishness etc... and sometimes if we can revive emotions such as empathy and kindness... then maybe there will be hope for un-slaving humanity...

... new anthem... in the meanwhile, we will be confronted with adverse situations that can start as early as in the family home to religion, dogmas, political ideologies, anthems and billboard advertisements... and the list can go on ad nauseum... the irony being, history has and will always repeat itself... though the outcome for humanity may be unsure... what is for sure is that the planet/universe will go on... with or without us... are we really that important in the grand scheme of things or are we just conceited...

## 2015/03/31 – Tuesday (Lisbon, Portugal)

... eternity... this long lasting cold is getting worst, I can't seem to get better... first fever and now, I have this rash developing all over my skin... must be an allergy, but to what... as I sit here in this ugly coffee shop, alone with my thoughts... sipping an espresso that will prevent me from sleeping again... but the reason why I'm here is because I fear going to bed and sleep... the loneliness and now my being sick combined... makes me fear to go on living... at my age of 55... I know enough  that there is no one woman who can ever make me happy... the solution is not an external one... but in fact something that needs to be corrected on the inside... feeling too sick to go and join Suzanne at her place... guess I'll stay alone in Lisbon tonight...

... living dead... is it because I'm alone and weak... that my head is filled with lost souls again... I'm tired of just feeling your anguish in my head... I need to see you... I need and want you to be good, despite my fears... I feel this is right... I've always known it, why do you torment me in the evenings... where are those who haunted me at home when I came back from the Camino... why home and not here and now... so many compassionate stories for humanity's strife... leave me in a perpetual restless state of being... I think the best approach for me... would be to share with you... what goes on in my head and surroundings... I am hoping this will give you some insight into me... but at the same time... I do fear you would find me boring... after all you are in another world... but is it better than this one... or are you still stuck here in some way... in my head to be precise...

... just the living... my line of work in home renovation... I deal a lot with elderly people, gays, single moms and plenty of single/divorce people... and I sense vibes... that all they want is some sort of acknowledgement... I have noticed that sometimes, some women even dress up when I come around for a second time... and I always say a kind word... though it is a small gesture for me, it seems to make their day... and perhaps who knows, it gives them the boost to get back into dating... on very rare occasions... I did pick up flirting tones and I know it was more desperation on their part than anything else... I cannot take advantage of their weakened state nor am I the solution to their anguish... if anything, I could just complicate matters... I don't think with my penis as it gets me in trouble.... I know, I am far from handsome... but I am funny with a certain charismatic appeal... and when I step into their homes in clean professional clothes and before seeing any customer, I spray a little perfume, and am in a healthy physical shape, etc... compared to most 55 year olds... I am one notch above most and I may come across as a catch... but I am not... inside, I'm so fucken flawed...

... lurking... the last job I did was the renovation of a 20+ year old bathroom... spent over a year negotiating this contract... the husband did not want to renovate anything, the wife on the other hand wanted the old bathroom gutted and re-built... money was not an issue for these professionals... one summer day, out of the blue the lady calls me to start the bathroom job... it was sort of an emergency and that I start it quickly... when meeting up with them, my experience told me he was not in a good mood but had agreed to the renovation...

... vengeance... the first day of work... I removed/stripped the bathroom... he had asked me to discard everything except the dingy 20 year old toilet... since it was the customers who had purchased the materials... I noticed there wasn't any new toilet... when I asked them where it was... he said to re-install the old one and I saw the silent tears on the wife's face... I thought he was joking... but in seeing her tears, I knew I was trapped in this spousal drama... for the next 8 days until I finished the job... she would drop in and see how the work was progressing... red eyes, sniffles and a running nose and heavy sighs was all I heard when installing the shower, vanity and high end ceramic tiles...

... latrine... with daily tears still flowing... should I cross the line and listen to her with a compassionate ear and/or offer her a hug… can I maintain my professional composure and not get involved… certainly, it is not me who can ease this pre-retirement couple's marital woes… my reasoning, are they together out of love or spite… the latter, by all accounts… with a brand new and shiny bathroom completed, the only outstanding item was the toilet… I offered the man to purchase and install a new toilet at my expense… he refused and insisted I install the old one… the old toilet was an eyesore to the new bathroom as he was/is to his wife…

… origins… the husband created such a negative atmosphere… every time he uses the bathroom he will gloat that he won some sort of power struggle with her… the bathroom to her, despite the extensive renovations… she will not see the beauty of anything, only the ugliness of the toilet… are they living dead souls still in a human form… not sure… what I am sure, once these people die… they will be like the living souls now visiting me in my head…

* * *

# APRIL

PART SIX

## 2015/04/01 – Wednesday (Lisbon, Portugal)

... uncanny... I'm plugged into my headphones... hoping it will distort all my senses as I walk around the apartment in pain and alone... not sure I have the flu, but something worse... if this is what retirement feels like when one suffers from an old age chronic illness... then please shoot me and put me out of my misery... also, and this I feel very strongly about too... if I ever walk around wearing Bermuda shorts, white tube socks and open toe sandals... then please and I insist upon this... shoot me too, put me out of my fashion *faux pas*...

... sympathy... I feel so miserably sick and alone... I feel like going back to Montreal... somehow I think there is someone there who can take care of me and even console me... I must be delusional to even think this... I'd be more alone in Montreal than I am in Lisbon... I spoke with Suzanne on the phone and told her I was still ill with the flu... did not tell her that I was in really bad shape... did not want to worry her... today, the weather outside is very hot and sunny as I sit on my 5th floor gallery... so much traffic noise below and above every so often I hear and see a low flying plane on its' way from or to the nearby airport... I try to replace my negative thoughts with happy ones...

... airport 2014... last November when I flew into Portugal... had to fly in via another European /London city as there are no more direct charter flights... met up with Suzanne once I landed in Lisbon and we drove to her home in Cascais... in the evening in the midst of all the excitement with regards to my arrival... we headed down to Dom Pedro for ribs... a few giggles, many caresses and lustful eyeing one another... all this marinated with several glasses of sangria... needless to say... as we walked back home... we needed each other for support, because of all the laughter, booze and fatigue... we were quite drunk... how we made it home is quite fuzzy as a memory... but I did remember her saying she needed to brush her teeth... but the next thing you know we are both slouching on the couch with only enough strength to remove our shoes and nothing else...

... airport 1981... on a return trip... it was a traumatic experience for a non-recovering member of AA such as myself... this was a while back, at Mirabel airport (returning from Portugal alone) I was waiting for my one suitcase... as I huddle against the luggage carousel with another Portuguese grandmother... her cart already contained 5 suitcases & 4 cardboard boxes tied with string and duct tape...

… obvious… I knew she was Portuguese cause she was dressed in black & had one long & wide eyebrow, a mole on the left cheek with tentacle dangling hairs… I remember this cause I switched sides to avoid seeing the mole… even though I was now on her right side… the mole hair was still within my peripheral vision… and of course, her delicate perfume was called *naftalina velha* or *old mothballs* for the rest of us…

… churn… as I was bending over to retrieve my luggage from the carousel… I sense an unearthly presence next to me… it was the Portuguese granny and her mole hairs brushing up against my face… I froze and felt shivers of repulsion running up & down my spine as I was grabbing my suitcase off the carousel… at this very moment she was going under my arm to reach her masking taped suitcase passing under me… with all this commotion I dropped my suitcase on hers…

… misplaced guilt… from this point on, things got worse… the bottle of moonshine I snuck in illegally broke inside my suitcase… and the whole area smelled like *agua-ardente*… or if you prefer moonshine… being quick minded, I now needed an innocent alibi… so I waited and helped the granny get all her luggage… and we pushed our carts together towards the last customs control… as we handed our customs cards to the last agent… this is where I pulled an actors' performance worthy of an Oscar…

… humanitarian… just like when you fart in public… and raise your head and look around pretending you did not fart and trying to figure out who did it… *just replace the word fart by agua-ardente in the previous statement*… with my nose making intense snorting sounds and my head held high in the gesturing/pointing towards our granny… she got pulled aside for baggage inspection and I went thru… as for the granny, odds are she was sneaking *chorizo* and *carapau* and probably deserved to get pinned… once home I got on all fours and licked any wet moonshine piece of clothing dry and then attacked soaking up the suitcase itself… maybe, my being sick now has to do with karma… maybe my whole life has to do with karma too… it sure feels like it…

## 2015/04/02 – Thursday (Lisbon, Portugal)

… magnify… the freshness of the toilet bowl water soothes my aching sweaty head… I spent the morning throwing up… I'm no medical genius but now I'm sure this is not a simple cold/flu… these rash marks are increasing too, every morning when I wake up there are more blisters... but it must be a good sign of sorts that my appetite has not been affected... so, I ventured out to the grocery store for supplies... I have this unpleasant feeling of being high from the fever... my head feels extremely morphine light... as I walk through the grocery store and I can't seem to remember what I needed to buy... picked up some fruit and ready-made food...

... sympathy... coming out of the store I look down the street to see if I spot my homeless man, as I wanted to give him some food I just bought... I'm walking home and looking backwards when I walk into a lamp post with full impact... I got startled from the crunch noise my nose made against the post... now, every time I touch my nose bridge, it hurts and makes a crackling sound... did I now fuck up my nose cartilage too... I wonder, would the homeless man be sympathetic to my suffering or would he just stick out his hand out as per usual... I believe there is a code of honor amongst homeless folks to help those in need...

... mockery... if a fly is trapped in a garbage can is it hell or paradise?... like a heart attack during an orgasm, are you coming or going... or in my case, being sick while on a sabbatical... mind you this is my second sabbatical... when I was a mature 20 year old... I shipped my motorcycle to Portugal and from there rode into Spain & France and hitch hiked into the UK... cause towards the end of my one year travelling sabbatical, money was running out too... what memories this brings back... travelled thru Europe on my motorcycle and spent quite a bit of time in the south of France... met a whole lot of people and we would spend long evenings drinking and smoking and listening to music... curiously, I was surrounded by so many new friends, yet I still managed to feel lonely...

... pain festival... I am sure I have done some great things in my life... but now all I can think of is my pain... will I remember Lisbon as the place I survived my wounds... is it this which identifies me as a person... a survivor... after cancer, why doesn't a person become just that *a person* and not a cancer survivor... grant you cancer is nocuous... but it does not merit being carried around as a badge of honor... are our wounds a banner/medal... I know when I was 20ish and had a motorcycle accident while traveling through Spain... I felt it was a benchmark in my life, but I never let go of the memory as it was one of several times in which I thought I was going to die... whenever I wallow in lamentable self-pity... ironically, I use this miserable time from my past to uplift my spirits today...

... 1981 - 05... I had been driving my motorcycle from France to Portugal... by this time I was in Spain and about 50 kilometers away from a city called Salamanca... with midnight ticking on my wrist watch and fatigue humming along to the ticking sounds... I found myself skidding into a guard rail... the impact shot me through the air and eventually on ground, all the while I was thinking as soon as I stop this trajectory, I'll get up and ride off on the motorcycle... after rolling for about 6 meters... the landing did not hurt nor the rolling... actually I did not feel any pain... it was only when I stopped my free-fall and took a breath of air, did all the physical pain kick in... so much pain and alone on the road too... I truly believed that this was a stupid way to die... I felt fate tripped me into falling and scraping my life away...

... side by side... this was not the moment to be a drama queen... even with pain, I argued with myself that is not the way I wanted to stay or even die here... I saw my motorcycle and made an effort to get up... the mind and body were not in sync... any attempt to move exasperated my pain... as I lied there for eternity... I see a car's headlights coming in my direction... the car goes by me and does not stop... am I already dead that the driver cannot see me... I just lie on the ground moaning and trying to flash through in my mind my pathetic life... another car comes up from behind me and stops in front of me... the woman ran off somewhere to get help, and the man came out to my aid... not understanding his Spanish speaking... I can only speculate he told me not to move or something to that effect...

... really high... some medic injects something into my arm... today I can only describe it as the wellness of morphine... an ambulance takes me to the city hospital in nearby Salamanca... a catheter was inserted into my penis... though this was painful, it was not as bad as when it was finally pulled out days later as it also peeled skin from inside my penis urethra... since there was no internal bleeding I was released from the hospital... with all my money left in my motorcycle saddle some 50 kilometers away... I had no means to get back to the motorcycle, let alone even ride it as my whole body was one giant ambulant bruise...

... fashion statement... the accident had caused me to also roll on the guard rail... the rail had sliced through my leather jacket and sweat shirt leaving only my t-shirt intact... basically I was now wearing a t-shirt... with a leather jacket and sweatshirt halter top combo... I knew my clothes were shredded, but I needed to feel the comfort of warmth, if only on my shoulders... since I was a foreigner with no money, the hospital let me go without paying, so I think... next, to pee or not to pee... with whatever dignity I could muster up... I went to the bathroom... the urine acidity trickled through my open wounded urethra scorching it with pain... no need to pee, as all fluids were coming out in form of tears via my eyes...

... grandmother alert... I walked into the emergency's waiting room, I needed to figure out what to do... walking was difficult but breathing was even harder... I could not inflate my lungs due to the massive bruises on my chest and the bandages... the waiting room was packed with people... not an empty chair in the horizon... the room looked like a sea of old ladies dressed in black widow garbs... not exactly a flattering or promoting picture for the hospital industry... is reality a cruel dream... before I know it, a wave of grannies are getting up from their chairs... after a few shuffle around... there are now 4 empty chairs in a row for me to lie down on... someone cared for me... these people acknowledged my existence... I felt human and even loved...

... cuddle... none spoke English and my knowledge of Spanish was lame... but they spoke amongst themselves with arms pointing in different directions... my mind was like a dark street with all the lamp post lights turned off... I had no idea what I wanted or needed to do... I felt like sinking myself into the chairs and disappearing... maybe be abducted by a UFO and taken away on a long spaceship journey... but even there, eventually I'd die of loneliness on the spaceship... from the dark cloud of grannies arises a smiling social worker... she spoke some English and gave me money for a train ticket to where I had the accident and had left the motorcycle... she also arranged for an ambulance driver to give me a lift/ride to the train station...

... wailer... whatever illness and even broken nose issues I have now... it certainly is easier to handle than what I went through back in Spain as a young man... maybe I'll call Suzanne for help... but more urgent... is that I need to find my homeless man and give him this food... he is worse off than I am...

## 2015/04/03 – Friday (Lisbon, Portugal)

... nauseating... *sick time* again and still no sign of getting better... to restless to meditate and/or even read... cannot think to clearly either... I just sit here wondering about odds and ends... my biggest pride and joy are my 3 kids... nothing can top these moments in my life... and as my physical pain and discomfort continues... I reach back into my memories for harder times where I managed to survive, but even with this I am not doing well... my body has an agenda of its' own... I must be delirious from the fever...

... silly thoughts... my mind wandered to when I was married... for 20 or so years when I did not have a motorcycle, as raising a family ate up my income... I took it seriously the responsibility to protect/provide for my family... but with every spring season I would whine/lament my chant... *everyone has a motorcycle except me*... then one spring, out of the blue, Emme (now ex-wife) pulls into our driveway and sees my brand new motorcycle parked... in her anger because I did not tell her beforehand that I had bought one... for 3 days she did not speak to me... how I enjoyed this quiet time back then... but right now, I would even enjoy her arguing with me... I must be in a very bad shape to be wishing this...

... deity... still sitting on this sofa and the day seems it's in fact full of long lasting minutes... when I had my motorcycle accident in Spain, back then I was an atheist and yet found myself praying while lying down on the gurney... now, I am simply arrogant that I will get over this pain/issue on my own... why bother god with my miniscule problems... in my experience life is nothing but a series of hurdles hindering a path to happiness... but all things said and done... as humans, at times we jump over a few hurdles at a time... this is my little victory...

... end of my rope... looking forward to Suzanne coming tomorrow... as I also asked her to book me an appointment with her family doctor... my head is lighter than air... why is it only in sickness that I appreciate the value of being healthy... am I the only one who does this... I think not, cause when I go to funerals I always sense people are making some sort of promise to change and/or appreciate their life... but I also feel these promises are no different from those done in a new year's resolution context... as humans, we have a short memory and lack commitment in our daily endeavours...

... Suzanne interval... time... no need for a wrist watch or a cell phones' additional function of time display... so many clocks monitored by the sunrise/sunset... I feel alone and miss Suzanne... my time is unlike all others, it is quantified by my being with her... and yes, time does torment me, when away from her... for every jerky shift of the dials... a little bit of me gets taken away to oblivion... those seconds of *me* where I am deprived of her... never knowing the beauty of being measured by her... time is unrelenting... it has no human emotions... for if it did, it would not tick by me as she is so far away... it would stop, and allow me to catch up with her... maybe, even cheat and go back in time... extending our time together...

... emotional... my Lisbon apartment is losing its' appeal and novelty... looking closely at the overall living room... neglected moulds, cornices and arches... the corduroy like burgundy sofa colors... the elongated chrome legged table with a white wash table top and the box of Kleenex... the rust color carpet... a patio door leading to a balcony... a red curtain and a fan... indicates this is a furnished apartment decorated by a single guy... as all the furniture and accessories are un-matched... nevertheless... I find myself sitting on this ugly couch and dosing off into a dream state every so often... would it be possible to write after I wake from the hallucinations...

... hallucination one... the ruins resemble and/or make me think this was once a church... especially the stretched out arches spanning the whole height of the room... and the nookies underneath the arches on either side... the guilt corner or if you prefer the confessional... and the round window at the apex of the gable roof... but the dead giveaway... are the children... from what most likely seems to be the remnants of a third world colony... the beauty, the epitome of imperialism along with the church... is that it is always short lived... but for a very short time, it still managed substantial damage...

... hallucination cont'd... hands tied with a rosary... so an emotional slavery of sorts... one foot is dug into the earth while the other skims the surface... perhaps she is in a state of confusion whether to stay or leave... there are 8 holes in which sunlight penetrates the wine cellar... I assumed it's a wine cellar... the cellar is at the bottom of an incline for the *coolness* temperature required to make quality/store wine... the window bars are dented inwards which without a doubt proves the wine which was produced here must have been exceptional... hence, a horde of professional drunk wine connoisseurs broke in, by pushing the bars... had they robbed the place during the day, they would of noticed the unlocked and ajar door... perhaps if hydro was paid, a night light could have been turned on... unless of course it had a cheap light bulb from a trendy one euro store...

... hallucination the end... to the right of the young lady's breasts is a shadowy area with another entrance passage... all I can hope for, is that she has a twin sister in the next room and who is not so melancholic and knows where the wine has now been stored... and feels like partying... and if she knows how to flambé *chorizo* with Portuguese *agua-ardente*... she earns my respect for such culinary extravaganza... the cellar is the reality, the room next door is my dream world... I choose the dream world cause reality here is too depressing and demanding...

... so, what can we conclude from all this?... I guess we only see what we want... the mind sort of has a selective viewing mechanism for self-preservation, no?... who am I kidding... this is all bullshit and just pure entertainment until supper is put on the table... subliminal... I know there is a message here in these dreams/hallucinations... a Freudian festival of sorts... but I am not qualified or care to exam it for a message(s)... what I need is a doctor ASAP... cause my rash is getting out of control...

## 2015/04/04 – Saturday (Lisbon, Portugal)

... fuck!... fuck!!... fuck!!!... woke up on the couch... another rough night... my whole body aches... but there is something curious about my rash this morning... it is concentrated on my upper right arm... the blisters are in a in row and sometimes in a clusters... there are about 19 at best count... the itching sensation is so intense I feel like ripping off my arm... went on the internet to see if I could find something that can explain my flu like symptoms and rash... shockingly... the rash is caused by flea bites... and to make matters worse... my body over-reacted to the bites which explains the giant rash/blister marks... rare, but all the symptoms I thought were related to the flu were an allergenic reaction to the flea saliva...

... inquiry & enquiry... spent the next hour or so on the internet researching the bug attack on my person... I feel violated... and such anger for not noticing the rash was indeed a series of bites... all my extremities were bitten... under this new light of information I now feel dirty and stupid... I want to peel or even rip off my skin... now that I saw all the ghastly pictures of flea bites... read all I could about the enemy... and now how to fight a bug which is no bigger than a pinhead and for the most part invisible to the eye... the more I read, the more paranoid I became... I felt my body was constantly under attack while I was reading... besides the itchy rash/blisters... I began to think Hellstrom's chronicle was not so farfetched...

... doorbell... Suzanne's arrival interrupted what was becoming an obsessive research assignment on fleas... though there are no pets in my rented apartment it was nevertheless infested with fleas which hid in the carpet... and bloodthirsty fleas too... upon seeing my bites Suzanne recognized the bites were of flea origins, as she already had pets of her own... *not sexy in any way*... she told me to strip down and put my clothes in a plastic bag and any other clothes I had lying around... she went out to the store while I showered... at first I showered with soap and rubbed vigorously... then I showered a second time and used Head & Shoulders dandruff shampoo on my body... the tingly sensation the shampoo left on my body secured me that no bug can survive attached to my skin... I rinsed my body with scalding water... at this point I realized I needed to get control of the situation... and not be a victim but go on the offensive...

... tactic... Suzanne came back from the store... she brought calamine lotion for the blisters/rash... apple cider vinegar to spray on ourselves while in the apartment as fleas are repelled by the acidity scent... the vinegar smell had me wishing for french fries... and environmentally unfriendly bug insecticide... my anger was such that I couldn't care less about the environment... I sprayed the insecticide into my suitcases and zipped them up... choke you *motherfucking bastards* who got into my suitcase... I vacated the apartment *permanently*... and before putting the suitcases in the car, sprayed them till kingdom come...

... easter weekend... Suzanne had come into Lisbon to pick me up and drive down to her parents for the weekend... but I was in no mood to socialize... and since she was unable to make an appointment with her family doctor on account of the Easter holiday... the doctors' office was closed for the week, *who knew doctors get time off too*... so... instead I asked her to take me to the hospital emergency... Suzanne left me in front of the emergency door while she went looking for parking... as I sat in the crowded waiting room... the images of the flea I had seen on the web were haunting me... the miniscule insect has black eyes like the gray alien pictures we see portrayed by the media... descendants and/or relatives?

... lab rat arrogance... are we on top of the food chain when an insect can unbalance me... sitting here, I think this hospital is as bad as anything we have back in Montreal... new anger was brewing in my head with regards to hospitals and schools... how can we claim we live in advance societies... electoral promises are a lie as they don't value life or education... a politician may start off with noble aspirations... but in the end it is all about bowing down to monetary profit... there is no immediate profit when investing in education and/or health systems... success in education or health is a silent victory which cannot be measured... every life should matter, regardless of age or circumstances... too bad I didn't see a politician in the waiting room...

... free... no matter what geographical, cultural or standing in society... if something is *free* we feel exultant... case and point is Suzanne as she found free parking... no sooner do I see her that I tell her I am not waiting any longer... we walk downtown instead and I buy over-priced aspirin in a tourist area pharmacy... hunger setting in, I popped four aspirins... we walked up the street heading towards *Castelo Sao Jorge* with lunch in mind... we stopped for lunch in a restaurant called Casa Madeira... the food was not the highlight but the fact that the terrace was across a busy street from the restaurant... the waiters had to cross the street back and forth to serve the terrace patrons... my highlight was watching these waiters dodging cars and tramways with plates in hand...

... organic kindness... after lunch, we headed up to the S. Jorge castle, I had never been inside... just like the hospital, there were lines ups for the castle... still not in the mood to wait, we head back to the car... as this point, the calamine lotion applied earlier was fading... and the hot sun was giving me a headache... we stop in a coffee shop called Café Pit... our waiter Tiago, has us trying organic hot soup served in a shot glass... after a concoction of soup, aspirins and coffee, I ask Suzanne to take me back to her place in Cascais... as I need to re-energize myself physically but mostly mentally...

## 2015/04/05 – Sunday (Cascais, Portugal)

... sunday & only... with a 3 hour drive Suzanne and her daughter went for lunch with family... she left me her car as it still contained my luggage... Easter is second to Christmas when it comes to family gatherings in this country... I'd feel like an alien dining amongst her folks with my white patches of calamine lotion plastered all over my body... I still feel disgustingly dirty and embarrassed for allowing a bug to violate my body... I feel I'd be a subject of curiosity and hypocrisy as people would talk behind my back and laugh at my misery...

... struggling... found a laundromat that is open on easter sunday... why would it be open on holiday easter sunday... because the owner had just opened the business a few months ago and is still struggling to keep his business afloat... being his only customer today, in a way I think he should be grateful for my flea misery... as I pull out the first suitcase from the car trunk, I spray insecticide all over the suitcase like a madman... the intoxicating insecticide mist made me cough up some of the anger in me... I rolled up the suitcase to the washing machine... did not sort out the clothes by color or whatever... dumped everything into the machine including most shoes... I felt myself thinking... *drown you mother fuckers...* I took the suitcase outside and sprayed it again both inside and outside...

... lunacy... as I sit on a chair facing the washing machine... I feel some sort of hypnotic contentment watching the clothes spin in the machine... but I also feel what I can only describe as *flea paranoia* creeping in my head... thinking, ideas such as... I should also shave my head and beard... when walking down the street I should think like a dog... that is avoid any lamp post or tree trunk where a dog would likely hang around... and where fleas may be lurking for an eminent attack on me... this flea ordeal is a violation and there will never be enough insecticide in the world to ease my resentment... I sound like a drama queen... for god's sake, lighten up man it's only bug...

... fool's literature... once my second suitcase has been unloaded into the washing machine... I now took the time to look around the laundromat... found a pile of old magazines and newspapers... this being a soccer country most of the magazines carried an article or advertisement featuring CR7... the man is a living legend promoting an endless array of commodities... I guess for the advertisers and the targeted consumer market it's happiness by association... flipping through a newspaper I read an article about spousal violence leading to death... I feel the article was almost an adoration of this misery with pictures and statistics of wives murdered... I didn't mind reading this and almost accepted this as normal... am I desensitized by my current anger as much as the husbands who killed their spouse...

... domestic... with garbage bags full of clean and sterilized clothes... and my throat itching from the previously inhaled insecticide... I head to downtown Cascais for lunch... on this easter sunday most businesses or restaurants are closed... but since downtown is basically a tourist haven... I'm sure whoring restaurants are open today... easter always meant having a festive lunch with my kids... I feel my life is just an empty shell without them around... even separated from my ex-wife, the *family man* is still alive in me... I feel sorry for myself because I'm alone... will I one day end up alone and homeless... I wonder if the homeless man who sat outside the grocery store in Lisbon whom I fed regularly is also alone today...

... lords and ladies... there are basically two family gatherings in the restaurant... one group are retired UK foreigners... easy to spot with their white skin complexion and a red lobster tan color... or is their red skin tone from consuming too much wine combined with high blood pressure... the other group is a multiple generation Portuguese family... judging from their clothes and moderate conversation volume, they are what I would refer to as having a *well to do* status in society... interestingly enough... the ratio of wine bottles on their table is almost a bottle per person... *well to do* indeed... gotta love Voltaire's expression... *don't think money does everything or you are going to end up doing everything for money...*

... moonlighting... is there anything more pathetic then sitting alone in a restaurant... but to add insult to injury, on an easter sunday too... even the waitress seems to be here somewhat against her will... I try to engage small talk with the waitress... not sure if I wanted to cheer her up or was it me who needed cheering up by talking to someone... the waitress is a single mom, who works in a daycare during the week and on weekends moonlights as a waitress to make ends meet... she left her children with her aging mother and is constantly worried about them and checking her phone... according to her, moonlighting and family support is the only way one can sustain some sort of living... but the frown on her face when she said this made it very clear, things are not going well for her...

... oxygen... I turn my attention to the other folks eating here... so many body variations of the human form, I still find this amazing... as I look at some toddlers I can't help think the grandparents were at one time little babies too... then there are the very young teenagers so shy and awkward in their gestures... youth insecurity is categorized by boy being shy to speak to girl... old folks insecurity is to end up alone, therefore talk endlessly... tipped the waitress which is not customary in this country... rolled the cash receipt she gave me into a cigarette shape... walked out with a paper cigarette rolled between the index and middle finger... life is about projected images... *me...* I'm cool as I pretend to smoke this paper cigarette while parading my loneliness on the cobble stone streets...

## 2015/04/06 – Monday (Cascais, Portugal)

... convoluted computation... it is only Monday on the calendar, not in my head... actually, everything in my head is slightly deviated from reality... actually even reality is deviated but only in my head... which brings me to another point, come to think of it, there is no other point except... *never argue with an idiot, cause he will bring you down to his level and beat you with experience...* on second thought it could be Monday... but only tomorrow as I am not there yet... but being a free-spirited eccentric... the day of the week, will be determined by my multiple personalities playing musical chairs in my head... I'm rooting for my-selves, I hope one of me will win and choose the day of the week... I cannot be ordinary and follow the calendar like everyone else... I was & am and most likely will always be unable to conform... perhaps, I should adhere to conventional and grounded knowledge and follow the calendar... oh! shit... the bastard in my head won the musical chair game... I'm insanely normal...

... fretful... woke up this morning feeling disoriented... slept in Suzanne's bed but she was not with me... she is coming back later today from her family gathering... the apartment is empty but I feel her energy lingering in every room... I'm still trying to calm myself and snap out of my defeatist mood... I feel like running away but do not know where... maybe this is a sign to start my Camino journey... this thought is contradictory as it conjures excitement and hardship... the pilgrimage is physically gruelling, and I am still feeling drained and weak...

... single-mindedness... been in Portugal for over 5 months... and in different cities/towns seeking writing inspiration... and the highlight of this trip and/or experience is attempting for a second time the Camino pilgrimage... is this pilgrimage a masochistic or spiritual endeavour... is there a difference?... Camino perfection is a setup for hardship... I still have no plans as to what I will do after the pilgrimage... and I find whatever I write isn't any good either... it's probably confusing and only clear in my head... at times I feel that what I'm doing has a purpose but today there is so much insecurity in my head...

... sms... Suzanne texted asking how am I doing and stating she will be arriving late afternoon... should I tell her I'm stuck with the thoughts in my head... these toxic thoughts which are of my own creation... where is my self-love and respect... I'm my worst enemy... just like frustrated office workers coming into work on a Monday morning when asked by colleagues... *how was your weekend*... the *shut the fuck up* answer is... *fine*... now leave me alone... but since her message was *a welcome* as it interrupted my negative thought flow... I sincerely responded with... *I miss you*...

... forty sofa winks... a something... it started with her *sms* words, of course... just written words, completely un-uttered except in my mind where each syllable vibrated... every word on my telephone screen penned by her was spellbound and only to be exceeded by an overzealous passion for more... in the book of love... the distance increased between words and there were no... pristine, white screens left to be poetized... her voice, now echoes the invisible words into my ears... such sublime, soul soothing sounds can only be whispered by an angel... my angel, crosses a utopian Tejo river and hovers over me as I dream of being with her… with only our finger tips connecting us, our eyes gaze upon one another… the words, voice, touch and sight are for earthly concerns… though apart we are but one… I do know…

… waiting end… with the windows jarred and the breeze slowly shuffled into the living room coaxed by the massive tree outside her 3rd story apartment… it's (tree) blocking of the ocean view… is quickly overlooked as it is a very hot summer afternoon and these persuaded breezes are a refreshing and welcomed breath of fresh air… I allow myself to nearly slumber into the living room sofa as *Madredeus* is programmed to play repeatedly on the cd turntable…

… late afternoon… too hot to be reading, while waiting for you to arrive… I just let the music run its' course… at first in my mind but as the melody & rhythm intensifies it overcomes me into an appreciative… very mellow mood… where having spent the day without you… time was our enemy with the sunset, now soon upon us… with a flick of the light switch, you enter the living room… blinded by the light, at first only your curvy somatic silhouette emerges from the radiant light… along with your perfume now encased by the breeze which fiddled tauntingly with me… your elegant daintiness lifts me up… and the clock is reset to zero as time without you shall not be measured, never again…

## 2015/04/07 – Tuesday (Cascais, Portugal)

… loving morning… Suzanne was like an express elevator into my skull… negative rambling thoughts were quickly gather and sorted for their utility… what are thoughts but a collection of ideas… in which some must be discarded as their origins and utility negate ascension to inner peace and disillusion the physical world… come to think about it… how absurdly ridiculous to let an insect phobia destabilize me… the new sexy male look are calamine lotion swatches… and with this, she is off to work and I activate my olfactory sense to find me a coffee shop…

… Dolce & Caffe… is a coffee shop for the locals, an extension of one's home, if you happen to live in the neighbourhood, of course… this is a working class ghetto, there is no better way to describe this area of Cascais… cars parked nearby do not exceed a certain price range… clothes hanging off window cord lines come from large area surface stores… and freshly cooked food scents filter through the now partially opened grimy shutters… the common thread for all these folks is that they live nearby the café... therefore an obligatory salutation is a must when entering the bistro... as anyone sitting here right now may be a neighbor and one day even friend... otherwise, to the rare lost passerby this is a bleep on a GPS... a beacon from where to initiate a reference point in order to get home...

... financier... a man in a pinned striped bankers' suit with a crisp white shirt and red tie, carrying a motorcycle helmet in his hand... and to add to this perfect GQ image he shaves his head... so he will never be cursed with helmet hair... practical fashion style perfection to the last possible detail... now, this guy sticks out like a sore thumb in this place... though he seemed at ease with the mille-seconds of silence from the patrons when he entered the bistro... one gets the impression this happens a lot to him... is he lost, or doing a foreclosure on some working stiff's home nearby...

... navigate friendly waters... he tilts his head up and back in a salutation mode as if he spotted an acquaintance in the bistro... as he manoeuvres the obstacle course of confused chairs & tables hosting patrons... he reaches a thin young man with very defined if not chiselled facial features... a handshake ensued but what I retain is the young man's upper arm being continuously rubbed even after the greetings... there is more here than meets the eye...

... lattice wall... running up the stairs at the age of 17 was easy... and besides living at that time in Montreal... where the city architecture is renowned for staircases, I was very agile... with money in pocket to buy an ounce of weed... the urgency was all in my head... as I reached the top of the stairs... the bedroom wall in front of me had its' plaster removed... through the lattice framing... I saw two young women in a very sexually charged passionate kiss... lesbians?... first time and what an eye opener it was for me... interesting indeed... but I did not know them and made a mental note not to gawk...

... trafficking protocol... Richard was behind me and pointed to the adjacent living room... we sit down on large dusty cushions as there are no couches and a crate convincingly acts as a coffee table... now, entering the room is a young man introducing himself as Daniel... he extends out his arm and we shake hands... he then drops a bag of weed on the coffee table... he leans over to Richard and puts his hand on Richard's shoulder... once the ergonomic stability gear engaged, they embark on a long french kiss... I really don't care that love comes in all shapes and rainbow colors... but right now I am kept apart from what I love, my future bride, the bag of weed...

## 2015/04/08 – Wednesday (Cascais, Portugal)

... respect... woke up again with very itchy *but old* flea bites... a head-ache and now even my nostrils and armpits are aching... amazing how such a little insect can cause so much allergy havoc... and I the supposedly smarter being cannot control myself from scratching the bite rash... I really wonder if we are on top of the food chain when something even smaller than a flea such as a virus/bacteria can cause chaos... I found, I over reacted to the bites both physically but especially mentally... last night I finally got around to meditating... had visions of the bubonic plague during the medieval mas-sacre... could it be I am reliving elements of a previous life form the dark ages... maybe my physical symptoms of this morning are not truly of this time in space...

... equitable... being Wednesday, I went down to the market to pick-up flowers to offer Suzanne... on my way I stopped at a nearby coffee shop for breakfast... a bit to the left of the bistro was a parked van improvising as clothing kiosk selling designer names... but since the van still has the motor running... one can only speculate his business hours will be short lived as the *designer names* are counterfeit... what is it with people and buying designer names... is it just for flash?... I fail to understand how someone can blindly buy a piece of clothing on the assumption of its designer name... I never bought a suit with a designer name, but instead had it made to measure... no designer suit can top tailor made comfort or quality... and I do not advertise on my t-shirts unless I get paid for it... with designer clothing made in third world countries how equitable is the designer when he/she drives a luxury car when their stock boy in their local company's warehouse has to take the bus to work because on the low wage he cannot afford a car...

... vanished... as a kid I remember the milkman leaving our milk on our door stoop... and at one time, we even had fresh bread delivered as well... this sort of commerce is no longer viable, as the costs are prohibitive... probably due to an increase in wages and profit margin greed, but also an increment in the standard of living... but I do admire the ambulatory merchant in a van packed with clothing and always on the move... it's almost nomadic and even a small sense of adventure as he must be one step ahead of the law... after breakfast, I walk down to the market and cut through an abandoned field doubling as an improvised parking lot on market days... and I think about my reaction to the events of the last few days, I feel foolish... and with this, I see a field mouse scurry across my path, probably forced out of its' home by a parked car... I stopped, and thought about the Black/Bubonic plagued being transmitted via fleas on rats... nonsense!... the mouse adjusts to his new surroundings and situation and so should I... after all, the only constant in life is change...

... market history... growing up in Montreal as a 6 year old kid... we also had markets similar to the one here in Cascais... even today, some still remain but are no longer archaic as per the past... notably the Atwater market, and/or the one on Amherst & Ontario streets... but the one I remember best was on the north-east corner of St.-Laurent and Rachel streets... authentic by all accounts... so authentic that the market building was a health hazard and would eventually be demolished...

... farmers, *the real ones*... would park their trucks on Rachel street and sell their *legumes*... the building also housed meat markets and live poultry for the killing... here is where the memory gets interesting... the building was demolished in 1966 the same year I had just started grade one... a wrecking ball crane had been brought in... it was parked for several days in front of the soon to be demolished market... and since the market was on my way to & from school... there was a buzz of anticipation in the air to see this mechanical giant in action...

... a happening... one afternoon, as the kids were set free by the school bell... the noise of the wrecking ball pounding the old market building was our calling... the kids that came out of the elementary school... placed their school bags on the side walk and sat on them facing the market building for a front row viewing... as it was being knocked down with the giant ball all the while being doused with tons of water to minimize the dust... uhs! & awes were heard from the kids... but the funny thing... is that as the building got pounded... rats would run out into the street and I guess some got run over by cars... but the rats that survived the street crossing... and whenever one came near us... we would scream like little girls and get up from our school bag seats... but once the storm of rodents passed... we quickly regained our seats...

... signs... back then I already loved architecture/construction... my only regret is I did not get into this line of work earlier in life... because sitting on my school bag I was hit with an epiphany... but it did not dawn on me... until later in life... destiny does not always have a direct plan or path... but whatever you have coming to you... you will get it, one way or another...

## 2015/04/09 – Thursday (Areia, Portugal)

... gone astray... decided to have breakfast at one of my favourite's bistro, called T*asca Tosca*... it has been a while since the last time... yet the waiter remembers what I always order for breakfast... it's one of those make you feel good gestures, is it not?... or maybe it's also a sign that I need to get a life and maybe go elsewhere... where I am not known... but for today, I will indulge myself into thinking I'm a *somebody*... my health is not the best, but it's getting better though I'm concerned with my shortness of breath...

... responsibility... history repeats itself... why am I here on another sabbatical year, and at my age too... basically, alone looking for something which I know is missing in my life... but not even sure what it is... my best guess or description is an *emptiness*... I know the loneliness is in my head as there are always people around me... I am not a hermit in any way... the events of the last few days in connection with being sick... made me realize I'm *responsible for this body*... and I need this vehicle to complete a mission... there is something in me that compels and drives me to follow this obsessive dream/ quest... a dream that I'll one day quench my *emptiness*... do dreams come true?... when will I know if I have reached my goal/dream... perhaps on my death bed?...

... 1980... at the age of 20, I shipped my motorcycle to Lisbon from Montreal... the goal was to take a sabbatical year and travel... at the time, I told my friends and colleagues that I was travelling because I felt that working 50 weeks a year to get 2 weeks off as a vacation time was unfair and unbalanced for a quality life... I thought my explanation was pretty *avant garde* with a socialist undertone... but in reality, I felt an intense emptiness that I needed to get away from and to a certain extent... I was getting away from me and where I was in my life...

... anxiety highpoint... was retrieving the motorcycle from the port custom offices in Lisbon... in addition, my motorcycle had arrived and was stored for 2 months before I was informed/notified... bureaucratic lunacy of self-importance was on display with endless tidbits of forms to be filled out... and of course the best erection feeling these bureaucrats ever felt, is when they hold a stamp and ink pad in their hands... and pound my insignificant forms with blotted ink... I spent three surreal days enabling these miniscule office workers with olive oil stains on their henpecked wife bought shirts as they jerked me around until I got my motorcycle... of course, their unhurried incompetence cost me storage fees too... what a bizarre place... no wonder it is walled up... must be to keep the lunatics at bay from society...

... conveyance... with the Lisbon customs clearing ordeal behind me... eventually/finally, I move to travel around... with my balls snuggled on the motorcycle... drove to and spent a few months in the south of France... made tons of new friends... love interests flourished and my sleeping shift was moved to the daytime... booze and drugs became a ritualistic diet... but here too I realized I was just numbing my emptiness... the people I met were really nice and some became lifelong friends... but I needed to find something that could amend my internal silent disruptions...

... retrogress... after spending some time in the UK and then back to France... I decided it was now time to return to Portugal... and seek calmness, as my mind was tired... maybe I could start over... take a different route to finding happiness... by this time I had figured out my emptiness was sadness... I also thought I was probably a manic depressive as I went from a high to a low within hours... starting in France I drove along the Mediterranean coast on my way back to Portugal... it was already night time when I started to have engine problems... everything electrical on the motorcycle was off... and soon after the engine went off too... I ended up pushing the motorcycle up and down the hill side coastal road... after a few hours the bike was heavy and I was exhausted but I knew the Spanish boarder was just a few kilometers away...

... *au revoir hope*... when I was pushing the motorcycle... and it came time to go downhill, I hopped on the bike and at times the engine ran for a few seconds if I popped the clutch... going uphill was now taking its' toll and it was close to midnight... at one point I look down towards the sea and I see what appears to be a building way down the hill and by the sea... perhaps a hotel?... I decide I had enough with pushing and would check into the hotel... as I coast down the hill towards the hotel... it's beginning to appear it is not a hotel, but more like a hospital... I later found out it was an institution for the mentally handicapped... as I enter the lobby the nurse Ratchet clone greets me... I explain my predicament and ask if I can sleep in the lobby... she speaks with her supervisor and returns with a glass of water and informs me I cannot stay as my presence would disrupt the serenity of the patients...

... one of them... on my way out I meet Henri... he was excited to see me, he was like a 10 year old at Christmas time... except he was well into his fifties or more... it was a long route upwards to the main road... I figured if I push the motorcycle just a little bit uphill, then I return down and pop the clutch... Henri could not be happier as he helped me push the bike up... and ran down after me... I did this a few times but the bike would not run long enough for me to escape this serene coastal hell... with great persistence, I had to explain to Henri not to follow me uphill and that he had to stay within his compound...

... king of the hill... I was a huge ball of sweat by the time I reached the main road... I just kept pushing until about 2 AM when I reached the last village on the French border side... not sure how, but I ended up by the sea... once by the beach... there was a park with a couple of benches... at this point and time this seemed like a five star hotel... as it had the sound of waves as music... besides the waves were the only thing I wanted to hear... I took up a bench as my bed, no reservations required... I fell asleep to the thoughts of Henri, the mental institution and Lisbon port bureaucrats and my misguided quest... some people count sheep to fall asleep... I on the other hand associate people with common features in order to fall asleep... the lunacy of my life was the last thought before falling under...

... eclipse... I woke up with some guy standing over me... he did not look like a homeless man in any way... in fact he was dressed in blue jeans and a black three button t-shirt... he was balding but with long hair and a beard... he kind of reminded me of a messiah type of hippie... but there was an air of distraught... he spoke in a broken Spanish... even though I was pretty sure I was still in France... he repeatedly asked me in Spanish *where were we...* it was as if he was an alien who lost his bearing... eventually... I managed to understand... he was a Spanish sailor who got lost at sea overnight or so I think... and now found himself in a strange land... to me he seemed more like a lost soul than a sailor...

... mundane... I did not care to get too involved with the issues of this lost sailor... I had problems of my own to resolve with my motorcycle mechanics... and I was still physically drained from pushing the bike all night... looking at him I noticed he was barefoot too... just my luck, now for sure he would not be any help in pushing the bike with me, pretty much a *tits on a bull*... I had a pair of black sneakers I bought on an impulse at a country fair back in France... actually I did not like the sneakers and they were protruding from my motorcycle satchel... I handed the shoes and they were such a contrast on his white feet... his skin seems too paper white for a sailor... I left him at the first bistro which we found open... explained his situation to the bistro owner and he stayed waiting for the police... also found out where there was a bike shop where I could repair the motorcycle... picked up my motorcycle and moved on...

## 2015/04/10 – Friday (Areia, Portugal)

... professor... being a father I always worried about my 3 kids as teenagers when out in the world... so, right from an early age... I shared my values & experience and emphasized the importance of *THINKING AND DOING THINGS FOR YOURSELF*... but, they were young and still not perfect like myself... so when they got out of control... I simply changed the door locks to teach them a lesson... but because I taught them to *THINK*... those witty little jerks, pry open the patio door or window and get in the house... I am so proud of them for out smarting me... though annoyed with myself for wasting money on new locks... but the following day I gave them the new key... and put back the old locks... they have to learn... seriously, were you expecting something profound or intelligent on how to raise children... ???...

... 1980 gust... after the motorcycle stalled just as I was approaching the France/Spain border... and had spent most of the night time pushing the motorcycle until I was able to have it repaired... with the motorcycle running smoothly I was in a hurry to get nowhere fast... after a day worth of riding, new engine problems surfaced... by this time I slowly coasted into Barcelona... at first I thought I would spend a day repairing the bike... but as I discovered the city the one day stay turned into three day visit... something about the whole place felt like a *deja vu*... I walked around as if the map of the city was registered in my head... especially the old quarters of the city... suspicion set in as I felt the whole motorcycle problems were a pretext to have me visit Barcelona when I had no intention too...

... revving... departing from Barcelona as one leaves a dear friend behind... I set my course for Portugal... my route objective is to reach Salamanca by nightfall... by this time I'm about 50 kilometers away from my objective... I'm tired and fight to keep my eyes open... as I enter a small town, I switch from high to low beams as I drive through the town... once on the outskirts of town I switch on the high beams and see a turn/curve on the road up ahead... though I'm driving over 100k... I slow down and lean into the curve... I feel the back tire skidding on gravel on the road's shoulder... with the sensation of slipping and being pulled off the road... and total loss of control, I hit the guard rail and tumbled... in slow motion throughout the air... there was an angel minimizing my accident and injuries...

... reappearance... from lying injured on the ground to being hospitalized in Salamanca and about a week later finally finding myself back in this small town again... through the kindness of a social worker in the hospital, who gave me enough money for the train fare from Salamanca to the nameless town... for some reason, I was naively hoping my motorcycle and gear would be parked by the side of the road where I had the accident... the train ride was a painful experience... as the train went over a track connection, my body shook and caused undue pain... once at the station, I asked anyone with a car if they could give me a ride to the end of town... I was on my own, but somehow had the determination to walk to the end of town by foot... with every step, I re-live the pain I felt on the train ride...

... logo... as I approached the end of town, I recognized the landmarks and even the road's intricacies... no motorcycle to be found anywhere, only some shattered glass from the headlight and reflectors... I see a restaurant a bit to the side... maybe had I noticed it the night of the accident perhaps I'd stop for a coffee... the place looks deserted and even creepy... as I approach the restaurant in my shredded clothes... a thirty something year old man comes out to meet me... he was wearing a jean jacket and t-shirt which he got as a souvenir gift... the logo on the T-shirt was of the Ottawa Parliament building... I felt like laughing tears...

... arrangement... the t-shirt man was a Portuguese fellow living and working in this Spanish restaurant in the middle of nowhere... he was on the scene of the accident the night it happened... and had seen my *Quebec license plate*... once I was carried off to the hospital... he took it upon himself to store my motorcycle and gear until I returned... I did not have enough money to get back to Portugal... also the motorcycle was in bad need of repair... I left him my motorcycle as collateral if he would lend me some money... with the money I would get myself to Portugal to recuperate and in the meanwhile he'd have the motorcycle repaired... if I did not return in a month the bike would be his... we shook hands symbolically... he even assisted me with getting transportation to the Portuguese border... it's commendable to think for oneself... but I must never forget I'm not an island... and his kindness cannot be expressed in words...

## 2015/04/11 – Saturday (Cascais, Portugal)

... phases... while reading the morning newspaper between coffee sips... the article of the week is a father who stabs his 6 month old son in the heart... the reason for the act, being a cocktail mix of marital difficulties, alcoholism and vengeance... after the stabbing the father had gone to a bistro for a glass of Port wine... something I had read years ago, also popped into my head... *people who believe in absurdities commit atrocities*... there really is no limit to our madness... we are simply an amazing species when it comes to cruelty and stupidity... the fathers' troubles are only going to start now when he has all the jail time in the world to reflect on his actions... if he is lucky, he will not have much time...

... parental... as a father, whether my kids relish in joy or fight amongst each other... I am there for them and if need be even intervene... I would think a god from above would have some sort of paternal instinct for us humans... but it seems more likely that we are simply lab rats... a scientific experiment of sorts for a god with large black eyes and a tight gray skin body suit... I guess we all have our qualities and beliefs required to survive... surprisingly enough my biggest asset first appeared to me when I was a young boy... *the capability to think for oneself*...

... spirited... after my motorcycle accident in Spain... I spent the next month in Portugal recuperating from my injuries... soon it was time to return to Spain, to retrieve my motorcycle... I hitched hiked my way back into Spain... not for lack of money but because I had the time and also for the adventure... since I was on my way to pick up my motorcycle I carried in my hand the helmet... and it played in my favor, as most drivers stopped to give me a ride thinking I had mechanical problems with a motorcycle... I had hitch hiked my way all day and now it was around midnight... and with only 40 kilometers left to go before reaching the small town where I had left the bike... I did not want to stop...

... halt... yawning as I stood by the side of the road with my hitchhiking thumb out... I walked a few meters and found a park next to the road... a few more steps away was a bench by a lamp post housing a traffic light... there was also a pedestrian crosswalk light which is activated by pressing a button... as I sat on the bench, I continuously pressed the button which forced cars to come to a halt with the red traffic light... when the cars stopped, I stuck out my thumb and hoped for a sympathy ride as I tried to make eye contact with the night time drivers...

... two's company... as I deliberately caused the traffic to stop... and no one would give me a ride on account of the late hour (I think)... my thoughts now turned to sleeping somewhere... as I sat there thinking, some old man stands next to me... to close for my comfort as I felt he was in my bubble... he asks me in Spanish *if everything is alright*... at first I figured at this late hour in a public park, this guy must be a gay seeking pleasure... so I respond in a combination of Portuguese and Spanish by saying *I was waiting for a friend to arrive any minute*... he then asks me for my passport... being a smart ass... I reply with a question... *where is your passport?*...

... wallet... he repeated his request for my passport... by this time I now figured he was not gay but a passport thief... next thing I know, he has his pistol barrel pressed against my temple... shit, this cold metal has me in a sweat... I tell him my passport is in my motorcycle boot and that I am getting it for him... with the gun in his right hand, my open passport in his left hand and the gun barrel on my temple freezing sweat... he tells me that he is from the *Guardia Civil (police)* and yet he is not wearing any uniform... as I struggle not to shit bricks... I ask him for some identification... he tells me once again he is from the *Guardia Civil* and that he left his wallet at the station...

... belief... irony has him press the button to activate the pedestrian crosswalk light... he also presses the gun barrel into my temple and tells me to get up from the bench... he swings the gun behind my back and is now using it to push me to cross the road... I naively hope some driver sees this and helps me in some way... once on the other side of the road we are joined by a short stalky man... the three of us walk down the road approaching a dark alley... I keep insisting with the gunman to show me some identification... we get to the dark alley and I now refuse to walk into the alley... he presses the gun hard into my back... in my adrenalin rush induced fear... I believed these were my last few moments on earth... my life did not flash before me in any way... why would it, I had not accomplished anything memorable... though I did remember my 4th grade teacher in a mini-skirt and how much I loved her legs in stockings and high heel boots... I still had warped humor despite adversity...

... dark alley... as the three of us stood in front of the unlit and very dark alley... I still think I'm safer where there are cars and street lights... then the thought of taking my motorcycle helmet and swing a hit allowing me time to make a run for it... but at this moment the stalky man, points to a sign up above on the wall... on the sign were the words *Guardia Civil* written... and with an arrow pointing into the alley... he runs into the alley and opens

221

a door to a small house like building... the gunman puts his gun away and signals me to move ahead into the alley... I like to think the smell of fear emanating from me had reached his nose... I was not able to make a decision whether I should or not walk towards the light coming from the building... I felt my heart pounding so fucken hard... I thought the heart pounding was to be my last memory on this planet... I was okay with this... as I now felt this body was never mine...

... irrational... as I go through the doorway... expecting a police station of some kind... instead it looked like a heroin flophouse... as I am guided to the center of the room... the gunman picks his wallet off the table and shows me his picture identification... he is indeed a police officer... I scan the whole room with one amplified glance... the room is about the size of a small bedroom... with one single bed in the corner... an adjacent table with one chair... one light bulb in its' socket hangs from the ceiling... as my glance is panning the room... the stalky man starts to frisk me... the thought of him finding my money or worse yet planting drugs on my person to be used as an excuse to frame/jail me... but then again, where would the jail be...

... surreal... as the stalky man frisks me... I keep hitting his hands every time he touches me... and I still had my helmet in hand as a weapon... all my senses are working overtime... not that events are running in slow motion... but more like my senses are attuned to every molecule displacement in the room... the gunman sits at the table... he slides a sheet of paper towards him... on the sheet is an ad for a circus... he folds than tears the sheet down the middle into two halves... on one half, on the reverse side of the circus ad... we writes my name and passport info... he then hands me my passport and tells me I have half an hour to get out of town...

... lunacy... all I know is that I now have my passport in one hand and helmet in the other... I slowly walk out of the flophouse police station... as I walk down the dark alley... I constantly look backwards to see the door entry... before I reach the main road, the door is closed and I no longer have light to see where I am walking... as soon as I reach the main road... I start running run like hell... did not know what else to do... but running kept my mind busy... in the far distance I see a taxi parked... I now had a destination...

... mockery... the taxi is parked in front of a standalone building with two turrets... kind of an odd architecture for this part of the world... the driver is sitting in the taxi... I ask him if he could take me to the small village down the road where I had left the motorcycle... not a problem, but first he was waiting for another customer pointing to the odd building... once this fare finished, he'd take me... I ask if I could wait in the taxi, and I sit next to him in the front seat... my eyelids are heavy and I close them while my hearing stands on guard... loud laughter outside... I look to see where is the commotion... I see a man with a smile from ear to ear... accompanied by three women wearing lingerie, garter belts, stockings and high heels... the taxi was parked in front of a bordello... as the taxi driver drove his customer, I did not understand all of their conversation... but the customer was happy, to say the least... facetiously... how is it that this evening both I and the customer got fucked...

## 2015/04/12 – Sunday (Lisbon, Portugal)

... definitely... the world is a very funny place... as people truly believe in dogma religions and some even kill for a belief system... is it because we fear being alone... that we have this imperative need to feel we belong to something or somewhere... in a state of being, that is more than us or at least appears to be bigger than we are... let's face it... if you want to believe in god... then it is within oneself where god could be found... not from another human being or organization who is/are as frail as any of us... need I bark the joys of *thinking for oneself*...

... seafront... the weather was nice and why not go into Lisbon for lunch... Suzanne and I wanted to take the commuter train from Cascais to Lisbon... as we would ride/coast along the Atlantic ocean... but once at the station... there were announcements of train delays... as we stood on the platform with other slightly more disgruntled commuters... I could not ignore the bond between platform strangers starting to form... without looking at anyone in particular... a woman said in a loud voice that *the train is late because it must be a suicide*...

... synchronization... the musical griping spread almost harmoniously... jumping rhetoric from one commuter to another... soon the vocalization context switches to a new rhythm/melody... *how inconvenient it is to wait*... no one seems to think it could be a mechanical problem with the train... nor does anyone care or even remember the speculative suicide... now, it is all about one's inconvenience...

... improvise... as we now drive the car to Lisbon... the *taking the train* idea is quickly forgotten and replaced by our growling stomachs as we ap-

223

proach the city limits... there is no other way than *weaselling* our way into downtown... road confusion is the norm when it comes to urban planning... personally, I think some city planner has a mischievous flair... similar to the city planners in the *Plateau* area of Montreal who promote the unremoved street snow as a tourist attraction... our late arrival, forced us to have lunch in the Rossio quarter... I broke my cardinal rule which is never to eat in restaurants that cater to tourists... and with good reason... surprisingly the food was good, but the waiter tried to jack up our bill...

... bandits... as we walked around aimlessly... our conversation topics revolved around the actions of our waiter... eventually we sat on a bench, I even wrote a little while Suzanne ran into some boutique... in the end we just watched people walk by... all shapes and sizes is one thing... but what gets me are the couples... what makes people pair up... in appearance some couples look dysfunctional... so there has to be something cerebral... or better yet a spirituality they are probably not even aware of that connects them together... perhaps we connect with certain people... because we already had a previous life together... I feel this is the case with Suzanne... since history repeats itself, am I repeating the same mistakes with her... ?...

... presence... I feel my body is a shell... nothing more nothing less... at times I feel at odds with my body... as if it is not mine and maybe I should share it... do we really die or do we simply change to another shell... maybe even in a new place and/or time... our essence lingers forever and maybe even everywhere... sitting on the hard bench, we notice a church with tourists flocking in as much as out... usually churches call to me as I find it is a place where I can meditate in serenity... but this church kind of gives me the creeps... even Suzanne feels uneasy with the building... as we approach the massive doors... a peculiar thought came to mind *why visit this place*... especially now as I'm still grinding in my head the waiters injustice...

... impartiality... no sooner do we take a few steps inside the church... Suzanne turns to me and signals in a whisper... the place is too sickening and motions her hand in a circular pattern gesture in front of her tummy... I whisper back, *drama queen, chicken*... then she steps out... but she was right as I felt gut wrenching sensation too... but at the same time I was seduced to stay... the church interior was basically in a rough stone... the decorative plaster which covers the columns/wall was long gone, only small blotches remain... even the few statues and paintings looked meagre for a church this size... my curiosity was aroused, what is this place and why does it feel familiar...

... infamy... now more than ever the whole place gives me the creeps... I feel uneasy and would go as far as to say agitated... I want answers to the questions I have not yet formed... near the opposite entrance I see a large bulletin board... on the board are photocopy clippings of old newspapers... the name of the church is *Sao Domingos* and was built around 1241... the church had survived a couple of earthquakes and restored soon after... then in 1959 there was a major fire where two fireman had perished... the restoration after the fire was minimalistic... which explain its' current state...

... curio... as much as I could read off the bulletin board... I felt if I'd meditate that I could get more... more of what I did not know... the feeling of the church being a déjà vu and empathy combined forced me to sit down... I tried to breathe slowly in order to start meditating but I could not calm down enough... new plan of attack... instead I just closed my eyes to see in my minds' eye what I could sense, if anything... I think, the images projected in my mind by the third eye were initially of injustice and empathy... but it soon turned to pain, revolt and anger... I could not really understand the images being shown to me, as they were coming in too fast... there were too many images being thrown at my minds' screen... it had an overlapping effect... it was a mass confusion... the more the images piled up the sicker I felt to my stomach...

... hoary... I wanted to scream in pain... but I was in a public place... I know I let out a grunt but I don't think anyone noticed... stop, stop, enough... I had enough... now, I just wanted to get out... outside Suzanne looked at me with concern... *you're white as a ghost*, she said... I'm not feeling well... I need to get away from here... we stopped at the first café and ordered drinks... I am not one for hard booze, but I ordered a brandy and espresso... fuck, I'm not in a good place... my head feels light or almost detached from my body... as I sat there trying to unravel the image layers I had seen in my head... Suzanne, was fiddling with her phone/internet and said... *the church was associated with the inquisition in the1500's...*

... home-based... Sunday night and feeling blue... Suzanne and I sit in front of the TV... we are surrounded by an intentional silence only to be broken by the television... it is always hard to go back to work on Mondays and/ or leave the weekend behind... but this Sunday had a disturbing afternoon for me/us... despite this I know I am lucky considering some people are worst off... I get the feeling things are going to get rougher during the night... I really hope I am wrong about my assessment...

## 2015/04/13 – Monday (Cascais, Portugal)

... voices... if I wanted to believe/learn a religion... I would turn inwards for answers and *think for myself*... or in a more risky fashion... I'd go to a church or some place for god worshipping purposes on my own free will as opposed to having a Jehovah witness ramming his mantra on me on a Saturday morning... *maybe we can share our fortune without demanding or expecting anything in return*... isn't this the concept of any given religion and/or faith... but the curse of humanity has not been religion but mankind's interpretation... maybe those who interpret the manmade rules, should know that rules only apply to themselves and no one else...

... dawdling... woke up exhausted and feeling weird... if it were not for Suzanne in bed with me... not only would I toss and turn perpetually but probably even spin in circles... there was no amount of lying in a fetal position that would ease my physical pain... every limb felt it was being stabbed or cut off... and such a stiff neck too... was constantly thirsty too, kept getting up to drink... yesterday's church visit left scars in me... I don't want to admit this, as I am scared that I bit more than I can chew... but I know something happened that put me in this disconnected state of mind...

... monday lunacy... I know we never die... the body does, but not who we are... this part of us lives on forever... some even comeback to the physical earth realm... otherwise I guess we float around in a different time and space, involved in new experiences and maybe even acquiring knowledge... the idea, I think is that we are all neighbours and should do our best to get along... but sometimes our different realms overlap and/or at other times we don't want to leave one realm for another... my first instincts pointed to not entering the church, in fact even to avoid the building all together... curiosity mixed with ego, is mildly toxic... but in the church yesterday it was lethal...

... ego... knowing, accepting and even partake in astral projections is still playing with fire... it is my human arrogance in thinking I know something... when in fact I will never live long enough to know... a sliver of a fraction as to what is out there around us... I'm so limited by my human senses... whatever source I tapped into yesterday, I kind of left a door ajar... that I now need to close it to bring my own being back to some sort of balance and harmony... I waited for Suzanne to leave for work... and then went on to taking responsibility for my actions...

... novice... using my empathy to sense vibrations in the church was amateurish... it was a lack of respect for other realms... at my age, I should know my place in the universe... in fact, this is a lesson for me... as I did not have control over my own being as I opened the flood gates to the beyond... I played with fire, no doubt... as I write this I have shivers of fear running down my spine... but I consider fear as one of my favourite emotions... fear is a trigger or guideline for me to proceed onwards... there is enough arrogance or blind stupidity to confront my fears... this is one way I think for myself and solve my problems...

... cool and collected... relax man... as I sit in my chair with headphones plugged to my skull... it blocks out all exterior sounds and I feed off the music's soothing notes... as I start *not* to feel my feet and then my legs... and as I carry this numbness from the floor throughout my body and all the way to my head... when my head feels so light it seems detached... I know I have reached a zen moment in my meditation... and am now ready to go further out seeking answers...

... elucidation... with my head floating in the clouds... and in a nonchalant tone, even humorous... my attitude was that this body I'm in is mine and it has a purpose and usage solely for me... this notion put me in an authoritarian position... and with this I asked to revisit yesterday's overlapping images which were projected by my third eye... but this time it had to be shown at a slower pace and without the sentiment of pain... each image was of a spirit like energy, but these energies were like black dust... the reason I felt so overwhelmed was because these black energies were coming at me and pushing one another to get to me and voice their pain...

... unsettled... I saw enough to understand there were massive deaths... *old*... I had this smell of old lingering in my nostrils... but soon, even in my mouth I could feel and sense *old*... I kept repeating the question... what does this *old* smell and taste mean... *sudden death a long time ago*... am I to understand these black clouds of energy or spirits have been here for a long time... death had come to the these spirits while in human form... either during the inquisition or an earthquake... these spirits feel they left with unfinished business... that is why the attraction to me when I was in the church... I think I was perceived, perhaps a guiding light of some sort...

... obligation... nothing happens without a reason... sometimes we do things against our better judgement... but we also forget our destiny was planned before we were born... and we came down to earth with a plan in hand... but once down here we wing it and improvise... but one way or another we complete what we had agreed upon to be our destiny and learning experiences when we re-surfaced on this planet... all this to say, there was a reason for my stepping into the church yesterday... perhaps on my next astral projection... I'll return at night and help ease their pain in some unknown way... I always knew and felt it was my duty while on this planet was to help people... I never thought it extended into other realms...

## 2015/04/14 – Tuesday (Cascais, Portugal)

... adrift... not an exciting day... woke up very tired but at the same time feel at ease with myself... but as I do my online banking budget and see the money going out... I wonder about what it is I'm doing with my life... I'm the *anti-poster boy* for all those businesses who want you to put money in the bank, buy insurance or retirement saving plans... you know the ones who sell you fear but disguise it as common sense... right now I have neither... though I still have the mindset that because I'm healthy I should be working and saving for a rainy day... taking a sabbatical year from the grind is not maximizing my earning potential... but it is one of the perks where I can say *this is my life*... and what if I say, I don't give a shit... the only money I should be saving is for Dr. Kevorkian fees, but then again he has moved on to the next realm... so, spend it while you got it and live in the *now*...

... ascetics... again this week... I went through my clothes and donated more clothes to charity... and as the month of May approaches I started getting psyched up for my Camino trek... there is a liberating feeling that all I'll own will be in my backpack... now, the perplexing question is what will I do after the pilgrimage... will I go back to accommodating the insurance or banks... or will I say *fuck off* to all the fear mongers... will all my bravura endure or will I soon be the *new poster boy* on how one becomes homeless... gutsy and/or suicidal as my balls may be... will I give up a lifestyle where I'm *uncomfortable in my comfort zone*... there is a recklessness about me and I wonder at times if it's genetic...

... vessel... my dad being the only son of three children... he had a care free life other than working on the family farm... a womanizer par excellence... athletic and agile as he would jump from roof tops to sneak in the nocturnal hours... into the houses of young women to seduce them all the while their/her parents would be sleeping in the next room... he was also at ease throwing his fists around when need be... it was never clear whose idea it was to emmigrate to Canada... was it my grandfather who was concerned my dad would not settle down and get married... or was it my dad who wanted adventure... either way... both my grandfather and dad burrowed money for the privilege of the debt excursion to Canada...

... cruise... with a job contract to work on a farm... my old man at the age of 27 sails off to Canada in 1953... first docking in Halifax and then moving on to Quebec City... he spent two days in the immigration offices eating cornflakes with water... as he had never seen cereal in his life and no one gave him milk either... one must remember that in his childhood once he stopped being breast fed... he was initiated to wine as the beverage of manly champions...

... ranch... in his village in Portugal... a rich farmer would own maybe 4 cows... the dairy farm by which he was hired had over 100... he was offended that when a cow died, it was dragged by tractor to a nearby field to rot... he felt disgusted by this lack of respect for the farm animals... speaking of animals... he could not get over the idea that the farmer's daughters were sunbathing instead of working the fields like his sisters did... his experience on the farm was short lived... one can only speculate which of the animals caused him trouble...

... vocation... it was not his calling... but he ended up working as a lumberjack... the idea of driving with his buddies from Quebec to eventually British Columbia in search of the most paying locations... it was not so much as cutting down trees and getting good money for it... it was more his growing sense of family... when it came to sending money to Portugal and help his dad clear the debts... and even being able to save money too... the family notion also applied to his own life... at 32 and single, living in lumberjack camps where ample food was no longer a substitute for happiness... he now wanted more... the nomad adventurer now wanted to settle...

... old maid... leaving Canada after 5 years... he is now back in his miniscule Portuguese village... being used to the open spaces of North America wilderness... his small village was limiting... the poor farm boy/man can now afford a to buy himself a Vespa and new clothes such as trench coat... he is such a dream, a true catch for any girl... so handsome wearing a trench coat while driving his Vespa... all the girlfriends he had ever known were all married... cause in those days women got married in their 20's otherwise they would be considered old maids... my dad felt his biological clock pounding his desire to have a family and children...

... juggle... my mother was jolted by her boyfriend after an endless wait... her wishes for marriage vanished when she was already a humiliating 31... she became an instant old maid with no prospects in sight... wait...

229

maybe there is hope, as her third cousin who just arrived from Canada is in search of love… an eligible bachelor with assets… and he is planning to go back to Canada to seek more fortune… could he be her dream man… no, of course not… but he could provide for her and take her away from where she has been humiliated… they will learn to love one another and it will all work out with time… but how can love grow when it was never sown…

## 2015/04/15 – Wednesday (Cascais, Portugal)

… equate… do young adults have the wisdom to raise children… they certainly can perform the sexual copulation procedure with very little training and pop a kid some nine months later… what about a woman like my 30 something year old mom… who within a year went from being an old maid to a wife and an overnight mom… would she be qualified to be a mother?… in the microcosm of her personal world…

… independant… in comparison when I entered grade one, I did not speak any English… I paid for my school supplies at the beginning of the year but the teacher confused me with another student and gave him my school books and materials… something about immigrants all looking the same… I spent the year without copy books and pencils and when it came to books I had to sit next to a student and share his text book… when I told my mother… according to her it was my problem… and it made no fucken difference if I was innocent cause if I had this problem… I must of done something wrong and brought it on upon myself… not easy for a 6 year old to deal with a manic depressive mom… since she never stepped in my classroom to resolve the injustice… I basically learned very quickly and started to develop the early concept stages of *think for myself*…

… entertaining… clothes and shoes were bought a few sizes bigger as we would eventually grow into them… it actually annoyed her that we grew out of our clothing and she had the burden to buy more… though my brother is 15 months younger than me… she always bought us identical clothes so that we'd look like twins… she insisted that we wear the same clothes so that we match one another… it basically deprived us of individualistic identities for a while… until I contrived her plans by wearing different garments and not being in sync with what my brother wore… toys in our home were a waste of money… for fun my brother and I would wrestle… it was all fun and games until we got too rowdy… at which point she'd come after us with a wooden spoon for a beating… the marathon dash was for my brother and I to get to the bathroom and lock ourselves in until she cooled off…

… coincidence… my mother was in a long term relationship with her ex-boyfriend called Fernando… *uncanny is it not as this ex-boyfriend and I share the same name*… their imminent breakup started when he left Portugal for Brazil to seek his fortune… so at first they continued courting via letters being sent by snail mail… his letters soon became a collector's item as they were becoming a rarity… so few were his letters that through the grapevine it was discovered he had married while in Brazil… upon hearing this, my mother's marital prospects were fucked… so, my mom at 31 was now officially an old maid, with an unamendable broken heart compounded by the sheer humiliation of being a laughing stock in the village…

… saga… about the same time my mother was going through her festival of bleakness… my dad, but at that time he was more of a prince charming gino… came to the rescue of the old damsel in distress… being third cousins, they instantly had their union stamped with the family seal of approval… after all, they both came from good hereditary stock… at least all the 4 parents thought they did… especially since my grandmothers were first cousins… friction was soon replaced by tolerance while waiting for love to kick in… initially it was a marriage of spite… but with the years and the advent of two children… things did not change in their relationship until they retired back to Portugal… by this time their union was a habit and now their only fear was to end up alone in their golden years…

… axiomatic… within hours of the phone call announcing my father's death… my brother and I flew to Portugal for the funeral… we were on a tight schedule cause within a few hours of our arrival we'd be attending the funeral… as we all sat at the dinner table, I looked at my mother… and placed my fingers on her face to open up her eye as I wanted to confirm her pupil dilation… I asked her what medication she was on… apparently her doctor had prescribed something to calm her… but she said she really didn't need it as she was ok with my dad's death…

… prime of life… as the years went by, she eventually moved into a retirement home… I would visit her annually… so, with every spring I would visit her in Portugal… I spent my afternoons with her and she would speak of my dad with fondness… did I miss something while growing up in the family household?… this was and still is a mystery to me… but with a new mystery and old one is resolved… having always suspected my brother was her favourite child… in the later years/visits… she would always call me by my brother's name... once I'd explain I was her other son, she would then ask about how my brother was doing... maybe, he reminded her of my dad... isn't love quirky...

## 2015/04/16 – Thursday (Areia, Portugal)

... pass time... of course besides arguing or loving Suzanne... when not writing I read more now than ever before... listen to TedTalks, why isn't this on prime time TV... ?... are we mindless after having spent the day working on probably a mindless job... even the concept of work is mindless... then again, thinking these thoughts is also mindless as it serves no purpose...

... bygone... this objective I gave myself to write a daily journal/entry story is taxing... I try to write about what I see and how it relates to me... but the *me* is always in the context of life on this planet... I always lived by and told my kids to... *the day you stop learning you might as well die*... sitting here today in the Tasca Tosca bistro and seeing the same crowd is not really inspiring me... at times I find myself opening up memories and/or events of the past... though I am writing, I still do not know what purpose these writings will serve... though during my first Camino pilgrimage I received an intuition that I must write... I do not take seriously what I have written so far... at best I feel it is egotistical escapism... my best assumption is that my kids will have these stories as a memento of their dad... insane dad?...

... Iran the country... back in 1992-93... I worked in Iran for a very long year... at that time I did *administrative* work within an engineering context in a mining facility... though this was both my title and job description... what it really boils down to is that I was a glorified filing clerk... can never take myself too seriously... *as it is my curse*... but, I was really well paid... one aspect of working overseas away from family... is that one is consistently homesick... along with missing my spouse and 2 young kids... it is the little things in life/culture we take for granted, that all of a sudden become so important... whenever I had time off from work and would return to Montreal... all of us, especially my kids were heart broken when I'd return back to work overseas...

... whoring money... sure it was a very interesting salary... for us as a new family it was like winning a lottery jackpot... initially I was trying to get a contract to work in Venezuela and where my family would come with me... but because of political turmoil the contract was cancelled... so, I was on the rebound in terms of work... as a lark, I applied for the Iran mining project contract... after months of interviews and medical examination, I was approved... considering the culture shock I had once I landed in Iran, I decided it was best to leave my family stay in Montreal... though the family remaining behind was an unmeasurable hardship... the flip side of the con is that I was in an exotic country...

... learn... fear is under-rated... I like fear because it keeps my pompous arrogant attitude in check, it makes me humble... everything, I have ever done in my life... such as my sabbatical year travelling in Europe on my motorcycle... to audacious career moves and even working in Iran... and now a second attempt at Camino... were all results of my fears... call it reverse psychology, if you want or perhaps there is even a touch of being masochistic...

... personal growth... it is hard to sum up in a few words what I experienced during my one year in Iran... but it was to say the least, mind boggling... during Ramadan, we had the chance to visit Persepolis... I am one to admit/believe, that nothing happens without a reason, call it destiny... but upon arriving at this historical sight... I had an epiphany, a *déjà vu* mind set/experience... was I back home from a previous life... ?... I do not claim to be special in any way... but I do know that I have a knack for feeling certain things...

... strip... take an ordinary Iranian... peel away the political labelling, religious cloaks, privileged university degrees and whatever propaganda you have seen on TV describing these folks... and you quickly realize they share the same fears and concerns like any of us... the bottom line is this... I regret not taking my family with me to Iran... we all could've learned something...

## 2015/04/17 – Friday (Areia, Portugal)

... classification... if you never lack food, this does not include junk food... but lack everything else in the home you are growing up in... and always lived in rented flats and moving every few years... would you be considered poor... we once lived in a flat where my brother and I would race out of bed to see which one got to the kitchen sink first... switching on the kitchen light... we'd surprise the roaches scurrying about... and we tried to drown them down the kitchen sink drain...

... priority... as kids, my brother and I did not know any better... though we witnessed a lot of arguments between our parents... we knew it had to deal with money but not much more... maybe we were on the verge of becoming homeless... maybe my whole life has been a set up for me to be eventually homeless... maybe this is it, when I'll finally fulfill my destiny... I apologize if I do not jump with joy... since I have this fear of becoming homeless, I will do my utmost not to make it happen... destiny or not...

... tradition... can tradition and destiny be inter mingled... my grandfather was notoriously known in his village for the beatings he gave my father... the purpose for this was... that he believed it introduced and educated my father to the concepts of responsibility and respect for authority... to a lesser extent my father kept this tradition and applied to it to my brother and I... now, coming back once again to the concept of *thinking for oneself*...

... king's festivities... we were all sitting at the kitchen table having supper... when I see a roach crawl under the food in my brothers' plate... I point this out and my brother panics... my father tells me I was seeing things and making up lies... and with this he slaps me on the face... I stand up... there was an intense moment of silence where only his eyes and mine spoke as we looked at each other... I saw fear in his eyes and he probably saw forthcoming retaliation in mine... but from that day on... he never hit either one of us... there was an understanding that even at 14 years old, I was already a man... maybe my destiny was not to follow our fathers' tradition but actually change its' course...

... respect... as a high school student... I had a part time job working in a bakery after high school... of course, the location of the store was smack in the middle of Montreal's red light district... as the hookers would be standing along the bakery building soliciting along the wall... we (students) would drop rings of pineapple, cookies and little silver sugar balls used to decorate cakes... suffice to say just about anything we could get our hands on, we would drop it on them... we got cursed at, along with the usual threat of... *tabarnac attends que je t'atrappe...*

... venereal veneration... my best moment was when we went on the roof of the bakery and threw sugar cookies at the rooming house across the street... it was a hot evening and windows were wide open and we saw a hooker and her client having sex... it was very hard to hold back the laughing all the while aiming/throwing cookies at the open window... in hindsight, the amount of sweet firepower projected through the hot summer air was enough to feed a diabetes convention... not!

... accountability... in the very early 70's I can still remember the roach infested house we once lived in being demolished to make room for a public park... which turned out to be a hangout for us... during the summer days we would play football/baseball... in the winter, boards were set up for the skating rink... and of course, we would help the french guy who took care of the rink... by clearing out the recently fallen snow... he would lend us shovels, we would skate and clean... and he got paid... also, next to the rink... there was a wooden shack, with an oil furnace... where we would warm up...

... responsibility... as time passed and we got older and wiser... we would later use the park to once again hang out... but this time until the wee hours of the night... we'd spin the merry go round so hard that it almost flew off its' axle... push the baby swings, so that they wrapped around the horizontal post/bar... and of course, the ultimate test of juvenile delinquency, try to smoke a joint all the while hanging upside down from the monkey bars... could one be any cooler?... absolutely not...

... injudicious... maybe I still required a few more beatings to appreciate the concepts of responsibility and respect... did my father fail in his parental duty...?... or did I as a son...?...

## 2015/04/19 – Sunday (Cascais, Portugal)

... culmination... what does my life sum up to... dysfunctional parents with whom I cannot hold a grudge because I understood their hardship... my failed marriage where I simply fell out of love with an incredible woman and mother of my children... how does one survive any hardships in life... with love?... may it be a placebo and/or an illusion which one faithfully believes so intensely as if it were a religion... maybe *love* is the real thing... the cure for ailments... too bad we interchange love and sex as being the same...

... tranquility... Suzanne's carefully selected music... mellow sounds ooze from the speakers... her words flow in my mind with lingering imagery... lying here and concentrating hard to forget or even stop time... my heart betrays me and pounds the beats of time... a heavy feeling... very melancholic right now cause we are embraced as one... but at the same time I feel restless with unrelated thoughts perturbing our moment... I find romance is so under rated... we tend to focus too much on physical sex and techniques that we forget the mind or like I prefer saying the spiritual essence of a person... the mind is and can be such a powerful orgasmic element...

... inexhaustible... am I the only one to blame for my restless & sleepless nights... where I want you from beyond too... in those few hours where we are both in bed... I hold on to the headboard... so that my body does not move or leave our bed... and my essence can now leave my body and go over and see you from a bird's eye view... I hover over you and can almost smell your perfume... and imagine my desire just to hold my cheek against your face... I glide under the blankets with you and feel your warmth... I want to ravish you... slowly, ever so slow... I am in you not physically, or mentally but metaphysically... our bodies become one for so many endless hours...

... sashay... a few days ago, it hit me like a rock... a thought came to the forefront... we are incredibly lucky... there are forces beyond my (us) understanding that are pushing this union/connection between Suzanne and I... the purpose/reason for this is still foreign to me... but you know what... I am just gonna sit back and truly enjoy the ride... cause I now believe everything will come into focus... maybe not like we wish... but I always found that in my life... everything I ever wished for always materialized... though never the way I wanted or expected it to happen... so, once again... my attitude will be to let this mysterious force guide me/us... are you game... ?...

... age-appropriate... upon reflection... we seem to be going through a wave of fatigue, Suzanne and I... at an initial glance, I had previously stated this was old age creeping in with the grumpy years... but maybe not... what if, all we have done throughout our lives was subconsciously... trying to find one another in this lifetime?... we endured neurotic parenting... difficult relationships... perhaps made some drastic mistakes over the years... or even the feeling of not belonging here... do you think all we did as individuals was nothing but filler until we would meet again...

... finish line... would it be accurate to say... that we both got to a point in our lives... where all we want is to be with one another... and that we have had enough of putting up with people in general and their social absurdities... are we or will we, become recluses?... clues or ideas such as our bedroom is our sanctuary... the children are now adults with wings of their own and our role as parents has diminished drastically... look at our current aspirations... we don't care what or where we will be as long as it is in a US context...

... presently... reflective pensive thoughts for the mind... a feast for the eyes upon seeing you... it allows me to breath away from the mundane and put you in the forefront of my life... as this is where you belong... to press my mind up against your body... to measure your shoulders with my eyes... to caress your body, your heart, your femininity, your scent, your beauty and sexiness... to indulge myself in your uniqueness, to appreciate it like probably no other can… is more than I have ever wished or even dreamed for… to have your body wrap me in our slumber… allowing my eyes to finally close and let go of reality… knowing, once open again will not see reality until they (eyes) have captured you as the first image of the day…

## 2015/04/20 – Monday (Cascais, Portugal)

… manic whiner… after the weekend… everyone I can think of has a Monday job waiting for them… my sabbatical year is a very, very modest financial lifestyle… I do not have a job other than writing what I observe and whatever thoughts and/or reflections I can associate with my observations, other than this I read, listen/watch TedTalks and meet up with Suzanne whenever possible… all my monies for the one year sabbatical are my savings divided into 12 monthly installments… and yet despite my meager expenses I will not have enough money to stay the full year… keeping in tune with my current mindset, I do not want to think about what I will do when the money runs outs… I will be the first to admit, this is the epitome of irresponsibility…

… contrast… found this new coffee shop called Buzio… in one of the more affluent neighbourhoods in Cascais… food and service is simply outstanding and add to this a spacious exterior terrace… almost tailor made for me to sit unperturbed with my people watching hobby… new modern condos surround the bistro… but beyond these high end condos are moderate ones… it is a reminder for the rich that they are surrounded by the poor majority and therefore must spend money on alarms and window bars… but for the poor majority it is a reminder that maybe god is unjust or does not give a shit about inequality… personally I think god is too busy to focus his attention on this grain of sand we call our planet… considering our infamous stupidity… we can irritate the best of any deity…

… target… lunch hour and no school kids walking home for lunch… what I see are plenty of single folks walking their dogs or high end luxury cars pulling out from underground parking lot vaults… one would think money would enable a family lifestyle… instead it creates leeches… a leech is someone who uses up oxygen for their sole benefit… I hope when they grow old or that they outlive their pets… and the money buys trinkets that fill in the aging voids associated with seclusion… it probably will as they have no alternative…

… coming together… finally… I see a seventy something year old couple walking by the bistro... they look in my direction at the bistro terrace... but only as a curiosity as they do not stop and keep on walking... the man is quite tall, with a full set of grayish hair and wearing prescription glasses with transition lenses which turn greenish... he holds her hand as they walk, her pace is much slower than his elongated strides... but she manages to keep up despite her hefty size... actually she wobbles from side to side when walking... as she holds on to his hand and pulls on his arm too... but this does not unbalance him or affect him in any way... one gets the feeling his body is used to this and compensates automatically like we do with breathing during a run...

... preserve... he wears a dress shirt and slacks... with a wool sweater hanging on his shoulders... his shoes seem slightly worn out on the heels... despite the signs of wear and tear, the shoes looked as if they are polished regularly... she is wearing a long skirt and a blouse with paisley print... her hairstyle is not of this decade, I get the feeling this is the same hairstyle she was born with... despite her plus size body and grayish hair, there is an air of confidence in her... one would think a woman this size with mobility difficulty would have a hunched back and/or leaning forward... but not her and neither the man she is with... which I suppose to be her husband despite not seeing wedding bands associated with their generation... as I study their clothing, it is abundantly evident these were bought many years ago... if I were their age, would I trouble myself with shopping for new clothes knowing I would not live long enough to wear them out...

... shopping bag... he is carrying two grocery shopping bags... the kind that used to be free in grocery stores and re-used to line garbage cans... until the ten cent environment fee came into effect... now we have to buy plastic bags with not just a sole purpose of being for grocery/garbage but also make the merchant richer... as they reach the roundabout intersection... in one of the street corners there is a small tree lined green space with a park bench... just one bench, it looks like it was a surplus from some other park... the bench seems completely out of place... but I guess, privacy and isolation is what they want as they brush off leaves and sit down...

... tupperware free... he places the grocery bags between them... she pulls two cylinder shape items covered in aluminum foil paper from one grocery bag... from the other he takes out a plastic water bottle but it has a red liquid... and also takes out two plastic cups/glass and pours the red liquid in them... he hands her a cup and they make a toast, now I'm sure the mysterious red liquid is wine... she partially unwraps the foil cylinder, and it looks like a sandwich from where I'm sitting... and hands it to him... he holds his and waits until she has also unwrapped hers... my eyes can see them... share a secret smile which is a message between them as it signals it is time to start eating... each bite is rich with flavour, respect, admiration, kindness and love...

... shivers... she hands him a spoon and from one bowl they dip both spoons in it... as the spoons make contact with their lips... he smiles but her facial grimace expression indicates it is a cold dessert... I don't think anything was said between them, yet he placed his sweater on her shoulders... unspoken secrets/requests are communicated by the souls as words are limiting and echo nothing... like when one dies, then the remaining spouse also dies inside as the remaining life is now also limited... the day a god touches whatever love there is between them, the interference will destroy the only worthwhile beautiful earthly occurrence... this is what we all dream off... true love...

## 2015/04/21 – Tuesday (Cascais, Portugal)

... morning... with Suzanne gone to work... I just lay here in her bed... the bedroom is an extension of her personality... there is nothing in here that associates me to a feeling of *belonging*... I feel homeless but still in a state of worldly comfort... with every *good night* wishes... brings me to another bad morning as I take in a panoramic view of the bedroom... soon, this bedroom will be a distant memory which I will remember as something pleasant even though in the present it's becoming unpleasant...

... bare... as I get out of bed in the loud silence of the house... only to be interrupted by the next door neighbour's toilet flushing... the thin walls have no sound barrier qualities of any kind... but as long as they (walls) block unrefined scented farts I can accept all other flaws... looking in the mirror this morning... there is no need to comb my hair as I'm bald... the bags under my eyes remind me that my body is deteriorating... despite the foolish thoughts emitted by my mind that I am young at heart... actually I look more like my father now... do I look more like him or is it the last mental image I have of him in his coffin that reminds me that I look like him... nevertheless I'm tanned and slightly healthy looking in appearance... maybe because I skipped a Canadian winter... so lucky, indeed...

... orthodox... yesterday was the first time I walked into this neighborhood... as I looked down the 4 avenues from the roundabout... I put myself in the mind frame of a realtor or land developer... and with this foreign mindset, I thought like these folks and logically walked down one of the 4 avenues where I thought a bistro ought to be... this is how I came to find the Buzio bistro...

... dreariness... just sitting in the bistro terrace... in order to sit here for several hours, my only obligation... with an espresso cup in hand... is to ensure two sips of the coffee are downed... then... what am I going to do today... this is what I ask myself every morning... what will I do with my life... I don't feel like doing anything... but I just want to be *okay*... but what is this *okay*... in the meanwhile I watch people walk in and out of the coffee shop... am I a stalker, voyeur or anthropologist?... so far all I have seen are single folks mostly from the retired age bracket... then, as if to break the monotony walks in a young, long haired, good looking brunette in her early thirties...

... ennui... in the time it took for her to sit down at the table in front of me... without any malicious intent but certainly with curiosity... I looked her over, honing in on everything no one else would care to think of... designer jeans with back pockets... though the pocket flaps are slightly different in size, so the jeans are defective or fakes... her blouse snugs her breasts but is loose over the tummy... a bit too loose, as if to distract from a tummy bulge and instead redirect our attention to her cleavage... she constantly nods her head and her long brown hair sways from side to side... almost like an insecure nervous tick... but her glued on finger nails are constantly separating hair strands... I have the feeling she is too self-consciousness to pull out a mirror... probably wishes she had sat facing the bistro window so she could see her reflection...

... mammon... certainly she does not wear them for the comfort of the stiletto heels... the plasticized gold color cloth is ungluing from the heel on one shoe... they seem fairly new but are an ill fit as the shoe material is cheap and cannot possibly contain her foot... her large loop golden earrings could be used to make artisanal dream catchers... also with rings on several fingers both massively bold and gold in color... the kind you buy in popular clothing stores... usually displayed by the cash register on your way out... where you end up making an impulse purchase decision... in her case in was intentional... so big are the rings that they can be used as a weights when scuba diving... but a diver would not dare to use it as such... for large fish can mistake the shiny golden rings as a fishing lure... also, in fish schools it is a gaffe to be fooled by shiny metal...

... coat-tail... in her cigarette loneliness... she leaves her lipstick trail on the cigarette filter and coffee cup... so much red innuendo clamouring financial love... the kind of love that feeds one's time in the shopping malls of empty abundance... the fragrance of an aspartame daddy with ease of red money... if she had a therapist he'd suggest she give up red meat... with aging time... eventually she'll wake up and still have her make up on from the previous day(s)... and maybe giving up on life when the mirror tells... that her beauty can no longer be reflected...

## 2015/04/22 – Wednesday (Cascais, Portugal)

... pudginess... all play and no work has added millimeters to my waist line... should I get a bigger mirror for the bathroom... one which can capture my expanding girth... perhaps get a re-enforced bathtub too... I spend my days trying to come up with ideas for my writing... I feel I'm boring and drained too... what can I possibly write which has meaning and substance for a human... every experience we have in life is based on something else, there is nothing about us in terms of originality... we repeat the same mistakes for eons after eons... so on a smaller scale... here I am taking time off to try writing when someone has already done this, for sure... and probably written something interesting...

... doting... today is my ex's birthday... I think she is off on a vacation somewhere in the Rockies... actually, I'm quite proud of her that she managed to move on and flourish... I have this paternal feeling for those I love and care for... let me see if I can explain this... after 33 years of marriage... *I love my ex-wife but I'm not in love with her*... I felt in the latter part of our marriage we were more like a brother and sister couple... despite our separation, if need be I would still hold her hand when a plane would take off...

... vibrations... my marriage was a mixed bag of emotions with the multiple facets of guilt being predominant... I have yet to come to terms with my guilt for causing pain to others and to a lesser extent myself... and couldn't continue to live in a world where deception was my religion... though religion may be a container for faith... in my case it was a colander... it was a clear example of... why do we know nothing yet think we know it all... at the end it was like ice skating as fast as you can and hit the snow bank in order to stop... lived my life like this until the snow melted...

... one-sided... my marital life was out of control... no, let me re-phrase this more accurately... *I was out of control*... it was a game convincing myself

I was in control even if my plans and behaviour were improvised every other second... how long can I fool those I love... as long as I could fool myself... it was a balanced equation, no?... living in my selfish mind... doing the perceived right thing was no different than my homeless man sleeping in front of an air vent for warmth and thinking this is a luxurious lifestyle...

... excursion... I'm still puzzled as to why I did the first Camino pilgrimage, two years ago... whatever prompted me to do it had to be orchestrated my divinity... I never felt alone on the walk of solitude... towering over my head... it's *them*... the unseen *them* by conventional eyes... but nevertheless, I see the invisible *them*...

... aftermath... with a second Camino journey next month... then what, after the pilgrimage... this lifestyle without work and only creativity... disconnects me from responsibility of the real world I was in... can I return to that world as I cannot manage in this one forever... this has been a life of privileged spiritual leisure... okay?... so where do I draw the line so that I may cross over permanently...

## 2015/04/23 – Thursday (Estoril, Portugal)

... itinerant... what am I doing when I hop from bistro to bistro... a spoiled brat, who goes around observing people... what does this contribute to improving mankind's existence... fuck all... certainly what I write is not a revelation either... it's more like fodder for my wasted time... and it's not as if what I see and/or write about satisfies my ego in any possible way... then why do I write about what I see... am I playing god when I write... I want what from these strangers walking by this affluent seaside café... who the fuck am I to do this... all I do is point out faults in others... can it be I learn from their mistakes... absolutely... as I see myself through their mistakes repeating history...

... egocentric... this coastal beach town oozes with money... it's a different kind of crowd where quite a few business people, TV personalities and politicians make it their home... it's also a playground for the rich tourists with its' casino... but despite the affluence one can still find extremely modest homes which were once upon a time homes for the local fishermen... dog walking is the past time as it allows one to be seen... chance meetings to schmooze with fellow upper class/crust residents... yet, so high are their noses turned up that they fail to see their dog's shit... and even if they saw the fucken mutt crapping it is beneath them to scoop it up into a bag... and what is civic contempt without cigarette butts being flickered on to the pavement too...

... destitute... do opposites attract... there is a beggar (elderly man) with both legs amputated at the knees... someone's leashed dog comes up to him for a sniff... he pets the dog... there is mostly a one sided conversation between the old man on the ground and the middle aged woman who is the dog owner... I can't hear what they are talking about... but I can sure make it up based on his gestures...

... interpretation... you are so right, a hug can do wonders for my soul... but throw in some money with a hug and I can get the peace of mind which I seek... please, certified cheques only... nothing more annoying than getting high hopes in seeing the cheque... to later find out there are no funds to cover it... even the hug will lose its' value... after such a fiasco of false friendship and a bouncing cheque... ok, you know what, just give me a hug... and let's leave it at that... this is good enough for me... seriously, it is never enough... throw in a kiss too... yeah, a hug and kiss... this sounds good... ok, a hug and kiss and you make my day... but if you have spare change... that too can sweeten the deal... hug, kiss and spare change... cannot go wrong with this winning combo...

... honey... is all honey sweet... am I in love or the idea of being in love... or is it that I simply do not want to be alone... am I experiencing another relationship difficulty with Suzanne... when I look at her, I see slow beautiful gestures and movements... she is graceful in every sense of the word... yet, I'm sure she has other qualities but I only care to focus on this right now... of course, physical beauty is not enough to sustain me... though I can see and feel the love she has for me... but her love can only reach or touch the outer shell I'm in... she cannot reach me inside... no one ever did... but she did come close...

... indulgent... bottom line is I don't want any attachment as it requires some sort of responsibility... I just want to be left alone... am I tired of being on this planet... it's absurdity and stupidity has taken its toll on me... or maybe am I prompting myself for a despair... what path am I on?... perhaps a masochistic one... is it the one we wonder about when we see a homeless person... it never fails, every time I see a homeless unloved person... I think, this was someone's baby at one time... maybe instead of succumbing to a depression in the making... be less self-absorbed and even read more (but I ran out of english books)... and why not exercise to keep my fucken mind busy...

## 2015/04/24 – Friday (Areia, Portugal)

… nailed… woke up again, shit I still have another day to live… I'm losing myself… no longer living or eating properly either… a diet of coffees… this being here in Suzanne's place is getting to me too… her motherly good intentions get on my nerves… but I am her guest and need to be civil… one cannot bite the hand that feeds you… I may be fucked in my head but I still have *savoir vivre,* even when I fuck her… for how long I do not know… again, as I lie in bed alone and she prances with getting ready for work… my self-indulgence asks… am I human or not… if not where do I come from as I cannot be a product of this planet… then, what am I inside this human shell… in the galactic bureaucratic universe maybe it was a mistake placing me here… as I look out the window and see the intense blue sky… my wish is to stand on the window ledge and fly away… not loneliness but agonizing aloneness propels me… I want to be with my peers whoever or where ever they are…

… distorted pace… walking and thinking… is it as lethal as pot smoking and drinking… can the mind distinguish between the two… as I walk around I see nice single family homes… I cannot see myself tied down to a dwelling… what would I do with my days… work during the day and come home in the evening… it would feel like two jails… besides I do not even have a picture I can hang on the wall… something that would say I belong here and this is my house… just like the rest of the world has and does… even with Suzanne taking my point of view and replacing it with hers as she claims to know where happiness lies… it certainly did not lie next to me, this morning in her bed…

… echo… need to wake up when this sabbatical ends… keep forgetting my objective for coming here in the first place… repetition is the best way to learn and remember… *is it a self-discovery and spiritual quest… * or is it my ticket out of here?… the last time I walked the Camino pilgrimage I had received an intuition that I would die… for the longest time I thought it to be my physical death… maybe the death refers to a lifestyle or as new agers believe… *that death is a rebirth…* it still does not change… we always hurt the ones we love… miss my kids… almost forgetting the life we had together… it does not seem like it was real… today is surreal and I'm trying to live off thoughts from the past… but how real were those thoughts… after all, perhaps it is a physical death as every memory is gradually becoming blurred… this would ease the transition to the next world…

… pair… is there really only two kinds of people… and this distinction is evident from the children I see and hear in the park... most of the kids growl and chase the pigeons to scare them off... a smaller group of kids stand in front of the pigeons but are ready to retreat if the bird approaches them... as a kid, I did not even want to disturb a pigeon let alone stand in defiance before it... this bothered my parents that I was not aggressive... their contrived words of encouragement simply introverted me more... it was like when we went on the only vacation as a family... the peace of sitting in the backseat made me invisible... and once at the destination I could... maybe re-invent myself for a little while, at least to please them...

... childhood... the drizzle does not bother me as I stand on this small dock... it was made by amateurs from what I can see... handsaw cut planks and I guess there was a shortage of nails too... as some planks have just one nail which serves more as decoration than utility... my prescription glasses fail to make me see things clearly... as water beads cling to the lenses... as a kid, I once took a shower still wearing my glasses... I had completely forgotten I was still wearing the eyeglasses... as the water set on the lenses I panicked slightly thinking I was going blind, but quickly realized my silliness and laughed out loud to myself...

... uninterrupted... am I still repeating my childhood but in an adult form... there is a small row boat moored to a post... the boat is filling up with rain water... what if I took the boat for a ride... rowing in this rain and I can't swim either, how far out into the Atlantic would I get... once out there would I still be able to see westernmost extent of mainland Portugal and continental Europe... since my Camino walk is to reach Finisterre, the most western point in Spain... why not row from there and leave behind thousands of voices who never heard mine... in my last breaths would my spirituality lead to aliens... beyond the universe... intelligent re-design... are we a lab experiment with incomplete features, a trial run of sorts... and maybe even a re-birth to get things right the next time around... instead of being one of god's mistakes...

## 2015/04/25 – Saturday (Areia, Portugal)

... fortunate... I keep forgetting how lucky I am to be living this experience of being in a foreign country... I spend my time observing and sometimes even admiring these people who cross my path in life... I have read more books in the last 5 months than probably in my whole life... unless of course articles in toilet magazines count... even newspapers are a novelty as I try to master the language... eventually, newspapers will only be sold in retirement homes... the art of reading a morning newspaper while sipping coffee will be a relic of the past... with their Wi-Fi mindset young people will not continue with newspaper reading... in fact, in their daily haste they even drink coffee standing up... with phone on the table, one hand on the espresso cup and the other tapping on a texture-less glass/screen...

... gait... there is kind of strut with the locals as they walk about... couldn't figure it out, why such high steps... then realized the high steps are because of the uneven stone pavement sidewalks... both men and women look like a *Joe Cool* walking with an attitude, including the folks who seem to be in the lower financial ranks of society... the underprivileged woman looking at window shops... only seeing beautiful things and never occurs to her to ask why she does not have them... maybe she is happy with her strut in life... when I lived in Montreal, snowstorms were an acceptable way of life which was dealt with accordingly... unlike the Torontonians who call in the army... in Montreal we toughed it out even with shabby snow removal in the plateau neighborhood...

... adults... don't see too many kids outside today... this being Saturday, I guess if they aren't obliged with school then they'd rather stay at home on a computer game... as a kid I shared the same values except we'd stay home and watch cartoons... that was until the advent of Portuguese school on Saturday mornings cut into our prime time cartoon viewing... but my parents insisted we learn Portuguese and expelled us from the house... but I also suspect they wanted us out of the house to procreate or maybe just peace of mind... since I went against my will to class on a Saturday morning... I spent my time in a mischievous state... teachers were not qualified nor had any training as teachers... and were unable to maintain order/discipline in the classrooms... put 30 or so rowdy anti-Portuguese language learning, cartoon deprived kids against their will in a classroom... is like lighting a match to a dynamite stick with a short fuse... institutions... truly, I was always anti-establishment... always questioning the *why* of everything... and it got worst with time too... as a teenager it was pretty much when I got out of hand... today I think I am more subdued... I think...

... high school... seriously, do you think in any way I would be part of the dance committee back in grade 7... ouf!... I was too cool, so I thought... but in reality I was a little nerdy guy completely disoriented and navigating through teenage confusion... and now as an adult I still do not know where

I am heading... but the fatalist in me is pretty certain it will be an economically priced coffin... why spend money on something... which in principal I will not enjoy... on the other hand I just hope... I would be able to purchase the most expensive coffin and charge it to my credit card... and watch creditors sweat it out collecting it from my grave... try to collect now, you bastards...

... distracted... secondary one (grade 7) was my first mixed classroom experience... up until then it had always been an all-boy classrooms... from which I retained such fond memories as eating sunflower seeds and discreetly disposing of the shells in some jerk's desk, usually a bully... *I was a vindictive sneaky kid*... and those 8 foot roll up window blinds with a rope... there was a student sitting in front of me who always placed his hand/arm on my desk... I tied the rope to his wrist and pulled the rope up... the blind went up and so did his arm/body... pretty funny, huh?... so I thought too... he didn't think so... it's ok, the bastard also ended up with sunflower shells in his desk... again, it was another one of my silent victories...

... lethargic... sorry, my story was heading into a left *sunflower* field... now, back to the dance committee in grade 7... of course the first school dance theme was Halloween... though I did not participate in the dance organization... I did envy those who did, cause they were excused from attending class... lucky bastards... eventually, I attended the dance... it was my first and I guess the same for most of my classmates... judging from the fact we were all pinned to the walls until a slow dance came on... in hindsight, there should've been more guys involved in the dance committee... especially when it came to the music selection... let's face it... Leif Garrett, Donny Osmond, and Partridge Family are nowhere near Black Sabbath's Paranoid christian music or is it devil music... not sure?, if you know please correct me...

## 2015/04/26 – Sunday (Areia, Portugal)

... silent rituals... I like churches without a priest being present and/or noisy weekend hypocrisy crowds... mind you not all church goers are phonies... just the ones who sit there constantly making sure their cells are on silent mode... one can never be too sure... but I can understand as I once upon a time attended Sunday mass... cause after consuming the host (or body of Christ) there is a moment of kneeling penance and some people have plenty of sins that need forgiving... me on the other hand I had no sins *I'm incredible this way*... therefore, I find the back rest of the bench in front of me makes for a perfectly good table to place my phone and play a game but cell phones had yet to be commercialized... then again I'm not sure if it is truly the house of god, but on weekdays it is quiet enough to be...

... motherly aureole... some people are coming out of church as if they received a message from the almighty regarding a looming earthquake... or was it the priest asking for a donation to help the Nepal earthquake relief... mention money and people will either run to it or from it... as a kid while in church we had to make the sign of the cross over our mouths whenever we yawned to prevent evil from entering... asking my mom... *are we not in church the holiest of places, what evil lurks here?*... her answer came in the form of a backhander directly to my halo free head for being a smart ass...

... nimbus... with another disaster such as rain on the horizon... I witness a mother already in the church parking lot... before driving away she opens her car trunk and retrieves an oiled stained white pastry shop box... two pudgy boys swagger towards her... not that I'm concerned with their dietary habits of deep fried meat pastries... these Portuguese finger foods are high in saturated fats and cholesterol levels so high that they can reach heaven... I'm in no way a dietary specialist here but I suspect, nor are they trendy gluten free... luckily the *host* representing the body of Christ is dipped in wine, just for the priest and not the rest of us... is it not a miracle, that wine has no adverse effects... especially if you drink a few bottles... everything seems so right... even the greasy Portuguese finger food becomes benign... wine, the cure for all ailments...

... parental wisdom... growing up as kids we were not regular church goers... only in time of crisis such as funerals or weddings... but whenever my brother and I were rowdy... my parents in their infinite wisdom figured Sunday mass would calm us down... in reality it did calm us down as we were completely bored... my parents had very busy social calendars on Sunday so neither one of them had time to take us to mass... dad would go hare hunting in the wee hours of the morning and once he got home in the afternoon he just wanted to sleep... as he entered the house mom was leaving for work... in hindsight this scheduling conflict also enabled the longevity of their marriage...

... responsibility... I kind of see mass in the same vein as my parents did... it also conflicted with my Sunday schedule... but because my dad feared god and mom equally... he ordered us to attend the 5 pm mass on Sunday afternoon... now the beauty of this afternoon mass was that it lasted only 30 minutes and not a full hour as in the morning sessions... still, 30 minutes is just too much time for an 11 and 12 year old boys... my brother and I would leave the house at the very last possible minute... once we got to the church, we'd watch the people go in and we'd stay outside throwing snowballs at one another and also commit ourselves to any mischief we could think of... when people started coming out of the church after the mass... we would then head home too... the old man would ask what the sermon was about... my brother froze with these questions... I on the other hand had a well-rehearsed lying routine... it always centered around the theme of *the kingdom of god and how we need to go to church*... so as to get into heaven...

... perpetuate... back in the day of kingdoms... European countries were keen on the idea of discovering new lands for profit/greed... and with this, the well-meaning notion of spreading Christianity... even today, when you donate to some Christian fund to help the famine relief in Africa... noble as their intentions are in helping the less fortunate... why do they send out a handful of missionaries with bible in hand to spread the gospel... just because someone is starving... does not mean they do not already possess a religious belief of some sort... it's a cult mind set to indoctrinate someone when they are at their weakest state... why can't we just help someone with no strings attached...

... reflections for the reader... might as well get on with your mediocre life... cause had it been a palpitating life... you would not be here reading this to the end... I know and you now know, I have hit a nerve... your existential-ism pursuit is now in question... oh shit, how banal are our lives... if I spend my time writing this important useless crap... and worst yet, you the reader are still here... reading this to the end... god!... you are worse off than me... tear out the page and put it in the recycling bin... or go to mass with this page folded into a little square and place it in the collection basket...

## 2015/04/27 – Monday (Cascais, Portugal)

... commute... if I did a count on which day of the week I'd call in sick most often... Monday would be a sure winner especially when I worked downtown as a computer programmer... the thought of hopping on the #44 bus from Brossard suburbia to downtown Montreal was enough to make me cringe... and at times the bus would arrive and I would stand back and wait/ take the next bus... somehow I was hoping for a miracle... wearing a fashionable shirt and tie, with a matching tailored suit… I befitted the corporate image indeed… my mind and soul were not up to par on this… hence my dilemma…

… water cooler… how was your *weekend* jargon… who the fuck cares… ask me how my *life is not* fitting into this metal framed glass mad house of an office… in the limiting cubicle world… where the greater the number of partitions it takes to build one's cubicle also determines the importance in the organization… that it is as long as your salary does not affect the upper management's *projected profit*… since when does a projection equate reality or why do we live by the man-made law of a projection… I was a male whore with 3 kids to feed and a home to maintain… all I wanted and worked for was the money… I only looked out for my interests as I'm number one in the corporate scheme of things… if the salary raise was unsatisfactory, a slew of CV's were shipped out in an efficient military aggressiveness…

… fine-tune… I invent my own rules and only if it makes sense for me… when it stops making sense… then it's time to change and every time, I do so in order to adjust to my current reality… this is how my brain is wired… I have been living in Portugal in this nomadic lifestyle for the last 5 months… I keep reminding myself how lucky I am to be doing this… and in a few days I should be starting the Camino trek… but though my mind is still somewhat young in its thinking, my body is not… the tired old man in me is showing up frequently… there is contradiction within myself… looking to settle but at the same time been there, done that syndrome… Suzanne was my last anchor to civilization where I had a home to stay in… now I'm a nomad where everything is not mine…

… single-mindedness… always moving and always writing… I spend my day with endless observations… at times my loneliness and aloneness drive me mad to tears… repeating my mantra how lucky I am is sounding more like a broken record… why do I think I want a home and a love… why do I fool myself that this is what I need… even if I had this I'm not sure I would recognize it… nothing is sure in my head or life other than I miss my kids… my coming on this trip made my children feel I abandoned them… this is a part of my life I feel I fucked up royally…

… full of shit… like a spoiled brat… filling my days with selfish self centered absorption… why do I look at everything on this earth as if it is for the last time… who am I writing for… who would read the whining crap I write… as I go back and read some pages my first thought is to scrap everything… is writing a catharsis process for my years of confusion… not even, it raises more questions especially with spirituality… as I get older things are not getting easier, in fact it is the opposite… maybe if I did not give a shit and sailed through life unhindered I would still get to the finish line… and maybe even happier… what can I offer the world… my share of sadness… I lost my wisdom, credibility and feel like a fool to those who knew me… I'm mentally tired and this is why I write this… is it?

… reflection… siting in this bistro… I see myself in the glass window… no one knows I'm here… if I were to disappear only Revenue Quebec would notice I were missing… why do I feel alone and don't like it but yet shun from people too… what is wrong with me… the human part of me wants to stay here and flourish… my spiritual side wants to hop on a window ledge and fly away… why aren't they compatible… ?

… daybreak… today my morning started off with these words to Suzanne… *my reality is this… I reached a point where my being with you hurts me more than not being with you…* how can the rest of the day go well… I doomed myself from the moment I realized I was still alive this morning… am I so bored of *being…*


## 2015/04/28 – Tuesday (Lisbon, Portugal)

… linger… arrived in Lisbon this morning and checked into a hotel which will blow my budget to kingdom come… my money/budget makes it to heaven but I cannot… as I step out of the hotel for a walk the thought comes to me… *am I wishing my life away…* with the IPod plugged in, I find my time is measured by the number of songs heard, as each song lasts about 5 minutes… nevertheless… the day is simply beautiful with summer like weather unlike in Montreal this time of year… and just around the corner is a small park alive with people…

… Jardim Constantino… is a small park in a residential neighbourhood… a green space in the midst of 6 storey apartment buildings… one can find an ice cream kiosk, a public phone booth, a playground with swings and some sort of rope climbing cage, which would've been banned in north America because of potential lawsuits… century old trees offering cool gothic shade… but for me it is the open air terrace bistro with large parasols and beer at 50 cents, espresso coffee and of course cigarettes are unlimited…

… ecological… green spaces flourishing with heavily fertilized shrubs which are only disturbed when dogs walk by to shit… there's also a free public bathroom, the building structure is about size of toolshed with a turret... and it is here to stay cause it was built solidly... with a brick and tile exterior, with a gazebo type of roof as a mini observatory... there is even a lady who works there full time making sure it is spotlessly clean... she showed me her little castle with so much pride... and yet on the other end of the park I had seen an old man pissing up against one of the fertilized shrubs...

... invisible partitions... during the day one can see toddlers with over-protective hovering parents (*dumpies the new yuppies*)... |||... and the older kids are on their own as one of their divorced parents are sitting on the bistro terrace concerned with their children's health by smoking from a safe distance... all the while refreshing their stale breath with coffee and cigarettes... also this morning's potent whitening toothpaste is no match for sun yellow colored teeth... too bad the cell phone on the table does not ooze reflective teeth whitening microwaves... as a *selfie* would just be too vain but quite suitable for an internet dating site... |||... seniors shuffle in hordes... expelled in the daily ritual from home by their complaining children... leaving a scented trace of mothballs behind to annoy the children living in the house/condo they paid for... an old *gentleman like* senior sits next to me on the terrace... I feel like giving him my eye glasses as he starts reading his newspaper 3 inches away from his face... at least he is not one of those trendy seniors one reads in the newspaper using hunting rifles to resolve domestic issues...

... fuckery... my ass and the bistro terrace are both centrally located in the park... and there are benches placed along the perimeter of the park grounds... come to think of it... I am sure in the nocturnal hours the park is a sanctuary for pot smokers... the benches are quite occupied... on some there are seniors feeling important in contributing an imaginary *something* into the air for another senior to hear... on other benches are happy people just talking, kissing or holding hands amorously... then there are people sitting alone on the edge of the bench... as if the space next to them is an invitation... their empty eyes stare into the crowded park emptiness... it's these, the sad ones I am drawn to... my empathy is in vain as I sit here alone... people are the same everywhere...

... unofficial... there is a man who seems to be a caretaker of the park... I'm not sure of this as he wears civilian clothes nor does he have a broom, garbage can or a florescent/reflective vest to his persona... but he did blow a referee like whistle when one of the playground kids was playing rough... the man is also going around and picking up discarded folded cardboard boxes which came from the nearby chinese no frills store... he inspects the cardboard and if still in good condition he places them up against a retaining wall... there is a bench reserved for the parking monitors/facilitators, these are drunks that guide passing drivers in search of parking... pointing to available street parking spaces in return for a tip... the day must be good, as there's 2 big beer bottles underneath the bench... the bench shade acts as a cooler... how simple is a drowning life when all you live for is alcohol...

... stacked deck... in one corner of the park there are three tables with 4 chairs each, and all permanently anchored to the ground... a bit to the side of these tables are 3 benches... the tree canopy provides the shade over this unique area of the park... this micro cosmos of the park is reserved for card playing, for mature men with protruding tummies or receding/graying hair... and it is a woman free zone too... the previously collected cardboard boxes are used to pad the concrete chairs and table tops... the cardboard on the table top is also written on to keep track of card playing scores... with 4 players seated there are no more than 2 spectators per table to act as coaches, referees or provide comic relief... on the nearby benches are players with injured egos or waiting in line for a seat to free up in order to play cards... it is not a penalty box unlike hockey...

... succession... splattered bird droppings are everywhere... pigeons flock to pieces of bread being thrown on the ground... the only pigeons who don't care about the bread crumbs are the cruising male pigeons... pumped up males courting/chasing females playing hard to get... at the other end of the spectrum... generational voices echo throughout the park as these people are beautiful in their differences... as I sit here and watch all these folks... I realize my thoughts and written words do not affect them... whether they are playing cards or supposedly watching their kids... my presence does not disturb them... and yet I'm feeling a fondness for all this around me... this park is the cycle of life with a toilet included...

## 2015/04/29 – Wednesday (Lisbon, Portugal)

... ritual... my ex-wife *Emme* introduced me to the art of coffee drinking... it's not just about the beverage but how you drink it... for one it should never be standing up or drank when in a hurry either... the location is an important element to this joy of life... funny as memories seem to lose their meaning with time... she and I had spent many hours idling over coffee and it was never seen as a waste of time... we had dreams like any other couple...

children, growing old, retiring and grandchildren... though our divorce was difficult it was extremely civil and our friendship is still strong... why couldn't I imagine myself as a senior with her... is it to deny death or is it because I believe I will never reach old age...

... distinctive... ending up in Lisbon's Versailles Café for breakfast... this café was built/opened in 1922 and pretty much maintained its' original appearance... with period mouldings, columns and 10 foot high ceilings... a 60 foot counter and hand crafted cabinetry... even the waiters wear pristine white shirts and black pants, a red vest with matching bow tie and elongated white aprons... truly a style from a bygone era... but the breakfast prices certainly do not come anywhere close to the ones on the opening day... if you get my drift... as I sip my coffee a question arises as a group of middle aged women walk into the bistro... *why does a woman sometimes stop being a woman when she becomes married and/or a mom...*

... connubial... never had chores until I got married... mind you, when first married it seemed like fun doing things around the house... but like everything else in life including marriage... the novelty quickly ran out... in my infinite wisdom... for me to do any chore, I had to be in the right frame of mind, otherwise it would not happen... what I consider wisdom, my ex-wife claimed it to be laziness... as I slouched on the couch watching quasi-lame sitcom re-runs, because it is to arduous to look for the remote... she figured she now had me as a captive audience and launched/recited a list of chores that required my intervention...

... astray... trust me her chore recital was far from melodic... but I did manage to get a few words in edge wise... I said, add to *your* list of chores... *get ME a beer*... I never saw the beer... instead I saw the raising of her hand as she wound up for a *potuguese bolacha* on my head... ouch!... that *wedding band radar* on her hand sure hurts... in order to avoid future matrimonial violence... we each had a chore lists posted on the fridge... my list was easy to spot... the white paper had turned yellowish from oxidation and the corners were either curled up or had simply fallen... once again in my comedic infinite wisdom... I managed to insert another chore on my list... *make new list as this page is now full...*

... playful... as to why someone would go down to the pool or even buy one is beyond me... personally, I just filled up my indoor pool as it was quite big... a full 32x60 inches, actually it is better known as a bathtub... once the water level reached half way... I ran into the kitchen only wearing soiled mis-matched socks *I match my socks based on thickness & not color* and my speedo that I got when I was 17... *it has shrunk tremendously since then... due to water exposure, I think?* and grabbed the Palmolive dish soap *lemon scent...* and dumped/poured the bottle into the tub... as dish soap bubbles expand beyond control... I ran back to the fridge for that ice cold beer(s)... and ran back/jumped into the tub... watching the bubbles splatter the ceramic walls... I drank and smoked...

... mishandling... my mind wonders euphorically, and my whole body feels ever so good... but just then, my future ex breaks down the bathroom door/lock and barges in screaming about the mess... as I crawl the ceramic wall tiles to help me stand up erect... I reply, in a defiant yet loving tone... *huh?...* with a smack sound and lights out... next thing I know... I am being wheeled on a stretcher thru the hospital by some bearded intern... my ex-wife running after us holding my clean underwear and nagging the hairy chap about me wearing clean underwear before seeing the doctor... seriously... I ask you... is this not spousal abuse?... what is wrong with wearing my speedo when seeing a doctor...

... corrective measures... though my ex never hit me in any way... I do think that maybe she should've of had... and that the beatings would continue until morale improves...

## 2015/04/30 – Thursday – (Lisbon, Portugal)

... romantic desire... sometimes the smallest words have the biggest impact... if one reads between the lines... I'm gonna take a gamble, let's one day get together for lunch... I'll gaze at you in awe while you speak... cause you know I now hold you in the highest esteem... your delicate scent will tingle my senses... your truly sparkling eyes will hypnotize me into believing life is beautiful... fantasy is so pervasive... but it'll pull me through another mediocre day...

... loser... why do I write... is it for my ego?... if so, then this is not a good reason at all... but writing and then reading about my actions... perhaps, I can learn something about myself... or better yet be able to recognize an opportunity when it shows up and not let it slide by... breaking up with Suzanne has left me vulnerable... I find myself reminiscing missed romantic connections when I was working in home renovation back in Montreal... right now being in dream state only numbs the pain... after all when it comes to romance there were so many bad decisions... all based and driven by ego...

... manhood... my paint job was behind schedule... to say the least it was a hectic morning... I skipped breakfast and even my sacred café au lait morning ritual... my stomach kept making growling sounds like an underfunded symphony orchestra using recycled paint cans as percussion instruments... I was hungry... looking at my watch, it was already past one... and the saying *time flies* would very well be a propos... my hunger was becoming loudly obnoxious but at the same time the idea of Italian food especially pasta began to stifle my growling stomach... heading down to a small Italian restaurant where the food is so good that there are always line ups... my consolation was the late lunch hour and therefore perhaps no waiting...

... queue... there were no line ups but the restaurant had a full house of *ties in suits* on some get drunk convention... so waiting by the door to be seated... the waiter looked at me and signaled two... not sure if he was pointing at me so I looked back and was stunned to see this woman behind me... so gorgeous in her business attire and her perfume was simply splendid... the waiter approached us and said he had just one table left... I sensed he was hoping we would agree to sit together... I turned to her and asked whether she spoke French or English and then explained that I would not mind sharing a table as long as she promised not to throw spaghetti strands at passing waiters... what a dumb thing to say... her mischievous smile meant a *yes*... the waiter jovially led us to our table and now he re-iterated not to throw pasta at passing waiters...

... member... we sat down and I introduced myself... at this very moment our waiter very graciously offered us house wine... with all the commotion of the wine pouring... during this moment of silence I stared at this ravishing lady... after establishing what her name was... I just had to tell her... *I say this with the utmost respect, but you are simply beautiful...* sensing my observation caught her by surprise, she seemed almost speechless... placing my hand on hers... I said that I did not want to make her uneasy... touching her long delicate fingers sent shivers up my arm... she smiled and through her rosy cheeks she said... *thank you...* and sipped her wine... we spent the afternoon talking about everything and nothing... like old kindred spirits who ran into each other out of the blue...

... putz... sometimes, I amuse myself and wonder how would I define the perfect woman... and come up with a list of quasi-impossible traits... she must be intelligent, sexy, sweet, sensuous, feminine, dainty, articulate, sense of humour and ad nausea... can she be the stuff dreams are made of... maybe I'm too much of a foolish romantic, but there was something extraordinary...

almost as if I was in another realm of reality... and all this was happening in me, just because I was taken by her presence... I wonder if she realizes the impact she has on me... as I sipped my espresso while watching her adamantly eat her apple pie... but when it comes to an infatuation... should I have faith in my intuitions... when they tell me this woman is actually a man...

* * *

# MAY

PART SEVEN

## 2015/05/02 – Saturday (Lisbon, Portugal)

... answers... so many questions and doubts... I need to get a grip on my reality... it's a constant reminder that my purpose here is to re-do the Camino pilgrimage... and yes, there is no rhyme or reason for doing it other than there is a little voice in the back of my head that I have to... *listen to?*... walking around Lisbon is no longer capturing my interest... I know it is not the city which is the problem but whatever grinds my wheels in my head... boredom of my life becoming a chaotic nomadic routine will be the catalyst which will propel me into making a decision about committing to the Camino... is it only my life which is a contradiction...

... grasped... ended up walking in a neighborhood called Arroios... once one becomes familiar with the neighborhoods by name it's a sign that I have been here too long... like every great nookie in this city, it is where one will find a public park... or if you prefer the last stomping grounds where trees can still handle the air pollution... a triangle shape park with a few benches, neglected sidewalks and trees with exposed roots... mainly because the park is on a hillside and the erosion of the land was never stopped or replenished...

... dynasty... some of the buildings around this park are very modest... neglected building maintenance is not only a sign of the difficult economic times, but of historical hardships as some houses seem over a century old with only fingernails grasping the fragmenting foundations... a very small park indeed... but even its' small size does not undermine the importance it plays... there is no playground, but an abundant pigeon flock competing with dogs who only request a small space to shit... there is also an elderly homeless woman... whose monopolized empire is still limited to two benches where she stacks her suitcases covered with a tarp... she must be the *queen* of the park as her disloyal subjects only flock to her when she inadvertently drops a handful of bread crumbs... and what would be a kingdom without a church...

... puzzling... located on one of the corners facing the park... is a church which has several layers of steps leading to an elevated paved patio/platform... and once one manages to reach the patio then there is another obstacle with a further dozen steps before reaching the church doors... mankind probably believes making god quasi-inaccessible is better for devotion... on the patio level there are finely dressed people... with shiny shoes, cellphones in hand and a festival quantity of group selfies... and most with cigarette smiles too... on the sidewalk are people also finely dressed including shiny shoes... there are no selfies being flashed but all cells are resting on ears... there is an air of boredom coming from their faces... whether they are high up on the patio or down below on the sidewalk... the common feature of these faces are that they look like they're trapped in life... where is the optimism of the little child in them... or was hardship imposed from the first breath...

... riven... at the sidewalk level there is a side entrance to the church's ground floor with a funeral hearse parked outside its' doors... a coffin is being pulled out... on the patio level a newlywed couple are showered with rice... leaning up against a bench in the park, as I want to feel something poking my ass to wake me up cause I must be in a dream state... I can't help but laugh at this fiasco... is this crass scheduling... which of these events could not wait... the newlywed couple are oblivious to what is going down below and even the deceased by this time could not give two shits either... whatever the occasion... it's a human get together... a happening for uniting family and friends... with all this going on, there are now fearless and daring pigeons diving for the rice feast laid out before them before the *park queen* kneels to scoop it up...

## 2015/05/03 – Sunday (Lisbon, Portugal)

... without... Portuguese mother's day... there is enough in the media to make you feel guilty for not having a mother... I don't remember this ever being a big thing in Portugal, but North American style commercialization of this day as well as any other shopping oriented agendas has set roots in the culture... long gone are the days when a kiss and a hug spoke endlessly to a mom... now we need to shower her with flowers, perfumes or clothing/lingerie... please allow me to fuck you up... imagine your mom and dad in a 69 position and her slurping his cock and loving it... do you still want to buy her flowers?... your dad should...

... loud silence... the city is dead... from my inn room I heard cars passing by all night... an exodus of sorts... the streets have been silent all day... truly a ghost town... everything is closed on Sunday... my usual restaurants are all boarded up... either I eat at McDonalds or I try the vintage café called Versailles as I know for a fact they are open... one step into McDonalds and the line-up pushes me out... in the Versailles café... all the waiters are men maybe it's a sexist cultural difference... the waiter brings me my white bread ham sandwich with crusts cut off... this is as close as I can come to mom today... as she had worked for a cater and liked the idea of no crusts as it was a classy thing... there are quite a few mothers also having sandwiches for supper too... and me *a son* on my own too... we're all wearing faces of struggle...

... investment... an anorexic spinster with her old lady... the mother is sitting down with her face almost in the plate... the old woman's nostrils are close enough to the soup bowl to cause tsunami type ripples... the daughter speaks and orders for her mother as if she were a toddler... and even knows how much and what she can eat... from the looks of it... the mother was pulled out of her retirement home... though today was not sunny, it was the first day in a very long time she came out for day light air... maybe Easter was her last time... she is already sporting the same make-up the under taker plans to apply to her once she hops into the coffin... the daughter leaves mom alone for a cigarette break outside... the old lady has tears in her eyes... is this outing of theirs an obligation or love... will the old lady be pushed into oncoming traffic after supper... luck is on her side as the city traffic is dead...

... genetic entertainment... a group of ten are seated at one table... the crowded multi-generation family consists of the grandparents, two sons and their respective spouses... and an assortment of grandchildren... and such a joyful contrived family awkwardness... the brothers are truly from two different social classes... the shirt and tie son has two calm university prone daughters... the other loud speaking son sporting a faded polo shirt (with a red football crest) has two rowdy sons already pre-set in life for struggles... a heated discussion over the restaurant selection and food is just scratching the surface... but what is really at stake is the price and dividing up the bill... just because you look like you have money does not mean you do...

... fondness... as a kid when it came to mother's day in our house... the old man was not too keen when it came to offering gifts... he had a policy where... if she wanted something she can always buy it... but if my brother and I insisted he'd give us money to buy her perfume from the corner drug store as it was the only shop open on Sundays... why did everything have to be complicated with my parents... maybe this is why I like the simplicity of just walking calmly in my Camino solitude... maybe I have a voice I never heard... hopefully it will echo something soothing...

... 69... stepping out of the café, I see a parked car with flowers on the dashboard pressed against the windshield... and wonder who bought these mother day flowers... was it the child or the husband...

## 2015/05/05 – Tuesday (Lisbon, Portugal)

... body versus mind... yesterday and even today has been difficult, being isolated in Lisbon... incredible city, but its' charm is dwindling... I know... I now need to get on with Camino... but my last six months in Portugal have made me soft both in mind and belly as I'm out of shape... the starting point for the trek is from St. Jean Pied de Port in France... several options presented themselves in terms of travelling to get there... having friends in both Madrid and Paris I was inclined to make my flying arrangements via one of these cities where there would be an air of familiarity... but at the same time, I felt I would be explaining or even justifying my sabbatical year to these well-meaning folks...

... carbon copy... not even the idea of the pilgrimage excites me... why is this... maybe because I feel empty inside, alone and with no one at the end of the road... what do I have to look forward to... what do I do after the Camino... for the last two years I focused all my energies to get to the point where I can do the pilgrimage... the first time I did the pilgrimage in 2013, I came out of it with several intuitions... that I must re-do the pilgrimage, write a book and *I will die*... (the critical and puzzling intuition)... it is this last intuition which has kept me unbalanced... so much so that I'm willingly unable to commit myself to any kind of relationship... I feel I'm a lost soul, why would I bring anyone into my world... as I'm still not sure (naively) what was meant by the intuition *I will die*... is it a physical death by accident or by my own hand... or is it simply a change to a new lifestyle... if so could it be happiness?...

... shade... everything I do today seems to be as if it is the last time... breakfast was a slow process... the last bite of toasted bread was done in slow motion... as I felt I needed both the visual and taste to be carefully and accurately recorded in my brain... like this was vital information for a later time when it would be useful... as I observe my own thoughts and actions... I think I must be fucking crazy... have I snapped and do not even know it... can't anyone else see I'm fucked and that I need help... even walking out of the metro station... coming out of the darkness to the light I had to walk a long corridor... as I walked along the corridor wall I thought to myself... if I rubbed myself against the wall I would eventually *erase me* and never see the light at the end of the tunnel...

... others... all I do is whine silently... even I'm tired of my nagging thoughts... I need to get off my ass and do something positive... all I need to do is shut the fuck up and look around and see who is really in misery and needs some sort of help… me, I'm still alive and surviving, even though the thought of my own death is soon approaching… as I raise my stare off the sidewalk and project it beyond the tip of my nose… a gypsy woman picks up a half smoked cigarette off the street as a white car honks a useless warning to the woman… the two tone white and rust small car was at one time someone's pride and joy… now its' white paint has faded and lost all its appeal… with a husband and wife driving in silence, she stares into the smokey blind distance… the drivers' window is slightly opened while he exhales cigarette smoke in an absolute calm… enjoying what seems like the only pleasure while driving in an automatic mindlessness… how can I help these people… in their own and unique way they too were fucked by destiny…

… unbeknownst… as a kid in elementary school, my son during gym class would place his watch on a bench and then he'd be surprised that when he'd come back to retrieve it, that it was gone… this happened to a couple of his watches which were gifts too… at the time he could not understand that there are basically two kinds of people… good and/or bad… to him in his mind there is no need to be bad in anything you do in life… to this day, as an adult he has not changed his thinking about people and he still sees only good in them… maybe he is the better human… the role model or even prototype for what the new human should be like… as I think about my son I no longer ask if it is a curse or a blessing to have Asperger syndrome… despite being watch-less he is always on time…

… faint… how empty is a life when there is no one to share with… *what I see*… as I sit in the train leaving Cascais, I plug myself to the headphones with Beethoven's 9th… the rails guide the train to Lisbon paralleling the Atlantic… with sunset over the ocean… last *early* supper with Suzanne… as my eyes shift between the coast and ocean… it is a melancholic good-bye to these summer towns and beaches lining the tracks… when the train pulled out of Cascais it was like a fading memory in the making… one day it may comeback but it will be blurred… despite my fears, she believes in my writing, pilgrimage and even me… with her parting words and hug I now feel privilege to be doing this trip… maybe I'm different because my life was meant to be lived this way…

## 2015/05/06 – Wednesday (Lisbon, Portugal)

… train in vain… I decided to take the train from Lisbon to Hendaye France… it is an overnight 13 hour train ride… I got myself a compartment with a bed too… since the airline company I wanted to fly with was in a labor conflict mode and with sporadic cancellations… why aggravate myself with someone else's monetary issues… besides, there is a kind of a romantic notion to travelling by rail… if nothing else, it is much different from flying as there is none of the neurotic airport security, custom processes and especially the endless waiting… the train leaves at 9:30 PM… and since I had to vacate the inn by noon… I will now have a full 9.5 hours of waiting… ironic is it not?…

… Europe endless… I purposefully chose to leave from the *Gare do Oriente* train station as it is located in the former Lisbon's 1998 World Fair grounds… with an intelligent architectural and functional station accommodating bus, metro and train station… also some of the former pavilions are still standing and there are quite a few restaurants and a mega shopping mall… and since this is my last day in Lisbon with time to spare… why not spend it on these grounds…

… inspection… mind you it is early afternoon but the grounds look deserted… the water view is really impressive but as I gaze back at the grounds it is nothing but open concrete flavored spaces… mind you the buildings are interesting… the shopping mall nestled between two residential towers that must have incredible views… yet these towering skyscraper luxury homes with balconies show no sign of life either… maybe it is me, but I find this place cold and dehumanizing… not enough green spaces for my liking, maybe it's because my mind is already set to the Camino forthcoming greenery…

… trough… my late lunch consists of a coffee… it seems to be my diet of choice lately… I never seem to be hungry… I base myself on the watch to fuel my body… it feels like an obligation feeding this *cellular* machine… the mall's food court is packed with people from all age groups… truly a cacophony of mostly unemployed voices… I cannot make out anything being said other than it is frantic and loud… cup in hand and looking for silence I step outside onto the large exterior terrace… a toddler struggles to escape from his baby carriage while a cigarette smoking mom looks at him and exhaling from the side of her mouth away from the kid… subconsciously she knows the smoke harms him, this must be love as she does not even have a few seconds to enjoy her smoke…

… runaway… heading back into the mall hoping there would be something more exciting to observe in order to pass the time... a man stepping away from a fast food counter drops what seems to be a bread bun wrapped in cellophane... the bun is rolling in the opposite direction from where he is going... a few people looked at the bun, but their surly faces indicated they were either annoyed by it or it wasn't there problem... dodging a few passersbys I picked up the bun and pretty much darted across the mall after the man... finally caught up with him and tapped him on the shoulder and handed him the bun... he looked at me surprised and asked where he dropped it... I said right by the counter... now he even looked more surprised as if I was either really nice or a complete idiot for wasting my breath...

... teenagers... Suzanne came down to the shopping mall... it was a nice gesture on her part to keep me company but our time together was eclipsed by those long moments of silence as we went for a ride on the funicular... my pensive mood stifled my vocal cords... any man would be happy to have her company but it was nice but no more than that... in the mall I noticed we were very social even when I felt like being alone... as we sat over coffees, I could not help thinking while watching shoppers go by... I feel these folks are boring or maybe it is me who is boring... either way, I'm truly on my own and probably it has been my whole life too... the train could not come fast enough...

## 2015/05/07 – Thursday (St. Jean Pied de Port, France)

... derail... for me, the gallantry of rail travelling is now officially something of the past... upon boarding the train and settling into my cabin... the floor carpet is filthy, cannot go about this two ways... I'm sure the mites have now settled in a lap of luxury and for life too... pulling back the blanket the white bedsheet has a footprint on it... generally speaking I have seen more hygiene while camping in a tent despite barfing from too much drinking... claustrophobia aside, the thought of a 13 hour trip had me seriously contemplating getting off at a Madrid and flying the rest of the way... since this trip nearly cost me 200 euros I swallowed my spiked contempt... isn't it something... being so financially deprived that it makes us submissive...

... weary... the small faucet/sink was adequate for brushing my teeth in two installments... all I had to do was decide which would I brush first... the top or the bottom ones... since I wasn't hungry I skipped supper as I had consumed several coffees during the day... eventually I had to pee... and made my way to the back of the train for the toilet... though I have a penis, I felt it safer to sit down just to pee... the train I was on was very shaky from old age... to the point I had no need to shake off the *good to the last drop* piss droplets... the saved prick shaking time... allowed me some free time to think... this is going to be a very noisy ride when it will come to sleeping...

... prose... the *Tell-Tale Heart by Edgar Allen Poe*... this is how best I can explain what trying to sleep on this train was like... unlike my competitor Mr. Poe I was not cursed by a beating heart under the floor planks but a non-melodic grinding of rusted metal under my pillow... I could not go mad, cause all the vibrating shakes prevented my brain to form a thought of madness or any thought for that matter... my body was sleep deprived but did not know what was going on as my brain for security reasons had to go into a shutdown mode and only left emergency functions such as breathing, running off an automated backup...

... curtains... the sunlight usually wakes me up... but it was still dark outside... it was so dark that not even my voice could be heard in my head... forcing myself back into a noisy sleep but failed stridently... so, with bad breath I headed to the dining room car... to my surprise the sophistication of a dining room car is now a converted 6 swiveling bar stools along a counter... the portly attendant behind the counter had a horizontal worn out streak on his tie from rubbing on the counter edge... with the morning silence of coffee in the train restaurant... where one tries to maintain some sort of non-spilled dignity... my only voice was left behind fending for itself on the pillow... in the train my loneliness is a silent bowel movement...

... devotion... the compressed air being released by the train brakes signaled the silent end... we were now in *Hendaye France*... there were more restaurant stools than people leaving the night time cabins... stabilizing my legs on the platform, I headed to the information desk... where I'm informed there are no trains to St. Jean Pied de Port (SJPP) my starting point (town) for the pilgrimage... there is an upgrade/repair investment to the rail system to SJPP... is this a government belief endeavor or an electoral promise to coffer tourist/pilgrim money and cut down on taxes... nevertheless... two bus rides are now in order, first to Bayonne and then SJPP...

... 99 bottles of beer... the bus ride to SJPP was in a somber mood... as if the pilgrims were all competing for god's attention and did not dare to speak to one another as there strategy may be inadvertently revealed... the only 2 people in the bus speaking were locals... once in town, I headed for a hotel... I wanted to have a shower and sleep in a real clean bed... registering at the front desk with the chatty hotel manager… complaining about how commercialized the pilgrimage has become, yet his business is booming… years ago before a pilgrimage association was created… it was a woman in SJPP, who set the pilgrims on their way if they had a letter from their hometown priest acknowledging they were worthy of undertaking the *spiritual* walk… I do not know what happened to this woman… but her office local has now been replaced by a tourist souvenir shop…

## 2015/05/08 – Friday (Roncesvalles, Spain)

… ritual… last night I walked around SJPP to scout the Camino route (to Santiago de Compostela) from my hotel and also determine/inquire which coffee shop would be open so that I may have a breakfast coffee… actually the first time I did the Camino in 2013, I had no idea where to go/start… so I just stood in the hotel lobby facing the doors, looked up to the ceiling and mumbled… *give me a sign*… and with this a dozen or so pilgrims walked in front of the hotel door and I just followed pretending I knew what I was doing… today's trek was of 25 km but because it was mostly uphill the energy expenditure was equivalent to 31 km… all this to say, that one cannot have a marathon/finish line mentality… I figured if I can pace myself at between 3 @ 4 km per hour… it is reasonable… after all the whole journey will probably take 6-8 weeks to complete as I plan every so often to stop and smell the flowers…

… them… within an hour of walking I run into this retired couple from the USA… friendly as can be, they remind me of those greeters as you enter any Walmart store… she is a chatter box and asks me how far have we walked… figuring it has only been an hour, so it must be about 4 km… I wasn't sure if I should tell her I had perhaps 7+/- hours to go… but at her pace she would see the sunrise before getting to Roncesvalles… we all laughed, but I wasn't kidding… though I enjoyed walking at their slow pace, my heart could not handle the slowing down and so I moved on… on the Camino one will see walkers, cyclists and horseback pilgrims too… also high up in the sky are vultures, for incentive… it's the vultures who are afraid of heights that concern me most… and with this I see four Portuguese cyclists… swearing amongst themselves when I joked if they were Benfica or Sporting soccer fans…

… oblivious… speaking with a handful of people on the route… most are here for the 800 +/- km to Santiago and have not met anyone yet who will go the extra 90 km to Finisterre... most came in with a 5 week return airplane ticket... most guide books recommend walking 20 @ 30 km daily to complete the pilgrimage in 33 days... no one takes into account that back home they only work 5 days a week and need the weekend to rest... somehow, here they plan to walk for about 5 weeks without a rest... in two weeks, is pretty much when the shit hits the fan... when the novelty and redundancy of the landscape no longer leaves them in awe... in fact the only *awe* will be coming from their fluctuating breaths when their exhausted bodies insist on taking a bus or train to Santiago...

... flock... but I have to admire the drive being displayed so far by these pilgrims including myself in having faith and determination to complete this journey... I can only speak for myself as I do not understand why I must do this walk, all I know and am sure of is that it must be completed as per an intuition I received on the first walk... there are basically two types of pilgrims walking... the ones who travel alone and are disconnected or want to disconnect from the world... they stop to look around without pulling out a camera for a nature size selfie... and the rest are basically vacationers either as a couple or in a noisy herd mode... walking by a pasture I see cows grazing... some are wearing bells around their necks and every time they bite into the grass the bell chimes... it must be annoying not to be able to eat in silence... all I can hope for is that they (cows) take turns with wearing a bell... or maybe in the cow world it is a status symbol of importance...

... magnitude... with over 4 hours of walking in an alone state... I'm pretty much ahead of the other pilgrims... for some reason I walk faster than other folks... the night before I bought some fruit and this morning picked up a warm baguette... lunch high up on the mountain side was breath taking... as I look down into the valley I couldn't help feeling my smallness compared to the view... after lunch, I just sat there and plugged my headphones on... I like doing this as I have a game associated to it... songs come on randomly on my Ipod and what played was *Brian Eno's - An Ending (Ascent)*... my god, how a propos... with music in my ears and the view, serenity circulated throughout my body via my veins... here I do not feel inadequate... perhaps it is my own inabilities that makes me feel like an outcast...

... luxury... in the first days of the walk, I prefer staying in a hotel... as there is a bathtub for soaking my aching body... usually I stay in the economical albergues (Spanish for hostels) but they only have showers, no tub... as I sat on the bistro terrace refueling with carbonated water... the pilgrims next to me were sipping beers and talking about the journey... indeed the 8 hourish day climbing height of up to 1200 meters trek was very difficult... the only thing that flowed as much as the beer were the ricocheting compliments amongst themselves... as if what they did was extra-ordinary and needed repeating... all they did was just walk and probably snap pictures as they are doing now... why do we need re-enforcement form others?... these merry folks are not pilgrims but they are one notch above a tourist... the lone ones contemplating the day's events are numbed by inner peace without alcohol...

... strategic... a toothless beggar was outside the church asking for money... he needed money to pay for his lodging... so, I gave him some... with my money making its' way into his pocket... dozens of pilgrims were exiting the church from the evening mass... as they walked by the beggar, only one chap actually gave him money... incredible... but maybe I'm using the word pilgrim in vain when referring to these church goers... why didn't more pilgrims donate... who are these ugly humans... who can only acknowledge themselves... then again why not give him (beggar) my spare bedroom in my hotel suite...

## 2015/05/09 – Saturday (Zubiri, Spain)

... breakfast... started off the walk with a festival of *chemtrails* in god's blue morning sky being deliberately sprayed for sinister purposes undisclosed to the general public... though the scientific community and/or government claim such trails are simply normal water-based contrails (condensation trails) which are routinely left by high-flying aircraft under certain atmospheric conditions... if so, then why are the chemtrails being sprayed in a grid format over my head... sometimes, I feel it is not the fear of dying but of living... still, I am human and have no one to comfort me other than these dark chocolate covered cookies with a gulp of bottled water picked up earlier from one of the public hopefully uncontaminated fountains...

... ingenuity... hand washed my underwear and socks last night but they were still quite damp this morning... I placed them in the microwave for a ten minute defrost cycle... perfectly warm and toasty on my scrotum and ankles... as I walked thru a forest I wondered if I fart in the forest, does anyone hear... so, I ripped a dark chocolate covered cookie scented fart... and did not hear it, mainly because I was plugged into my Ipod... a safe distance later I sat by a river with feet soaking in water while I ate an orange... as I looked at my backpack it has a side pocket on each side... on one side I place my 1.5L of bottled water... on the other side pocket I took an empty water bottle and cut out the neck/spout... I ended up with a plastic cylinder where I can store 3 oranges...

... show and tell... during the day ran into a Korean woman a couple of times, who seemed out of breath and even felt she was walking against her will... her husband was always far ahead and she walked alone... every time I intersected/passed her I wondered if she/they ever rested... or were they living to the full extent martyr's roles... nevertheless, as I passed her I would clap my hands and exclaim *vamos* (move it) which made her smile... also ran into some Canadians whom I had met yesterday on the camino... one of them had passed out from a combination of heat exhaustion, jetlag and probably not being physically fit... after leaving them in the shade, I made my way downhill quickly into town and had the restaurant owner contact an ambulance to pick her up... all things said and done, everything is fine... my good Samaritan gesture got me free chicken wings and a beer from the restaurant owner... two elderly German pilgrims and myself shared a table... as they were raving about the virtues of being vegetarian my chicken wings flew in and landed on my plate...

... gas... whenever walking through a town, often stopping at a coffee shop for carbonated water... sitting back into my chair, I can't believe how glorious... is the chair invention... was it invented with pilgrims in mind... reading posted pre-election flyers on a telephone pole, claiming the existing party is corrupt and favours the rich... were they like this before elected or did they become corrupt once in power... what about if the next elected party is the one now distributing flyers... will their new greed and power also be in some future flyer... grandmothers pushing baby strollers with hairstyles that gives them height are now blocking my view of the posted election flyers... double parking the baby strollers... I think the grandmothers are discussing hair maintenance as they seem to point to one another's bouffant hairdo... with flat shoes being the norm... no heels to propel them to have their fancy hairdo rubbing clouds... one cannot risk pre-maturely undoing the expensive hairstyle... as it's got to last the month... with a quick peek into each other's strollers accompanied by a polite smirk these experienced voters move on as I do...

... evening optimism... there is a party down by the Arga river... people soaking their feet in the water... plucked guitar strings... even the homeless man from the previous town is here begging too... anyway... the party mood will be short lived because of what I call the Cinderella syndrome... *albergues* usually have a 10 PM curfew and these pilgrims have to make it before the palace doors to the dormitories are sealed until 6 AM the following day... the restaurant/bar was packed with boisterous pilgrims celebrating day two of *el camino*... since I did not have reservations, I asked the owner if his cook would be kind enough to make me a sandwich to go... the owner said to me even though I did not understand why... *that I was polite and therefore found me a place at a shared table*... I was so glad I had supper and was not eating alone... it is evident the *el camino* is becoming commercialized... but it still has aspects of pious decency...

## 2015/05/10 – Sunday (Zubiri, Spain)

... sympathy... woke up to the silence of my voice... as if I had made a vow to myself never to speak again... all I heard were my barefoot steps walking and cracking the floating floor in the room... I was going over the dream I just had a few minutes ago which propelled me to wake up... there was a murder rampage in the hostel I was staying in... I managed to escape and warned the police... but the killer finally caught up to me and shot 2 bullets through my forehead... he had aimed for my third eye... I felt the warmth of the bullets and even saw his face between shots as he was shooting... all his concentration was focused on aiming... as if all that is involved in killing me is aiming accurately... it was ok, the man was just an empty shell too, as I am... there is no loss here, nor anger towards him... there is no him...

... flippancy... it's just a dream so I thought... if it has some sort of meaning I do not feel like dwelling into it... as a kid whenever we woke up with bad dreams either me or my brother... my dad would promise us we'd get Delmonte canned fruit later in the day... actually no sooner are we out of bed the manual can opener is spinning sparks as the can opens... dad had to play the role of King Solomon when it came to the one cherry in the can... WTF, less tasteless seedless pale grapes and more sexy red cherries... is this asking for too much?...

... yep!... as if I have any imagination to come up with such a tall tale... once upon a time and once again... anyway, as a kid... my old man would heat up red wine, pour it into a cereal bowl and drop 2-3 healthy tablespoons of white sugar into the mix... then, we would take a paposeco (Portuguese bread for those born into the wrong culture... take this up with god, not me) and break it into pieces and dip the bread into the wine and sugar mix...

mmmm, so sweet and tasty... curious enough, I was never able to finish off the bread or the wine mixture... I soon fell asleep, actually it was more like passing out... the next day my mom would struggle to get me out of bed in order to go to school and hopefully learn something other than a hangover makes one's stomach queasy...

... ferment... with all the yummy bread/vinho combo from the evening before... now brewing in a classroom and setting this premature mix into a volatile expulsion through the mouth and nose... ah! relief for me but not the school janitor... sure, this being 1967, a school nurse was still in the conceptual stages of development and let's not even go there with calling my mom or dad on the not yet invented cellphone... what?... make them (parents) pick up their kid at school and lose half a days' pay because their little bastard threw up... *if it didn't kill him, it will make him stronger*... was the attitude my parents took towards their kids in the 60's... go ahead laugh, as you think about the wimpy kids you raised... anyway, even though I did have my own house key... I was not allowed to leave the school premise and had to wait for the school bell to ring and sound off legal responsibility...

... stool... so, I sat in the principals' office... my chair was placed in the middle of the room just in case I threw up again... no human in the vicinity would come into contact with any remaining vomit mixture... finally the bell rang and headed home... to tell you the truth I was kind of hungry... once home, the bowl of wine from the night before was sitting on the counter... now, even at age seven I was smart enough to know that the paposeco/wine combo had made me sick... so, instead I got Weston sliced white bread... as my old man always complained that this was not real bread... there is no cure for alcoholism and such stupidity probably deserves to be shot in the head too...

## 2015/05/11 – Monday (Pamplona, Spain)

... hosts... one can almost understand the Spanish family value system through their habits... groceries, especially bread are bought on a need be basis... nothing is bought ahead of time and frozen for later... going to the market daily, for fresh food is the only way to be in small towns and even a city like this... these medieval towns I have walked through the last few days still have a foothold in the past as it is what defines them... streets are deserted between 2 and 6 as every possible shop closes up… minus the restaurants and bars which seem to be open eternally…

… modern… just like the Portuguese the Spanish are no different… in bistros the festive mood of people multi-tasking is evident with talking loudly, holding a drink and a cell phone… yesterday while having a 7AM breakfast watched TV (volume was off) more gruesome news footage of the Nepal earthquake all the while the radio blaring the song *It's a Wonderful Life*… a married couple in their 60's and what seemed to be the husbands father… were having what I like to coin as the breakfast of champions… the men were having red wine and the woman a coffee… maybe she was the designated driver for this meal…

… three way… there are those who walk because they had some spiritual calling, which from my observations is the majority… why would anyone want to walk 1 000 km with a heavy backpack and with difficult creature comforts every night… when for the same money one could go to a *Club Med*… then there are those who have no calling and just want to hike to accumulate non-rewarding air-less miles… but the funniest are the weekend walkers (clean underwear pilgrims) on tourist package junkets who have their luggage transported to hotels and carry a child size backpack with snacks and treats… often travelling in herds and always accompanied by relentless chatter and giggles… rule of thumb… I never greet/talk to pilgrims walking on their own as they are in a reflective interiorized mood and not in a vacation mind set…

… sole/soul… meditated in a park but felt it was not enough… having walked a few more kilometers wishing for a quiet spot I came upon a river… I quickly found serenity in this setting… initially all my thoughts are from the exterior world… as I sink deeper the images are coming from somewhere in my interior… I can feel my soul struggling to get out… it seems to pull out/away from on top… where the neck meets the back… asking why?… the chatter and giggling of how and where to pose for a picture interrupts my request… fucken tourists!… it's not their fault as my quest is spiritual and not like theirs in the pictures they take… am I anti-social?… or is it my answers will not come from these people… yet, all said and done… I enjoyed the improvised supper with these picture taking strangers in the evening setting…

… soul/sole… why the feeling of my soul wanting to escape… the thing with my meditations is that the information comes in images… and it's as if my brain is incapable of handling all the images in one lump sum… is it a feeble human intellect?… I am left with a lot of blanks which I try to rationalize or fill in with my own understanding… what if the my soul has multiple lives going on at the same time… in human and alien forms, both in time and even space… as if a soul is fragmented to accommodate all these entities… I imagine my soul is like a fist and each finger is a lifeform somewhere in time and space… is it possible fingers or fragments of my soul overlap?… since a fraction of my soul is here through me to learn and experience something it needs to progress in for its' own growth… is it possible just like me my soul is not perfect… considering we have good and bad bacteria… good human spirits and ghosts… even with aliens we have good and bad ones… everything is fucked up in the universe… maybe this is why no matter how bad it seems we have it here on this planet… maybe it is better than what is out there and this is why we negate death…

… who else… a common feature to all these medieval towns seems to be the proximity of water, higher grounds usually mountain sides and of the highest possible church steeple… height being the town's affirmation to being close to god… having a construction background, I can appreciate the buildings and especially the time in which they were built in, considering the tools and materials of that era… as humans we have made great strides coming from painting on cavern walls to tactile screens… but where did the technology of pyramid building disappear to… these churches with crumbling structures are a far cry from what we can see was done on pyramids… and even with pyramids constructed all over the world and great as they are… how come there are no other structures as impressive surrounding them… surely, if an advanced pyramid building society can build colossal structures… it should have also developed impressive social housing concepts and not just mud huts…

## 2015/05/12 – Tuesday (Pamplona, Spain)

… perception… the restaurant waitress and owner are a couple in early 60's… he has the same *David Cassidy* hair style of the 70's… she is small and perky with short hair but with her long bangs to one side she is constantly swaying her head to keep the hair out of her eyes… she is wearing a pant and loose blouse, almost maternity like… with her high heels she bounces to the sound of jingling jewelry… this is their restaurant or to be correct their lives… the walls are full of pictures of them posing with celebrities… a showcase of others fleeting adoration for the couple… though they physically pose together with celebrities in the framed wall picture... they are not together... maybe in the night time bedroom, the banality of their lives has them talking about the business until falling asleep...

... pulse... stepping out of the celebrity café with no picture of mine framed... I wander the streets in early morning as a free man... watching small vans daring to circulate on pedestrian laneways... busily delivering bread, beers kegs and crates of vegetables to restaurants... the noise of empty bottles being dropped in recycling bins... pilgrims walking out of the city hunched under their backpacks... the city is waking up as store shutters are being pushed up and away... a store owner unlocking the door, looking left/right for robbers or maybe a waiting customer... another shop owner cleaning her store front windows through the metal grills used to protect the glass from bulls?... a street sweeper with a parked, dirty maintenance trolley... with broom in hand and an intense nauseating body odor smell... now the delivery vans are looking awkward as bistro chairs and tables are deployed outside with matching parasols...

... alphabet... faces smeared with sunscreen, pressing up against their cameras... pilgrims wondering what to snap... is it a church, a roman architecture influenced edifice different from their home towns... or is it the streets with no sidewalks... even the abundant use of the letter X in Basque signs is of interest... what these pilgrims want and are not able to capture is that this medieval town is alive and there is not one picture or video that can record the vibration... me, I block myself with the headphones as their world is not my world... maybe I do not love myself nor am I happy... I know, I do not believe this...

... shattering... I'm a nobody here... actually I'm an invisible nobody... so much loneliness in me... I need to talk to people, anyone!... I just need to hear my voice so that I know I'm still alive... but if I did I'd probably monopolize the conversation... I know my soul is tormented with being here... but fuck it's not my fault... why am I being tormented and dragged thru hell... leave!... stop the wrecking ball... the only control I have is I can decide to die at will... is it in my control or was it already destined... maybe if the plug is pulled out of my whining ass I'll deflate my soul...

... throng... at the end of the working day these folks head down to *Plaza del Toros* and I follow suit even though unemployed... it's an immense city square with bistros and small shops... I have a preference for *Café Iruna* as its' décor still dates back to 1888... sipping a cold beer and wondering whether or not I should go to the *Burger King* I had seen on my way here... nostalgia of Montreal was creeping in but I decided not to make a decision until my beer(s) had it's say in the matter... a gangly and tall homely woman with a Romanesque protruding nose steps out of the bistro with a hop in her steps... hair pulled back tightly into a ponytail held with a rubber band more fitting to hold broccoli stems... she is in love with a man just as cute as her, as he stays sitting in the café waving her a good-bye... he loves her to no end as shouted by his eyes when they locked upon her... our gangly love interest passes by another woman who is old and wrinkled... this earthly woman now cast to an eternal earthly solitude with her dog...

## 2015/05/16 – Saturday (Estella, Spain)

... sunrise... I see eyes with a red stare looking at me from within the mirror... who or what is there on the other side of this reflective glass... is my reflective view physical or mental... yesterday a dog had been walking behind me for a few kilometers... he didn't seem to lack food or water... it felt that he was just keeping an eye on me when the thought of *what if I fell off the cliff edge* lingered in my head... will I then be food for him, so I thought humorously... then wondered if I'll eventually be one of those *epiphanic moment crying pilgrims* who stop in the middle of the path... where one's loneliness of the road continues in a bistro/restaurant to the warmth of a touch screen device... where the screen is the closet contact one now has to humanity...

... bubbling... with the sounds of river water running through the city... pedestrian streets leading to a city square in the evening bustle... baby strollers of all sizes and color equally pushed by parents or proud & glowing grandparents... bicycles with training wheels... kids of all sizes running after soccer balls... and on the perimeter are bistro tables with matching chairs and logoed parasols... all this, is a thing of beauty... and the voice vibrations echoing throughout the pulsating earthly mortar-fied heavenly pavement... and even though no one listens they are all understood... of course...

... waterworks... what's an evening city square without a few injured crying kids... a 7 year old girl with massive lipstick lips, taken from her mom's purse... teenagers boisterous in both language and clothes... things which have come in and out of my life... I'm gonna miss these humanity sunsets... a kid running and hopping from one bench to another... the free spirit acrobatics of innocence which have not yet been compressed by a daily routine...

but may be released when he becomes a grandfather and breaks free again... this is the beauty of the tears in my eyes...

... overpass... the heated evening solitude displaces me above the cold river air as I stand on the bridge... leaning comfortably against the railing as my support for jotting notes... written thoughts seeking a voice, even permanence... empathy for the water ripples below me are interrupted by them, their combined energy is not of a couple in love but one of childlike innocence... she stood next to me, maybe wanting to see what I was writing... without looking up from my notes... her voice was friendly as I listened to her from the side, still without looking at her... she had a radio voice, a singing voice, a voice that simply soothes... his echoing convivial *hello* got me out of my notes and smiling... such an energy for a man who had spent the day walking... the protocol being, we introduced ourselves... these two pilgrims were Janis from the USA and Ayaan was a Catalonian... she/they apologized for interrupting my note writing... the interruption was a refreshing blessing in disguise as their being together stirred something in me...

... her... Suzanne, can I make her real again... I cannot feel her... as if she was just a creation of my imagination cause all I have as a memory of her is a blurred visual... there is no sound, smell and even less a touch of her skin or lips... was she real... am I real... I'm dying inside am I not... again with the headphones... loud music slows down my dying... quieting my mind with loud music as I lean against the coolness of a brick wall... I'm not all bad... yet I feel my soul trying to pull out of me again... like some insect struggling re-birth... to come out of its' cocoon... what will be left when it (cocoon) bursts... a *me* carcass integrating itself into the mortar of a comforting wall built with clay brick blocks... with an un-tormented hollowness...

## 2015/05/17 – Sunday (Los Arcos, Spain)

... schedule... a French breakfast in Basque country... coffee and croissant... everything feels like the last time... as I feel all the time I have left, is on the camino... at times I find myself walking very slowly... I feel or have an overwhelming feeling of dying if I stay too long in the same town too... one cannot cheat death... my reality is what counts now, this very moment and I plan to savor it... and with this thought I get myself a second coffee... maybe additional caffeine will jolt me of my morning negativity...

... triangles... whether the croissant or the upside down coffee cup...

I see triangles everywhere... and it always brings me back to Egyptian pyramids... as if I had been there and actually have a say on this matter... at times I find/feel I was a revolutionary fighting injustice... other than the Egyptian rulers why was everyone else living in mud huts... with mastered pyramid techniques... there should be remnants of social housing reflected in their construction technology... perhaps these super structures were built by aliens for their own purpose... maybe by a dwindling minority of aliens who stayed behind and played rulers of this planet... is this what Egyptian royalty was all about... but maybe some of us did not care to be royalty and stayed behind too...

... gullible... on my route I'm stopped by another pilgrim... she asks me if I know where the *fuente de vino* (wine fountain) is located on the route... I check my map and it's on our way to Los Arcos... she goes on to explain it is a miracle fountain as wine comes from an underground spring... wow!... the chicken that lays golden eggs... as we arrive at the so called fountain... it is a promotional exterior tap promoting local wines... there are two taps/faucets... one provides water while the wine faucet must be on a timer/quantity controlled dispenser cause nothing was flowing out... we both laughed at the absurdity of this fountain while taking pictures... as I step back on the road I run into Ayaan from last night... we ended up walking the rest of the route together... since he had been walking with Janis for the last five days... I teased him he had downgraded with walking partners by being with me...

... worms... early birds catch not a worm but an albergue cot in the next town... it's a first come first serve scenario... Ayaan and I split up to find accommodations and meet up in town for beers... stepping out of the inn... I literally felt myself being lifted up... my feet did not leave the ground but I could swear they felt as if I had... I'm not in my body am I?... I carried this thought with me for the rest of the afternoon...

... round one... being first to settle in... I'm now waiting for Ayaan and sitting in the shade drowned terrace sipping an ice cold beer watching pilgrims coming into town... they all come in with a look of bewilderment... as if it is the first time they enter a village... their faces light up when they see someone they had met in an albergue or the camino... even if their first meeting lasted only seconds and was no more than a vocal bon camino... it was enough to establish a connection and now a comforting feeling of familiarity... they are not used to being alone...

... round two... other exterior bistro tables are along the square facing the church building and basking in the sun... the plastic chairs are so hot they burn when first sat on... the tables are practically all filled with pilgrims... sipping beer or wines... as church goers come out from a children's first communion celebration... now also struggling to find a table/seat... with church bells adding more noise to the cacophony of voices in the square... confusion reigns...

... round three... local women are wearing their Sunday best and in heels elevating them closer to a celestial goddess of beauty, desirability and why not even sexiness as they now prance in the plaza square looking for no one... and men with phone, drink and cigarette in hands admire these delicate creatures testing the engineered structural integrity of the high heel spike... is there anything more phallic than a necktie... perhaps a heel?...

... round four... on the outdoor bistro tables, pilgrims leave behind half full glasses of wine or beer heating up in the sun... they order these drinks because they are tired of drinking fountain water found on the route or maybe they want to be cool like the locals... but unlike the locals who drink alcohol in the shade... and always leave a glass empty...

... it started... by this time... myself, Ayaan and Juan a Spanish fellow who we just met at the bar... and we're all having beers... and no sooner we finish a round... we see Janis walking into town who must stop for a beer too as Ayaan tugs her backpack... as we spoke banalities... I felt myself invaded with intuitions... just sounding off at the top of my head... as much as I wished these intuitions stayed in my head... they found their way to the ears of these strangers... telling Juan his deceased wife was with him and that he would never make it to Santiago... for Janis there is a baby spirit roaming around her... and for Ayaan, apart from his kindness and his search for something missing in his life, the answer is close at hand... what am I doing with these people... I feel this was a setup, my being here... why do they listen to me... but better yet why am I talking to them or am I ?...

... knock out... what made sense, in what I just told them... very little... big deal, so I felt Juan is a widower as his wife passed away and since her death he decided to walk only part of the camino route... Janis already has a daughter and at 34 years of age does not see another child in the making... Ayaan, just got shivers when I spoke of him...

## 2015/05/18 – Monday (Viana, Spain)

... another sunrise... the night before I had scouted which coffee shop opens early... 7AM was the best time I could find... I helped the owner unlock the doors... I was anxious to get out of my room not that I was scared, far from it... there was a shadowy black smoke like figure of a person standing in the corner of the room... I could not see its' feet nor was its' face defined... at best it was a see thru silhouette... I sensed it looking at me as I looked at it... it was all curiosity on both sides... without any fanfare it blended into the wall... and I went for a long overdue pee... yesterday's cervejas finally got filtered thru my body...

... news... the morning quiet is broken with the TV news cast... as if we all wanted to be informed what transpired during our sleep, as if we missed something important... all I know is I woke up and am still here, I'm grateful... I'm also grateful the TV is anchored to the wall or it would fly out the fucken window... walking in a country where I barely understand the language... with images of violence on TV nothing gets lost in translation as stupidity crosses all borders... a sextet of pilgrims walks by... I wonder how can they walk on a spiritual path when your own spirit requires your full attention... when all you do is spend your fucken day talking, stopping to take your daily quota of 5 000 pics... and eating and endless series of hobbit meals... why are you scared to be alone, probably for the same reasons as me?... despite what my cynicism hones in on, there are more great folks here too... more in one day than one can see in a life time... cafe com leche por favor...

... traffic... Juan steps in for an espresso... we greet and chat... I apologize if I spooked him yesterday and as I say this another intuition prompts me to tell him to laugh today... in an awkward farewell gesture we shake hands but I had a feeling he was looking for a hug... nearly tripping over my own backpack on the floor as I attempt to sit down... in comes Janis and asks to sit at my table... the adjective beautiful keeps repeating in my head... I repeat it to her but emphasize it has nothing to do with her physical appearance but what is inside her as a person... intrigued she asks me if we can walk together...

... just me... I had expected/hoped to walk alone today as I had walked a long portion of the Camino yesterday with Ayaan... I really wanted time to myself, the last 24 hours threw me a curve... but I also sensed Janis had not yet walked the camino alone... she was always with Ayaan except yesterday... she is not comfortable being here alone... I was hoping the person/woman with whom she walked yesterday would show up now... with all this I figured it is an upgrade for me to walk with her as opposed to Ayaan, we laughed at this shared observation... the walk turned out better than I thought, she needed to vent and maybe I am some sort of father figure for her... she talked about her singing career and how she sees it also being a business and should be handled as such... actually I was impressed by her savoir faire... taking into account her border line poverty family/background...

... making sense... the question was straight forward, and no eye contact was made either... she asked what happens to a spirit if the baby is aborted... I am far from qualified to answer this... but it did not stop my mouth... if the spirit wants to come down or has to, it will find a way... why would I even think let alone say such a thing... almost reaching our destination of Viana... Ayaan meets up with us and the three of us walk the last few kilometers together...

... over lunch... we had lunch together in Viana... they were planning to continue walking but not I... as we parted after lunch... I told her to remember she is beautiful... cause now this made sense to both of us... she has always been verbally mistreated and put down by her family... I then caught Ayaan to the side and told him that if he and his girlfriend decide to have a baby, that this baby would answer his existentialist questions and that also, it would be the favorite grandchild for his father... with goose bumps on his skin, he said his dad always affirmed... if he had a child that his kid would be the favorite... he hugged me intensely and so did she... as they walked away I knew our paths would never cross again... this was not a co-incidence meeting... though I felt it but did not mention it to either one, is that the baby spirit hovering around Janis will move on to Ayaan... this is why they met... is there connection, a spiritual mating... a transference of sorts... ?...

... shadow... with them gone, I focused my thoughts on this morning's shadow... I did not fear it at all... it was a non-chalant encounter... but I can almost say it planted a thought in my mind... if a homeless man has a fragmented soul, but all the fragments are in the one physical body... it explains why the homeless man is at odds and argues with himself... if a fragmented soul is found in different bodies and even in different time spaces and realms... are the bodies that house these fragments of souls complete... ?...

## 2015/05/23 – Saturday (Santo Domingo, Spain)

... making sense... in the last few days oddities have transpired... both my ex-wife and myself have been experiencing out of the usual encounters...

I sense there is a message here but have not been able to connect the dots... all I can do for now is re-group our email exchanges between her and I... and see how this whole thing unfolds with time, if ever...

*Sunday May 17... email from Emme (ex-wife) located in Montreal, Canada...*

Hi Fern,

This morning (Saturday) I was supposed to meet someone for a walk up Mount Royal park, she was a no show, so I went up the stairs solo, when I got to the top, sat down, taking in the beauty of flowers (tulips) and noticed a group of people with hiking sticks from afar (about 30 people, all age groups), didn't think much about it, just assumed it was some Meetup thing.

I started my walk, minding my own business, when this gentleman Lucien started walking next to me, looked me over from head to toe, and asked if I was part of the group; I hadn't noticed they had caught up to me, I replied no and asked what is this group, when he told me I laughed out loud and got a little creepy... he said we're pilgrims, we are a group called "Du Québec à Compostele" and he continued to say, it's an info association for people who want to prepare and go to Compostela, and that he's been to Compostela several times and that they meet up a few times a year to hike/walk... he introduced me to several people in the group and I walked with him for about an hour; I told him about you and asked him if I could take a picture of him to share with you, he proudly agreed and wanted to make sure I got his feet in the shot too ( that also gave me chills)... He looks frail, but he's not, he's a good walker, could keep up with me... very spiritual too...

Now here's the comical part about Lucien, he tells me he smokes pot and whispers that the other pilgrims do not, that he is a pure laine PQ... he's ok with ethnic people speaking their own language amongst themselves, but not English... He was trying to remember some politician's name and he couldn't and says to me... I meet a lot of people and have a difficult time retaining names, but the only name that keeps rolling in my head over and over again is your name Emme, I don't know why... and he goes on telling me that I impress him and that my French is really good and I'm a good walker, that I should do Camino and that I shouldn't give up on smoking pot LOL... that my body would get used to it and if I have an outer body experience just hold on to who you're with, and he laughs, but that it was ok if I choose not to... when it came time for us to split ways, one of the organizers informed me, that they will do another walk in June, if I want to join them it would be nice... That's when Lucien shook my hand and says in a sweet/cute flirty way (mischievous eyes) to bring a friend... deux femmes c'est toujours mieux... Lol... Now, why did this small framed, white bearded man cross my path... of all the people that were walking around us/me, he picked me... I don't know if I should say this, but here it goes; at one point when he's speaking to me, I looked into his face and saw... future Fern... one of my gut feelings I get sometimes...

Take care,

Take care of your feet (I feel like, that's the message Lucien had to convey),

Emme

*... Tuesday May 19... my response to Emme (ex-wife)*

hi Emme...

... hope all is well... kids and all... I wish our kids would acknowledge my undertaking...

... I read your email several times over the last few days and studied the picture too... it left me slightly perplexed but at the same time I feel it has some sort of meaning for you, me and even Lucien... but what this connection/message may be I have no idea... time will tell...

... when I studied the pic... a creepy feeling of loneliness and solitude came over me... to tell you the truth it disturbed profoundly... the Camino will be over in a few weeks... I keep busy with the book project and am filled with self-doubt if it is worthy of reading/printing... after the Camino I still have a few weeks of proof reading to be performed on the manuscript/notes... along with your Lucien pic and what my inner core tells me... my life is still set for more chaos... to tell you the truth, I am tired and at times scared too...

Ciao...

*... Saturday May 23... email to Emme*

... hi Emme...

... 2 days ago met a pilgrim called Victor from Lithuania... he's physically a clone of your Lucien... he wears an old double breast gray suit similar to one I once had... his long legged pants are rolled up and he has decent hiking shoes... and he sports a straw hat... he drank black coffee for breakfast and had a big glass of cognac with it... I had to stop and speak to him... I could not resist... when looking into his eyes... I was set back with him as he instantly reminded me of my grandfather (almost a clone)... red watery eyes... shape and all...

... don't know what is going on... with these old men... but when I said good-bye to him this thought entered my mind… if you see the kids… ask them if I died now… would it make a difference in their lives?

ciao…

## 2015/05/24 – Sunday (Santo Domingo, Spain)

… demographics… church bells summoning all gray hairs to their spiritual calling before earthly time runs out on them… who is gonna fill the collection baskets… yesterday I got annoyed as I wanted to visit the Santo Domingo Cathedral but had to pay 3 euros to get in… mind you it has a museum too, which is justified in its' charging… but I do not care for the museum I just wanted to go into the church and sit there quietly… is this temple now a place for commercial activity… would god really require payments from us when he has already deposited in his Vatican bank account enough to pay for all temples to be free of charge… once upon a time, even his son was outraged when he also ousted commercial merchants from a temple… so the story goes…

… international… one cannot help but meet people from all over the planet being called to walk the el camino… some of the most fascinating are those who do not speak English let alone Spanish… and yet fuddle their way through this country when something as simple as a menu is a nightly challenge… the handful of Brazilians I've met are here to fulfill a promise they had made with god… almost like a contract, such as an illness kind of thing… if god spares some family member from a terrible illness they promise to walk el camino… though there must be pilgrimages in South America… but I guess it is holier here and more jet set too… after all this is Europe…

… WIFI… the four letter word that connects the world… it seems every hostel now offers a wifi connection to the pilgrims who want to disconnect from the world while remaining connected… is this the new spiritual pilgrim… could be, as I met a few who are here because a Hollywood movie inspired them… the technically advanced pilgrim can find his way with a GPS and even convert kilometers into miles to get a better understanding of spiritual distances… every so often though, actually every other day I see/ meet a pilgrim walking in the opposite direction… is this a sign or even a protest of the Camino's commercialization…

… branding… walking along vineyards… with chemicals being sprayed on grape vines I would think twice about drinking water from the public fountains as it could contain chemical runoffs... if lost on the camino, one could always follow the foot prints on the wet ground laced with a CSI identifiable chemical residue... even here one can walk along with a chemical corporation's foot prints... maybe one day pilgrims will have corporate sponsored credentials (pilgrim passport ID)... where one can now get an endless stamping of the credential at every corner no longer just albergues... like kids collecting useless trinkets from fast-food restaurants...

... seeking... well rested and relaxed... I latched on to the bed post... with 60 + km walked in 2 days and a 12 hour sleep marathon coming to an end... the body was in such a relaxed state I can attempt to travel astrally... in a meditative state... the imagery of a warm water flow is magically soothing... I'm alone in this place, alone in your world... I found myself in space... a black mess but still non-threating and even soothing... it was not a thought of wonderment I had but a repetitive and puzzling one to look for myself... are there two of me... look for me?... what me, do I have a twin(s)...

... protection... upon my return form a meditative experience... one must be careful not to bring back undesirables... some will project upon themselves a self- induced white light for protection... but this is no different than a prayer... with me, it is a simple fuck off as this is my body and not yours... I find this is as effective, if not better... anyway, re-thinking what I heard and saw... why do I have to look for myself and why am I barefoot and searching for me in different places... how can one be happy if they feel incomplete... I think I've had enough and yet I'm still here...

## 2015/05/25 – Monday (Villafranca, Spain)

... caffeine sleuth... what if my dream of this morning was a lecture of sorts... actually not a dream nor a lecture more of a warning bordering on asking for my help... groggy images of souls being split/fragmented and distributed in different bodies either here or other realms and in time and even space as if to maximize their (soul) learning process... but at the same time it was also a punishment for the soul to be especially associated to earth... what if my loneliness is not mine but that of my soul... what if my soul rebels and is fed up with learning and being split up or scattered in different bodies... is my rebellious soul going against the norm... its' quest is now to re-unite itself with its other fragmented soul parts and I'm in the way... as all his learning of love is one thing but witnessing or experiencing earthly violence is point-less… maybe it just wants to get out and move on…

… Q&A… so the soul goes around collecting its' fragmented elements… and if souls were so perfectly divine… then they wouldn't need be here to learn through us… but maybe being on earth is the equivalent of a soul hell… what if this so called learning is really inmate therapy or counselling for souls… suppose it (soul) wants out… why?… why not just get out of me and move on… why am I being dragged into misery, which is probably not mine in the first place… am I caught in my soul's drama?… and why now all this morning's thoughts inspired from a dream?… did I spook my soul yesterday with my surprise astral visit?…

… intersection… at certain points, in some infinite wisdom of a bureau-crat… the camino has us walking along side with traffic on the highway… immense trucks zoom by us… as the numerous trucks passed by so did my opportunities of jumping in front of one… the impact would cause me a slight short lived headache… it has always been a life of so many mistakes… everything I have done was always improvised and at times recklessly too… maybe ending everything here or at Finisterre would be the first thought out decision… do I have a death wish… waiting is the hardest effort… the rest of the day was one of silence for both me and in my head too…

… signs… as I finally got off the highway with a sigh of relief as I wiped my tears… I felt I was safe from myself as I would no longer test if I had the courage/audacity to jump in front of a truck… walking into a small town… a chained German Shepard dog drops a blue rubber ball as close to me as al-lowed by his chain… I tap it back to him with my foot… and he comes back with it in his mouth to play again… we played a few times as it made me smile… did he sense my highway mental ordeal… but as I walked further into town I see a limping cat and another small dog missing a back limb… maybe this is a sign that getting hit by a truck… I would live and probably be crippled too… with this thought in mind I see several doves fly vertically straight up into the sky… odd…

… switch… overlooking the valley below… in the evening loneliness of no love finds me in the small plaza… am I accepting the fact of my own death… am I giving up… have I stopped fighting and/or have I accepted my destiny… there now is an ease in my mind… nothing, absolutely nothing is important here… even the stupidity of the married couple over heard on my way here is irrelevant… life is so simple… without love in your life nothing makes sense… I miss my family life… it was a good thing but I blew it…

desperation set in to just having one love of any kind again… so lonesome for love that I'm even willing to die for it…

## 2015/05/26 – Tuesday (Atapuerca, Spain)

… all apologies… don't hate everyone cause you hate yourself… am I a grouch because my chamois towel would be ideal for wiping a car dry but not my hairy ass… and those whores of the camino… the non-spiritual bus load of silent and digital flickering camera shutters… they make so much noise in my ears and head… I need a fear free night's sleep… I'm tired… need to plan my next trek just pass Burgos… maybe to some hotel… I'm so sad it is crippling… sitting in a bar watching Spanish trash TV and feel I understand what is being shown/said… I'm alone again… another storm in the making… all alone all the time… my passing line of the day for the people I meet is… I wish you Merry Christmas… they laugh at my silliness… I no longer find it funny…

… pissing contest… after the truck madness or as I like to call it my theoretical suicide attempt… my head is quieting down… did I spook my soul… bet you did not see that coming you mother fucking soul of mine… did I thwart your plans… us humans on earth, we help the less fortunate people and the more driven good hearted people at times give their lives in those war torn and /or famine countries… it is the same about souls… in their realm, things are not perfect either, after all if souls were divine they would not be learning through us… maybe some souls help invisibly and others come to help us via the human body… where do I stand with my soul in this scenario?…

… bosom… how I would like to lie next to a woman… to smell her perfume as I sink myself into her bosom… where I could get a restful sleep in her arms… where I can feel I'm a person both cared for and loved… how I dream to be touched and be human again… the Spanish beauties at the next bistro table with their cigarette and cell phones… their perfumes struggling for sexiness with the cigarette smoke rings puffed out of those luscious red lips… oozing with desire bestowed upon any man who allows himself to fluctuate his impulses between carnal desire and self-control respectability…

… green cross… the pharmacy sign is flashing 30 degrees Celsius… reminding us to drink as it is a hot evening… and any fallacy this evening could be remedied by the pharmacist in the morning… the cigarette smoke dissipates her humanity... with the eyes of a Cleopatra, does she know the carnal desires she stirs in men and perhaps even women... the reverberating church bell shouts the 10 PM Cinderella lock down of the albergue... the Spaniards are out playing while the pilgrims are soon to be fast asleep... too young for me, but very beautifully desirable indeed...

## 2015/05/28 – Thursday (San Bol, Spain)

... my special... when I walked the camino 2 years ago I had stopped here at this albergue... the place spoke to me again, as it was near here I had a spiritual epiphany about a kilometer up the road... back then it was raining hard and I came upon an intersection where four roads intersected... the rain did not bother me in the slightest... there were mounds of accumulated rocks at each corner... I sat on the north/west mound... I looked at my watch and it was 2:15... I decided I would rest for 5 minutes and closed my eyes... I felt my feet blending as one with the ground... I knew I was not asleep nor dreaming... I found myself going down in a blue vortex spiral... I just kept going down, this was all I could remember... then I heard a voice tell me it is time to go... when I opened my eyes I saw the time was 2:35... I knew I was somewhere for the last 20 minutes... it was not until I made a hypnosis regression a year later that I knew I had connected with my parents and one grandfather who were guiding/helping me on my difficult journey...

... so far... revisiting the intersection I felt at peace... my body and mind were calm, especially my mind... I sat across from the stone mound as I felt it was nothing special in itself, as I was what counted... so I just looked at the mound... grasses of all kinds invaded it... I felt that whatever I write in my journal and publish it... it will help someone... on my way back to the albergue, I felt this wave of emotion over me that it brought tears to my eyes... I felt like a little boy who is wearing a big body suit that does not belong to me... white butterflies fluttered around me and back over the wheat fields... they were like kids running after one another playing tag... there was silliness in their flight movements...

... pristine... the San Bol albergue can only accommodate 12 guests in one dormitory... it is so remote that solar panels provide electricity and it has a round table for 12 pilgrims where we have our communal supper... but it also has a natural spring water fountain with a basin for washing clothes or dipping your feet... along with picnic tables for passing pilgrims to rest...

and with this, there were about 20 senior citizen tourist pilgrims... with yellow handkerchiefs around their necks and who had stopped to rest/eat... the herd mentality was grazing in the albergue grounds licking each other's blistering foot wounds but the reality is they care for one another...

... male... restless and prancing senior males were walking in circles... but had to wait for the females who were still sitting and resting their plump bodies... except the jaw appendage as this is self-sufficient energy wise and does not require resting... security in numbers perhaps but time/life is passing by those who can and are ready to walk... they are like little kids reminding one another to drink water... is it they care or are they so insecure that they need to talk constantly to feel heard and/or acknowledge... or is it that the fear of loneliness equates silence...

... support... they love their walking poles... lining up near the courtyard gate... the guide gives them a pep talk... the men are already stomping their poles on the ground revving up for the departure just like a race car at the starting line... and one last reminder from the guide letting them know in which direction to go... comically, as there is only one way out, anyway... finally at the speed of a human pace car... the guide sets the pace for the walk to the next village...

## 2015/05/29 – Friday (Fromista, Spain)

... eastern sunrise... this morning I woke up early because a married couple sleeping near me got up at 5 AM to start walking... their discreetness was subtle... after gathering and packing my backpack in the near dark... I was standing at the albergue doors at 5:30... as I opened the door to leave, I was struck by how dark it was... the stars were still in full display and in no hurry to be invisible to the day time eye... with both feet on the cement balcony, I took in a deep breath... I felt tears come to my eyes... not from the emotion of the night time sky... but in true Canadiana style... I expressed a verbal sentiment of... fuck it is cold... and how cold was it?... so cold that the sunscreen on my face crystalized and flaked off...

... desires... I watched this early bird married couple yesterday, walking about the courtyard of the albergue... they are in their 50's... she is not too pretty but she is cute... a gym enthusiast for sure... one had the impression they were walking the camino to rekindle their couple... but from the body language it was obvious this was gonna be a long trip together... luckily they both kept their masturbation scented fingers busy with their cell phones... I felt her sadness and a desire for affection... during the night after having been to the bathroom, on my way to my lonely cot... I saw her looking at me from her cot... I felt our feelings/desires were mutual... suffice to say it was particularly hard for me to sleep in the cot next to hers...

... segregation... as a priest waves good-bye... two plump women limp to a taxi with backpacks on one shoulder... their boots are not on their feet but shoe laced into the backpack... this morning my 10 toes were in a complaining mood as I tried to get them into my boots... some were upset being next to toes that had leaking blisters... I told them to get along or during the walk, I'd drop a stone in the boot to cause chaos... still not clear why priests cannot marry... being good men, odds are their kids would also be good people if he marries a woman from the parish... if he marries a hooker it's a crap shoot as to what his offspring will be like... but if he marries a shemale, then any child born to them is of an immaculate conception... why does the Vatican stop this proliferation of possibly better human beings...

... arias... a group of Italians are singing at the top of their lungs... opera by the sounds of it... a few sit down on a bench and with a lighter to sterilize a pin... are now piercing the blisters on one of their colleagues' foot all the while another is filming this foot surgery... this is the madness of these pilgrims... a deadline was established for the camino and no pain will delay the objective as they need to be back home on time... why the martyr notion of the camino... 36 days of non-stop walking stupidity because of work... is your work of more value than yourself... ?...

... lining pockets... the church facing my inn room is now open... to the right side as you enter is a glassed booth where a man sells tickets to go into the church... for a 1.5 euros you get a ticket stub and a palm size flyer with a description... and this transaction is performed with the elegance allowed to the clerk when he can turn away from his desk size computer featuring football news on the internet... the polite pilgrims hang on to these pieces of paper, a memento of sorts until they find a recycling bin either here or a drawer bottom in their home country...

... selective... probably the benches outside the church were built and anchored into concrete blocks... with the wood planks of varnished chestnut color stain... an extension of the benches inside the church but for the poor who could not add to the collection basket and were not worthy of a seat inside... swallows fly frantically in a circular pattern over the church sky... never landing on the church building or grounds as if they did not have a parking permit... was not even able to coax them to land/stop with yesterday's stale bread served to me as toasts this morning...

## 2015/05/30 – Saturday (Fromista, Spain)

... playing with fire... saw a man sitting alone on a stool outside of a bistro... with a look of disappointment as he switched his eyes from the losing lottery ticket in his hand to the dusty street of a very small town that limits his world... as I walked passed by him... feeling his disappointed despair... found myself returning on my steps and walking back to him... pointing to the ticket, I said two weeks... my voice broke his pensive mood and I repeated two weeks... gesturing he would win money... he looked at me stunned and almost sheepishly smiled... he wanted to believe me, but was not sure... the two weeks statement was not mine at all... it came from an intuition... who is playing with fire, me or the ticket man...

... stepping down... families here include all the generations when they go out for meals or just drinks... it is touching to see grandkids hovering likes flies while the parents physically support the grandmother, one by each arm to help her fragile body move in what we take for granted as walking... the parents parrot each other as they tell her there are steps leading up to the restaurant... the old lady raises her leg in vain as there are still 5 paces before reaching the step... she has the frailty of a newborn... a baby rebounds from falls, she probably would not... would she mind?... will I ever be a senior... ?...

... counting... I spent most of the day in bistro terraces as the day was extremely hot... I slept quite a bit this morning and was in no mood to stay in my room... I just sat drinking carbonated water as I felt my body was tired and dehydrated... the tables around me had locals coming and going... it's a ratio of four chairs per table... but folks drank in a social context and would come in large groups of 6 or so... politely, I was asked if they could take one of my chairs to their table... it was not long before I was sitting at my table with no chairs for any of my friends... the irony being I have no friends... I'm completely alone in life... my numerical hero could only be a zero...

... when... a couple with old age slowness... but she is in shape as she puts out her arm for him as he comes down the two steps from the restaurant... his cane combined with a weak grasp of the railing has him at risk of falling... the Band-Aid across his forehead is evident of this reality... but it's her that impresses me… is this an addendum to her commitment for better or for worse… does she still see the young man she married… who now has blotchy forehead skin… the once upon a time unified pigmentation is now fragmented… fatigued cells giving up on re-generation and the rest of the body follows suit… does the mind follow suit… I'm not sure…

… pity… a man walks on to the terrace platform… he's surely over 6 foot tall… with dark rings under his bulging eyes… maybe it is from perpetual masturbation over computer porn and indulging in sweets from the size of his protruding stomach… I wonder if his mom puts a box of Kleenex next to his computer… no sooner does this nasty but funny thought enter my mind… that a woman with one leg shorter limps on to the platform and sits next to him… the weddings bands are now evident… she is pretty/cute for a 40 something… but I'm sure in her youth men did not flock to her… from the looks of him he courted her desperation for a married family life as this was pressured upon her as being a romantic fantasy… of course, she was his first and only too… as he is no prince charming either… they simply settled and learned to love with time or maybe just respect one another as they felt they were short changed in life… a comfortable love as they hold their glasses and toast…

… martyr… am I desperate not to be alone… everyone I see now is a potential candidate for love… am I becoming bitter now that I have concretely realized I'm alone on this planet… the smiling faces of pilgrims will be my last human connection to this place… their milliseconds of affection for me is not enough to feed my hunger… I want tenderness from a woman… the man in me is just a little boy in a big suit… I am alone, very alone… tomorrow I will walk like a madman… pushing my physical limits… to forget…

… whine… I have something to say before my end no matter how insignificant I may be… I'm here on the terrace invisible to everyone even to myself… fuck, do I exist if I can't even see myself… did my soul leave me here connected to the headphones blasting Sex Pistols… guitars and pumping bass drowning out my emotions… at least there is temporary peace in my mind as I watch couples of my age holding hands… as I do not envy them but instead am happy for them… they have someone to sleep with… like the comfort of a baby's ear listening to their mothers' heart beacon of security… I don't have that now and wonder if I ever did… I can no longer stay sitting here as I need the comfort of a pillow to absorb my tears…

* * *

# JUNE

## PART EIGHT

## 2015/06/01 - Monday (Sahagun, Spain)

... visions... I woke up in a perpetual restless state of being... how can one wake up and need silence immediately... I'm tired, what have I been doing to get to such a state... and I have some 20 kilometers to walk today... is it the evening with its' sunset that leaves me alone in the dark... talking in my head and rehearsing full conversations... in the odd chance someone knows I am here... alive with a beaten heart... I feel my walk will involve a crying breakdown again... when I think about what I have written... it is not my hand writing... it is another *me* who writes and cries... if I walk fast with music loud... it will not allow the other *me* in my head...

... pause... this being a bigger town with about 2 800 inhabitants... pilgrims tend to take a day off here... better food, sights and hotels with bathtubs amongst the more valid reasons... how can you spot a pilgrim in the evening... pilgrims walk in sandals to release their feet from the confine of hiking boots... with foot pain, walking/limping through town in solitude... if you come here looking for something and/or an answer to which you are not even sure what the question is then you got fucked wherever you came from... dear pilgrim, the problem is where you come from, look there too... may be that limping is the badge of honor for pilgrim's devotion... they are still in the physical stage of the pilgrimage and it is all about shoes, equipment and pain... the mental and spiritual stages are yet to come...

... one... probably some pilgrims are going through some sort of self-justification that resting is an acceptable trait, and that they are not on vacation mode... as is the case with the woman next to my table... every familiar face she sees she chants her sore foot blister litany... and her friends are no better off... pain is the subject flavor at their table on this bistro terrace... then I wonder... doesn't she realize she's not hiking but walking... her credit card with wear and tear of the raised plastic gold lettering elevating her unhappy status in society... with which she purchased her expensive hiking boots... as the smart ass store clerk asked *how much are your feet worth to you*... and with this premise scanned plastic money was no object... and those bloated blisters with so much puss that it drowns the ants roaming around the table for crumbs... then again what better cure than rest and pints of beer...

... self-image tourist... despite her blister litany... she is about in her 40's and kind of pretty but she let herself go physically... especially in the midsection... though in her voice one denotes kindness and also genuinely very caring... with the hot sun overhead I close my eyes and just hone in on her voice... not on what she says but on her vocals as guiding waves for empathy or even my intuitions... why do you fear silence?... is it the sound of your voice that chokes your loneliness?... does it make you forget the contempt you feel for yourself when you put on makeup... ?...

... self-image tourist reflected... walk alone until your well of tears dries up to the point that when you look in the mirror you do not see the reflected body... but plunge into the dry eyes in front of you... as you enter deeply into your very own eyes... you'll see how beautiful you are... and no one can dare tell you otherwise as you no longer need their acclamation to validate yourself... as the little girl in you with shiny eyes is still very alive...

## 2015/06/02 - Tuesday (Sahagun, Spain)

... repetition... after checking into the inn yesterday... my slew of orchestrated questions ensues... is there a grocery store, barber or laundromat nearby... 2 out of 3 ain't bad... there was a barber and if I hurried I can get a haircut before he closes up for siesta time which lasts from 2 to 5 pm... no luck for a laundromat... so once again I place my clothes in the shower while I bathe and my feet act as a washing machine... stomping the clothes into cleanliness... funny thing, as the barber trimmed my beard, the touch of his hands on my face made me feel human... I'm a person of flesh and blood and not just thoughts...

... the pulse... as I walk down to Plaza Mayor for breakfast... it's an open square with bistros of all kinds gracing the perimeter... a waitress is sweeping her area of the plaza/esplanade... she was here last night serving me supper and now at 8 AM is serving me breakfast... I gestured with my hands placed together, next to my cheek, do you ever sleep?... her smile was a term of endearment... with her motherly hand on my shoulder she guided me to a table... she stands a little over 4 feet tall of feistiness... in her 50's with very dark hair and pale complexion which emphasizes her red lipstick gloss... whatever task she is doing, it is done effectively fast except when she speaks to me...

... with routine... breakfast with sunshine just on my table as it is unprotected by the awning's reign of cool shadows... trivial as this may be the OJ is freshly squeezed and not bottled as the one on the table next to me... can you sense motherly love from the waitress, I know... I'm adorable... pilgrims walking thru the plaza in search of a morning meal... with their oversized and over stocked backpacks... who cannot and will not discard anything to lighten their burdensome load for fear of losing something of themselves... as if the t-shirt with a message slogan to *BE CALM blah, blah, blah...* sitting at the bottom of the backpack which has yet to see sunlight is an extension of who they are... are we ants in colorful and matching clothing but with backpacks too...

... zoom by... the cigarette leaves a dust trail as a young mom pushes the baby stroller... just like a blurred photograph the cigarette smoke leaves her face unfocused blocking my view of her anxiety... still the body posture of heaviness cannot be masked by the smoke... another mom running late with 2 small children struggling to keep up with her... a daily ritual it seems... perhaps the mom should be the one behind her children and appreciate their small pace of life...

... visible longevity... the two city workers sweeping the plaza wearing navy blue pants with reflective yellow bands below the knees... methodically dance their brooms into every nookie dragging out any dust particle from where it does not belong... as if the plaza is their pride and joy, even an extension of their being... with so much respect for the plaza as they sweep about with cigarettes dangling from their chapped lips... their own self-worth is short lived unlike the plaza which was there before them and will be there after them too... their efforts are an investment in concrete durability...

... on the other side... the still quiet of the plaza is disrupted by the metal chains being removed from the stacked aluminum chairs... as the chairs are being distributed and reunited with the also recently freed tables... a delivery van with a picture of bread on its' side pulls into the plaza carrying with it morning freshness... the faceless driver steps out and opening the back doors of the van saturates my sense of smell with the neatly stacked crates of breads and sweets... this may be just a job for him... for the rest of us it is a necessity of joy...

... without routine... students walking thru the plaza on their way to school... also carrying backpacks full of copybooks and maybe even some borrowed school books... eventually the copybooks will wilt in the back-pack from the time summer vacations start and to the beginning of the next school year in the fall... at which point they'll look at their past homework and wonder where did time go and with the same breath of thought discard the scribbled paper into a recycling bin... time gone by and old copy books are of no concern, in fact they hinder their optimism of the future...

... reality... with no money to spare for a coffee a young woman opts to sit on a bench with a cellphone in hand and a cigarette on the other... she reads her morning emails/texts and in an executive fashion butts out her cigarette on the pavement with her foot... with her right hand now free she types out digital messages... filling the voids in her life with trivial mis-spelled words which only perpetuate the errors in her life...

## 2015/06/03 - Wednesday (Releigos, Spain)

... another... morning of hollow emptiness filled with intuitions... but there is an ease in knowing I have no one nor a so called *home* to go to... my backpack is an extension of me and it is pretty much all that will remain of me... will they go through it to inquire/discover who and what I am, will my legacy be a series of assumptions as to who and what I was... why am I thinking of this, why does it matter, is it simply a human tendency for a perpetuity of some sort... walking here on the *Camino* is like when I walked about town in *Aveiro*... by walking, my mind relaxes as my heart pumps my body... in doing so, it opens and even floods my imagination... or is it messages from beyond as when walking I'm also more receptive... can I categorize/classify my madness... ?

... black balloon... as I walked around town, I came across ancient houses built/dug into a hillside... almost like hobbit houses... though impressive... is this the best they can build with Greece only two countries away... where extra-ordinary palaces were built not to mention the Romans too with their functional city architecture... all of a sudden and pretty much out of nowhere the Greeks excelled into a great civilization with impressive buildings and of course the Olympics... where men competed in sporting events as if they were thoroughbred horses... could it be that mankind was being genetically modified... as if mankind were like pets to the Greeks gods who lived in the heavens and came down in their fiery shiny metal chariots with bright lights... these celestial gods helping and watching them evolve and then stopped... why?... did they fuck up and left us to our own demise... or were they just here creating slightly better human machines to accommodate souls...

... board game... the feeling of jumping out of the body is persistent... as if trapped and fighting for dear life... a man is complete if he has a soul... or if he feels something is missing, then he has an incomplete or half soul... why do I know this as if it were factual... how does a soul re-unite or is it even possible to?... as long as I am alive the soul (or half soul) is stuck with me... it (soul) must be fragile on every realm overlapping time and space... because of this I know my world is amiss... somehow when I get fed info from my soul on different plains and times as intuitions... like snakes and ladders of life... I have no home to return to... my days are counted... skin wrinkling to what it was like when I was a newborn... and the garbage bins here smell like the ones back in Montreal... it's the same everywhere... when we die we're all the same...

... seriously, dare me... came to a highway overpass and opted to sit on the railing as massive trucks revved below my asshole world... how easy it was for me to calculate the right moment to jump for maximum impact, so that a truck can disintegrate me... other than maybe a messy reddish mist on the truck windshield, it was fool proof and sound... I felt empowered... got over the railing and stood on the edge, my backpack was caught on the railing and pulling my lower back against the cold metal, which did not feel that uncomfortable as I was slightly sweating... fuck, there is never a truck when you need one... when I see in plain daylight the shadowy almost human form glide in the cold morning air in front of me... it slows down in front of me as if to obstruct my view of the oncoming trucks... the highway went dead silent, as if time stopped... the shadowy form disappeared in front of me and only to reappear to a pilgrim a few meters away... as the blackish shadow hovers over him... I see the pilgrim raise his head in alarm and quickening his pace towards me... fucken bastard!!!!... back on the railing, I get my camera and pretend to be taking a pic... the pilgrim eases off on his quick pace...

... thoughts... I kept walking a few more meters until the next village... wondering about what I had just done on the overpass and even my commitment to the task... in retrospect my historic lack of dedication, had me sleeping in on a rainy Monday morning instead of attending the final high school math exam... as I chuckle to myself, as I can recognize the humor in my own actions from back when... I see the shadowy form sitting in the bistro terrace... can no one else see him?... he/it was pissed... I could feel the anger... I snickered as I passed by he/it and went inside the bistro... when I came out with my bottled water he/it was still sitting outside and I sat at its' table... I could still sense anger in it but my attitude was one of *fuck off*... it/he was not in his world but mine... and with this thought the chair emptied into clarity as it/he vanished... not sure if it/he can walk but with me it'll be walking on eggshells... why does this shadow want me alive... is it the other half of my soul?... am I worth more alive than a suicidal corpse... wait!!!... it must need me... why... ?

... borders... where are the boundaries between earth and heaven... who is feeding me these revealing intuitions and daring strenght... is there some heavenly agenda and I'm a pawn... maybe it is not so heavenly after all... it's seems to be as petty as the earthlings on my planet... could it be there is dissidence in the heavenly realm... ?

## 2015/06/04 - Thursday (Leon, Spain)

... baffled blur... woke up later than usual, about 2 hours of extra restless sleep... and in a state of melancholy I walked aimlessly for about 3 hours in Leon... before realizing I was hungry... it was my hunger that brought me out of my thoughts... last night met and had supper with a French Canadian woman from nearby Montreal... though our supper conversation was frenchly animated... she inadvertently reminded me of what I had when living in Montreal but especially everything I lost... as I thought about the people I loved at one time in my life, they now seem inexistent... what is happening to me, how can I disconnect so bluntly from people yet remember city landmarks amongst other trivia... their memory seems to flicker in my mind... why do I feel guilty for missing them when I cannot even remember them in detail... if my thoughts are a blur, then so must be my life... no?

... the last good-bye... my soul is going to leave my body soon... this is what I feel and I have very little choice in the matter... and I don't know if it will return or what will become of my essence... I wonder about people who commit suicide, is it because they are just a shell once their soul abandons them, is their emptiness so unbearable that the body and mind are dis-oriented to the point of a temple gun... where is the sanctuary of a temple when one is free falling and it is not a Sunday morning when the doors are opened for business... just maybe, is this the same feeling of an inmate on death row too... this is the feeling flowing thru me but without fear... no point in hoping for a pardon as there is no turning back for me... I have been set-up and played... holy shit, I'm being fucked...

... brittle... my skin is dry, no one has touched me in a long time... it aches for tenderness, I am still human as I drift in loneliness with guilt and without Suzanne being here... we had a lot of US plans and dreams about travelling or at least I did for us... things did not work out for us as I fucked up royally... the more she cared for me, the more alienated I was... and yet here I am shivering in the hot sun, as a newborn without the mother's love...

shriveling into a prune... old and ugly before my time... a hug, just a hug to make me feel I am still a person and not just another soulless body in the crowded city street... the smelly homeless man with a paper cup in hand gets more affection from passersby through metallized tokens of affection... I know I still exist but I cannot locate myself in me...

... coded scribbles... I have done nothing all afternoon other than sit on this bistro chair facing the cathedral... for what purpose do I have a pen and paper as what I am scribbling are not even my doodled thoughts... come to think of it, even the handwriting seems foreign to me... in the confusion of the written scribbles of blue ink I see chaotic beauty... faces looking at me from the paper... no sooner do I focus my glance back at them they disappear and show up disguised as another face somewhere else on the paper... I know these faces want to tell me something but they do not last long enough to talk to me... with my brown eyes feeling blue... I look up to the sky and back down to the plaza facing the cathedral...

... plaza rhythm... an elderly nun in a blue garb with a skirt just below the knees... she is wearing blue running shoes... the shoes look as if they were bought with her meager allowance at some riff raff country fair or Chinese knick knack store... are her shoes the only visible extension of her personality and fashion taste... did her religious order overlook this rebellious statement of non-conformity, to think for oneself when choosing the shoes... or in their infinite wisdom, toying with her in allowing to be slightly human... the question that now beckons, is this radicalism extended to underwear too... nevertheless, the shoes are now part of the uniform, is this officially Vatican approved?... tourists are entering the cathedral because they have a camera in hand with trigger happy fingers, freshly pulled out of a nostril or ear... somewhere or someone told them the cathedral is a thing of exquisite beauty that must be seen... they come here and yet they fear being alone and must be surrounded by people at all times... as they selfie themselves into a picture...

## 2015/06/06 - Saturday (Villavante, Spain)

... scalp sunburn... the day was a long one... physically draining but also feeling mentally tired to the point where my temples ache... I decided to cut my walking day short and find a place to sleep... the belief here seems to be, one does not come to the Camino... the Camino calls you whether you are a tourist or not... or whether you finish the walk or not... the fact that you are here is special enough a reason, as one has been chosen... this town is on the map because it makes for a nice dot in a barren area... suffice to say, the one Albergue and the one local bar/restaurant were both filled to capacity... I moved on to the outskirts of the town hoping to find accommodations in a B&B...

... silent doorbell... if the word kindness in the dictionary had a picture it would be of the B&B inn keepers, posing in front of their property at Molino Galochas... of course the inn was full... but to help me out... they invited me to stay in their home's guest room... the beauty of their home is an extension of their kindness... out of respect for them, while in their home I limited my displacements between my room and the bathroom... there is a beautiful sink on a natural piece of wood acting as a vanity... looking at this hand crafted artifact I realize that... I have nothing of beauty in my life... all I have is my backpack and smelly boots but this is just a lame excuse to ease my nothingness which I seem to have in abundance... and a head full of intellectual bullshit materialism...

... paces... as I walk the grounds... the two adjoining buildings are laid out in such a way that one is parallel to the river and the other building (inn) is over the river... a series of arches over the river support and act as the buildings' foundation... it is a thing of pure architectural beauty and to a lesser extent for the eye an engineering feat... but later at night when sleeping, the sound of the running water soothed me as I slept in a fetal position... I see things of beauty as I walk the Camino but have no one to share them with... so, for whom would I take pictures?... do I belong in this idyllic B&B paradise lost in nature... is this my last pleasant memory of being on this planet or am I coming back in another form... I do not want to go back to the real world... but this is a quasi-permanent year long vacation that should end with my death either by my hand or accident... no?

... into the white light... the guests are all pilgrims... with ensuing conversations over the perceived refinement of wine drinking... discussing their interpretation of what divinity means to them and for some it is even factual... have they learned nothing while walking other than re-affirm to themselves that my god is the right one... they look at me for an opinion but I'm not in the mood to talk... in fact there verbosity tires me and at the same time would they be able to grasp what I think and also believe to be factual... even I'm just as naively foolish in my beliefs as they are... life is about pleasure and pain... this is what the soul is seeking as a learning experience by using me and my physical body... I am a whore on this planet, as I am getting royally fucked... there is no doubt in my mind this is hell, at least for humans... unlike the soul we have no way out of here...

... imposter competition... in the evening there was a communal supper in the dining room overlooking the rippling river as it flows underneath the inn... new faces for whom I am new too... how will I project myself this evening... what will I create as the imposter flavor of the day... can they see I have no personality... I fake my intelligence as being wise and paternal... all bullshit!... if anything I'm depressed and cynical... but all those at the table are optimistic pilgrims... or at least this is the image they try to convey... not to worry, the moment I think I'm the worst/best there is always someone else who beats me at my imposter game... one pilgrim brags about the Camino and that it makes him fall more in love with his wife... yet earlier he had claimed he also spends 12 hours at work and hardly sees her or the kids... and better yet he is here on his pilgrim vacation... I sense/intuit he has a mistress... why do I want to be wise?... will I be quiet or will I shoot my mouth exposing his lying stupidity... what I really want is adoration, what a whore I am... I will keep my mouth shut and not seek adulation at his expense... who am I to play god...

... enable... the stewed pork was delicious, truly... as I waited for my espresso to cap off the supper orgasm... it dawns on me the cruelty of my food pleasure... as I look at my plate, there was nothing but invisible pain left on it... I can see and now even feel the pain of death... of the animal and vegetable energies on my plate... now, I feel like throwing up... how can I eat and even have enjoyed this as what I eat is death... why can't I get my nourishment from the sun like my soul... I do not like the real world... maybe this planet is a vacation for souls but not me... again should it end with my death either by my hand or accident... what the fuck am I thinking?

## 2015/06/08 - Monday (Astorga, Spain)

... realization... this far into the Camino... pilgrims racing to meet the 30 or so day deadline to Santiago... have now slowed down... as fatigue and intense heat along with the reality that reaching Santiago will not be any time soon... and I am no different, but I fuel my body with an endless combination of espressos and carbonated water... one is for the sugar/caffeine rush and the other for the salt content in the water... all I know, is after this cocktail I zoom on my two feet... with speed in my feet, I leave behind pilgrims alone in my dust... my Ipod songs are my last connection to this world... (note to oneself, press play)... they (songs) are the only ones who speak to me... I have no desire nor do I want to talk to people when walking... as my head has more messages or conversations than I can handle...

... déjà vu... well this city is a déjà vu because I was here two years ago... when I walked my first Camino... it had impressed me with its' rich history dating back thousands of years before the romans... of course churches are a staple of this historic city, roman ruins and so is the chocolate industry... but along with all these tourist niceties, it also has an energy that leaves me with an impression that I was here in a previous life and now want to be here for a while... so, I had promised myself that I would check into a hotel... first to soak in a bathtub... and second to find a Laundromat in town to wash all my clothes... if not, I will wash them by hand in the room... as this is the lifestyle of the rich(not) and un-famous pilgrim...

... plastic money... checking in at the hotel reception... the clerk swiped/ scanned my credit card and simultaneously dislodged the encrusted dust particles which had settled from lack of use... actually she had to swipe the card twice as the dust on the magnetic band had interfered... it occurred to me... I could live like a king by maxing out my card, and let some honest person pay for my defaulting with high perverse credit card interest rates... isn't this what royalty does, fuck money out of the honest workers with taxes so that may have unimportant necessities like yachts, parade designer clothes, attend benefit galas and pretend they contribute to society as they are chauffeured around in both rich and poor countries...

... overview... my hotel room has a small balcony that if I don't fart I'd be able to stand on the deck... it is facing the plaza square... the very first time, two years ago when I was here... the plaza was filled with vendors as it was the monthly fair... travelling merchants selling, clothes, shoes, kitchenware and improvised vendors selling fine collections of knick knack crap... but this is a dying tradition and/or way of life... as everything that was for sale could be bought for cheaper in a one euro Chinese store almost 24/7... the only thing which will never be replaced or eliminated are the food vendors... when it comes to food, tradition still lives on...

... invisible history... the plaza is a scenic tourist picture paradise... and justifiably so, with all its bistros and neatly, if not anally aligned chairs and tables sprawled out on the plaza... the clock tower watches over these multitudes of locals and tourists alike... history is written daily... in the morning freshly clean and energized pilgrims leave town and in the evening a whole new horde of dirty and smelly hunched over backpack carrying pilgrims drag their feet in paw like steps... whatever history is being written, the tourists snap away pictures endlessly... if only we could go back in time and see the public hangings/burnings nurtured by the Spanish inquisition... today the plaza is serene in its' modern décor but it wreaks pure malevolence and injustice... am I the only one who can feel this?...

... when before... again, I find myself walking the streets... I was not able to stay in the room, the feeling of confinement made breathing almost impossible... kids are coming out of school and grandparents are at the door waiting for them... this is family life... I had this too, but it seems so far away and I can remember certain images of my kids but not the emotions that go with the images... walking around I see a shoe store window display... small size and very colorful kids' running shoes are displayed... the bolder and brighter the colors the more likely they would end up on my little girls' feet... what would be a silly color to my eyes would be a smile on their faces... every step in the new shoes offered them the possibility to see their reflection on some window shop... reflecting images of them wearing the new shoes... the reflections I see are the ones of their eyes widening with the color of joy... I can remember this invented memory...

## 2015/06/09 - Tuesday (Astorga, Spain)

... wrong side... I don't, I don't, I don't, I don't know who the fuck I am or what I am... talk about waking up on the wrong side of the bed... my eyes are bewilderedly wide open when I realize I'm still in bed... gradually I begin to acknowledge and feel my body... there was a moment of uncertainty... like when one runs the bath and pulls the knob on the spout to engage the shower... the milliseconds it takes the water to change direction from the spout to the shower head... I had to wait for my mind to acknowledge all my body extremities were accounted for... I felt and knew, I was on my way back into my body... and often as before, could not remember exactly what had transpired during the night...

... breakfast delight... since the sun rose again just to piss me off... might as well have my morning ritual of coffee, toast and newspaper... but since I don't read Spanish, I'll improvise my ritual without a newspaper and look at people instead... I close my eyes as I sip my coffee... I don't need to see the people around me as I can feel them... people are ugly and all pilgrims look goofy too... what a blessing my soul has given me... the ability to emphatically see/feel people... is this gift to torment me more?... to show me a side of human nature which most of us cannot and do not want to see... is it to expedite my desire to surrender back my remaining soul from this body from this physical entity which is, me?...

... musical chairs... what's this bitterness in me... I feel contempt for humans and a while ago all I wanted was to help others... where is my old self?... my thoughts are strangled by her nauseating shrieking voice... the voice of a know it all... this generously plump pilgrim woman with her heavy duty clayed on make-up, disgusts me in every sense, to the point of vomit... an adamant self-proclaimed atheist very proud and arrogant pilgrim... I recognized my old self in her after we parted... she fucken disturbed me all day... I too used to be self-assured and in the illusion of control... but now I am fragmented and my thinking is chaotic... for what it is worth, if giving up eases my anguish then I'm ready to die... this living is just fucken unbearable... this dragging disease called life is killing me slowly... and in the end, this repulsive preposterous woman with her loud speaker mouth and irritating appearance, all she wants is to be loved... to my eyes she did not succeed in her attempt to camouflage her sadness and loneliness...

... fishing lure... walking around, it is obvious there is some incredible history in this town as it is also the European birthplace of chocolate... one can only imagine conquistadores bringing back the cocoa bean in exchange for an oppressive reigning regime and imposed Christianity on the good folks of the hot Americas... with drizzling rain and I do not want to wet the 3 strands of hair remaining on my bald head, I step into a church for shelter... the church interior is typical... with endless statues and carvings trying to convince god almighty that those who come here are heaven worthy... hellloooo, I'm here!!... I sit and rest for a while in the aloneness of a Tuesday church... focusing my eyes on statues of monks... they look slightly effeminate... is this the benign look of their time?... or perhaps the sculpting artist swung his chisel both ways... the more I stare at these statues, they seem to nod their heads at me... or is it my suggestive mind playing tricks...

... introverted empathy... fragmented memories of what I did during the night are coming back to me... I met my complete soul, in the sleep time darkness... my half of the soul re-united with the other half which was lurking here in this darkness... I was able to read its' thoughts with my mind... I stared at him or at least where I thought he was... this time shivers of fear ran through my body, I saw it (body) jerking on the bed... his energy was too intense for my cellular body... fuck you... I thought... the only thing it can do is prolong my pain, not add more... I on the other hand can kill myself and he loses... it/he is the one who should be scared and instead is bluffing me with his circus tricks... fuck you... you fucken piece of shit... I want to know what is going on... speak up you silent whore?... or I'll fuck you so hard it will kill all your family if you have such a thing...

... celestial office politics... we (humans) are being used by souls for their selfish experimenting/learning... via us for emotional ranges such as; from love to cruelty and physical body sensations (sex too)... like my soul, some are opposed to this... soul dissidence is punished by fragmenting into several physical bodies... I don't remember being consulted for my role as an emissary... my intuition gift is for communicating with my soul, but inadvertently it also allows me access to the humans' mind... there is an overload of intuitions from everyone around me... I'm no longer in the forefront... I cannot drown out the intuitive messages... I have reached the maximum loudness on the headphones... how do I manage them, messages and humans?... my soul is it too close to my earth plain and does it want to drive me insane... how long can I keep fighting myself... souls are not as divine as I thought...

## 2015/06/10 - Wednesday (Rabanal del Camino, Spain)

... any day... one day I'm going to die, but what about the other days?... the morning newspaper has now been replaced by the Camino guide book... in this nameless establishment which is a general store, coffee shop, and bar combination, this little booklet is my guide in this limited world... last night I slept well, and woke up feeling serene but not necessarily happy with what is going on between my soul and I... nevertheless, all I want right now is to sit here alone at this table of five and sip my coffee in silence, but the sound of people next to me makes me cringe... and their syllabic voices make me think... do I live in a world of madness... is it real or just in my mind and which world is mad... theirs, theirs or theirs... it has to be theirs as my mind is accounted for...

... vicious... do I control my thoughts or are my thoughts controlling me... and who is the creator/owner of these thoughts, me or my soul?... who cares?... I still feel beaten as my thoughts slumber in the darkness with no illuminated exit sign... I'm tired of walking and need to rest my feet, my legs... shit!... my whole fucken body... with this summer rain and thunderstorms, pilgrims get off the road and seek shelter... as the metal frame supporting our backpacks acts as an antenna for lightning strikes... as if I care... I sit outside on a road bench leading out of the nameless last town... the bench is in front of a 2 meter high retaining stone wall composed of rocks piled with no apparent mortar... I opt to sit facing the wall... so many stones of different sizes piled/stacked together resisting/defying time and rain erosion to form a something... and here I am with so many thoughts of emptiness forming my non-existence... am I a collapsed wall?... am I tired of living?... like a wall I would need help to re-build... there is no one on the road and I know what I want... I need to die but this is not my thought, is it?...

... scare tactic... a few nights ago I had this dream... a semi-buried coffin has 2 half doors... and it's about six feet under already with its' top door closed and covered with earth/buried... I keep it clean as I go down the hole and in thru the bottom door... I crouch in and slide myself through the coffin by pushing against the bottom/end panel... once thru I struggle to turn around and lay on my back... I am now in the appropriate traditional resting position for a coffin... the daylight disappears as earth is pushed in one swoop down the hole... my legs are crushed by the weight as I forgot to close the bottom door... the oxygen darkness is now trapped with me and I'm ok with letting go... I can now remove my headphones as they are useless as they never had music... I breath in the dust and cough myself to sleep... I was so tired, I really was... with such a nightmare one should startle and even wake up... but I didn't...

... illusion... life is beautiful, is it not?... who believes in choice, not I... we don't make the future, how one deals with the present moments is what determines the future... so this is it, how I'm going to impact the world, by writing in this journal and let people know there is a war in the heavens... do souls come from heaven?... they're such a chaotic lot too, how could they be from a divine celestial heaven?... if they (souls) impact our daily behaviour and existence... and as I look around me with what goes on this planet... they cannot be divine in any possible way... at least not all of them...

... deprived... over 2 years in the making... I've been shun by my family... losing everything for an obsessive soul who wants the world to know what is going on up above... a rebellion which is not mine but I'm involved in... since childhood I've been tormented without knowing why until now... sometimes you end up waiting, just like when your parents bought you shoes one size smaller just because they were on sale... all that connects me to the world is the backpack lying on the ground... its' content are the last remnant of my earth life... it is still more than what I started life with... looking around, this nameless small town whose dot on the map is bigger... I wait for my boots and socks to dry... there was so much rain today that my socks got washed in my boots...

... new rules... the irony of life is that nothing lasts forever... this applies to misery as well as happiness... every person one meets in their lifetime has a purpose... most of the time we do not understand why we meet... but as time passes and maybe if we reflect upon the encounter we sense that our life hopefully improved in some way... sometimes ever so slightly... it is this little improvement that helps us deal with the future... but since I do not see a future for myself... what is the purpose of talking/listening to these pilgrim blurs on the Camino... this is where my new rules applies... it is not what I can get from these pilgrims but what I can contribute to them... even if it is just a smile and hello... as I am still in charge...

## 2015/06/11 - Thursday (Ponferrada, Spain)

... somewhere in there... I look skinny and old as I reflect myself in the morning mirror... is 55 old?... my reflection is dialoguing with me... the soul needs to re-unite to be whole as it is in soul hell when fragmented... a tormenting punishment... why does it want to re-unite... is it not happy with me or is it feeling incomplete too... if incomplete could it be unhappy like me... I know/realize a bit of my soul managed to escape when I was a kid and another fragment on the last Camino... at times I am so sad and lonely it feels like hell... am I in hell, is my soul in hell too?... hell is not for us as humans but for our souls... is earth just their hell?... how can it be, this planet is so beautiful... why am I being pulled into their drama?... I'm not a soul...

... my 2 cents... today's Camino had me passing thru the Cruz de Ferro site/mound consisting of an iron cross, sitting on top of a 5-metre wooden pole, and surrounded by a pile of stones that have been left at the site by thousands of passing pilgrims over several past centuries... it is a symbolic gesture for a pilgrim to bring a stone from their place of origin... for me, the true pilgrim is the one who stands at the base of the mound and places his stone with an attached thought... on this particular day and much to my disappointment... some blasphemous pilgrims ruptured the serenity of the place... it was worse than the garbage truck winding its' way through the adjacent tourist car/bus parking lot to pick up the overflowing garbage dumpster...

310

... in french... there is an exuberant festive mood with all the picture taking... from a group one can even hear group hugs... these are stones placed by pilgrims over decades and yet these people climb the 10 foot mound to stand next to the extended pole supporting the metal cross... they snap endless pics while holding a glass (plastic cup, trashy) of red wine... am I over reacting to this?... not all of us share the same spiritual beliefs... but this mound is not created solely by Christians but also folks who were seeking something missing in their lives or a memory of someone dear... there is an energy and even a reverence to this place... can they not feel it?... maybe when they get back home, it will show up in the pictures...

... north american... a young woman on top of the mound picks up stones and looks at then in a judgmental manner, and tosses them back down... what is she looking for or expecting from her stone hunt?... she picks up another and says to her nearby friend this one is ugly and with these words, throws it down below onto the field... her friend shouts it belongs to someone... with this realization our young woman goes down the mound and looks for the stone in the grass field... picks up the ugly stone and heads back to the mound... as she is going up the mound again... she makes the sign of the cross while holding the stone... once on top she drops the stone and laughs foolishly making sure her friend sees the stone is back... for me, this girl by all accounts is an enigma...

... iberians... cyclists take their bikes up on top of the crowded mound for a picture session... impatience setting in between one of the cyclists and the fellow taking the picture... vulgar portuguese swearing ensues... I was embarrassed by the language used... especially because it was on the mound... once they came down, I approached them and asked them in portuguese if the vulgarity was necessary considering where they were standing... I caught them off guard with my question/language... and in a panic mode, they apologized profusely... I said every stone has/had an owner and the apology is not for me... after they left I felt bad, cause I had no business reprimanding them... and thought if I see them again on the Camino I would apologize for my pompous and intrusive behavior... in the late afternoon I spotted them in a bistro crushing beer cans on the table... I kept walking and moved on...

... stoned... in the late afternoon... I sat in a park bench and reflected on the day gone by... and the stones I placed on the Cruz de Ferro site... I left stones dedicated to my kids, Suzanne and also for a few friends including my ex-wife... with all the trampling going on the mound, how serious is this place?... is it just a tourist curiosity, but I did feel energy as I approached the site... it is a special place, I want to believe this as I also said a prayer for my-self... a belief system is an insurance for me to stay alive...

Babylon?... is it my curse to understand and speak these 3 languages... it was no joy to be multi-lingual and witness the stupidity at the Cruz de Ferro site... what is it about humans and no matter our origins... that makes us so callous at times... but at the same time, I saw so many good people and they outnumbered the bad ones I mention here... there is hope, I believe this...

... natural selection... the park bench faces a courtyard adjacent to a school... there is a class of young teenagers playing dodge ball in the court... they are easy to spot/identify as most would make prevalent candidates for a dramatic life crisis acne commercial... I had forgotten that dodgeball is an ag-gressive game/sport... based on the player's personalities or lack off... there seems to be a pecking order where the players stand in the playing field...

... the girls in the back... are insecure, nervous on unfamiliar territory and not athletic... but want to be liked by boys... and mother the boys with their words of encouragement...

... the boys in the front... competitive and arrogant... play rough as it's physical strength that dominates... over-reacting gestures and shout when someone does not come to par with their  perceived abilities...

... girls in the front... here to compete... thin and athletic with swaying hair being constantly pulled back to the side/back... athletic but not all retain their femininity...

... the boys in the back... so shy and will occasionally shine with one good play... until they fumble and will be remembered for the one mistake, forever... may connect with a girl standing in the back but will forever wish and desire a girl who is up in front...

... will the Camino one day call any of these kids... which will the Cami-no call?... since, one does not go to the Camino, as the Camino calls you... though I do not understand why those pilgrims were at the Cruz de Ferro site this morning... maybe the Camino is like a god and does not explain itself and works in mysterious ways... one has to rely on faith... this is hard to swallow though I want to believe... and why was I called?...


## 2015/06/12 - Friday (Ponferrada, Spain)

... computing... woke and felt too tired to walk... it seems, I am the boss of none, not even oneself... but fuck it... I'm gonna linger around town today, anyway... I'm in a coffee shop and in my headphones... the music re-invents what I see... I have Einaudi on repeat... only piano and no vocals as the sound of the human voice irritates me... I pop open my portable computer and see the webcam eye, I wonder what it sees?... cannot go back in time to what I had but I sure don't want to go on either, I think... I like this I think doubt, it is one of hope... I just need those few seconds of courage to finally have control of my life... if I had any of those seconds of control... maybe I would not allow my soul to deteriorate my life to this point where at times I desperately seek abolishing it... this cannot be who and/or what I am...

... flight echo... in the plaza the scarce benches are crowded... except the one shaded bench under the tree... an old lady feeds the pigeons... she sits in the middle of the bench with her purse close to her almost hindering her movements when breaking the bread into bird size crumb pieces... even with her generosity the pigeons fight amongst themselves for the crumbs and she shouts at the pigeons reprimanding them for their impolite behavior... is this what this planet is all about... fighting over crumbs as with the pigeons but what about the humans... is there anything we do not fight about... with who is the old lady fighting with to have the bench all to herself... her foe is not here right now or is it... does being here, out of her house's solitude connect her to the world when feeding meager crumbs to pigeons... picking her purse she gets up and dusts any crumbs of her skirt... she looks at her pigeons while holding her hunched back with the support of her closed umbrella... her baby steps lead her out of the plaza... the pigeon truce is over now that she is gone... their true fighting nature over food returned with a vengeance...

... no vulgarity... I dreamt about Suzanne and it was so pleasant... me in my simplicity and snuggled in her kindness... is this what I need to restore hope?... we were standing face to face... with our arms stretched out, and our hands tangled in a chaotic fashion as only lovers can decipher its' dis-entan-glement, but not just yet... we allow ourselves to sway to the music, the area rug is our dance floor... with the blinds rolled up so high that they seem to disappear... the sun floods the living room highlighting only us... and yet no prying eyes could see us... for they would not understand or even know how to deal with our energies bonding us as one... our four legs, criss-crossing to allow an air tight contact between our chests... two hearts listening to one another and synchronizing to beat as one... with eyes closed, we dance to the music as our cheeks caress one another, we grant our senses to fall in love too... our lips meet, and the outmost of a sensual kiss is shared... the gentle-ness of our lips tells and may even remind us how important it is for us to be

313

lost together... upon waking this morning, I wanted to run back to her and cry myself to sleep in her arms...

... answer me?... a mother and her 10 year old son... he is on the scooter moving with speed and dodging folks in the plaza... as she sits at a bistro table with her hand supporting her chin... she came out for him... surely... as her mind is in a reflective mood as the little boy zooms by her but she is not aware of him... unless he falls and cries, here his sound of distress may pull her out of her thoughts... so much body language sadness in her as she walks away with the little boy holding and pulling her hand... who is the grown up in this pair?... at the other end of the plaza is a church with a pair of giant ornamental doors... but in one of the doors is a smaller door... and a priest steps out through the smaller door followed by a dozen senior citizens, mostly women... no young people in sight... who will carry the torch to guarantee a job for this priest once this shrinking older generation passes on... and even though they ignore the gypsy beggar outside the door... she too may need to relocate in order to survive... will she cue in to the global economy?... why do I want to help them all???...

... elucidation... resting allows me to re-think, remember and re-charge... maybe driving me to fatigue prevents me from making a sound decision... just like those clothing stores in the malls with loud music to clutter one's thinking when deciding to buy overpriced designer clothing... am I so friendly and helpful because I want to be loved... it is a desperation for something I cannot feel... a little boy in a man's body... soul searching with this writing (pardon the pun)... what I write in this journal/book will only attract losers who will recognize themselves in me... maybe they can save themselves... cliché as this may be... my best memories are of my kids as toddlers and the women I have loved where I felt needed... my life has been good... I will set my half soul free... it'll be my last act of kindness... but isn't this being at the mercy of my soul?...

## 2015/06/14 - Sunday (Villafranca del Bierzo, Spain)

... sleepless sunrise... my feet trundle across the floor, invisible to my ears... the faucet is alive as I wait for the hot water to flow through... I think of the familiar faces of the camino are gone as I stayed behind and they moved on... new faces are on the horizon but I do not care to start mingling again... but I know I should and I shall... deep inside, I know I like people and always cared for their wellbeing... am I a bleeding heart loaded with empathy... is this who I am... yet, I feel like getting off the Camino radar... is this my desire or my soul's?... I miss my children... I wonder if they will contact me in the upcoming father's day... do they remember I exist... all I feel is sadness... right now, do I know or remember any other emotion... maybe a coffee will bolt me out of this melancholy...

... cultivate... usually when walking I eat light... but yesterday I got lost and deviated off the Camino into farmland... with a trail no longer in sight... I had two choices... one, was to go back on my tracks or the other was to follow the telephone pole/lines running across the field... I knew the telephone lines either went or came from a civilization... I followed the telephone lines as I will never go back on my tracks and my life is about taking risks and living with the consequences... with so much insecurity I finally reached a small town called Cacabelos... and wouldn't you know it, it was a blessing in disguise as I got back on the Camino and also found a quaint restaurant called Casa Gato...

... progenies... I sat in the terrace alone... had lunch with my backpack, sitting across the table from me... should I name my backpack Wilson?... unlike my lunchtime companion, I had a vantage point of the Camino and could see pilgrims go by... the restaurant owner spoke French which made my meal experience easier... a family restaurant with his son running the kitchen... along with its' Spanish music this was a touch of class in a rural area... I ate slowly indulging in every bite... a simple pleasure accompanied by wine and that I will cherish... saw a young pilgrim couple with a toddler walking by... the mother had the toddler on her back (pack) and the dad was carrying the supplies in his backpack... later in the day I caught up with these American pilgrims and asked why the Camino... they simply believe... what is or has been important in my life?... I miss home but do not even have one and besides not sure what it is anymore now that I'm divorced... if there's one thing I thought would never end, it would be my love for my kids... how wrong was I... at times, they too are now a series of faded memories... ... I hate myself for this...

... timing... there is a plaza in every town, no matter the size... a rallying center for the locals... an open air community center unlike the shopping malls in North America... as I stand in the entrance way of an inn... I have Einaudi –TheEarth Prelude in repeat mode and loud, coming out of my headphones... as I pan the plaza from left to right looking at the parasols, tables and chairs moving about in all directions as patrons try to shelter themselves from the hard hitting rain... the serenity of the music contradicts what I see but at the same time it's simply fantastic for my senses... the plaza is in turmoil but there is peace in my head as I realize... soon, I will no longer be one of them running frantically... I'll be free of this chaos... is this what someone on death row feels once execution day arrives... is/was waiting the hardest part... ???...

... fanfare... there is a religious procession crossing the plaza... there aren't too many spectators... for one thing it is raining and most of the town folks are in the procession... horn music and drums disturb/compete with the sound of rain... I kind of hoped the tuba player would choke on the rain as it accumulates in his instrument, it would be funny... little girls and boys dressed up in their Sunday best are now soaking wet with their hair dripping down... adult men and women who have no significant role in the procession other than it gave them something to do on a Sunday, walk piously carrying their umbrellas... pall bearers, the elite in the procession carry a bigger than life size statue of Christ in agonizing pain... one of the pall bearers is shorter than the rest... he is not carrying the statue but hanging on to the pole/bar instead... the coup de grace is the priest... he walks under an awning supported by four corner posts... with one man at every post, they are somewhat sheltered from the rain... but still get wet as the priest is blessing and swinging holy water at anyone who tries to get shelter under his awning... not sure how accurate this is, but it seems like so...

... eagerness... I can feel my soul is excited as its' day of freedom is soon upon us... as I more or less promised by claiming my last act of kindness... it knows I keep my promises... whatever skill it takes to be happy I know I don't have it... then why should both me and my soul suffer... at least one of us could be happy... is this love, when one does more for another than oneself?... lately... I now find I sleep a lot... is it fatigue, poor nutrition or neither... am I practicing for the final rest?... at times I am scared to finish the walk but I also don't care for the Camino anymore... and it is no use connecting with pilgrims... the last few days are mine to reflect...

## 2015/06/15 – Monday (Linares, Spain)

... revival... last night while walking in the midnight moonlit insomniac air... as I stood under the medieval bridge and put my hand on the stone pillar... I could feel the intense labor it took as each stone block had to be chiseled and painstakingly snuggled into place... balancing oneself on the rudimentary scaffolding while setting the stone block with mortar... with rushing river water deviated by manmade earth dams to allow the rickety tree trunk scaffolding to stay in place in the muddy river bed... my eyes look away from the stone and back to the river... I feel the earth dam caving in to the river and washing away the scaffolding and anyone or anything on it... even if they were available, in these situations hardhats are no more than a status or of a decorative use... I ought to know... as I was there when it happened... it was the last thing I saw...

... grasp... at a time when my 3 kids were still toddlers and my then wife worked the graveyard shift... in the evening I had our kids to myself... we were more like 4 kids but every so often I would assume the role of a responsible parent and turn off the Sex Pistols CD... sitting here in this gloomy cavernous café/bar... harping away at a chipped finger nail with my teeth... I remember sitting in the backyard with my kids and I'd clip everyone's nails including my own... it was a grand total of 80 nails... my youngest would never sit still, how I miss her and our struggle... and with this a young pilgrim woman walks into the bar... she looks so much like my youngest daughter and on her backpack is a Canadian flag... I engage conversation and discover she just graduated from university in fine arts... the same program my daughter is now attending... she spoke incessantly but I did not mind as she even sounded like my daughter too... in the end we hugged as we parted... and for a brief moment I felt it was my daughter who I was hugging... after, I refused she take my picture... I didn't want this moment recorded, it had to remain as surreal... because the Camino does not give you what you want but what you need...

... depiction... as a 12 year old vacationing in Aveiro (Portugal) with my family... I'd risk a beating whenever I'd take my dad's 35mm camera... mind you beatings were the norm as far as I knew in my Montreal ghetto neighbourhood... all us imported kids accepted it as being a way of life... as we became fathers ourselves... only a few of us realized that this is not the way... pain is not love, it simply cannot be... nevertheless, since a beating was inevitable either for taking the camera or anything else my parental units could justify to vent their miserable frustration... I took the camera and with a film roll of 36 Black and White (B/W) frames... one had to be selective in what to photograph... of course, the beauty of this ancient technology is that one only got to see the pictures, weeks later once they had been developed... it is at this time where my joy of seeing the developed pictures for the very

first time even if they were thrown on the floor as a beating was also imple-
mented... once the old man realized I had used his camera... as he whips me
with the belt, I force myself to be within viewing range of the pictures... as
he fucks me in the ass with his genuine leather belt... the pain is irrelevant as
I look at my 36 B/W pictures on the floor and tell him it is worth the pain...
I'm a misunderstood fucken artist but also with a sore ass on my backside...

... atoms... in the solo solitude of discovering with a camera, I came upon the
Aveiro city cemetery... I hesitated going in, fear of some sort I guess... but
at the same time standing near the entrance gate I could see the graves were
very nicely decorated with real flowers not plastic and on the perimeter were
elaborate mausoleums... armed with my dad's camera, curiosity got me and
I creaked the gate open... even as a kid, I appreciated these morbid structures... one of the mausoleums had a glass facade... one could see the coffins
stacked in triple, with the picture of the deceased on the coffin... I peered
through this glass mausoleum, but kept a safe (?) distance... not sure why
I did not get closer but I did sense an inviting peacefulness and now in hindsight, think I even envied their silence...

... one of the living... there is a sunken cellar like mausoleum... with
collapsed stairs halted by a steel gate which leads into the crypt... creepy as
this may be, it is the nearly 3 meter high copper green statue on top of this
mausoleum which I photographed incessantly from every angle... ended up
using my 36 B/W frames on this one subject... it is a statue of the grim reaper
pointing with his right arm/hand to the sky, his left arm is about to embrace a
woman with generous voluptuous curves... the woman's statue is a of a young
woman with her right hand placed over her heart in a mea culpa pose... her
left arm is dropped to the side and is holding some kind of torch (looks more
like a vibrator)... she is wearing a very loose gown/toga where it drops down
under one breast and one can see a nicely exposed nipple... I wonder if ancient Greeks and/or Romans would have considered this art, since to them
the beauty of a female form was in the subjects' voluptuous curves... would
they place it in a cemetery?...

... turning tables... I guess, art is a reflection of the current society trends,
with the statue being about a century old and even though my pics are over
40 years old and in black & white for a more visual effect, I think today both
would still be great and survive the test of time... anyway... mind you, and
correct me if I am wrong on this... but, as a male... once you see a pair of
breasts we want to see all of them... and this obsession with breasts started
with breast feeding way back then... and with this disrespectful tone, I got the

beating not for my misappropriation of the camera, but for photographing within the cemetery walls...

... defiant... while on the camino I find myself walking fast... I stay in my head... every so often I leave my head and come down to see if my body is alright or maybe that it needs water... but most of my time is spent in my head... the body is walking on automatic... and this allows me for endless conversations with my soul... I'm scared to write these thoughts/ideas/ intuitions as I feel I'm playing with a fire which is not even mine... as it will be controversial if these pages are ever read... and get me in trouble when I want is to be low key... when faced with fear I go against the current and face my fear and deal with it... whether wrong or right I make a decision and live with the consequences, at least this had been my philosophy, but now I am no longer sure... is this to undermine me, when talking to pilgrims it drains me... as I hone in on their energy and for most I feel their pain... it saddens me that I cannot help them...

## 2015/06/16 – Tuesday (Barbadelo, Spain)

... thirty three... with 33 symbolic kilometers already walked I was ex-hausted from the dusty heat and wish for a Mary Magdalene to wash my weary feet... no such luck, for one I do not wear leather sandals like the other guy's son who was down here working while his father almighty was on hia-tus... my hiking boots along with economical budget socks (bought by the half dozen) that are never washed but thrown out after use... just the smell emanating (like burnt meat) once the boots are removed can render some-one unconscious if they don't take precautions (safe distance) when exposed to my feet... as I continue pushing myself and walking through what seems to be a one town albergue/hostel and bar/restaurant... and both are full to capacity... with hunger and fatigue I move on to the next town... as I know there is a bed and breakfast, but I'm taking a chance without having made reservations...

... leftovers... am I shy or is it I do not fit in with people and/or pil-grims... I feel dumb and very ignorant... they don't have a chip on their shoulders where as I'm always fighting something... mostly in myself... I'm not happy... so many unhappy moments in my day but in reality my day is a glimpse of my life... soul or no soul I do not want to be here anymore... why can't this planet be like a primary school where all one has to do is raise his hand and asks to go to the washroom or in my case, exit out of the body... with a fuck you all, I'm outta here... what is the protocol for establishing I'm tired of living and want to move on... I can leave anytime as what weighs me down are memories not possessions... and any possessions such as my pen-nies in the bank... I can forward them to televangelists and in turn will be used as seed money to save those who stay behind... another fucken humani-tarian good cause for the parasitic conniving leeching rich televangelist...

... soul free... what if souls did not exist in the first place... what would we be like without a soul?... for one, emotions that are not mine are removed... what would I be like... still intelligent, would live life without competing with the Jones'... would mate to procreate and physically feel the pleasure of an or-gasm... would I be like pigeons in a spring time park... and also crap, without regards for whom it may affect... at work, things would progress and flow without competition between colleagues and mistakes would be corrected without the guilt trip... orgasms are already good in themselves... and then reproduce and have kids... mate based on biological seasonal needs and not on appearances or sexual innuendos... invisible border lines between countries would actually be invisible... efficient barcodes instead of names... no need for a religion... skin colours are insignificant... and death is no more dramatic than an expiry date on a bread tab... we would be like the drawings of happy goofy kids found painted on the gated exterior daycare barred windows... and this soul marketing bullshit claiming that we have free will... whatever free will there is now comes with constraints... souls are parasites feeding and using us... if dolphins, whales, dogs and even crows can manage without a soul, why can't we?...

... nonsense... I find myself avoiding eye contact with other pilgrims because I'm sure they can see my fragmented soul, my madness and even my loneliness... it would frighten them to get near me if they saw inside of me... I need bigger and darker sunglasses... do I talk about this or do I keep quiet... silence kills, no?... am I human and mortal... or am I mortal and human... but for me if I commit suicide it's as if I bring this journal/book up to date as I already consider myself dead... the more I discuss my death in my head without the interference of my soul... the conclusion is always the same... why am I getting fucked out of my life... my soul's dissidence and its' fragmentation penitence is not my problem... I did not ask for a difficult life on earth... and at the same time I did not have a quality life either... I have to let my body die naturally,... if a traumatic death is incurred... then the remaining soul is fractured even more and difficult if not impossible to harvest back into a whole unit... my beastly impulses demand I stay alive... what can I learn from this?... do I take charge of me and rebel against my soul... do I stand a chance against a goliath... right now, I'd say no... but what do I have to lose...

### 2015/06/17 – Wednesday (Portos, Spain)

... unprofessed... walking in snorkeling silence, the only thing I hear is my drowning breath... feel sadness regarding the end of the walk... feel detached from the world... it is no longer my home and why not, I have no one or nowhere to go when I finish the Camino... tons of married life memories flashing in my head with no interference by my soul... my kids and their silliness and humor... with them everything was a pretext for laughter and I concurred... where is that old me... just as my kids age and I get closer to death, maybe my old me has already died... they (kids) are the only good thing I did and now even that I lost too... in a few days I'll have reached Santiago...

thinking about whether I will have the last supper in Santiago or am I walking through the city to Finisterre and leave behind 95% of all pilgrims... for sure the Camino after Santiago will be desolate, and so what... just as amusing, is that my interior will be in sync with the Camino exterior...

... don't mind... walking along/alone on the Camino... insects bathing in the evaporating morning dew... sun rays guiding my shadow in dodging horse shit... off key, melodically swollen bird's chest chirping... the now freshly showered insects fleeing for their lives as they make a seductive foreplay snack for amorous birds... add to this the rumbling sound of a young Asian man going by on skateboard at top speed down the road... with a Camino scallop shell fluttering off his backpack... is this a non-reflective sign?... in the sense that the camino is now something one must do fast... and get it over with... at a slower pace I met an American minister who lived in denial about his job... as he said it made folks nervous and even scares them away... we did not discuss godly issues per se other than he believes Hillary will make a difference... (when I thought of this woman, only a feeling of intense sadness came to mind)... no soon is the minister a spec in my dust trail... a herd of 40 students fooling around and talking/shouting loudly monopolize the road... they're horsing around and grabbing each other's hats and throwing them in the garbage bins on the side of the road...

... resorts... I used a binder paperclip as a marker in my camino guide book... it no longer holds the pages as I approach the end of the booklet... actually if keeps falling off the book, as there aren't enough pages to justify its' usage... the book is thinning but not as fast as I have thinned out... all my bones are protruding... poor nutrition and insufficient rest are all contributing factors for my weight loss... I always thought the best way to lose weight was to do volunteer work in starving countries... scooping up the dead into wheel barrels and dumping them into mass graves (small children should go in first to maximize the bucket usage/efficiency of the wheel barrel)... instead of pushing a grocery cart and having difficulty distinguishing which grocery store isle has the dog food or the potato chips as the bags are now the same size... mind you, a court appointed summer vacation in a third world country, would put things into perspective for a juvenile delinquent too...

... heard in vain... graffiti is modern art as it reflects society to the masses without the nonsense of an entrance fee... but since most believe valuable art cannot be free, then nor is graffiti modern art... I saw this graffiti message on the camino to Santiago... starting in Sarria isn't the real thing... what does this mean?... if you only walk the last 100 km (starting point is the city of Sarria)... you are entitled to collect your Compostela certificate from the pilgrim's office in Santiago... but if you walk the first 800 km but not the last 100 km... you are not entitled to the Compostela certificate... the absurdity of this ludicrous regulation is art in itself... and now... the short lived concentrated joy, in meeting fellow vacationing pilgrims... as most are partially bussed to Sarria in order meet/expedite the 3 day deadline to Santiago as determined by the package deal offered by their travel agent... what could be more fascinating then dodging herds of pilgrims blocking the camino who just arrived in a bus... with still visible price tag and shoe size stickers on the soles... exchanging stories and wanting to turn strangers into friends for life... if of course they are not on their cell phones... such as, explaining to some lame husband how to make spaghetti and even telling him where in the kitchen cupboard he can find the pasta... and I'm stuck in this shit herd...

... tonight in the night... wrong or right, I always advocated to my kids... make a decision and move on... with this mind set, I decided that once I reach Santiago I will do... I have no fucken idea what I will do... the human curse, is that we all go thru introspective quests at one time or another some easier than others... I am hoping to appease the void of my mundane life once in Santiago... no pity is required here, it's simply a case of the funny man is really a sad soul man... maybe there is too much oxygen in my head... I must be delirious... nevertheless, I dread going into Santiago as it will be the festive mood... where pilgrims even clap in the cathedral after the service... a festival of souvenir trinkets, t-shirts, shot glasses, bags, wallets, key chains and the Compostela Certificate if one has all the required stamps in their Credential (pilgrim's passport)... useless paper as if the humility of the camino has to be framed in a dollar store bought frame and hung to dry in one's dark escapist apartment entrance hallway... perhaps lucidity will come to me in the darkness of the night time bed before I get to Santiago...

## 2015/06/20 – Saturday (Santiago, Spain)

... wired... again, woke up exhausted and numb... cannot remember what night activity I was involved in... suffice to say, I was not myself where ever I was or went... this morning all my limbs felt loose as if they had been pulled away from me... I do remember the struggling feeling of being hugged or more likely pinned down... am I to believe my soul, that I am an emissary to inform earthlings of the souls' wrong doing... or is my soul toying with me for his personal gain... who are the guardians of this planet, who are the good souls?... are they the ones protesting against those who are guided by money, greed and war... there are good people on this planet, I have seen this... not all souls are bad as not all humans are bad... they go hand in hand... all my thoughts are disconnected and not lining up to flow smoothly... I don't know what to think let alone believe... I wish I could cry but my tears are blocked...

... everybody... when I was living with Suzanne during the cold winter nights... we had this electric blanket in our bed and a few minutes before calling it a night, we'd switch it on to warm up the bed... but the only problem is that it was a small electric blanket and it would only warm up the foot area of our bed... Suzanne was mischievously always the last one to get into bed... I'd be lying in bed in a pre-shiver mode trying to warm up and she would lay herself on top of me to avoid the cold sheets... I'd quickly forget the cold sheets, and melt under the warmth of her delicately small framed body on top of mine... my palms fluttered over her skin from the shoulders down to her inner thighs... body heat ensued and we'd switch off the blanket and lights... the bright stars shot their light through the crispy night air... the brilliance reached our bedroom window unobstructed... in awe of the woman lying next to me and the magnificence of the nocturnal vision... I felt there was something outside the bedroom window... there was something there and I know we were not alone... this I am sure of... was it the other half of my soul?... was it waiting for me to go out and play?

... 30 000 steps... today I walked about 30 km... a below average walking day for my pace... but it was all that was remaining to reach Santiago... should I be impressed that I have walked the official 770 km +/-... nope, I swerved lots of U-turns and O-turns on my heels... (O-turns are like U-turns once you realize that initially you were going in the right direction)... so the kilometer count is much higher, but still not impressed... as is the wear and tear on my boots... upon entering the city I posed in front of a Welcome to Santiago billboard... and posted the pic on Facebook... got what seemed like an endless number of compliments for walking nearly 800 kilometers from my FB friends and even some strangers... but since none of my kids commented... this adulation means nothing to me... what is the walk about?... I don't think I have learned enough to match the time and energy expenditure invested on the camino... as my world is in chaos, whatever I put into the camino, I should never expect an equal return... and I never treated my kids equally but fairly, as they are not equal but unique... and with this notion, I was hoping my kids could see that I'm not a conventional parent...

I am a man first with fears and insecurities and then a father trying to deal with his own drama all the while providing assurances to my growing children... there lack of response means I failed...

... indoor plumbing... this being the weekend the city is full of tourists... with smart phones in hand... snapping pictures into a storage cloud in a virtual sky which will be viewed as long as the vacation memory is still fresh in their nightfall or Facebook post minds... these pics will probably re-surface at Christmas time and then disappear into oblivion... my almost penthouse boarding room is around the corner from the cathedral... as I sit on my window ledge... observing the silently invisible noisy click sounds created by the camera/phones and the photographer's combination of voice and gesture instructions telling the poser how to stand/smile... it is clear, all we want is to be heard, seen and maybe even remembered, simply said loved... no matter how far up or down we are in life... it is so simple, what we need to fuel a human being is give it wings to soar... but even this we fuck it up... my penthouse room is a shit hole with walls... a shower stall, a sink, a useless closet armoire with jammed doors, a TV screen no wider than my ass, a solitude bed and the shared toilet is behind one of the doors in the hallway... as if I'm getting up in the middle of the night to piss in the toilet, the shower will double up as a big urinal befitting my cock's ego... now, I pushed the bed in front of the shower stall and lying down on the bed with only my feet in the shower stall... I cooled off my burning paws from being so much on the ground...

... blizzard... the broken TV antenna isolates me from the world, or am I to believe the fuzzy screen on every channel is a snow storm... why do I need to keep my mind busy?... what is wrong with silence?... what is wrong with me being with me?... why can't I just hang around... instead of filling my time with trivialities to feel as if I have something to do... planning the fruit and/or water shopping or buying Band-Aids for the blisters or eating out as if these activities are the milestones in my day... too much loneliness, there is just too much loneliness... compounded by the ability of empathy... now, I am too sensitive to others people's misery... and I end up feeling their misery is now my own... is this the goal of my soul... to make me realize life is hard and not worth living for... for me to relinquish my life so that he (soul) may be reunited and happy... will he succeed in coaxing or choking me into releasing the half soul?... at least someone comes out as a winner in this equation... but it requires me to being unselfish... so yeah!... people are weird, sad and even mean... so what, nothing is perfect and imperfection is actually better than nothing... hope, on the other hand is perfection...

... black sun... in the plaza below my boarding room window is a bar... a very rowdy and noisy bar and I have not been able to sleep one wink... fatigue is not potent enough to put me to sleep... the changing numbers displaying the time on my Ipod rest more than I do... loud conversations are carried up to my room by the cigarette smoke... it is now past 4:30 AM... there is one man's loud voice and several other voices hushing him to be quiet... this is soon muffled by the aluminum bistro chairs and tables being stacked and chained... no sooner do I recognize the sound of silence... that the city cleaners appear, driving the vacuous water hosing sweepers... they are tediously efficient and thorough as the sun light is now pointing out where the dirt lies... now, with the clear thought process of a sleepless night... what and where is my life?... is it all about the kilometers I walked... and what is my hurry to get back... to where?... and to do what?... I have no idea if my book/journal is worth shit... I can't even remember anymore what I have written... is it worth anything other than the paper and ink... I grabbed my gear and as I packed decided to walk to Finisterre...


## 2015/06/21 – Sunday (Vilaserio, Spain)

... trivia... if I were to translate the name of this town into English it would be as follows... seriously, this is a town... miniscule is a grandiose term... it's major attribute is that it is on the Camino and it has two albergues... one of the albergues is a former elementary school, with misleading newly painted exterior walls... as one walks in, the dust on the floor is disturbed and I can see my footprints behind me... as the sneezing changes the direction of my gaze... it is still under renovation, nothing positive can be said about the showers facilities and sleeping on a concrete moldy and dusty floor is for anyone but me... no attendant is on the location... almost a self-serve and honor system as pilgrims in principle are good people with values and morals... but this hardly explains a woman's predicament when in another town a few weeks ago she had her boots stolen... it's not as if someone made a mistake and took the wrong boots... there were no left over or forgotten boots to replace hers...

... vast empire... the second albergue is run by the owners of the only bar in town... no grocery store of any kind but the bar may provide you with some basics... no restaurant either, but the bar does improvise meals at 7PM... the albergue was top notch, quite new too... all the facilities a pilgrim could want in terms of laundry, showers, kitchen and bedding... it even had kitchen facilities but of course there is no grocery store in town and unless you can convert water into wine or in this case boiling water into soup... nevertheless, I give credit where credit is due... with the smell of deodorant/soap and wet hair... a mass of pilgrims step out of the albergue and make our way to the bar for supper... supper was fried ham and eggs with fries (I beg to differ but ham does not qualify as pork steaks as per the menu)... in most countries this is considered breakfast... maybe I was getting a start on the morning meal by having it before bed time... before supper arrived, I went into the bar and bought some fresh bread... well, it was fresh maybe 2 days ago... and I know by tomorrow's walk it will be hard as rock and its' only utility would be to ward off roaming dogs... I did see the deep fryer behind the counter... if the oil in the fryer was in an automobile, the manufacture would void the car warranty if it were not changed immediately...

... magnificent seven... as I chew endlessly on my greasy supper meal without being able to swallow the slippery mush... I look around and what do I see sitting next to and shadowing me... what are these men who only see work as their raison d'etre... working hard, smoking and beer/wine fill the void of their lives as alcohol induced obesity sculpts their spherical bellies... shopping cart pushers they are not, as their arms are not long enough to reach beyond their stomachs or even pat the waitress's ass... pretty but a flirty waitress she is not... there was a hard edge to her as she seems at ease on how to down play alcohol induce advances by this Viagra boys club... seven men who work hard and will eventually go home expecting supper... with their cigarette and alcohol breaths they slump into bed... at random any one of them could... places his limp arm over his wife and touching one of her nipples arouses the man in him... as the nipple rises up as she sleeps... and with the thought of the cute waitress in mind, he maneuvers himself upon his wife... using his fingers tips in a brail fashion he hap hazardously finds his penis... then again... maybe they (men) will not go home for supper as this is the town's only gathering location... and tonight the whole town is meeting here to celebrate the Saint John the Baptist Christian holiday... pilgrims are not invited... while we are locked in our albergue by the 10 PM curfew imposed on pilgrims as we are also expected to live like monks... but they did share with us the noise and the delicious smell of BBQ'd meats until the early morning hours... of course, some of us are squirming in bed awake and wishing we had had antacid tablets for desert...

... karma-o-matic... I was on my way to take the bus back home... through the downtown core I walked on Ste.Catherine street, a busy shopping artery of Montreal... with a wide range of consumer products in window displays... is also an unquantifiable number of beggars and/or homeless people on the street... again, how much of anything is enough... maybe if these beggars were victims of an earthquake in a foreign country I would help without judging... so, I passed them by leaving their raised left hands still weightless... then, the stench hit me before I had a visual of the another homeless man sitting on the sidewalk... he was leaning against the wall and did not have his hand raised or even a hat/box as a collection plate... his watery eyes were off in the distance... empathy or intuition I will never know which, but I felt his pain, this grown man was a little boy... in a frenzied state I quickened my pace and felt like a chicken without its' head running aimlessly... I looked up and saw a Burger King and walked in and the girl behind the counter asked me if I wanted a Kids Club Meal... why she asked me this I will never understand... I said I wanted two... I came back to him and leaned down and held the two bags in front of him... I broke his distant stare, he smiled and I placed my hand on his shoulder... tears lubricated my eyes, I felt awkward... but a serenity also came over me... I think the food was trivial... he wanted to feel human... or maybe was it me who wanted to feel human?...

... don't panic... in my serene and safe neighbourhood... there was a series of vandalisms on construction contractors like myself... my van amongst a few others, were vandalised over the weekend... they broke a window in order to get into the van to steal my tools... there is a lucrative market for this... the irony is that the previous week my van had been in the paint shop for repairs... hence, why I was walking downtown, to catch the bus home... and prior to dropping it off at the garage, all its' contents (tools) were moved/stored in my living room (my dear ex-wife thought it made for an eclectic décor, yeah right!)... when I got the van back, I procrastinated in putting back the tools right away... what a surprise for the thief, to break into my van and see it completely empty, the shock must have been so grand... cause he could only steal my pocket flashlight from the dashboard... I guess to see that his eyes were not deceiving him... is this luck or karma?

## 2015/06/24 – Wednesday (Finisterre, Spain)

... dawdle... again, I woke up late... the closest thing to the human touch is my hand with its' pillow warmth, touching my face... today's walk from Cee was about 20 km and did not take more than 3.5 hours... for a man with nowhere to go I sure walk fast... so, with time as my friend or even time to kill, I stayed in bed till midday... as a young man, between the time I woke up and actually got out of bed... I used this semi-awake time to reflect on the day to come and later in life, this time was replaced by meditation... and this morning, I used it to discuss my fucken current affairs with my soul... this is now a celestial hi-tech communication, progressive intercom bullshit time... I was re-reading the pages of this journal/book... why is it I write best when I'm in emotional pain... one day the pain will be more than I can handle... and I will shred my page to death... this is what you want!... for me to give it up for you... not just yet you motherfucker...

... unknown man... I walked thru Finisterre (town)... this beach sea-side town reminded me of a Caribbean resort town... but I continued on to Monte Facho with its' lighthouse where it was (or even is?) believed the sun died and the worlds of the dead and the living became closer according to the romans and/or pagans... since I'm in an irritable mood, Cabo da Roca (Portugal) is the cape which forms the westernmost extent of continental Europe and not Monte Facho... nevertheless, with my backpack still in tow I reach a stone pylon with the Camino scallop and a plaque indicating 0.00 km... but the coast is still another 100+ meters... the walk from Santiago to here, plunged me deeper into my own madness, there was no serenity only solitude... I was hoping this place would be more serene than Santiago... no somber/joyous event or location is complete without rowdy teenagers... others are drinking... there is a symbolic tower and bonfire... the tower is just a mere post with memorable unimportant names... as for the fire, a pilgrim's intoxicating smouldering plastic, underwear and socks garbage... there are a scattered handful of disconnected pilgrims sitting quietly looking into the ocean blue distance... what do they see out there?... I envy them... as I slump on a rock... I'm a disappointment surrounded by disappointments... sure as hell it is not the destiny... then it must be the fucken journey... all I need is a volume control to raise the sound of the ocean waves... there is too much noise in my head...

... appreciation... for the last 38 years, since the age of 17+/-... I never went to school or worked on my birthday... I used this me day for reflection and maybe catch a movie, love the feeling of an quasi-empty theatre... whenever my kids arrived from school, they would make sure I knew it was my birthday and overwhelm me with hugs and kisses and tell me about the chocolate cake in the fridge which they and their mom had baked the previous night... and I would tempt them to join me in eating the cake as a snack and not after supper where I'd get candles to blow out... they would scream/shout after me as I pretended to go to the fridge... in the later years all the best wishes posted on Facebook simply humbled me... love yourself and everything will fall into place... and I need that today, would feel like a birthday... I do...

... wasting time... I was able to calm myself down with happy thoughts (my kids, Suzanne) and accept whatever would happen next, the Camino is now over... now what?... so I walked back to Finisterre, I stopped at a restaurant that does not offer a pilgrim's menu, a real restaurant where a local would eat in... a pilgrim's meal menu usually consists of 2 plates... one induces diarrhea and the second plate constipates... it's not good Friday but the waiter is pushing sardines... fresh salted sardines on charcoal with kale and boiled potatoes all swimming gleefully in olive oil... delicious as it was, it left me thirsty... nevertheless... give a man a fish, and you feed him for a day... right now, this is good enough for me... let the working class deal with... show him how to catch a fish and you feed him for a lifetime... soon I will not have the luxury of time... with sardines gurgling in my stomach, I feel much calmer... I gave up fighting with myself, it's a human thing to fight and I don't feel very human... maybe never was, as I never felt I belonged on this planet...

... where I belong... my shadow slowly spreads out in all directions as the sunset dominated the landscape... I left the restaurant and made my way to find an albergue for the night... the albergue had a bus load of high school students... and I looked at the attendant and simply said... nope!... and walked out... as the early bird gets the worm but only if alone and in the morning... my routine for the last few weeks was walking into a town, find an albergue/hostel, shower with my clothes on to wash the clothes and myself simultaneously and have supper... this no longer applied as the Camino was over... so, I headed down to the beach to figure out what to do next... amazingly, I was surprised with my calmness... off to the side of the beach was a plank dock with an anchored row boat... unloaded my backpack and hopped into the boat... sitting on the center plank, it had the comfort of a wheelchair but on a positive note, there was also an outboard motor... I clutched the handle on the motor and it felt like my Yamaha 650 motorcycle gas throttle...

330

for a few seconds I fluttered my lips to make an engine sound and pretended I was off into the unlimited true darkness… with the joy of a little boy in me, I grabbed my backpack off the dock and placed it in the boat and figured this is a good place as any to sleep…

… kiss them for me… I sat on the boats' center board with my back to the shore… for some reason I felt free with no problems in the world as I looked into the abyss colored in dark… and in reality, do we really have problems?… oh!… dream on, of course we do but right now I don't give a shit, cause I can't see them in the abyss… this boat thing has me smiling so wide, that my teeth may become permanently visible… almost like a TV evangelist flashing teeth on a late night insomniac show, where with the same breath the dollar and Amen are farted… honest like a TV evangelist, I feel under the seat plank if maybe a key is hidden for the lock or even the outboard motor… no such luck… but I do see two oars on the bottom of the boat with a rope going through a hole at the end of the poles… as I follow one end of the rope as it goes up through a metal ring bolted to the dock and back into the boat… this is where I see the rope ends meet and where there is a loop at each end… the two loops are joined together by a combination padlock… I turn the number dial on the padlock and used my intuitive abilities to guess the combination number to unlock, but in the end I used my pocket knife to cut the rope… yep!… the musical swoosh swipe of the knife sounded like an unchained melody…

… ready to go… giddiness abounds as I anchor away… it's not easy to row the boat… I go mostly in semi circles… it seems I keep getting closer to the shore then away… if I row fast enough… can I get away from shore and even my soul… maybe he (soul) can't swim or walk on the water like the other hippie nor can he turn all this ocean water into wine as I'm thirsty from the salty sardines… when I stop rowing, I seem to move more, so I let the current guide me… as long as I can see the shoreline, I'm ok… even if the Camino is over, I open my laptop to make a daily journal entry and eventually I will send off my last few journals to Suzanne… I see my reflection on the screen and shit I look bad with long messy hair and a beard… cannot waste battery time, looking at myself as I have limited charge and an internet USB pen… worst case scenario, there's the Ipod… with the laptop off and now it is really dark and the shoreline seems to have less lights… I think it is late and folks turned off their lights as they retire to bed… anyway… I stare into the dark and wonder what those pilgrims on the coast had seen when they looked into the distance... maybe they were looking in the right direction... but at the wrong time...

## 2015/06/26 – Friday (Atlantic Ocean)

... curvature... the problem with our planet is it's quasi round... and for this reason when I woke up I was not able see the shore line... what am I now, a homeless man at sea, there goes the neighborhood... of course, things can get worse as in having only one oar left... hunger is rummaging through my backpack... a few dry figs, two oranges, a banana and bottled water... in my pocket I find the receipt from the sardine meal... so, the memento from that great meal is a fucken receipt, an unquenchable thirst and bad breath... after snacking with no coffee, I roll the receipt into a paper cigarette and pretend it's a joint... the only fire is in my mind and I pinch the wannabe paper cigarette joint between my index finger and thumb, inhale, hold the smoke, exhale the smoke and cough as if my throat was irritated... my whole life is an unlit illusion... and the worst thing is that it was dominated by ego, my human pettiness interfered with my not doing/being more good... why do I realize this only now...

... dress code... sitting on the plank seat, I look around for my boots but only see one at the bottom of the boat... last night I left the boots on the seat, and now one boot eloped with the oar... with the aerodynamics of a bald head in a convertible, the second boot joined the oar at sea for a ménage a trois... lost my balance and fell into the water... too my surprise the water was very warm, almost hot... with comical difficulty I managed to get back into the boat... it was as if I was lifted up by the back of the neck... like a cat picks up her kittens... I felt very light too... was it my soul leaving by the back/neck, did I miss it leaving me?... I laughed out loud at my wet misery... with no dressing rooms in sight, I got completely naked and pulled out my jeans and my favorite black t-shirt which according to Suzanne makes me look handsome, it's classy T-shirt with 3 buttons... I have no socks left... shit, my feet are whiter than my bleached notepad paper... wtf?... I turned on my IPod to see if it got damaged by the water... I guess it was because the indicated date was Friday when it should be Thursday... I sit down on a plank like bench to assess my situation... humm?... let's see I'm in the Atlantic probably in a warm Caribbean water current and have no idea which way to land... in addition I'm a lonely sailor stuck on a boat and checking out the oar with curves… everything is funny, once fear is no longer part of the equation… I feel like laughing as if I'm no longer carrying the planet on my shoulders… and now that I laugh out loud, can anybody hear me?…

… vortex… I'm paddling with the left oar and I'm moving in a right circular direction… if this is not in the vicinity of Australia, then it must be near the Bermuda Triangle as sometimes compasses spin in the wrong direction causing planes and boats to disappear… but I moved a lot and got nowhere… shit, this is funny but I still need help with getting to shore… my soul is nowhere to be found… I want a life back on shore and I don't want to sound selfish but it cannot be all about you… maybe this is what you need to learn as a soul… mysterious ways?… I see there is a red/green combo button near the throttle of the outboard motor… as simple as it is to press the green button… the motor starts running and having no idea which direction takes me to land… I go with the warm water current, but within a few short minutes the motor is gasping for gasoline… no panic, since I cannot walk on water, the current will eventually get me to land, hopefully on time to make my credit card payment otherwise my bank CEO will get a bonus to top of his 15M salary, hahahaha… my laptop battery will soon have the same fate as the outboard motor, maybe me too… I never got around to write a book, all these journal entries which were a basis for a book will never be used… nevertheless I have and will send them to Suzanne, maybe she'll put them together for a book… I'm not even sure she is getting my emails since she does not reply nor can I get on any chat and ask for help… later in the day I meditated just to pass the time… as I sat down, I felt myself plunging into deep trance… and going down perpetually in a vortex manner… for certain, I was not asleep, this is all I can remember but where ever I was/went I only re-surfaced about 4 hours later, and these words were jotted on the back of the paper cigarette… is my soul in some sort of re-hab?… fuck, even this is funny…

… convoluted surfacing misperceptions… where is my dear soul who has been driving me mad?… divinity is never around to help us when you need them… are you my soul's supervisor, his celestial elite to whom I can complain… I wish to speak to one of his elites?… they are for the most part in some rehab center or something similar covering up their mistakes… on second thought, perhaps it is better not to mingle with these higher ups… somehow I feel this is not good for my mental health having elites like them in my vicinity… what if you somehow think you are so intelligent, that you can understand what I am writing, would you then feel superior (elite) to those peasants who still hold an ink fountain pen with a left hand and constantly look for a pencil eraser to correct the correction they had corrected previously?... I know, how you feel, reading this shit... and wondering aloud that you should stop reading it now... because it is going nowhere and yet you are drawn into this babbling text and you refuse to stop reading, even if it means salvaging the last shred of common sense still within your reach... I am pulling you into my world, my elitist world... what happened to you?... you had so much will power and potential, and yet you are still reading this verbose splodge... admit it, your world dispenses a false sense of sterility... that is why you are drawn to this, to see if it is better here...

... reversed empathy... I was doing the pilgrim look into the distance thing and panned a full 360 degrees... the more ocean I saw the smaller I felt and now lucidity prevails as the reality of my importance has been defined in such a way that I could understand... I feel empty but not sad... as if the slate had been cleaned, but still functional... is this bliss, to worry about nothing as if I know everything... I felt myself being nudged over to make space on the seat... bright phosphorescent colours, almost glowing too, it basically felt like happy colors... I almost didn't recognize my soul... correction, a new and improved complete soul... long gone is the black mass of bitter smoke... the colored shadow looked at me and I understood/felt what it said... hey bearded hippie... I enjoyed having his company and felt his warm glow against my right side... but it was short lived, the warmth went in and out through me... he had seeded my mind with a message... day of death is now final and non-negotiable... but the time is of your choosing... almost like a prisoner on death row I'm granted a last wish... or as I prefer to think, the last year you believe the Santa Claus in the mall is real and will bring you your Christmas gift... I never went to a mall until I was an older teenager, we were that poor... on this planet and being human... your vibrational level is so dense that it takes you a long time to receive and understand information... your end is a new beginning...

## 2015/06/27 – Saturday (an Ocean)

... role model... I just am, I don't know if I slept... what I do know is that my head is full of the most minute details... from my married life, but especially of my children... little people who came in our home and filled me with a purpose in life... it was no longer about me, it was all about them... regrets?... plenty... time went by too fast... or was it I who did not seize every moment?... I learned more about myself with them than anyone else... where I was arrogant, they taught me humility, patience and especially love... life was about taking in oxygen and enjoying this privilege... as I miss all of my kids... my life without them now lacks substance...

... loner... I actually liked being married and having a family life... for a while I felt I belonged to something important... my ex-wife as a mother was simply incredible... her parental skills left me in awe... for the most part I just coasted and sometimes struggled just digging myself out of some mess... definition of what is a privilege?... a special advantage not enjoyed by anyone else... and I find I have had 3 of these privileges in my life... on a typical Saturday morning of TV watching... they had their stuffed animals sitting on the sofa... they would push them aside and tap the sofa with the intention for me to sit down next to them... without fanfare we'd watch TV, at some point I'd initiate adult conversation topics... I would tease and say... considering that you only have 50% of my genetic code... imagine if you had 100% of my genes – I know... unbelievable, right?... they'd respond with... ssshhh daddy!... we're watching TV...

... irony and/or absurdity... as I re-read some of the past journal pages I have written... it was evident that I was not living nor experiencing life in a conventional way... by all means, I will be the first to admit this... being in a foreign country(ies), moving around all the time with no place to call home... where ever I lived, was initially limited to my 2 suitcases, and a computer... and now, not even a full backpack... this is pretty much all I own... add to this, that I was on a sabbatical year trying to give meaning and orientation to the remaining years of my life... but the biggest chunk of absurdity was my thinking there was a future with my ex-girlfriend Suzanne... and the hindsight irony coup de grace... was now finding this letter written some time ago... for me, once in love forever in love, I'm adorable this way... too bad, our personalities just clashed too much...

*... outta know... :*
*... the beauty of being us, is that we were not introduced to one another by a third party as in... **this is my friend...** nor did we meet at a social gathering, cause as in any gathering, there is always a theme and by default we would already have something in common... also with us living in two different continents, I in Canada and you in Portugal... we did not have the opportunity to meet face to face and instinctively establish a connection... no, our connection was extremely subtle... an exchange of indirect posts on a Facebook (FB) page*

*of our former high school... where small nuances in our posts, though oblivious to the masses, we on the other hand honed in to what was written/shown/heard, between the lines...*

*... perhaps it is because we seek and therefore see beauty in the most remote recesses and are appreciative... most importantly, we do not take it for granted and let's face it, there is a feeling of being privileged... maybe I'm too analytical, but as I came across your posts day after day, I began to discover a real person behind theses posts and not just another FB acquaintance... from a static to a beating heart... you managed, to leave a mark on me and for the longest time, I felt it was not reciprocal, but it was nevertheless still ever so good... you cannot believe the joy/feeling in knowing, that you were entertained/amused by what I had written on FB... someone actually listened, isn't this what we all want... some sort of acknowledgement, recognition that we have an impact somewhere...*

*... the distance between us... forces us to re-read every word we have written to one another... it is, as if we want to re-live and savour every moment of the first impact the words had on us initially... the down side... is we may allow our imaginations to manipulate/mould our perception of what the other must be like, simply based on the messages... expectations can be wonderfully surprising, but we must not forget to breathe in and out and remember that after all we are still, very humanly fragile... regrets... I do have... the difficulty in remembering you when we were in primary/high school, before you moved to Portugal... wondering about the fun we could've had... or maybe the timing was not right...*

... in the end... in retrospect when it comes to us... with oceans separating us... each having spent the last 40 or so years absorbing cultural values... which moulded us into the adults we now find ourselves to be... and through incredible obstacles and when we finally met and the intensity of our physical contact... and then our failure to take our relationship to a higher level... and in the end I am left with the thought of not a broken heart but a harden heart that... with so much adversity... love does not conquer all... but it does not mean we cannot try again in the next life time... maybe we'll get it right...

## 2015/06/28 – Sunday (somewhere near Atlantis)

... so am I... though the oar has nice curves, there is no physical or emotional attraction... she was too rigid and set in her ways with paddling/

336

swinging only in one direction... and besides she does not fancy me, as my feet are shoeless and ever so white... I wanted to baptize the oar with the name Wilson, but it's not girly a name... I laughed out loud as only I can understand my warped humor... and then I laughed at myself for laughing out loud... no more need be said... utterly, the oar was holding me back so I ditched her cause the boat slowly sails in the ocean current... eventually it will reach a shore... as it has an agenda of its' own or perhaps it's blind faith... everything from now on is blind faith... I don't know if I slept or not but it's already Sunday... it must be like a dog, when left at home all day while the owner is working, the animal has no notion of time... anyway, I'm gonna have to make an effort to keep track of the days and not rely on the laptop as the battery is low... not sure how/when this happened, but my two front teeth were next to me on the seat... my first reaction was I have no pillow under which to place them for the tooth fairy... this would be an easy gig for the tooth fairy as we are now on the same vibrational plain... where is that bitch, I can use her company...

... cathedral echoes... nobody loved me better... Suzanne used to call me ET as we stood in front of her bathroom mirror... she touched my naked body with her mind and claimed I was never part of this planet... even my children often said I was an inattentive father... I miss them all, I miss everyone I took for granted... the only beacon guiding me back to them is the flashing red light low battery warning... this will probably be my last journal entry... as my only friend is my journal... it (journal) is the only one I can talk to, but isn't this me?... anyway I'll email it (journal) to Suzanne... I hope she does something with my journals... just like a musician with a guitar who wants to reach people and optimistically change the world for the better... I'm now the same with these words... but these words are probably lost in the ethereal plain and the idea of being a writer is dragging right behind the never read words... always said that if it doesn't fit in the coffin, you don't need it... once the laptop expires, I will dump it in the ocean and why not my backpack too... which speaks louder, words or actions...

... diablo duel... with my head down and my face buried in my palms... and wondering what am I still doing in this boat, I feel like I'm in a waiting line... all of a sudden I feel empty and sad, even fearful... I miss my kids' arms around my neck and those moments when Suzanne and I just hugged in consoling silence... through the cracks between my fingers I can see colors... raising my head I can now see/feel my colorful gaseous soul cloud all around me... it (soul) is squeezing into me from all directions and it gives me a shivering effect... I lower my head back into my palms and my mind goes blank, like a clean slate... but is quickly filled with thoughts created by my soul... the emotion you're experiencing is a separation from love... the realization that the people you connected with are slipping through your fingers permanently... just like a handful of sand palmed on a beach... it can never be duplicated again... every life is a new experience to be learned from... as you close your heart the fears will subside... I know this because I live the same fears since Atlantis...

... fooled again... I'm not even sure if it is the old me or the new me who is here... basically this goes for all species with slight variations for mankind... on our planet the barbaric concept of life is that we are killed (for food) or we die... it was not always like this... the only thing which is ascertained is that nothing lasts forever because... and let's face it... this reality isn't the best neighbourhood in the universe... luckily, even failure does not last forever... I'm still too low to move up in the universal scale... this parallel universe on the boat is fine but my next life is waiting for me... I've got to get out to get in so as to move on to the next life... my soul and I are now one... there is a feeling of rejuvenation and wholeness as thoughts are exchanged between us... Atlantis is where we started together... we did not do well and we have a lot of karma to contend with... we caused the white steam to float over land and water... white feet, falling teeth and then the sinking of the continent... we are both going back again... we need to...

... tits on a bull... sorry asshole, but I will not forget this life and will remember it (current life) for the next life too... simply said, mistrust my soul as it has his own agenda and it's covering up some fuck it/he did... where is heaven, hell or even a judgement day... are there no higher ups, or a god of some kind?... am I to take what he says at face value... it/he has been fucking me for 55 years and probably all other versions of me walking out there in time and space... it/he has no credibility... cannot trust my soul as it lies to me constantly... need to trick my soul cause this time I will remember and more than I did the last time too... and the other two me, I will find them too... come to think of it... it's all show and no substance... this cannot be my soul but some fucken evil that has been paralyzing me from a young age... did I stand up in line for this... a bad/lost entity posing as a soul, my soul...

... tomorrow, start today... humans are damaged... and we spend lifetimes trying to correct ourselves and still fail... and will always fail, because we are not and will never be perfect... so what!... but even with all our frantic behaviour... there are still beautiful moments and things on our planet...

and I don't know how but I'm coming back and try to make it better for all those who cross my path... it's not much, but it's a start cause I'm bound to this beauty... my paper cigarette is all soggy and I think I can even taste the ink... as I sit in an almost fetal like position, my stomach feels hollow and it hurts... there is an emptiness happening in my mind too... I'm losing memories, they're being slowly erased... but I'm not going back empty handed... the memories must be archived, they were of who I was... the low battery warning light is flashing a beautiful red lipstick color, this is my signal that shortly... jumping ship will be inescapable for a clean start... I love insanity... it's so liberating... will you recognize the stranger from paradise in your coffee shop holding a paper cigarette... with peace in his mind, love in his heart and probably money in his pocket because this is still an unevolved planet called... earth... as if anything is final... and in a un-final conclusion... I am what I am... and maybe I was a empath in denial, no more...

I will never spend another Christmas without my kids.

* * *

**Fernando Marques**

… the repetitive orchestrated sound of the wipers, squealing against the wet glass, transport him if only for a brief moment to a numbing serenity…

… to wash the chicken and get it cooked for the ungrateful family supper… of all those who will be at the table for dinner… the chicken is the only one who washed…

… I'm the anti-poster boy for all those businesses who want you to put money in the bank, buy insurance or retirement saving plans… you know the ones who sell you fear but disguise it as common sense…

## about the author…

*… didn't think I'd get this far with the book project… after all it pretty much started off as a lark but since it's a prerequisite that I say something pro-found about myself that will hopefully inspire you to take this book home and by the same token secure my pension fund… so, here goes… I'm a 57+ year old moderately romantic single chap and a Pisces too… very creative and extremely unpredictable…in cold winter days, I open the car door for you…*
*so that you may get out to push the car… the door latch is broken from the inside… also love cuddly romantic evenings by an electric or gas fireplace, as long as I get to hold the fireplace's remote control…*
*my dilemma is me loving myself that is always short lived and I drag the onesI love down into my conundrum… actually, I just wanted to use the word conundrum in a sentence…*

CPSIA information can be obtained
at www.ICGtesting.com
Printed in the USA
BVHW031704220419
546191BV00001B/4/P